K-HRM

Korean Human Resource Management

for Leaders

GYUCHANG YU · WOOSUNG PARK

CHANGMINSA

About the Authors

Dr. Gyu-Chang Yu is Professor at Hanyang University's School of Business and served as both the dean of the business school and the dean of the business school until June 2022. He served as president of the Korean Society for Ethical Management and the Korean Human Resources Management Association, and currently serves as an advisor(former president) of both societies. After he received his PhD in human resource management from the University of Wisconsin-Madison, he served as a Research Fellow at the Korea Labor Institute, where he experienced not only theory but also practice and government policy. Since then, he has moved to a university and focused on research and lectures in the fields of human resource management and leadership, while serving as an advisor to leading Korean companies such as Samsung, SK, LG, Hyundai Motor, CJ, and POSCO. He also often serves as an advisor to government agencies such as the Ministry of Employment and Labor, the Ministry of Economy and Finance, the Ministry of Personnel Management, and the Ministry of Trade, Industry and Energy.

Dr. Woo-Sung Park is Professor of Management at the School of Management at the Kyung Hee University. He received his PhD in human resource management from the HEC(Ecole des Hautes Etudes Commerciales) in France. Prior to joining the Kyung Hee University, he served on the research faculties of Korea Labor Institute, a leading national institute of research in labor policy. Believing that people are source of fundamental competitiveness, he has been actively doing researches on the theories and practices of people management for 30 years, and published many papers and books. He is now focusing himself on HR strategy in the aging era and the technological revolution. He has published 「4th Industrial Revolution: Changing Work and Management」 (co-author) and has published a number of papers on human resource management in the age of artificial intelligence. He provides HR advice to major Korean groups such as SK, Samsung, LG, and Lotte, while making efforts to develop the leadership of their talent. He is also very interested in corporate social responsibility and ethical management. He has served as the president of the Korea Ethical Management Association.

K-HRM for Leaders (Korean Human Resource Management for Leaders)

Published by CHANGMINSA, Room 401, 46, Changjeon-ro, Mapo-gu, Seoul, Korea.
Tel: 82-2-3272-1243, Fax: 82-2-3272-1245
E-mail: cmbooks@hanmail.net

ISBN: 979-11-92272-05-4

Preface

This book is the English version of Human Resource Management for Leaders, published in 2017(3rd edition, 2022). Although many overseas business management textbooks have been translated into Korean in Korea, it is very rare for Korean textbooks to be translated into English. The authors met for the first time as colleagues at the Korea Labor Institute in 1996, and have been doing research together for a long time and consulting with companies. We agreed that human resource management textbooks for leaders were needed in Korea. And years of collaborative work led to the publication of Human Resource Management for Leaders as a textbook. Going one step further, we felt the need for human resource management for global leaders. Korean companies have recently emerged prominently in the global market, and from an economic point of view, Korea has already become an advanced country. In addition, Hallyu, such as K-pop and K-drama, has established itself as a global phenomenon. Against this background, the number of people from all over the world who want to know Korea is increasing, and in particular, the demand for learning about Korea's greatest strength, human resource management, is increasing. This book was promoted to meet this global demand.

The features of this book are as follows.

First, we tried to explain human resource management from the perspective of leaders who directly manage subordinates in the field. This is to reflect the functional change of human resource management that is actually taking place in the corporate field. Until a few decades ago, human resource management in companies was centralized by the HR department. However, with the emphasis on competitiveness through people and the role of leaders for this purpose, the idea that human resource management is the exclusive domain of the HR department is being challenged. And the human resource management roles and responsibilities given to leaders are increasing day by day. However, the preparation of leaders to take on such a role is largely insufficient. That was the problem the authors felt while diagnosing the human resource management capabilities of many leaders over the past two decades.

Second, we tried to reflect the specific situation of Korea as well as the universal theory in the textbook. In other fields of business administration, such as finance, production, and MIS, the size of the company or the characteristics of the industry may be different, but there will be no problems without considering the unique characteristics of Korea. In these areas, it may be more important to quickly introduce and learn new theories or practices in developed countries. However, human resource management is an area that deals with people, and institutional aspects such as culture, values, practices and customs, and labor laws differ considerably from country to country. If these cultural and institutional differences are ignored, it is difficult to provide practical help to leaders who have to manage people in the field in Korea. Therefore, we tried to explain clearly the Korean context and problems that leaders, who are interested in Korean HRM, must understand as much as possible. In particular, the Korean labor law covered in Chapter 2 will be difficult to find in other textbooks.

On the other hand, we tried to contain both the Korean particularity and the theoretical universality. The basic principles and theories of human resource management have universality that can be applied in any country. The theoretical framework that competency and motivation determine performance has secured universality through long-term research. Managing people requires an understanding of people and what they do, and therefore, related theories and explanations are described from a universal perspective. It is expected that leaders' human resource management competency and insight will be enhanced by thinking about how to implement human resource management in consideration of differences in each country, corporate culture, and strategy on top of a universal theory.

Third, it has been explained in an easy-to-understand manner as much as possible. Rather than using technical terms or academic descriptions, we tried to write in a simple and everyday way so that even those who do not know the contents of HR management can understand. In addition, the authors tried to explain the content clearly by digesting it in depth so that the accurate content could be delivered. In the process, beyond the simple transfer of information or knowledge, the authors tried to understand the context and situation in which human resource management problems occurred so that the readers could share the problem awareness of the authors.

The Korean version of Human Resource Management for Leaders lacks many aspects, let alone the English version. Nevertheless, it was courageous to publish to meet the growing global demand. Constructive criticism for improvement is the greatest gift a reader can give authors. We look forward to feedback from our readers. Finally we would like to take this opportunity to sincerely thank Changminsa CEO Yoon Dong-gu, who faithfully helped to publish the English version as well as the Korean version.

Contents

CHAPTER 1 People and Competitiveness

CHAPTER 2 Labor Law and Human Resources

CHAPTER 3 Strategic Human Resource Management

CHAPTER 4 Person and Job

CHAPTER 5 Staffing

CHAPTER 6 Performance Evaluation and Performance Management

CHAPTER 7 Human Resources Development and Training

CHAPTER 8 Compensation Management and Pay Structure

CHAPTER 9 Pay for Performance

CHAPTER 10 Designing and Administering Benefits

CHAPTER 11 Turnover

CHAPTER 12 Globalization and Human Resource Management

CHAPTER 1

People and Competitiveness

1. Business, Management, and Human Resource Management
2. Historical Development of Human Resource Management
3. Human Resource Management and Competitiveness
4. HR Manager vs. Line Manager
5. Basic Model of HR Management
6. Scope of HR Management
7. Structure of This Textbook

Learning Objectives

1. Understand the position of human resource management in corporate management.
2. In a modern sense, the development process of human resource management can be explained.
3. Factors that are the source of corporate competitiveness can be suggested.
4. The role of line managers in human resource management can be explained.
5. Describe the factors that determine the performance of a company.
6. Can explain the relationship between human resource management, labor relations, and human resource development.

Introductory Case

Junsu Lee was recently appointed as head of the regional sales team of a Korean branch of global car company. The regional sales team is a strategic sales department and is an important part that has a great influence on the overall performance of the company. Team leader Junsu Lee was famous for his outstanding sales performance when he was a team member. He was very diligent in customer relations, and the repurchase rate of customers who purchased a car once was very high. He contacted the customer (not only the customers who purchased the car, but also the customers who visited him once even if they didn't buy it) at the appropriate timing so that the customer would not bother. When relatives in the countryside sent organically grown sweet potatoes, he deliberately visited and gave them to customers as small gifts. In return for these efforts, he received the best evaluation from the sales team, and was selected and promoted earlier than other team members for his contribution to improving the sales team's performance, and became the team leader. Team leader Lee was full of motivation as he became the team leader. He passed on his know-how to other team members, and set a vision for his sales team to become number one in the entire company. Team leader Junsu Lee had a swelling dream of becoming the head of the global sales headquarters. Team leader Lee has set a vision of being number one in the global market, and accordingly, he revised the goals of the regional sales team. In addition, each team member's goal level was raised. Some of the team members seemed to be dissatisfied, but because of the charisma of team leader Lee, they could not say anything and followed. In the first few months after taking the lead, the organization seemed to be moving as intended. Even though the team leader did not have to go out for sales by himself, he personally met with customers and helped the team members who had poor performance. Because of this, team leader Lee was very busy and busy, so he was insatiable. But overall sales performance was excellent, so he was confident that his method was correct and pushed it. However, over time, the team members' performance began to decline rapidly. When the team members left the office, they met in a small group and began to share the team leader's gossip. Some of the team members, known as excellent salespeople, were also told that they were thinking about moving to another company, and in fact, team member Kim Tae-woo actually moved to a competitor. However, team leader Junsu Lee was frustrated because he did not know the cause, and he insisted on the method he had succeeded in as a team member. Eventually, after the end of the year, when the sales results for one year were compiled, it was worse than last year's performance before team leader Lee took over. The decline in the performance of the regional sales team had a negative impact on the company's overall performance as a result.

Discussion Questions

1. What's wrong with the company's human resource management?
2. What factors determine the performance of the company's sales team?
3. What is the role of team leader Junsu Lee?
4. What to do if you give advice to team leader Junsu Lee?

1. Business, Management, and Human Resource Management

In order to understand human resource management, it is necessary to understand management, which is the upper concept of human resource management, and business that is the goal of management. Regardless of the size, most modern people live in organizations. Small neighborhood restaurants are organizations, as well as such large global companies with more than 100,000 employees as Samsung Electronics and LG Electronics. Human resource management is one of the many management activities these various organizations need to achieve their goals.

1.1 Business

The development of human being has evolved rapidly with the creation of modern organizations. Organizations are places where people with specific purposes come together to perform their respective roles.[1)] The purpose each organization pursues is called business. One of the main goals of the business is the profit generation of a profit organization. Generally speaking, when someone says 'doing business', it is considered 'do something for making money'. But to define the purpose of a business profit-making is a very limited view of the business. P. Drucker, praised for the founding of modern management, criticizes that it is wrong and even meaningless to say that the purpose of business is profit-making.[2)]

There are a wide variety of organizations around us, and business as diverse as various organizations. For example, universities also have an education business. It is difficult to say that universities are conducting education business to create profits. Of course, sometimes, exceptionally corrupt university founders may conduct education business for the purpose of money. We know that most universities don't. In other words, it doesn't mean that business is just for profit-making. Business is meant to achieve the various goals pursued by the organization.

These objectives are generally described in the company's mission statement. For example, "Preserving and improving human life through pharmaceutical business" (Merck: multinational pharmaceutical company), "Making all information in the world easily accessible and usable by people" (Google: multinational internet company). or "To make the world happy with unique technology" (Midus IT: Korean construction structure design company), etc.

1.2 Management

Management is an activity that an organization needs to carry out its business successfully. You can't do business successfully without having anything. For example, in order to do an educational business, there must be buildings, classrooms, blackboards, etc. In addition, there should be professors or instructors who can give lectures, and staff who can provide administrative support are also needed. In order to do a food business, you need to have ingredients, a kitchen, and a chef who can cook. In order to carry out such a business successfully, various elements are needed, and these are called resources. There are various type of resources: physical resources, tangible resources, intangible resources, and human resources.

The resources required are inevitably different depending on the purpose of the business. However, these resources needed for business cannot be supplied indefinitely. Most of the necessary resources have to be supplied from outside at a cost. In addition, there is not only one company pursuing the same business, there are many competitors, and all competitors need resources. Therefore, it is not possible for an organization to receive an infinite supply of necessary resources for its business. That is, resources are limited. Because resources are limited, it is called management to consider deliberately and study how to use limited resources to achieve the purpose of the business. The school of business or college of business in most universities has been established for the purpose of learning the management. In other words, in business school, students learn a variety of management techniques necessary to conduct business well.

When looking at the fact that the limited resources are utilized well through management in more depth, it has two meanings, specifically efficiency and effectiveness.[3)] Efficiency is the efficient use of limited resources. Efficient use means that you must be able to use as few resources as possible to achieve the same goal. Efficiency is related to cost. Organizations strive to achieve their desired goals with minimum cost (cost minimization).

On the other hand, resources also must be used effectively. Effectiveness means that the use of resources should directly or indirectly contribute to the achievement of the business' objectives. Effectiveness has to do with value. The resources used by the organization should have a clear direction. It is important to consider how the organization can use its resources to maximize value. In particular, the value most important to today's organizations is customer value. The different expressions of efficiency and effectiveness can be called productivity and creativity.[4)] Productivity is finding ways to put a minimum amount of resources on output, while creativity is finding ways to increase the value customers feel in new ways. Both productivity and creativity are important in management. Managers are people who achieve business goals by increasing productivity and creativity through efficient and effective resource activities.

1.3 Human Resource Management

Management is said to be the efficient and effective use of limited resources. Just as resources are diverse, organizations need various management. For example, financial management refers to the management of financial resources, that is, the flow and use of money so that it can be efficiently and effectively performed. Marketing management refers to the efficient and effective management of market resources such as customer information and desires. Production management refers to the efficient and effective management of the flow of a process from input raw materials to final finished products. Human resource management to be covered in this textbook refers to the efficient and effective management of people who are members of an organization, that is, human resources.

By combining the business and management discussed above, we can define human resource management as "all activities to efficiently and effectively utilize limited human resources to achieve the purpose of the business pursued by the organization." Various activities covered in this textbook include hiring to recruit excellent talents, evaluation to judge whether members are properly achieving their given goals, development for fostering support for members to increase their competence, and compensation to motivate members. Finally, there is separation that ends a relationship with the organization after employees have fulfilled their role.

2. Historical Development of Human Resource Management

Human resource management has traditionally been referred to as personnel management. With the creation of a modern organization and systematization of management, personnel management in a modern sense emerged. The importance of personnel management increased as the times passed, and the term human resource management was coined to reflect this. In this chapter, we will briefly look at how human resource management has been developed.

2.1 Pre-Personnel

In the Unified Silla Dynasty Era 1500 years ago in Korea, it would have required a lot of materials and manpower to build the Bulguksa Temple in Gyeongju. Thousands of years ago, when there was no modern organization, it was possible to create pyramids in Egypt or huge temples in Greece. Perhaps thousands or tens of thousands of workers, mostly slaves, were mobilized. How would so many heritage of human beings, both East and West, be created? Since it was before the development of industrial revolution, most of it would have been completed by human hands. Of course, they would have thought about what experts were needed for what kind of work. And they would have

Figure 1-1 Development Stage of Human Resource Management

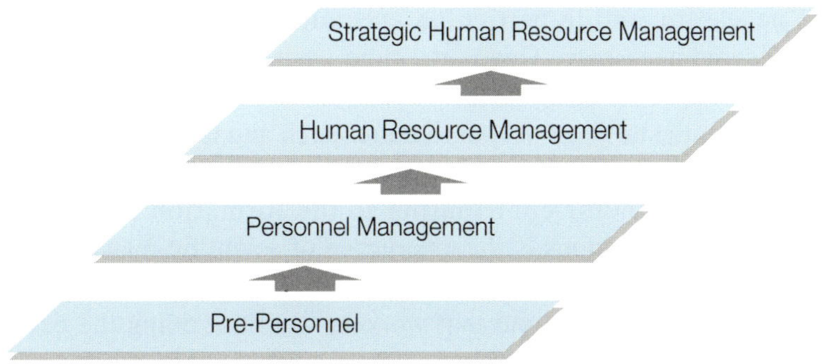

tried to find experienced experts, and if they couldn't find the right people, they would have made up for the lacking field by training. As such, human resources management in this modern term was not known and used, but in a practical sense, human resources management always has been with the history of mankind.

A more systematic and scientific approach to personnel management, which has been with the development of human civilization, has been in full swing with the advent of companies along with the development of capitalism. As the Industrial Revolution broke out and large-scale factories were created, a lot of labor was required. In the early days of the industrial revolution, it started in a field like the textile industry, but over time, huge corporations were formed in various industries such as petroleum, steel, railway, construction, and automobiles. And in these companies, the need to systematically manage numerous human resources has increased. However, until the end of the 19th century, when companies in the modern sense began to spread, it was still common to hire necessary manpower and pay wages directly to workers at the site, mainly by the hands of managers in the field. At that time, the required manpower was taken from the labor market and remained at the level of use by paying a daily wage. Since the organizational system had not yet been established, no division by function occurred, and even in large-scale companies, the function of personnel was not made into an independent department yet. At this time, the general affairs department took charge of the miscellaneous matters of the company including hiring manpower and wage payments.

2.2 Personnel Management

As the scale of the company grew, the functions were differentiated, and employees' expertise was strengthened, the role of personnel management began to become more important. In addition, as the desires of workers gradually increased, it became necessary to respond to them. A few progressive large corporations focused on improving the living standards of workers and working conditions in terms of welfare. Civic activists advocating for workers' welfare came into the corporations and dreamed of welfare capitalism. However, this movement did not spread significantly. Rather, the labor union movement took place as workers rebelled against poor working conditions, exploitation by child labor, and various unethical behaviors of managers, resulting in intensifying labor-management conflicts. Against this background, systematic personnel management has become necessary, and in particular, specialized functions to cope with labor unions have become necessary. This is the time when the modern sense of personnel management that we are studying today was formed.[5)] In view of this practical need, a major was created in the business school to do research and teach personnel management professionally in the 1940s and 50s, mainly in the United States.[6)]

Another important factor contributing to the formation and development of personnel management functions is the emergence of scientific management. Scientific management, devised by F. Taylor, has revolutionized productivity. Taylor, who was the manager of the steel mill, found that workers were not doing the best they could. Taylor then began systematically analyzing their work, hiring and assigning the right people for the job, and providing appropriate incentives to motivate them. It has been found that productivity can be dramatically improved. Although criticized for the scientific management method as an inhumane management method, Taylor's intention was not. Rather Taylor criticized managers for not doing their job and focusing solely on exploiting workers easily. He stressed that it is the manager's duty to make sure that workers can reach their full potential.

> "The manager is not doing his job properly, but is only trying to get the workers to work hard with low wages by wielding a whip over the head of the worker. Managers must ensure that each individual worker performs the job that best suits them and does not lose personality, while exhibiting their abilities in their respective fields, while maintaining originality and creativity."[7)]

In Korea, the modern personnel management system began to be established in the 1970s, when the economic development plan was implemented and the economy developed, and the scale of companies began to grow.[8)] In the early days, the main focus was to guarantee the life of workers, who were responsible for the livelihood of their families, and to solve basic food, clothing and shelter such as dormitories, medical facilities, or night school. In addition, the main purpose behind this was the suppression of complaints about low wages and stability of labor-management relations. However, until the 1980s, it was difficult to say that it performed the function of systematic personnel management. It was in the late 1980s that the personnel management of Korean companies took shape in earnest when they accepted the desires of workers that erupted along with political democratization in 1987. Especially during this period, the illegal activities of trade unions exploded.

2.3 Human Resource Management

The emergence of the human relations school was an opportunity for the paradigm to shift from personnel management to human resource management. The School of Human Relations, triggered by Professor A. Mayor's Hawthorne experiment, which was conducting research on scientific management methods, has contributed to greatly broadening the understanding of human behavior in organizations. People who had previously been regarded as a tool of productivity became more than just tools. This is also a time when understanding of human behavior in the fields of social sciences such as organizational psychology, industrial psychology, organizational sociology, economics, public administration, and political science greatly expanded. It is also a time when organizational behavior, a sibling in the field of human resource management in business administration, began to be established as a discipline.

In the business field, Germany and Japan, the defeated countries of World War II, were newly reorganized and began to join the ranks of the advanced countries. German and Japanese companies dominated the existing market by breaking away from the traditional management method of mass production by machines, armed with new management methods that maximize the capabilities of people. Competition between companies intensified, and now the focus of competitiveness was on people. People began to be called human resources, and the function of personnel management has been renamed to human resource management. Especially during this period, the field of human resource development was greatly expanded. Academic research such as career development, education and training, teamwork, leadership, etc. and its application in companies were actively conducted. Throughout this period, human resource management subjects and majors were opened not only in US and European universities, but also in almost all business schools in Korea.

The rising demand for human rights in society also influenced the development and change of human resource management in companies. In the United States, since the 1960s, discrimination against women, religion, race, age, and skin color has been strictly prohibited. Accordingly, the human resource management system was improved so that companies do not discriminate against reasons not related to performance in hiring, compensation, promotion, evaluation, etc.. It became an opportunity for companies to need more HR experts. Also, in Korea, starting with the Equal Employment Act in 1988, discrimination based on gender, disability, and age in human resource management is prohibited.

2.4 Strategic Human Resource Management

Human resource management experienced changes once again as the 1980s passed. Competition around the world is accelerating, and developing countries such as Korea and Taiwan have eroded the global markets with low labor costs. As the international trade environment became the WTO system, it was intensified to the point of calling it infinite competition or cross-border competition. In the academic field, as reflecting this, the field of strategy emerged in business administration. Bestselling books such as M. Porter's Competitive Strategy in 1980 and Competitive Advantage in 1985 showed this trend symbolically.

This trend was reflected in the management of human resources, and it was argued that management of people should also be made from a strategic point of view. Strategic human resource management means dealing with existing human resource management from a more integrated perspective. The integrated view is built on two aspects.[9] The first is vertical integration. Strategy is necessary to achieve the mission and vision that reflects the purpose of the business pursued by the organization, and human resource management must be carried out in connection with this business strategy. Human resource management, which previously remained at the functional level, must be raised to a strategic level. For this, a company's HR strategy must be established. The second is horizontal integration. Recruitment, evaluation, development, compensation, and separation, each of the functions of human resource management, do not play separate roles, but must be organically combined with consistency and congruence to achieve the strategy and goal of human resource management.

In the case of Korea, since the 1998 financial crisis, more and more companies are approaching human resource management from a strategic point of view. In the process of overcoming the foreign exchange crisis, globalization and open market took place rapidly, and foreign companies entered Korea in large numbers. At the same time, companies representing Korea have grown into global multinational companies. Companies that have recognized the strategic importance of human resource management have opened and prepared training courses to foster HR experts (for example, Samsung Group, LG Group, Hyundai Motor Group, SK Group, Doosan Group, and CJ Group).

3. Human Resource Management and Competitiveness

The changes in human resource management discussed above are deeply related to the changes in the source of competitiveness over time. We motioned that management is finding a way to efficiently and effectively utilize limited resources. Why is such a management activity necessary? Because there is competition. Competition is a law of nature. Just as all living things in nature have to compete fiercely to survive, so an organization must win the competition to survive. Of course, not only competition is necessary for survival, but cooperation is also important. Judgment and decision-making on who to compete with or when to cooperate is an important role for top managers. The discipline developed to deal with these issues is the management strategy.

The place where competition takes place is the market. The marketplace is where the trade of products or services takes place, and customers choose the products and services. The reason to manage limited resources well is to be competitive. Competitiveness arises when we have a comparative advantage over competitors in the market. According to the resource-based view of E. Barney, a professor in the field of management strategy, a survey of organizations with comparative advantages found that they were competitive in resources compared to competitors. Prof. Barney summarized the research results and suggested the following four conditions of resources to gain a comparative advantage over competitors in the market.[10)]

① Must have Valuable resources.
② Must have Rare resources.
③ Must have non-Imitable resources.
④ Must have Organizable resources

This is called the VRIO model after the first letters of the four resources in English.[11)] The VRIO model emphasizes that companies with four resources have a competitive advantage in the market and thus have a competitive edge, and many empirical studies have been generally supported. What is particularly deeply related to the human resource management we are dealing with is that most of the resources with the four characteristics of the VIRO model come from intangible and human resources, not from tangible resources. In particular, human resources are important resources in themselves and contain intangible resources. For example, when a company says that unique technology is an important competitiveness, technology is both an intangible resource and embodied in people. It is also the background in which companies make great

Figure 1-2 **VRIO Model and Competitive Advantage**

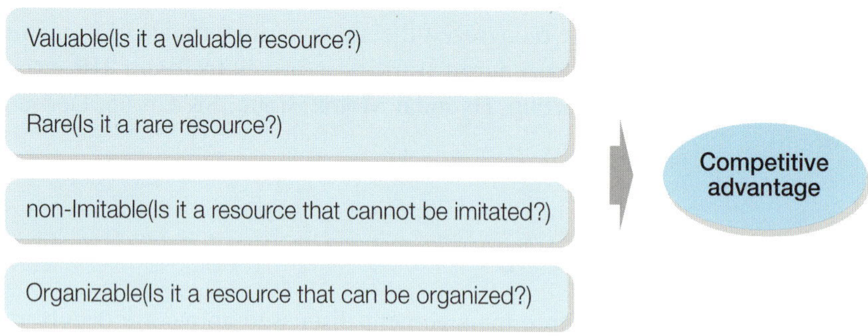

efforts to attract excellent talent while recognizing the importance of human resources.

4. HR Manager vs. Line Manager

Human resource management was defined as all activities related to the efficient and effective use of human resources to achieve the purpose of the organization. If so, what we need to understand here is who is the subject of all the activities to utilize human resources. In general, large corporations have departments that specialize in HR management. As shown in the general corporate organization chart in the figure, the HR department belongs to the management support headquarters along with finance, accounting, and legal affairs. The support department is called the staff department.

The role of staff members (called staff employees) is to professionally support the activities of those who play a pivotal role in achieving the business objectives of the organization (called line employees). Of course, the most important responsibility for achieving business objectives rests with the CEO, and it is linked by a control-and-command system as it descends from the top to the bottom of the organization. In this way, the department that is connected up and down and is responsible for the pivotal activities of the organization is the line department, and the head of the line department is called the line manager. The staff department is responsible for supporting the activities of the line department, with the CEO as the top, and the HR department is a representative staff department.

Then, is the HR department, a staff department where HR experts gather, the main body of HR management activities? If the human resources department is the main body of HR management activities, wouldn't the HR management activities be conducted in the case of a small organization without a HR department? Not like that. No matter how small an organization, it has to hire and pay employees. Perhaps, in the case of a small organization, the CEO, the representative of the organization, will either hire people or pay directly. For example, even a small restaurant that can be found in any city requires staff, hires and pays. Because it is small, the boss will probably have to do it himself. As such, it should be said that the main body of HR management activities are line

Figure 1-3 **Organizational Chart of the Company**

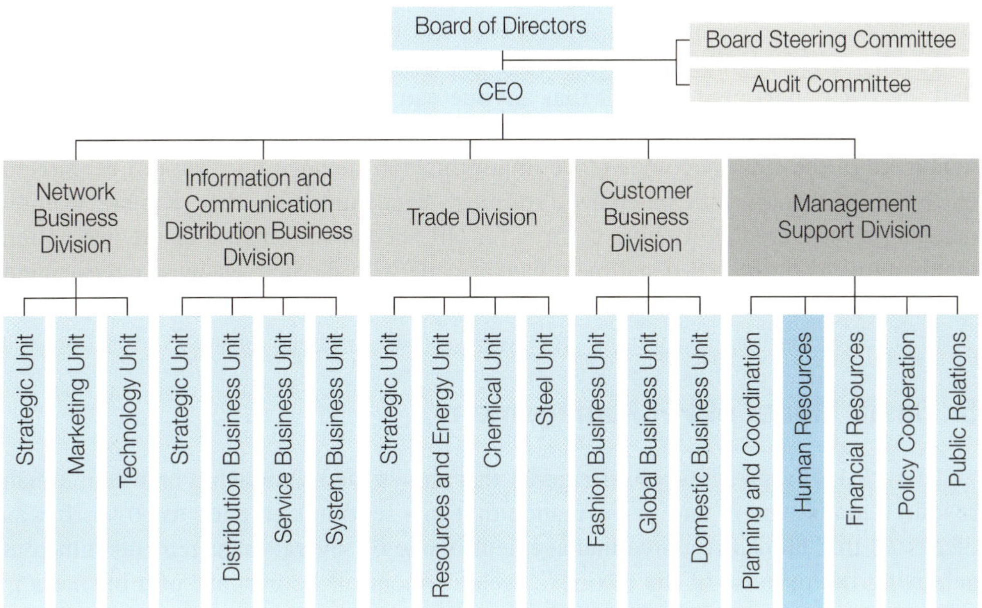

managers including the CEO. As experts, the HR department plays a role in supporting the HR management activities of line managers. Line managers and experts in the HR department have a mutually cooperative relationship.

There are many misunderstandings about HR management in the workplace, and these misunderstandings often come from ignorance of the nature of HR management. In particular, this phenomenon is more severe in large-scale companies with the development of professional skills in the HR department. Arguably, HR management should not be a task dedicated to experts in the HR department. The design of the HR system is carried out by the HR department with expertise. However, the actual operation of the HR system should be carried out by managers of unit departments (ie, line managers) in the field. In particular, as human resources become an important source of competitiveness, HR management in the field becomes more important. It is not the HR department but the line managers that actually operate the HR system.

In order to see the intended effect of the system, it must operate well. The operation is carried out by both the head of the department and the members. No matter how well the system is designed, it is meaningless if it is not operated. On the other hand, even if the system has some flaws, it can be used to improve performance if it is well operated. Even under the same system, performance varies depending on the leader. The design of the HR system is carried out by experts in the HR department, which is a staff department, under orders from the top management. The HR system is the setting of rules and regulations for recruitment, evaluation, development, compensation, and separation. Small-sized companies can operate without a system, but as the scale grows, certain rules and regulations are required. In addition, new systems are introduced and existing systems are revised or supplemented according to the strategic direction of companies.

Finally, another misconception about HR management is the tendency to think that the HR department is a job that anyone can do without special expertise. As the importance of human resources becomes more important, the competence of managers in the field becomes more important. HR management should be carried out by professionals with specialized training. As mentioned earlier, Korea's leading companies have created training courses for HR specialists because of the perception that employees in the HR department cannot cope with the new business environment without expertise.

5. Basic Model of HR Management

[Figure 1-4] represents a basic model that shows the relationship between human resource management and performance that this textbook intends to cover. It was discussed that human resource management is one of several managements aimed at achieving the purpose of the business. Achievement of the purpose of a business is influenced by a number of factors. For example, a construction company's business is directly affected by the construction economy, the real estate market, and government regulations. In addition, A wide variety of factors affect indirectly: e.g., the political situation, population structure, economic environment, consumer psychology, exchange rate, international situation, climate change, and sudden disease such as MERS and CV-19. Although these environmental factors have a profound effect on business success, they are difficult for managers to control. Managers should predict environmental factors as accurately as possible and actively respond to them, but most of them are unavoidable. In this respect, the most important thing that managers can do is to achieve business goals by increasing organizational performance.

Organizational performance is expressed in various indicators. Sales, output, return of equity (ROE), return on assets (ROA), return on investment (ROI), customer satisfaction, market share, and stock value. Managers strive to achieve the purpose of the business by enhancing the various organizational performance through efficient and effective

Figure 1-4 Human Resource Management Basic Model

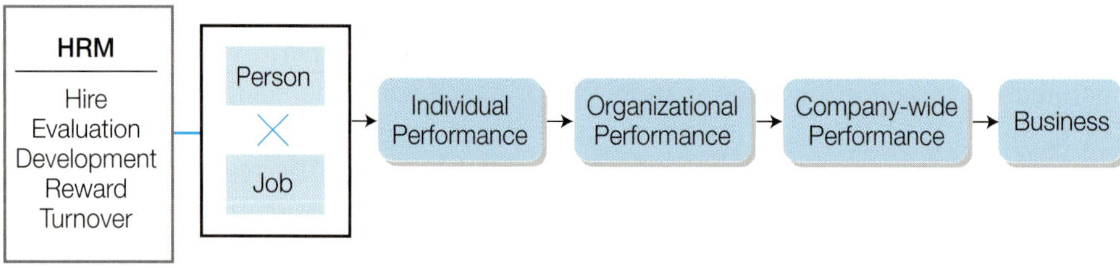

management of resources. It is not too much to say that the level of management in a company is as same as management competence.

However, an important factor that affects the performance of an organization is the result of the efforts of individual members. This is called employee performance. Of course, simply adding the achievements made by individual members does not lead to organizational performance. In reality, the sum of member performance may be lower than the overall performance of the organization. On the other hand, due to the synergy effect, the organization's performance may be greater than the sum of the member's performance. It is also the manager's role and responsibility to connect the performance of members to the performance of the organization and maximize the effect. At this time, managers must demonstrate good leadership.

It was said that human resource management is to achieve the purpose of the business by managing people, efficiently and effectively. To put this concretely again, human resource management can be said to contribute to the organization's performance by enhancing the performance of each member, and thereby achieve the purpose of the business. Improving the performance of members is an important role of human resource management, and what this textbook aims to address is what and how to improve the performance of members.

More details will be covered in future chapters. In this chapter, first of all, it is necessary to understand how members' performance is determined. The member's performance comes from the individual's behaviors. For example, let's say that a salesperson's performance is to increase sales. To increase sales volume, salesperson must meet with customers frequently. And based on professional understanding of the product, he or she must explain to the customer kindly to increase their understanding and persuade them to induce purchase. Only through these activities, that is, actions(behaviors), can produce the result of increasing sales. Management induces members' behaviors in a direction that can improve performance through HR management. The introduction of a salesperson incentive system could be an example.

Then, how do the behaviors that improve performance come about? Through a number of studies, scholars have summarized that competency and motive are the factors that make individuals perform behaviors that increase performance. Competency here means the power to do something (can do). Competency is a collection of knowledge, skill, and ability (KSA). KSA is a core element of competency, but there are many other factors as well. For example, personality traits can also be an important influencing factor. However, since various other factors are less direct than KSA, the main target of human resource management is the KSA. Motivation refers to the will to do something. Other expressions of motivation include effort and passion. Motivation also comes from external factors such as money, good food, a pleasant environment, and a spacious office. This motivational factor is called extrinsic motivation. External motivations are not the only factors that influence members' behavior. There are factors that do not appear outwardly, such as a sense of meaning, a sense of accomplishment, a sense of satisfaction, and a sense of stability in a relationship with others, but are still in people's minds. This motivational factor is called intrinsic motivation. Human resource management deals with internal motivation factors as well as external ones.

Just because competencies and motivations have a significant impact on performance doesn't mean that everyone needs the same competencies and motivations for everything. Like the words of the right person for the right place, the work that suits the person's aptitude increases motivation and performance. In other words, successful human resource management requires that the work required to improve the performance of the business is clearly defined and appropriate people are assigned to the work.

Another expression of work for the purpose of HR management is job. When it comes to work, it has a broad meaning that encompasses various things that people do in their lives. It includes chores, cleaning, service, and doing for hobbies. What we want to deal with in HR management is what is needed within the organization to achieve the purpose of the business among these diverse and comprehensive tasks. These specific tasks are imposed on individuals within the organization and are defined as duties. In other words, a job can be said to be a task imposed on an individual by an organization to achieve the purpose of the business. For example, tasks such as consulting with customers, writing contracts, negotiating prices, and post-customer management are given to sales workers, and these tasks are grouped into a job called sales.

It is people who perform their duties. If the job is the tasks necessary to achieve the purpose of the business on an abstract level, it is the people who actually put it into action. Of course, not only humans, but also machines and animals can do what is needed. In particular, in the case of physical labor, animals such as cows and horses replaced what humans did, and agricultural machinery and automated machinery were replaced with the development of mechanical civilization. In recent years, with the development of computers, even mental labor is increasingly replaced. Moreover, with the 4th Industrial Revolution, artificial intelligence may be able to replace even specialized areas. Managers must make important decisions about who will do what the business needs. In academic fields such as production management and industrial engineering, mainly machine-related content is dealt with, whereas human resource management mainly deals with the case where a person performs the job.

In human resource management, the term "people" means the subject that performs work. A person is an incumbent who possesses the competencies and motivations required to perform a job. For example, a person who needs to perform a sales job is a person who has the ability to do business well, such as customer management, and a person who has a will to do it. In HR management, these people's characteristics are identified and selected through recruitment. In summary, as shown in [Figure], human resource management strives to increase the performance of each member in order to improve the performance of the organization. A member's performance is the result of acting well by exerting the competencies and motivations required by the member's job. The organization conducts human resource management activities such as recruitment, evaluation, development, compensation, and separation to manage this.

6. Scope of HR Management

Human resource management is a field of study that deals with issues related to people in an organization broadly. This is a field of interest not only in business administration but also in psychology, education, educational engineering, sociology, economics, political science, and law. In addition, human resource management in business administration is actually receiving a lot of help from research results in these adjacent academic fields. Within individual companies, there are adjacent areas related to human resource management. For example, activities related to people in an organization can be divided into three areas: human resource management, human resource development, and labor-management relations. Sometimes all three of these activities are collectively referred to as human resource management in a broad sense. In smaller organizations, all three activities may be performed by one department or one or two persons in charge. In large enterprises, it is common for each activity to be divided and there are separate support departments. In this case, human resource management is used in a narrow sense, and human resource development and labor-management relations are independently operated as separate departments or functions. In the business school curriculum, it is common for the three subjects to be offered independently. A brief look at the three areas is as follows.

① **Human Resource Management:** Includes all activities for efficient and effective use of human resources such as human resource planning, job management, recruitment, evaluation, compensation, training, career development, and separation management.

② **Labor-Management Relations (or Industrial relations):** It is divided into individual labor-management relations and collective labor-management relations. Individual labor-management relations deal with all issues arising from individual employment relations with individual workers and organizations, such as labor contracts, working hours, grievance handling, worker participation, and non-discrimination. Collective labor-management relations deal with issues arising from collective employment relations, such as labor unions, labor-management councils, collective bargaining, wage agreements, productivity agreements, labor disputes, and dispute settlement.

③ **Human Resource Development:** It is divided into 3 areas: organizational development, career development, and individual development. It includes activities to identify current problems and improve them to achieve the desired future of the organization. Organizational development deals with activities to increase performance at the overall level of the organization, such as organizational vitalization, change management, and performance management. Career development is an activity to match each member's career needs with the needs of the organization, such as career management, career planning, coaching, and mentoring. Individual development deals with activities to improve the competencies required of members now or in the future, such as orientation of new entrants, incumbent training, manager development, and leadership development. In large corporations, separate organizations are created to professionally support human resource development. Examples include Samsung Group's Samsung Human Resources Development Center, LG Group's Inhwa

Figure 1-5 Human Resource Management and Adjacent Fields

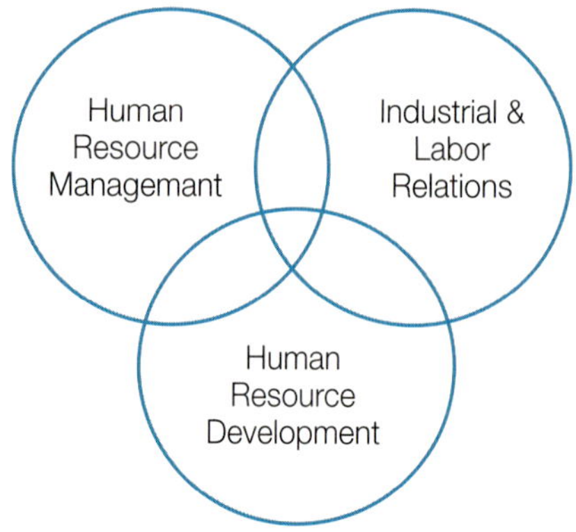

Center, SK Group's SK Academy, and Hyundai Motor Group's Human Resources Development Center.

As shown in the figure, the three areas of HR management, labor-management relations, and human resource development are independent, but closely related. For example, wage agreements dealt with in labor-management relations must take into account the compensation of human resource management. In human resource development, career development and individual development can be said to be a mutually complementary relationship with development of human resource management. In addition, the priorities and importance of these three areas may change depending on the change in the business environment. For example, when the conflict between labor and management intensifies, the importance of labor-management relations among the three areas is often the highest.

Among these, this textbook deals with the field of human resource management in a narrow sense. The human resource management areas covered in this book are briefly summarized as follows.

① **Human Resource Planning:** It includes the process of establishing an action plan to resolve the discrepancy between supply and demand by predicting the demand for human resources necessary to achieve the organization's strategic goals, and by analyzing the flow of personnel in the organization to predict supply.

② **Hiring:** Refers to all activities to secure excellent human resources required by the organization in the labor market. This includes recruitment, a process that draws out a pool of applicants who are qualified for the job they need, selection, a process that determines whether applicants who applied through recruitment are suitable for the company, and socialization, a process in which new employees are familiar with the company's policies and procedures and the job performance expected by the company.

③ **Evaluation:** Refers to a systematic process of identifying elements to improve organizational performance, and measuring and managing employee performance according to this standard.

④ **Development:** Refers to systematic activities that enable people to have the necessary competencies for their current or future jobs.

⑤ **Compensation:** Refers to a systematic activity that provides psychological or monetary value to motivate workers. These include a basic salary that provides compensation for workers' work, performance pay that provides incentives based on individual or group performance, and fringe benefits that cover the health or vacation of members and their families.

⑥ **Separation:** Refers to all activities to overcome management difficulties and minimize the departure of excellent talent. This includes voluntary turnover, in which members themselves leave their workplace for various reasons, and involuntary turnover, such as dismissal caused by reasons attributable to members of the organization or dismissal for managerial reasons in which members are collectively dismissed for management reasons.

7. Structure of This Textbook

This textbook consists of 12 chapters. It is divided into three parts. The first part, from Chapters 1 to 4, is the basic part for understanding the whole concept of human resource management and establishing a theoretical framework. Chapter 1, People and Competitiveness, examines why human resource management is important and is a source of competitiveness in companies. It also examines how human resource management has developed under capitalism along with the growth of companies. Chapter 2, Labor Law and Human Resource Management, deals with the system and types of labor law, and the contents of labor law that line managers and HR managers in charge must know. Chapter 3 Strategic Human Resource Management is the starting point of human resource management activities in enterprises. It is emphasized that the HR strategy, which determines the direction of human resource management of a company, must be established in alignment with the internal and external business environment surrounding the company, including strategy. Chapter 4, Person and Job, examines in detail the person and job, which can be called the building blocks of human resource management. Chapter 4 takes some examples to understand the theoretical background of competency and motivation. In the job section, the basic contents of the job that leaders must be familiar with, job analysi and job description were explained in detail.

The second part is from Chapters 5 to 11, and examines each function of human resource management in detail. Chapter 5, Staffing begins with a human resource planning that must be followed to make a hiring decision. Human Resource Planning is an extension of the Strategic Human Resource Planning in chapter 3 and examines specific methodologies. Subsequently, the hiring process was divided into recruitment and selection, and theories and practices were presented in detail with examples. Chapter

6 deals with Performance Evaluation and Performance Management. It explains the difference between performance evaluation in the traditional sense and performance management in the modern sense. And the elements of personnel evaluation that a leader must understand are explained in the theoretical framework of 6W1H. In addition, the process of establishing, checking, and evaluating goals with members was explained with examples. Chapter 7 Human Resource Development and Training examines why organizational leaders should pay attention to the improvement of employees' capabilities, and what are specific methods. Chapter 7 will also provide an opportunity to reflect on what students who have not yet had experience in organizations should prepare for competency development during school days.

Chapters 8 through 10 are compensation management. Chapter 8 Compensation Management and Pay Structure looks at the entire compensation management and system. In particular, it examines the principle of the basic salary, which is the compensation for the employee's work, and various alternatives. Chapter 9, Pay for Performance, deals with performance pays. If the basic wage covered in chapter 8 is a fixed wage, the performance paye has a characteristic of a variable wage that depends on various performances. Here, we look at the different types of individual and group incentives and discuss how to use them from a strategic point of view. Chapter 10, Benefit Management, is also a part of compensation management. In some cases, benefits are treated as small sections, but in this textbook, they are treated as a separate chapter in consideration of the proportion of benefits management in corporate management. It looks at various aspects of welfare benefits, including the four major insurances, the legal welfare benefits that leaders must know, and the non-statutory welfare benefits that companies voluntarily introduce. Chapter 11 is Turnover. If the recruitment in chapter 5 deals with meetings between individuals and organizations, this chapter deals with separation between organizations and individuals. The reason why a company should manage turnover is that it is as important as hiring and the side effects that occur when mismanaged are large. Separation management is divided into voluntary turnover and involuntary turnover.

The third part of this textbook is Chapter 12 Globalization and Human Resource Management, which examines how each function of human resource management covered in chapters 5 through 11 unfolds in a globalized business environment. Students study various international human resource management issues arising in the process of globalization of companies.

CHAPTER 2

Labor Law and Human Resources

1. Understanding of Labor Law
2. HR Decisions and Labor Law
3. Sexual Harassment in the Workplace
4. Workplace Harassment
5. Environmental Changes and Labor Law
6. HR Department's Roles

Learning Objectives

1. Understand the characteristics of labor laws.
2. Understand the basic contents of divers labor laws.
3. Understand the legal requirements regarding staffing and separation of human resources.
4. Can explain specific behavior that correspond to sexual harassment and workplace harassment.
5. Can explain the threat of privacy invasion caused by technological change.
6. Can take preventive actions to avoid labor related law suit.

Introductory Case

Team leader Kim, who is in charge of the HR team at a large domestic company, has a lot of worries about low performers these days. This is because the management has placed an order asking whether or not the employees who are repeatedly receiving the lowest evaluation should be released. Even if not directed by the management, he is well aware that each team leader is struggling with the problem of low performers in the field. However, he is worried that it is difficult to find a good idea.

According to the Fair Personnel Guidelines released by the Ministry of Employment and Labor in 2016, it is stated that fire decision should be based on absolute rather than relative evaluation, and that employees who received the lowest grade at least three consecutive times can be dismissed. Such guidelines don't really help him much. This is because it is not easy to change what has been relative evaluation so far to absolute evaluation. It might be possible to make absolute evaluation only for the lowest grade, but in that case, it is questionable whether the field team leaders will try to give their subordinates the lowest grade.

Also, getting the lowest grade for about 3 times means that an employee with a problem can keep the position for at least 3 years, during which the team leader have no choice but to be patient and work with them. The problem is that the under-performer is not only unable to do his job as expected, but also adversely affects other collegues' work. After contemplating, Kim decided to contact consulting companies for their advices how to proceed the low performer management asked by management.

Discussion Questions

1. How serious is the problem of low performers in Korean firms?
2. Is the HR personnel guidelines mentioned above a legal norm that must be followed?
3. What conditions must be met in order to be considered a dismissal with good cause?
4. What are the pros and cons of voluntary retirement to release the under-performers?

In a capitalist economy, companies conduct business activities by freely combining capital and labor in order to generate profits. Firms hire necessary personnel from external labor markets, evaluate and reward them and develop their competencies, or even fire them. These human resource management activities must be carried out while complying with labor laws protecting workers' rights. Violation of the law will have a very negative impact on the company's performance, not only by penalties or sanctions under the law, but also by making customers or employees feel that the company is unfair. A proactive approach making an effort to prevent such problems from occurring in advance is more important than using competent labor attorneys after a company makes a legally wrong decision. For this, it is essential that leaders have a basic understanding of labor law.

1. Understanding of Labor Law

The Labor Law is a collective term for legal norms governing labor relations so that workers can live a human life in a capitalist society.[1)] Korea's labor law has different characteristics from other laws in the following points.

1.1 Characteristics of the Labor Law

1.1.1 The Right Prescribed in the Constitution

An important feature of Korea's labor law is that the basic principles or rights of labor law are clearly declared and guaranteed in the constitution, the highest norm of the state.[2)] The constitution states that "all citizens have the right to work". This means that the state must protect the unemployed while working for the employment of workers. In addition, the constitution stipulates that "the standard of working conditions is determined by law to guarantee the dignity of human beings", thereby giving the government a policy obligation to set the minimum standard by law in determining working conditions. Lastly, the constitution sets the basic principles of collective labor relations by stipulating that "workers have the right to independent organization, collective bargaining, and collective action in order to improve working conditions."

1.1.2 Protection of Workers

Labor law basically aims to protect workers whose economic status is poor and subordinate to employers. This differs from civil law, which governs the relationship of free contracts between independent economic actors. In the arena of labor, principles of the civil law could not be applied because the relationship between employers and workers are not actually equal, leading to poor working conditions such as low wages and long hours of work. In particular, young people and women had been abused due to their inferior positon in the labor market, thus caused serious social problems. Labor law thus stands on the basis of a very active recognition of the need for the state to intervene in the protection of workers.

1.1.3 Regulations on the Minimum Standards

Labor law sets minimum standards for the protection of workers. The minimum standard for living a life is enforced by law, but for the better conditions, the free contract between employer and worker is recognized. The legislative intention is to to protect workers without overly intervening in free management activities. The Labor Standards Act establishes and regulates minimum labor standards, and the Minimum Wage Act also stipulates the minimum wage level that all employers must abide by. On the other hand, it is possible to set conditions that exceed these minimum standards through collective agreements between labor and management or individual labor contracts.

1.2 System of Labor Law

Labor law is based on labor-related laws and regulations, but it is a complex institutional system in which treaties, collective agreements, labor practices, court cases, and administrative interpretations coexist, and this makes it difficult for leaders to understand labor law. Although these are different in nature, they are all called sources of law in the sense that they are the criteria or grounds that are considered important when judges make decisions in order to resolve disputes under labor law.

1.2.1 Labor Law System

It is the labor-related acts and orders that form the central source of law in the system of labor law. The acts and orders are intended to realize the obligations and rights of the Korean people to work stipulated in Articles 32 and 33 of the Constitution.

Figure 2-1 Hierarchy of Labor-Related Laws

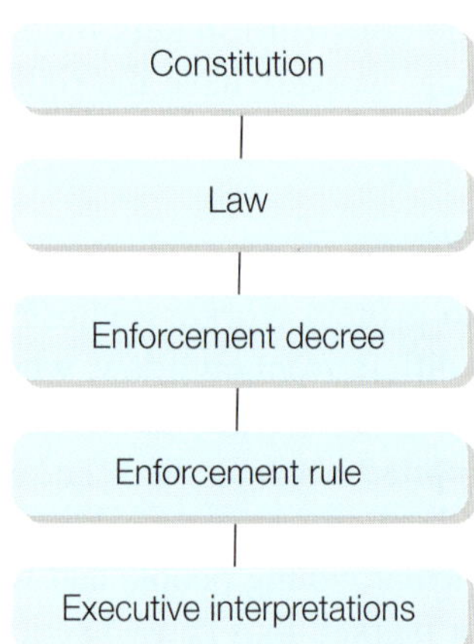

The Constitution is the basis for the formation of labor-related acts and is considered important in the interpretation of labor-related laws. Acts are labor laws enacted by the National Assembly and orders are made by the executive branch. In orders, there are enforcement decrees and enforcement rules. They decide the details necessary for law enforcement in accordance with the mandate set by the law.

Administrative interpretation, such as guiding interpretations and responses to inquiries, has not a legally binding force as it is an internal guideline for the relevant department or public official established for the efficient supervision or enforcement of laws and regulations. In reality, however, it also plays an important role, in particular, when the laws and orders are not clear about some issue. For example, it is the Ministry of Labor's internal rule that excludes fixed bonuses from regular wages for a long period of time. According to the Supreme Court decision in 2013, regular, uniform, and fixed bonuses have been recognized as regular wages differently from the precedent interpretations of the regular wages. On the other hand, treaties such as the International Labor Organization (ILO) Convention concluded and promulgated by Korea according to the Constitution have the same effect as domestic laws and are therefore considered as important labor law standards.

1.2.2 Collective Agreements, Employment Rules and Labor Contracts

Collective agreements, employment rules, labor contracts, and labor practices are not laws, but are used as important grounds for governing the rights and obligations of the management and unions representing employees. A collective agreement is a contract between labor union and an employer and has the effect as a contract between the parties, but at the same time has a normative effect that invalidates the contents of employment rules or labor contracts inferior to the working conditions stipulated in the agreement. Employment rules are set by employers to unify the application of working conditions or workplace rules to a large number of workers. Employers employing 10 or more regular workers are obligated to prepare and report the employment rules to the Minister of Labor.[3)] Labor contracts are contracts between workers and employers stipulating concrete conditions of work including wage and working hours. Lastly, labor practice refers to what has been taken for granted in the field for a long time without being specified in collective agreements, employment rules, and labor contracts. Practices that continue without objection from the parties may be recognized as valid as agreements or contracts.

1.2.3 Judicial Precedents

Labor laws stipulate the basic contents, but cannot be made with all possible circumstances. In reality, administrative interpretation can be used to supplement the areas not stipulated in laws, but it does not have legal effect. Therefore, disputes are settled by a court decision. The judgment of the court can be regarded as the judge's interpretation of the law and is legally binding on the case. However, precedents on labor cases are not the norms that other judges must follow. This is because in Korea, which adopts statuteism, it is not necessary for judges to follow precedents, and if it is not the same case, they are not bound by the precedents of the superior court. However, higher court precedents, in the sense of filling the void in labor-related laws or clarifying the meaning of the laws to be applied, constitute an important labor law norm. In particular, in the case of the Supreme Court case, it is the final judgment on the lawsuit and thus acts as a very important labor law norm that unions, workers, and employers must consider.

1.2.4 Priorities between Norms

As discussed above, legal norms or standards are wide and diverse, and in the case of conflicting norms for the same object or issue, which one to follow becomes an important issue. The criteria for determining priorities are the higher law priority principle and the favorable condition priority principle. The former means that the higher norms must be followed in case of conflict between different norms. As already mentioned earlier, labor law norms constitute the hierarchy of the constitution, laws, enforcement decrees (orders), collective agreements, employment rules, and labor contracts. This principle implies that higher norms have priority over lower norms and that lower norms violating the higher norms are considered to be ineffective.

On the other hand, the principle of preferential conditions is that in case of conflict between norms, the norms that set favorable conditions for workers are applied first. For example, if the labor contract is more favorable to the worker than the Labor Standards Act, the labor contract will be applied first. If the labor contract is more favorable to the worker than the employment rules, the labor contract will be applied first. This principle is a special principle of labor law that is difficult to find in other legal fields, and it can be said to be a legal mechanism to realize the purpose of the labor law to protect workers who are relatively weak compared to employers in the labor market.

1.3 Types of Labor Laws

Labor law is divided into individual labor relations law and collective labor relations law according to the subject of its regulation. The individual labor related acts regulate the contractual relationship between individual workers and employers or the working conditions of individual workers. Labor Standards Act is a representative example of this kind of law. On the other hand, the collective labor related acts are a statute that regulates the social position of the group of workers, including the labor union, and the relationship with employers. These laws include the Labor Union and Labor Relations Adjustment Act, and the Act on Promotion of Worker Participation and Labor-Management Cooperation. Each law can be viewed at the National Law Information Center (www.law.go.kr) operated by the Ministry of Legislation. Hereinafter, we will briefly look at the major labor laws that leaders must be aware of.

1) Labor Standards Act

The Labor Standards Act aims to guarantee and improve the basic living of workers by setting standards for working conditions. Since the working conditions stipulated in the Labor Standards Act are the minimum standards, labor contracts that violate or fall short of those standards are, in principle, invalidated. The Labor Standards Act applies to all businesses or workplaces that employ five or more permanent workers, but does not apply to workplaces using only relatives who live with and domestic workers. Some provisions of the Labor Standards Act apply to workplaces with four or fewer permanent workers.[4)]

2) Employment Insurance Act

This is a law aimed at contributing to economic and social development by promoting the stability of workers' lives and job search activities. Through the implementation of employment insurance, this law has a purpose to prevent unemployment and promote employment at the same time, and to develop and improve workers' vocational skills. When workers are unemployed, allowances necessary for life are provided by the employment insurance. Workers and employers pay 0.8% of the monthly standard income respectively as for unemployment insurance benefits. For vocational competency development, insurance premiums of 0.25% to 0.85% are charged to employers depending on the type of business and size.[5)]

3) Wage Claim Guarantee Act

This act has a purpose of contributing to the stability of the lives of workers by taking measures to guarantee the payment to workers who separated from the company without receiving wages due to difficult business situations. In Korea, employers should offer severance pay when they let employees out of the company, and sometimes employers could not pay it though because they go bankrupt. According to the law, the Minister of Labor shall pay unpaid wages on behalf of the employer when the latter could not pay wages due to reasons such as bankruptcy. And for this purpose, the Wage Claim Guarantee Fund was established and operated.

4) Industrial Accident Compensation Insurance Act

It is a law for the purpose of contributing to worker protection by promptly and fairly compensating for workers' occupational accidents, installing and operating insurance facilities necessary for promoting rehabilitation of injured workers, and conducting accident prevention and other projects to promote workers' welfare. Insurance business is administered by the Minister of Labor, and insurance is applied to all businesses employing more than one person. The Korea Workers' Compensation and Welfare Service manages and maintains insurance records, collects insurance premiums and other levies, determines and pays insurance benefits, installs and operates insurance facilities, and performs workers' welfare promotion projects. The employer becomes an insurance subscriber and pays the insurance premium.

5) Act on Equal Employment and Support for Work-Family Reconciliation

This Act guarantees equal opportunity and treatment of men and women in employment in accordance with the constitutional equality principle, and promotes maternity protection and employment of women, thereby realizing equal employment for men and women, and supporting the balance between work and family for the workers. While article 6 of the Labor Standards Act prohibits discriminatory treatment in the application of working conditions to workers who are already employed, its contents are comprehensive and abstract. On the other hand, this act specifically prohibits gender discrimination in recruitment and employment. It was enacted in 1987 in the name of the "Equal Employment Act of Men and Women", and there have been several amendments. The revision of 2007 introduced maternity leave for spouses.

6) Act on Employment Promotion and Vocational Rehabilitation for Disabled Persons

As the name implies, this law was enacted in 1990 to promote employment and vocational rehabilitation for the disabled. According to this law, public institutions, governments and local governments should hire 3.4%, and private companies employing 50 or more workers must employ 3.1% of the disabled of the total number of full-time workers, When the mandatory employment rate is exceeded, the employment incentive is paid, and when it is not met, the obligation to pay the contribution is incurred only for employers employing 100 or more employees excluding the state and local governments. Based on the contribution, a fund for the promotion of employment of the disabled is created, and various employment promotion activities for the disabled are carried out using the fund. The operation of all tasks necessary for the implementation of this act is undertaken by the Korea Employment Employment Agency for Persons with Disabilities, established under this Act.

7) Act on Prohibition of Age Discrimination in Employment and Aged Employment Promotion

This law was created to correct the reality of frequent discrimination in employment or dismissal due to age in the labor market while the number of elder people increases with the progress of aging society. The purpose of this act is to prevent employment discrimination on the basis of age without reasonable reasons, and to contribute to the stability of employment for the elderly and the development of the national economy by supporting and promoting the elderly to have jobs that match their abilities. Elderly persons under this act are those who are 55 years or older, and employers should not discriminate on the basis of age in all stages of employment, such as recruitment and hiring of workers, payment of wages, welfare benefits, education and training and placement, transfer and promotion, retirement and dismissal. Indirect discrimination by applying criteria other than age that results in adverse consequences for certain age groups is also prohibited.

8) Trade Union and Labor Relations Adjustment Act

Based on the workers' right for organizing, collective bargaining, and collective action guaranteed by the Constitution, this act seeks to maintain and improve working conditions and improve the economic and social status of workers, and to prevent and settle labor disputes through fair adjustment of labor relations. This law is aimed at maintaining peace and contributing to the development of the national economy. The collective agreement concluded between the labor union, the representative organization of workers and the employer, plays an important role in maintaining and improving working conditions. Working conditions that are above the minimum standard of the Labor Standards Act are secured through the agreement between the labor union and the employer. And working conditions that are not specified in the Labor Standards Act are clearly established by the agreement. To this end, this act deals with the conclusion and effect of collective agreements, along with the contents of the establishment and operation of unions. In addition, it stipulates institutional rules that can reasonably adjust labor-management conflicts, such as mediation of labor disputes, and includes regulations on unfair labor practices.

9) Act on the Promotion of Employees' Participation and Cooperation

This was enacted with the aim of realizing industrial peace and contributing to the development of the national economy by promoting the common interests of labor and management through participation and cooperation. In accordance with this act, establishment of a labor-management council is obligated in workplaces employing 30 or more regular workers, and the management has to consult with the council how to share the productivity, recruit and place workers and train them, prevent labor disputes, handle grievances of workers, etc. Unlike unions, the labor-management council is a consultative body that basically deals with issues for the promotion of joint interests between labor and management, but it also plays a similar role to a union in workplaces without a union.

10) Labor Relations Commission Act

Mediation of conflict or dispute between labor and management is very important for industrial peace, and the labor committee is the organization dedicated to it. This act stipulates the organization, composition, operation and authorities of these labor committees. The labor committee consists of three members representing workers, employers, and the public interest to determine or coordinate important matters in labor relations. The labor commission is established so that labor disputes can be resolved fairly, quickly and reasonably using the specialized expertise of labor issues. For individual workers, the Labor Relations Commission is important because it is in charge of applying for relief from unfair dismissal. Workers who are unfairly dismissed can file an remedy application for unfair dismissal within three months from the date of dismissal, and if the Labor Commission determines that this is unfair, they can be re-employed or receive financial compensation if the worker does not want it.[6)]

2. HR Decisions and Labor Law

Human resource management activities are closely related to labor law. This is because the HR decisions that companies make should be fair and not discriminatory, and an important criterion for determining whether such decisions are fair is the labor law. All HR activities such as hiring, evaluation, compensation, and dismissal are directly related to the labor law, and leaders must fully understand the principles and

Must the flight attendant wear a skirt?

Although it is not generally related to working conditions under the legal regulation, there are cases where the dress code for members becomes an hot issue. A typical example is the obligation of wearing skirts by female flight attendants, imposed by the management. Since its founding in 1988, Asiana Airlines has provided only skirt uniforms to female flight attendants to wear them. However, in February 2013, the National Human Rights Commission of Korea judged the company policy as gender discrimination. Accordingly, the company decided to allow female flight attendants to choose between a skirt and pants uniform. As Asiana Airlines, the only one airline insisting on a female skirt uniform, gave up this, the company's female flight attendants now have a choice to wear pants uniforms.

standards set by the law. Since leaders are not experts in labor law, it is not necessary to familiarize themselves with all the contents of the law, but they must be acquainted with the basic principles, and it is desirable to seek help from labor law experts such as certified public labor attorney and lawyers.

In the case of hiring, it is very rare for an unselected applicant to file a lawsuit against the company. In the national examination, it is possible to confirm the reasons or grounds for disqualification by filing a request for information disclosure, but in the case of private enterprises, such a system does not exist. However, discriminatory hiring is a very important issue in which applicants are deprived of opportunities, so discrimination related to hiring is not only legally prohibited but also leads to deterioration of the image of company. Among the areas of personnel management, labor law regulations and litigation are concentrated in the dismissal. Dismissal is the most threatening and serious situation for an individual who is already employed, so many requests for relief or a lawsuits occurs. Therefore, it is necessary for the management and HR department to educate leaders to prevent unreasonable or unfair decisions regarding hiring and dismissal.

2.1 Hiring Discrimination and Labor Law

Litigation related to hiring rarely occurs in Korea. This is because when applicants fail, it is difficult to know by what criteria they actually failed. Like medical disputes, the asymmetry of information that exists in the hiring process plays a role in greatly reducing the possibility of litigation. In addition, when considering the cost and time required for a lawsuit, the size of compensation itself is not large enough even the case of winning a lawsuit. Under this circumstances, it makes sense for the worker to look for other jobs rather than filing a suit against the company. In the case of the US, where problem solving through lawsuits is more common than in Korea, there are relatively fewer cases of lawsuits related to hiring compared to dismissal, promotion or compensation. However, it should be noted that discrimination in the hiring process is strictly prohibited by law in any country without exception.

2.1.1 Legal Regulations on Hiring Discrimination

Article 11 of the Constitution declares that all citizens are equal before the law and that no one is discriminated against in all areas of political, economic, social and cultural life based on gender, religion or social status. Therefore, discrimination without a reasonable basis for hiring is against the Constitution. Laws that clearly prohibit discrimination in relation to employment include the Act of Basic Employment Policy, the Act on Equal Employment and Support for Work-Family Reconciliation, the Act on Prohibition of Age Discrimination in Employment and Aged Employment Promotion, and the Act on Employment Promotion and Vocational Rehabilitation for Disabled Persons.

- Article 7 of the Basic Employment Policy Act

When recruiting and hiring workers, employers should not discriminate on the gender, faith, age, physical condition, social status, area of origin, education, school of origin, marriage, pregnancy, or medical history of the job applicants.

- Article 7 of the Act on Equal Employment and Support for Work-Family Reconciliation

An employer shall not discriminate on grounds of gender in recruitment and hiring of workers. When recruiting and hiring female workers, the employer shall not present nor demand certain physical conditions, such as appearances, height, weight, etc., and unmarried conditions shall not be required for performing the relevant duties.

- Article 4-4 of the Act on Prohibition of Age Discrimination in Employment and Aged Employment Promotion

An employer shall not discriminate against a worker and a person who intends to be a worker on the grounds of age without any reasonable cause in the following areas: recruitment and employment, provision of wages, and other money and valuables, and welfare benefits, education and training, assignment, transfer or promotion, and retirement or dismissal.

- Article 5-2 of the Act on Employment Promotion and Vocational Rehabilitation for Disabled Persons

Employers shall not discriminate against any worker in personnel management, such as hiring, promotion, transfer, education and training, merely on the ground that the worker is a disabled person.

2.1.2 The Reality of Hiring Discrimination

However, laws and regulations are not always well followed. In reality, there are still many different types of discrimination. According to the results of an additional survey on the status of non-regular work by the Korea Labor Institute,[7)] groups that were largely exposed to discriminatory practices appeared in the order of 50 years old or older, married women, women, high school graduates, and disabled people. In addition, the smaller the size of the business, the more severe the discrimination against women, disabled or elderly persons. According to another survey of 545 job seekers,[8)] people experienced a lot of discrimination in the order of age, school or education, appearance or physical condition, and social status.

When you search for the media articles, irrational discrimination is still easily found. For example, An aircarrier, which is said to have abolished the height limit set at 162 centimeters in the qualifications for female flight attendants, does not actually select if they are shorter than this.[9)] And there are still cases in which the age of eligibility for application is explicitly specified to a certain age during the recruitment process, thereby preventing employment opportunities for the elderly.[10)] Meanwhile, the constitution guarantees freedom of faith, but there are cases where faith acts as a discriminatory factor in employment. This is because some companies do not recognize the qualifications for non-members of a specific religion.[11)] And gender discrimination in hiring still remains. In the process of selecting an in-house attorney, there are cases in which a skilled female applicant cannot be hired because of concerns about job vacancy caused by marriage and childbirth.[12)]

2.1.3 National Human Right Commission and its Role

The National Human Right Commission was launched in 2002 and plays a very active role in resolving discrimination related to hiring. The committee is responsible for investigation and remedy not only for hiring but also for discrimination against the widespread violation of equal rights as prescribed by the Constitution. Individuals who have been discriminated may file a complaint with the Commission, and the Commission may investigate and recommend correction to the relevant employer or institution. Although the recommendation for correction has no compulsory effect, it acts as an important social pressure and it can be beneficial to the complainant if he decides to sue.

In addition, in accordance with the recommendations of the Human Rights Commission, administrative departments such as the Ministry of Justice and the Ministry of Employment and Labor may issue a corrective order on the matter, and a fine for negligence will be imposed if the correction is not implemented. One of the recommendations made by the Commission recently was the case of gender discrimination related to the open recruitment of candidates for police officers. While recruiting candidates, the National Police Agency allocates them by gender, and the Commission made clear that it is a gender discrimination.[13)]

2.1.4 The Role of Companies and Leaders

For the elimination of hiring discrimination, companies' voluntary efforts are the most necessary. In the case of companies, there has been a lot of effort to recruit excellent talent, but relatively less effort has been put to solve the problem of discrimination in the hiring process. However, neglecting the issue of discrimination can lead to stronger legal regulations. For example, the government announced a plan for blind recruitment and, accordingly, this practice quickly spread among public institutions nationwide. In addition, a bill has been proposed to institutionalize blind hiring when hiring employees. If the bill is formally passed by the National Assembly, job seekers cannot be asked for information that is not directly related to the job in the field to be hired. Even if it is not legally regulated, hiring discrimination can deteriorate the image of a company and make the mistake of missing out on talented people. Moreover, it is important to keep in mind that the loss of key talents due to discrimination can affect the success of the business. Therefore, the following efforts are needed to eliminate discrimination.

1) Job or Performance-Based Recruitment Standards

If the purpose of hiring is to recruit people who can do the job well, the criteria for recruitment and selection should be reasonable accordingly. From that point of view, requesting the submission of documents unrelated to job duties or requesting unnecessary personal information should be avoided. For example, unless it is absolutely necessary, it is suspicious of hiring discrimination in itself requiring information such as family member's education, occupation, property situation, family type, or physical condition such as height and weight. It is advisable to create and use a resume or application that excludes such information. Instead, the alternative is to hire based on information about competencies, skills, and careers that are highly correlated to job performance. In the end, it is necessary to use a hiring method with strong validity, and the details are explained in Chapter 5 dealing with staffing management.

2) Reinforcing Education for Business Leaders

Considering that a company's compliance with the law is the most basic of business activities, it is important for leaders that they should not discriminate in hiring. Moreover, it is necessary for the leaders to have a clear understanding of non-discrimination principle. Keeping in mind that all applicants applying to companies are potential customers, making efforts to avoid unfair discrimination in the hiring process is an important role and responsibility of both the HR department and line leaders.

3) Open Culture of Organization

One of the important reasons for employment-related discrimination is the company's closed culture which makes it difficult to accommodate a variety of human resources. For example, companies with a strong male-centered corporate culture tend to avoid hiring female workers. Even if the management or HR team tries to increase the number of female workers, there could be a lot of resistance from line leaders. In addition, even if HR team ignore the opposition and choose female workers, line leaders and employees do not welcome and support them. Therefore, there is a need to change the culture of the workplace to be more open. It could be very helpful to allow leaders and other members to experience the strengths and effects of the diversity of workforce.

4) Fair Recruitment Process

The hiring process must be conducted fairly in accordance with legal standards. The Fair Hiring Procedure Act prohibits false advertisements, and stipulates that the recruitment process be fair by notifying the recruitment schedule and the recruitment process, and promptly notifying the results when it is decided. In addition, it is forbidden to change the procedure unfavorably to job seekers after the job advertisement is published, or to change the offered working conditions after hiring. Violation of these provisions will result in a fine for negligence. Therefore, it is important for the HR department to conduct the recruitment process fairly and promptly so as not to violate the law.

2.2 Dismissal and Labor Law

Dismissal is a situation in which the dismissed tend to feel anxiety and anger most strongly in employment relations, and relief applications and lawsuits by workers are very frequent. This is because dismissal can be a very serious threat to the individual's economic survival. The employers have the right to fire employees if necessary. However, the law sets certain procedures and standards to prevent such decisions from being abused.

2.2.1 Different Types of Dismissal and Legal Regulations

Dismissal is an involuntary turnover made against the will of an employee. There can be many reasons why companies let people out. In some cases, a dismissal may be due to managerial reasons, or dismissal may occur due to serious faults or excessively low performance of the individual workers. Depending on the reason for which a dismissal occurs, applicable legal regulations and standards or procedures to be followed will be different.

1) Dismissal for Managerial Reasons

In order to overcome a serious business crisis, people are sometimes sent out. This is called collective dismissal for economic reasons, and in practice it is also called layoff. Unlike dismissal due to personal reasons, in this case the cause of dismissal lies not in the individual's fault or problem but in the company's economic difficulties. This kind of dismissal is specified in Article 24 of the Labor Standards Act, and in order for dismissal to be regarded as justifiable for managerial reasons, the following four conditions must be satisfied.

First, in order for an employer to dismiss employees for managerial reason, there must be an urgent management need. Not only severe sales decline but business transfers, acquisitions, and mergers to prevent business deterioration are considered to be of urgent business need. Second, even if the necessity of dismissal is recognized, the employer must make every effort to avoid dismissal. Third, reasonable and fair standards for dismissal should be established and the target person should be selected accordingly. In this case, discrimination shall not be made on the grounds of the gender or age. Fourth, the union or employee representative must be notified 50 days prior to the date of dismissal about the method to avoid dismissal and the criteria for dismissal, and they have to be consulted in good faith.

2) Normal and Disciplinary Dismissal

Dismissal may occur due to personal reasons, such as misbehaviors or low performance of individual workers. Normal or ordinary dismissal means that the employer terminates the labor contract if the worker fails to fulfill the obligation to provide labor and it is attributable to the worker. For example, when it is difficult for the workers to perform work due to illness, injury, or physical disability, dismissal is possible. However, the company should confirm whether the job can be performed through appropriate accommodation making the job less burdensome. A hasty dismissal is likely to be considered unfair dismissal. Remarkably low performance can also be a reason for dismissal. However, there can be a difficulty in securing objective standards for how to judge that the work performance is remarkably low.

Meanwhile, disciplinary dismissal is the termination of the labor contract for violating workplace order. The company may dismiss an employee if his behavior seriously damages the workplace order. The specific reasons for disciplinary dismissal can be very diverse, such as embezzlement of public money, drinking alcohol or taking prohibited drugs while working, assault, disobedience to work orders from the boss, and absenteeism without notice. In South Korea, where normal dismissal is difficult, disciplinary dismissal is often used as a means of dismissing poor performers. However, it should be noted that the dismissal may be nullified if the employee's violation of order is not serious enough to justify dismissal.

The criteria for dismissing underperformers are not clearly stipulated in the law. According to the judicial precedents, the justification of dismissal can be recognized only when the work performance is objectively poor enough to be unable to maintain the employment relationship. And whether it is impossible to continue the employment relationship is determined by comprehensively considering the following matters along with the provisions of collective agreements and employment rules.

① Evaluation based on objective and reasonable criteria
② Consistent and repeated low performance
③ Offer of opportunities for performance improvement
④ Possibility of improvement in the future

2.2.2 Unfair Dismissal and Legal Remedies

Unfair dismissal is dismissal without justifiable reason, and a worker who has been unfairly dismissed may file an unfair dismissal remedy to the Labor Commission or file a lawsuit against the court. Relief through the Labor Commission takes less time than through the court, and because the Labor Commission has expertise in labor, it is more efficient for workers. However, if the employer disagrees with its decision, they have to file a lawsuit with the administrative court again, which may result in more time and cost. A worker who has been unfairly dismissed may file a request for relief with the local labor commission that has jurisdiction over the location of the dismissed company within 3 months from the date of dismissal. If worker or employer disagree with this decision, they could file a lawsuit with the administrative court within 15 days of being served with the decision.

When an application for relief is filed with the Labor Commission, the Labor Commission conduct an investigation, and hold an interrogation meeting within 60 days. After that, 5 commissioners consisting of 3 representing public interest, and of each one representing labor and management, participate to conduct an interrogation on the applicant and the employer. When the interrogation is over, three public interest members make a decision. If the employee's request for relief is approved by the Labor Commission and the company accepts it, the company will reinstate the employee. If the unfairly dismissed employee wants, the company can compensate an amount equivalent to the salary for the period after dismissal instead of reinstatement. There are many cases in which the working relationship is terminated by monetary compensation. This is because it is not easy to go back to the company and perform work in an unfavorable atmosphere.

On the other hand, an unfairly dismissed worker, apart from filing an application to the local labor commission, could implead the employer to the local branch of the Ministry of Employment and Labor. Local labor offices do not make legal judgments on unfair dismissal, but have thc function of taking administrative measures or sending employers to the prosecutor's office for those determined to be unfair dismissal. If a worker files a petition or complaint with a local labor office for unfair dismissal, and if a relief order is issued by the Labor Commission, the local labor office gives the employer a corrective order. And if the employer does not comply, the office indict him to the prosecution.

2.2.3 Role of the Leaders

The occurrence of unfair dismissal means that personnel management is not being properly performed. In a company where legal disputes over unfair dismissal are frequent, it is difficult to expect that the competencies and motivations of its members will be fully exhibited. To prevent that from happening, leaders need to make the following efforts.

1) Understanding and Compliance with Dismissal Laws

Leaders must be familiar and comply with the rules stipulated in laws, collective agreements and employment rules. First of all, it should be noted that the declaration of intention to dismiss must be made in writing: if not in written document, dismissal has no effect. In addition, the dismissal procedures stipulated in collective agreements or employment rules must be followed. If a worker is dismissed without going through such a procedure, even if the reason for dismissal is justified, it may be invalidated by violating the dismissal procedure. Lastly, for dismissal, a notice must be made 30 days in advance. Otherwise, a normal wage of 30 days or more must be paid. If this is violated, the employer may be criminally punished for violating Article 26 of the Labor Standards Act.[14)]

2) Operating a Fair Evaluation System

The evaluation system is important for competency development and motivation, but it is also very important to avoid unfair dismissal. In principle, evaluation of workers' ability and performance is recognized as the employer's personnel management rights. However, evaluation should be made fairly so as not to abuse discretion in dismissal. To this end, the evaluation should be based on the work ability and performance of workers as objectively as possible. In addition, quantitative evaluation is a principle, but if qualitative elements are inevitable due to the characteristics of the work content, non-quantitative evaluation can be appropriately included in some evaluation items. The fact that the worker received the lowest grade through evaluation cannot immediately imply that he is significantly short of work ability or performance. This is because in the relative evaluation system, even if the performance is not markedly insufficient, someone has no choice but to receive the lowest grade. In order to avoid unfair dismissal, it is advisable to perform absolute evaluation to the lowest grade. Lastly, in a company where evaluation is conducted in a way that usually gives good scores to those who are to be promoted, the dismissal based on the evaluation results can be questioned as unreliable and unfair. It is therefore important for leaders to operate the evaluation system fairly and strictly.

3) Preventive Measures against Under-Performers

While it is important not to do unfair dismissal, leaders must make an effort in advance to prevent under-performers from occurring. To this end, it is important to carefully review and evaluate whether members have the capacity and motivation to fulfill their role from the early stages of their careers. If a worker is not performing enough, it is advisable to identify the reason and provide an opportunity to demonstrate one's competence through job transfer. If he does not match the core values of the company or there is a problem with his attitude, it is necessary to support his turnover so that the person can obtain new opportunities in other companies.

3. Sexual Harassment in the Workplace

Sexual harassment in the workplace is a much more frequent incident than discriminatory hiring or unfair dismissal. However, it is rare for employees who have been sexually harassed to formally raise issues. This is because they are afraid of having a bad reputation for themselves or of having to quit the company. However, if sexual harassment is neglected, the working atmosphere deteriorates and communication and cooperation among members are hindered, which negatively affects the organization's performance. According to the Gender Equality Employment Act, employers, supervisors, or workers are not allowed to engage in sexual harassment in the workplace, and employers should conduct education to prevent sexual harassment in the workplace and to create conditions for workers to work in a safe working environment.[15)]

Table 2-1 **Major Laws and Contents Related to Sexual Harassment**

Framework act on gender equality	• Definition of sexual harassment in the workplace • Obligation to prevent sexual harassment of heads of state agencies and employers
Equal employment and work-family balance assistance act	• Definition of sexual harassment in the workplace • Prevention and prohibition of sexual harassment • Victim protection and resolution of disputes
National human rights commission act	• Definition of sexual harassment in the workplace • Relief Procedure for Sexual Harassment

3.1 The Concept of Sexual Harassment in the Workplace

Sexual harassment is dealt with in various laws, but the most important laws are the Framework Act on Gender Equality, the Equal Employment Opportunity and Work-Family Balance Assistance Act and the National Human Rights Commission Act. The main contents covered by these laws are as follows.

1) Definition of Sexual Harassment in the Workplace

Subparagraph 2 of Article 2 of the Equal Employment and Support for Work-Family Balance Act says, "the term sexual harassment on the job means that an employer, a superior or an employee causes another employee to feel sexual humiliation or repulsion by sexual words or actions by utilizing a position in the workplace or in relation with duties, or providing any disadvantages in working conditions and employment on account of disregard for sexual words or actions or any other demands." Not only employers, superiors, co-workers, and subordinates, but also employees of business partners, customers, partners, workers, dispatched workers, and job seekers can be perpetrators of workplace harassment.

The victims of sexual harassment in the workplace are generally women, but legally, both men and women can be victims. Sexual harassment in the workplace is established when the position in the workplace is used or when it happens in connection with work. "in the workplace" is not a place-specific concept, but refers to an action that takes place within the scope of the employer's command. Therefore, workplace harassment can occur outside of the workplace, such as business trips and dinners.[16)]

2) Types of Sexual Harassment

The U.S. Equal Employment Opportunity Commission(EEOC) categorizes sexual harassment into conditional sexual harassment (Quid pro quo sexual harassment) and hostile work environment sexual harassment. Conditional sexual harassment is to give a disadvantage in employment due to failure to comply with sexual language or other requests. In this case, 'disadvantages in employment' refer to dropout of employment, reduction of salary, dropout of promotion, change of job, suspension, one-sided disadvantage of working conditions etc. On the other hand, environmental

Table 2-2 **Examples of Criteria for Determining Sexual Harassment**

Physical behaviors	• Physical contact such as kissing, hugging, or hugging from behind • Touching specific body parts such as chest and buttocks • Forced massage or caress
Verbal behaviors	• Making obscene jokes or telling obscene and vulgar stories (including phone calls) • Conducting sexual metaphors or evaluations of appearance • Inquiring about sexual facts or intentionally disseminating information of sexual content • Forcing or contributing to a sexual relationship • Forcing to pour alcohol by making to sit near at a dinner table
Visual behaviors	• Posting or showing obscene photos, pictures, graffiti, publications, etc. (including the use of computer communications or facsimile) • Deliberately exposing or touching a specific body part related to sex

sexual harassment refers to an act that makes the other person's working environment remarkably unpleasant and impedes the display of job skills, even if there is no employment disadvantage. Both types of sexual harassment are included in the definition of Korean act on equal employment.

3) Specific Behavior of Sexual Harassment

Behavior that can be sexual harassment is defined as those that causes sexual shame or disgust, but it may not be clear what specifically constitutes sexual harassment. To resolve this ambiguity, Article 2 of the Enforcement Rule of the Equal Employment Act divides the criteria for judging sexual harassment into physical, verbal, and visual behaviors, and presents concrete examples of behavior as follows. When judging whether sexual harassment exists, the subjective circumstances of the victim are considered first, but it is also considered together how a reasonable person in the victim's position would judge and respond to the behavior in question.

3.2 The Reality of Sexual Harassment in the Workplace

In Korea, sexual harassment in the workplace emerged as a social issue for the first time in the case of the assistant Mrs. Woo at Seoul National University, which started a lawsuit in 1993. The lawsuit could not be completely finished until 1999, six years later. In this case, the court admitted the perpetrator's responsibility, but not the employer's responsibility. In 1999, the same year, in order to solve the problem of sexual harassment in the workplace, a prohibition on sexual harassment was newly established in the Equal Employment Act, and sexual harassment prevention education became mandatory. Nevertheless, sexual harassment cases have not ceased since then. What brought sexual harassment back to the fore as an important social issue was a lawsuit against the CEO of the company by female members of Lotte Hotel union in 2000. This case drew a lot of attention in that it was Korea's first class action lawsuit of sexual harassment with

180 victims. As the demand for social measures against the sexual harassment problem grew, the law amendment in 2007 explicitly included employer responsibilities and punishment provisions.

However, the reality is that sexual harassment is still prevalent. If you click on the search term of sexual harassment on the Internet portal, you can easily find a lot of incident articles. Several survey results show that sexual harassment that Korean office workers face is very widespread. According to the survey of the Ministry of Gender Equality and Family on the sexual harassment,[17)] the number of respondents who experienced sexual harassment at least once during the past three years at work was 8.1% of all respondents, indicating that women, younger people, irregular workers, and social service industries had a high experience of sexual harassment. Sexual harassment perpetrators were mainly 'superior' (61.1%), followed by 'colleagues' (21.2%), and most of the sexual harassment were done by male (83.6%). 'Dining place' (43.7%) and 'office' (36.8%) are the main places where sexual harassment occurs, and workers who are victims of sexual harassment shows 'disappointed at work' (28.7%), 'lower willingness to work' and 'health deterioration' (8.2%). Surprisingly, 81.6% of the victims of sexual harassment responded that they did not report it to the company. They think it is not so serious issue or they do not expect the company would be willing to solve it for them.

3.3 Employer's Legal Obligation

First of all, the employer must not engage in sexual harassment on his own. The equal employment act stipulates that employers, supervisors, or workers must not engage in sexual harassment in the workplace. In addition to these passive responsibilities, employers should actively endeavor to prohibit and prevent sexual harassment. To this end, the employer must provide training to employees to prevent sexual harassment at least once a year, and if sexual harassment is confirmed, disciplinary measures must be taken against the offender without delay. In addition, employers shall not dismiss or take other adverse measures against workers who have suffered damages in relation to sexual harassment in the workplace or workers who allege sexual harassment damage.

The Framework Act on Gender Equality makes it mandatory for the state and local governments to provide an official window for counseling and handling grievances related to sexual harassment, and to designate a person in charge of sexual harassment grievances (Article 31 of the Act, Article 20, Paragraph 1, No.5 of the decree). However, disciplinary action and victim protection are not directly stated in the law. It stipulates that the Minister of Gender Equality and Family may request disciplinary action of the person concerned in the event of concealing a sexual harassment case or secondary damage to the victim.

In the case of private companies, non-judicial dispute resolution procedures that victims can use in relation to sexual harassment include local labor offices, labor commissions, and national human rights commissions. In addition, victims of sexual harassment may file a civil lawsuit claiming compensation for damage caused by sexual harassment. At this time, the claim for damages is possible not only for the wrong-doer but also for the employer.

3.4 Role of Company and Leaders

It is natural for the company to comply with the obligations set forth in the law. However, in order to prevent and eradicate sexual harassment, the company must make more proactive efforts than now. Sexual harassment is a very dangerous behavior that undermines mutual respect and cooperation among members of the company and destroys trust in management. Fortunately, education and punishment for sexual harassment have been greatly strengthened recently, in particular, in some leading companies. It is desirable for companies and leaders to work in the following directions to avoid the deterioration of the company's image and the atmosphere of the workplace by sexual harassment.

1) Strengthening Sexual Harassment Education

According to the law, companies are required to conduct sexual harassment training at least once a year. However, this alone is not enough. It is important to conduct sexual harassment education for the new employees. It should be clearly understood to members who are starting a new organizational life why sexual harassment must never be committed. In particular, it is important that leaders make efforts to prevent sexual harassment from occurring through continuous observation and communication.

2) Installation of Hotline

In the case of a victim, it is difficult to tell the facts to their boss, especially when the aggressor is the boss himself. Therefore, it is necessary to establish and operate a hotline with a person in charge. It is very important to ensure that reports can be made early so that sexual harassment is not repeated and persisted, causing further problems or damage. If the initial response is delayed, the intensity of the damage or the number of victims may increase, and the company's responsibility increases accordingly. In addition, anyone who discovers sexual harassment, even if he is not the victim, should

The largest sexual harassment damage compensation ever

In the United States, which has a punitive alimony system, the scale of compensation for damage is sometimes very huge. The largest claim ever related to sexual harassment in the workplace is the lawsuit filed by Ani Chopourian against Mercy General Hospital. She, who worked as an assistant in cardiac surgery, received constant sexual harassment from doctors and staff for three years from 2006 to 2008. She kept sending e-mails to the human resources department asking for resolution, but she had to be fired. Since then, she sued the company, and after four years of lawsuits, the federal court brought the company \$125 million for punitive damage, \$39 million for mental damage, and \$3.5 million for unpaid wage. (ABC News, April 3, 2013). This case gives un important lesson for US companies to respond quickly and fairly to sexual harassment in the workplace.

be allowed to report it immediately.

3) Rapid Investigation and Corrective Action

When reports of sexual harassment come in, prompt investigations should be made. In this process, care should be taken not to expose the identity of the victim. Those who are designated as perpetrators need to be carefully and accurately investigated. In addition, if sexual harassment is confirmed, corrective or disciplinary action should be taken immediately. Otherwise, the victim's complaints are amplified and actions are taken outside the company to solve the problem.

4) Intolerance Policy

For sexual harassment that occurs even after sufficient education, a very strict penalty principle should be established and implemented. It should be recognized by all that anyone who engages in sexual harassment is subject to strong discipline without exception. In fact, an elite manager of one company, who was expected to be promoted to the executive position, was forced to leave the company due to sexual harassment, and as a result, the awareness of not committing sexual harassment was greatly raised to the entire company.

4. Workplace Harassment

In any society, there is always discrimination or harassment against people with values or behaviors different. This phenomenon is the same within the company. Workplace bullying in a company can be caused not only by differences in values or behaviors, but also by low ability or under-performance. People show a critical gaze or disregard to the individuals who are hindering group performance because of their lack of skill or poor work. People who are the target of bullying tend to experience social disconnection, such as not talking to, and may self-depreciate themselves or show severe mental depression. As a result, they sometimes make an extreme choice. The case of nurse Park Seon-wook, who committed suicide in 2018, is a prime example. After working as a nurse at Asan Hospital in Seoul, she fell from an apartment and killed herself. It was caused by bullying at work and the resulting stress.

As her death caught the attention of the media, the serious reality of workplace harassment came to the fore. In 2019, a provision banning workplace harassment was newly established in the Labor Standards Act and came into force on July 16. In addition, the Industrial Accident Compensation Insurance Act was also revised so that diseases caused by mental stress from workplace harassment were included as occupational diseases, thus opening the way for victims to receive compensation. Article 76 (2) of the Labor Standards Act refers to harassment in the workplace as "an act of causing physical or mental pain to other workers or worsening the working environment by using the superiority of the employer or worker's position or relationship in the workplace" and prohibits such behavior.[18)]

In addition, Article 76 (3) of the same Act stipulates the obligations that employers

Examples of behaviors that could be considered workplace harassment

- Don't acknowledge or ridicule worker's ability or performance without justifiable reason
- Discrimination in training, promotion, compensation, and routine treatment without justifiable reason
- Unlike other workers, only specific workers are repeatedly given difficult tasks that are not specified in the labor contract, which everyone is reluctant to do.
- Giving only chores or hardly work that are not specified in the labor contract
- Excluded from the process of making decisions or from providing important information related to work without good reason
- Exercise pressure to prevent vacation, sick leave, and various welfare benefits without justifiable reason
- Unlike other workers, overseeing only certain workers' behavior if he is work or rest
- Constantly and repeatedly instructed to do things related to superior's personal daily life such as private errands
- Forcing to move or leave the department without good reason
- Spread back talk or rumors about personal history
- Inflicting physical threats or violence
- Saying swear words or threatening words
- Doing words and actions that insult the worker in front of others or online
- Forcing participation in drinking, smoking or dinner regardless of the worker's opinion
- Group bullying
- Do not provide major equipment (computer, phone, etc.) necessary for work, or block access to the Internet or corporate network

Source: Ministry of Employment and Labor (2019), Manual for judgment, prevention and response to harassment in the workplace.

should take when harassment occurs in the workplace. According to it, if anyone becomes aware of the occurrence of harassment in the workplace, he can report it to the employer, and when the employer becomes aware of it, he must conduct an investigation to confirm the fact without delay. Employer shall take appropriate measures to protect the victim, and take measures such as disciplinary action to the wrongdoer. If a disadvantage such as dismissal is given to those who report or alleging the harassment damage in the workplace, a criminal punishment equal to a sentence of up to 3 years or a fine of up to 30 million won may be imposed to the employer. In addition, employer must have a voluntary prevention and response system in the workplace and stipulate in the employment rules necessary measures to prevent and deal with the harassment.

The revised Labor Standards Act, however, does not impose direct punishment against the offender. Instead, it requires employer to set the employment rules and take prevention and corrective measures according to the circumstances of each workplace. The government offers a guideline book helping to understand the definition of workplace harassment and the behaviors susceptible to harassment.[19] According to the manual, in order for harassment in the workplace to be established, it is required that the offender has to take advantage of the position or relationship in the workplace, and his behavior exceeds the appropriate range required for the job, and it cause physical or mental pain to the victim or worsens the working environment. Harassment in the workplace can vary widely, making it difficult to list and define all types of behavior. The manual provides specific and diverse cases that can be judged as harassment in the workplace.

The enforcement of the law does not mean that workplace harassment will soon disappear. Even now, there are still cases of victim of workplace harassment. The Labor Standards Act stipulates that it is the duty of the company to investigate and take appropriate measures when harassment occurs in the workplace, but there are no sanctions that can be enforced if the company does not perform such a role.[20)] However, considering the intent of the law, it is most important for management and leaders to actively try to prevent harassment in the workplace. If harassment is neglected in the workplace, the deterioration of working atmosphere and decrease of productivity are inevitable, and if a lawsuit occurs, there is a high risk of worsening the image of the company.

5. Environmental Changes and Labor Law

When the environment changes rapidly and new social problems arise, laws are enacted to regulate them. Criticism is high about the law that cannot keep up with the reality, but the law tend to follow the reality because we can't regulate problems that don't appear. Important environmental changes to be considered by labor law are the aging of the population and the development of digital technologies. While diverse legal response prohibiting segregation based on age has been adopted, the problem of labor law regulation caused by technological advancement is undergoing various discussions without clear direction to be taken.

5.1 Aging Workforce and Labor Law

Everyone knows that Korean population is aging at the fastest rate in the world. As a result, its average age of the employees is rapidly increasing. Socially, it is an important task to increase the employment rate of the elderly. At the company level, the task is to keep the organizational vitality from falling down and protect the company's unique tacit knowledge and skills from disappearing with the retirement of the elderly.

5.1.1 Law Related to the Elder Employment

Representative law regarding elderly people is the Prohibition of Age Discrimination in Employment and the Promotion of Elderly Employment. This Act aims to contribute to the stability of employment and the development of the national economy by prohibiting employment discrimination on the basis of age without justifiable reason, and by supporting and promoting the elderly to have jobs that match their abilities. In this law, an elderly person is defined as a person aged 55 or older. What should be noted by HR managers in this law is that workplaces with 300 or more employees are obligated to make efforts to hire seniors with a standard employment rate or higher (Article 12).[21)]

However, since this is a duty of effort, there are no sanctions even if the employment rate is not achieved. The Act also implements a system to pay employment subsidies to the companies hiring new elder people, or exceeding a target employment rate of elderly people, or keep maintaining the employment of elderly people. The Ministry of Employment and Labor also provide employment subsidies when the companies consult on wage system change and job redesign for the purpose of stabilizing and promoting employment for the elderly.

5.1.2 Legal Extension of the Retirement Age

The most important revision of the law in relation to the elderly is the extension of the retirement age. In 2013, the retirement age of workers was extended to 60 years through the amendment of the Act on the Prohibition of Age Discrimination in Employment and Promotion of Elderly Employment. To be precise, the employer must set the retirement age of a worker to be 60 or more, and if the retirement age of a worker is set to be less than 60, it is regarded as having set the retirement age to 60 (Article 19). Therefore, it can be said that the retirement age of 60 is the legal minimum. In order to alleviate the burden on companies due to the extension of the retirement age, the law requires necessary measures such as reorganization of the wage system according to the conditions of the business or workplace, and if such measures are taken accordingly, government offers financial support under the form of employment subsidies.

It is clear that the extension of the retirement age is a necessary policy to cope with the aging of the population, but it is also true that the burden on companies such as an increase in the labor cost was not small. Under this situation, many companies have introduced and operated a wage peak system to reduce the burden of labor costs caused by the extension of the retirement age. It is effective in controlling labor costs by reducing wages by 10% every year after freezing wages at a certain age, such as 55. However, it is also true that there are side effects such as lower morale and productivity of workers subject to the wage peak system.

5.1.3 Challenges and Tasks

If aging progresses at the current pace and Korea enters a super-aged society soon, how to keep the elderly people engaged in economic activity becomes a very important social issue. In order to prevent the collapse of pension system and solve the social problems caused by unemployment of the elderly, the elderly population must continue to carry out economic activities. To this end, it is highly likely that the legal retirement age of workers will be extended more than the current 60 years of age some day. Or a plan to impose the obligation to continue employment as in Japan could be implemented. Japan mandates companies to maintain the employment of workers until the age of

65. And as a method, companies can either extend the retirement age or terminate the existing employment relationship at the time of retirement, and then enter into a new employment contract and hire until the age of 65. Therefore, existing workers who want to work can continue to work until the age of 65.[22] Considering these social and legal changes, it is urgent for Korean companies to prepare a system and culture in which people can work regardless of age, if they have ability and motivation. For this, the compensation system based on seniority should be changed to work and performance-oriented one.

5.2 Technological Change and Labor Laws

Advances in technology, such as the Internet and social networks (SNS), create various challenges in the protection of workers and regulation of labor. Among them, the most representative of the things that leaders must understand is the problem of infringement on the break time, and the use of personal information existing in the online space for hiring purposes. It is a matter of privacy invasion.

5.2.1 Prohibition of Contact and Order after Work

The technological progress represented by the Fourth Industrial Revolution is the era of hyper-connectivity. Being connected and connected anytime, anywhere has many advantages, but it can pose a serious threat to workers, resulting in pain and long working hours. In fact, according to a survey, it is found that Korean workers have a very large number of overtime hours per week, 11 hours per week through smart devices.[23] This kind of problem occurs in any country in the world, and Germany and France are already trying to regulate it through legislation. In Germany, after the Minister of Labor proposed the anti-stress law in 2014, it is being reviewed. In the case of France, amendments to the labor law are done to thoroughly guarantee the rest time of workers by advocating the right not to be connected.

In the case of Korea, on the other hand, in June 2016, some members of the National Assembly initiated a bill to ban work ordered by KakaoTalk after working time. The revised bill stipulate that employer should not infringe on the freedom of privacy of workers, such as giving instructions on work by using various communication means such as telephone (including mobile phone), text message, and SNS at hours other than the working hours prescribed by the Labor Standards Act. This initiative did not pass through National Assembly, and similar bill is being prepared now.

There is skepticism about whether legal regulation will be effective, but leaders need to clearly understand these social needs and respond proactively. In light of this perspective, some companies have shown voluntary actions prior to legal regulation. LGU^+ has decided to prohibit the use of KakaoTalk to give work orders after 10 pm in April 2016, and to dismiss the managers in case of violation. Considering that excessive labor hinders the normal reproduction of the workforce and negatively affects productivity, it can be said that efforts to make the rest unhindered by the hypertrophy of the work area can be also beneficial for companies.

Digital cleaning

In the case of social networks, deleting or withdrawing an account does not mean that all past information is deleted. In addition, there are many cases in which one's personal information or video is widely circulated on the Internet without even knowing it. This is not just for celebrities. There is also great concern that personal opinions or comments that they have posted on the Internet in the past may adversely affect the employment process. There are professional companies that performs digital cleaning to protect customers' personal information, and is sometimes called an online reputation manager. They use big data collection programs to correct client misinformation or remove inappropriate information. However, the disadvantage is that service costs are not small, and all information cannot be completely removed through this service.

5.2.2 Use of Online Personal Information and Privacy Issue

In the process of collecting applicant's information using SNS and big data, there is a possibility that lawsuits related to infringement of privacy and protection rights for personal information may arise. This is because if the company uses the result or information of an individual's free expression activities for hiring purposes, it can be regarded as an excessive infringement of the individual's private rights. There is already a growing concern in advanced countries including the United States and EU that such social recruiting can invade individual privacy.

On the other hand, due to such concerns, some people delete personal information or the details of his activity in online space in the past. Such digital cleaning has a certain self-defensive nature to protect themselves in the technology age. However, it is a problem that individuals, who are potential victims, have to pay a considerable amount of money for their own information protection. A more fundamental alternative is to regulate companies to protect individual applicants' information and to impose penalties for failure to comply.

From the standpoint of management, it is very important to proactively respond to the controversy over privacy invasion that can be caused by the use of SNS and big data. This is because if management responds passively, it will be difficult to get out of controversy or lawsuits, and it can adversely affect the corporate image or brand. Specifically, it is necessary to establish a clear policy on the extent and level of use of personal information. It is important to establish, through a review by legal experts, clear guidelines for the source and scope of securing personal information necessary for hiring without infringing privacy.

6. HR Department's Roles

Businesses are important institutional actor of society and have an obligation to comply with the laws set by society. In order to comply with the law, it is necessary to understand the purpose of the law and the contents of the regulation. In addition, it is also important to comply with the law in all personnel management decisions. The most basic of corporate social responsibility is compliance with the law. For this, the human resources department must perform the following roles.

1) Clear Policies and Guidelines

In order to comply with the law, the company must establish clear policies or guidelines for anti-discrimination. In particular, in the case of dismissal, it is desirable to ensure that such content is specified in a collective agreement or employment rules. The policy to prevent sexual harassment should also have specific policies and procedures.

2) Communication and Education

Established policies or guidelines should be clearly communicated to all members. Communication and training need to be carried out on a regular basis every year. In particular, it is necessary to make special efforts so that business leaders can clearly understand the company's policies while actively promoting the purpose of the system themselves.

3) Documentation

Data and documents are important to avoid legal disputes and defend the company's position in the event of a lawsuit. Therefore, key personnel decisions should be documented and kept as far as possible, including the basis for judgment. In particular, evaluation-related data are the most important. Therefore HR department must check whether the evaluation data are distorted or inconsistent.

4) Use of Experts

Human resources managers and line leaders are not legal experts. Therefore, it is necessary to seek the help of a legal expert such as a lawyer or certified public labor attorney. But it is dangerous to leave everything to them. This is because effective personnel management is not achieved just by following the law. Before proceeding to legal solutions, efforts to communicate with the parties must take precedence.

5) Prevention Perspective

Once a legal dispute arises, it consumes time and cost, and it deteriorates reputation and image of the company. No matter how well the legal dispute is resolved, it is worse than preventing it in advance. For prevention, the role of front-line leaders is very important. This is because they are in a position to know the issues of the employees most quickly. When leaders are aware of a problem in the field, they must notify the HR department and make active efforts to resolve the problem early.

Ending case

Former CEO gone to Jail for Hiring Discrimination

In the Supreme Court appeal against Mr. Park, the former CEO of the Korea Gas Safety Corporation, who was accused of manipulating interview scores in an attempt to disqualify female candidates during the public recruitment process, he was convicted and finalized four years in prison. He was charged with forfeiting female applicants by manipulating rankings during the hiring process in 2015 and 2016, and was also convicted in the first and second trials. The Supreme Court ruled that there was no problem with the precedent court judgment and confirmed a four-year prison sentence.

In January 2015 and May 2016, Park was handed over to trial on charges of unfairly selecting employees by arbitrarily manipulating scores grades with the help of five people, including HR managers. HR managers were instructed by him to manipulate the scores and rankings of the applicants and presented the modified data to the personnel committee. As a result, the interview scores of 31 candidates were manipulated, and 13 failed candidates passed, and 7 female candidates who were in the passing ranking failed. It turned out that he was doing this to his conviction that male employees are better than female ones. He was also charged with receiving money and goods from a specific company in exchange for enacting and revising the gas safety certification standard (KGS code) during 2012-2014 while serving as a director.

In this appeal of former CEO Park, who was accused of violating the gender equality law, the Supreme Court sentenced him to a fine of 300 million won and four years of prison, saying his behavior greatly undermined social trust in public enterprises. In the process of the investigation, he admitted that he ordered to change the rank of interview scores of some candidates, but argued that four of the successful candidates would have passed even without changing the rank of interview scores, and that such change was a measure taking into account the specificity of the jobs in the company, not his own unilateral and biased decision.

Discussion Question

1. The supreme court judged that former CEO Park had violated the act on gender equality of employment. Specifically, which article of this law had he violated? Also, what are the penalties for violating this provision, which is stipulated at the penalty provisions of the law?
2. As a prosecution related to hiring discrimination, it is very unusual for a manager to be sentenced to prison penalty. That is why this verdict attracted a lot of attention in the media. Do you think that heavy punishment was appropriate?

3. Former CEO Park admitted to the allegation of manipulating interview scores of female applicants in the course of the lawsuit, but consistently insisted that such actions took into account the characteristics of the Corporation's work. Can his argument be justified? What are the conditions for such a claim to be justified?

CHAPTER 3

Strategic Human Resource Management

Learning Objectives

1. Can explain the difference between traditional human resource management and strategic human resource management.
2. Can explain what HR strategy is.
3. Understand the options available in each area of HR to establish strategic HR.
4. Suggest five conditions for an effective HR strategy to improve organizational performance.
5. Explain the difference between the cost reduction strategy and the differentiation strategy, and give examples of HR strategies suitable for each.

Introductory Case

As Vice Chairman Nam Yong took office as CEO, he tried to transform LG Electronics, which was too conservative, into a global company. He recruited a large number of new executives from McKinsey consulting firms to make a strong change. The company-wide strategy was left to new executives from these consultants. And immediately, he recruited foreign vice presidents into the CEO group (level C) in turn: Johnson & Johnson's Dermot Borden to CMO (Marketing), IBM's Thomas Linton to CPO (Purchase), HP's Didier Chenneveau to CHRO (Human Resource Management) and P&G's James Shedd to Chief Go-To-Marketing (CGTMO). Of the seven C-level positions, five foreign vice presidents, excluding CTO (technical) and CFO (financial), joined the top management team.

Vice Chairman Nam instructed all meetings to be held in English and empowered foreign executives who were recruited. As such, Vice Chairman Nam pursued strong cost reduction measures while reinforcing leadership and pursuing organizational change. He grew up in the group and had experience as CEO of LG Telecom before coming to CEO of Electronics. Vice Chairman Nam focused on reducing unnecessary costs enough to advocate the creative management innovation of "eliminating waste" even when he was the CEO of LG Telecom. At the beginning of the change, the tension of the organization was very high, and the members seemed to move in the desired direction. However, as time passed, he felt that the launch of new products and various decisions were delayed.

> "In January 2007, I took office as CEO with the aspiration to make LG Electronics a global top 3 company. In 3 years and 9 months, there have been significant changes and achievements, but as the core business failed to lead the market change and fell into sluggishness, the efforts so far became half of success and half of failure." (Digital Daily. September 30, 2010)

What was the problem? In the fall of 2010, Vice Chairman Nam, the CEO, was regretted after finishing his farewell speech. Vice-Chairman Nam, who succeeded former Vice Chairman Kim Ssang-soo in 2007 and became CEO, made LG Electronics the highest performing company in the company's history in the year he took office and the following year. It didn't take long for the results to plummet. The mobile phone business has been so competitive that it is difficult to overcome for a while. Eventually, not a single foreign vice president remained and all resigned.

Discussion Questions

1. What is the relationship between human resource management strategy and corporate competitiveness?
2. What kind of HR strategy did LG Electronics pursue during the tenure of Vice Chairman Nam?
3. Why did LG Electronics' HR strategy fail?
4. What conditions were necessary for LG Electronics' HR strategy to succeed?
5. If you were the CEO, what HR strategy would you have pursued?

In Chapter 1, we defined human resource management as "all activities to efficiently and effectively utilize limited human resources to achieve the purpose of the business pursued by the organization." In this chapter, we will discuss the direction of human resource management. The reason why direction is needed is that there is not only one activity to efficiently and effectively utilize human resources. For example, in hiring talent, you need to answer the following questions; will we mainly recruit novel new employees and cultivate them well for our organization, or will we hire experienced employees who have already been proven to have considerable competence in the market and entrust the work required to the organization right away? Judgment on the direction of human resource management can be made differently from time to time, but more desirable is to carefully review and proceed strategically how to conduct human resource management activities. This is called strategic human resource management. Managers should endeavor to ensure that the organization's human resource management is carried out strategically.

1. Characteristics of Strategic Human Resource Management

In Chapter 1, the change in human resource management was explained in four stages, and most recently, it was emphasized that the concept of human resource management was expanded to strategic human resource management. Then, what is the difference between traditional human resource management and strategic human resource management? Of course, the basic framework and principles of human resource management remain unchanged, but they show a big difference in how they approach them. This applies not only in terms of the academic approach to human resource management, but also for designing and implementing human resource management in enterprises. As shown in [Figure 3-1], the traditional approach and the strategic approach show differences in approximately six areas.

1) From a Cost Perspective to an Asset Perspective

The emergence of strategic human resource management is because the source of competitiveness has changed. In an organization, members are both a cost and an asset. Both aspects are important, but the viewpoint as an asset is becoming more important than in the past. Not all companies will do this, but you will have to move away from the more traditional cost perspective, especially if good people are the source of your organization's competitiveness.

2) From Micro Focus to Macro Focus

This is where the goal of human resource management is set. Traditional human resource management focused on individual units from a microscopic point of view, prioritizing the satisfaction, attitude, behavior and personal performance of members. On the other hand, strategic human resource management focuses on the entire organization, which is a strategic unit, so that managers are interested in the impact of human resource

Figure 3-1 Comparison of Traditional HRM and Strategic HRM

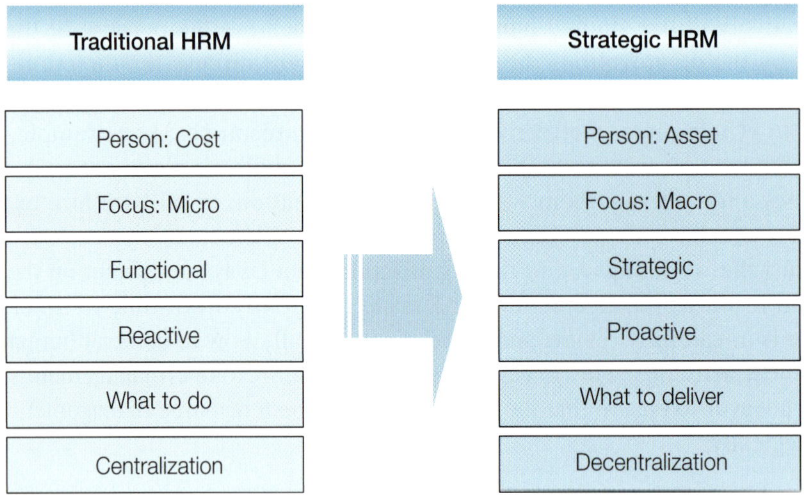

management on the overall performance of the organization beyond the individual.[1]

3) From a Functional Perspective to a Strategic Perspective

In traditional human resource management, each functional role, such as recruitment, evaluation, compensation, development, and turnover, was considered important. It was considered that if each function was performed well, the goal of human resource management could be achieved. On the other hand, in strategic human resource management, it is more important whether it is contributing to achieving the strategic goal by consolidating each function in one direction. Reflecting this aspect, many companies have a chief human resource officer (CHRO) in their organization's group of chief executives.

4) From a Reactive Perspective to a Proactive Perspective

Traditionally, human resource management has been dominated by a passive perspective that responds to business needs. It has been functioning at a level that does not cause problems as much as possible. On the other hand, in terms of strategic human resource management, there are many cases in which it is necessary to proactively carry out preemptive activities to secure the competitiveness of the organization. For example, in the process of mergers and acquisitions (M&A), HR played a major role in reorganizing the HR system of acquired companies after mergers and acquisitions were made. On the other hand, from a strategic point of view, a preemptive judgment is made whether the competency or organizational culture of the members of the acquired company can create synergies with the organization. If it is judged to be inappropriate from the viewpoint of human resource management, mergers and acquisitions may not be possible.

5) Focusing on the Customer of what to Deliver from the Action of what to do

Traditional human resource management focused on what it did. For example, the evaluation system was improved. An incentive system was introduced. Or, education and training were provided to managers. This aspect is viewed from the perspective of the HR department. On the other hand, in strategic human resource management, the focus is on what effect it has or what change it has made to customers. Here, customers are mainly members who are internal customers. For example, in strategic human resource management, the following questions are important. Has the leadership of managers changed through education and training? Did the introduction of incentives increase the motivation of the members?

6) From Centralized Decision Making to Decentralized Decision Making

As already mentioned in Chapter 1, in the traditional aspect, major decisions in human resource management are made in the personnel department, the staff department. On the other hand, in strategic human resource management, human resources should be treated as assets, not costs, so managers, which serve in line departments, should be in charge of important human resource management decisions.

2. Overview of Strategic Human Resource Management

2.1 Vision, Strategy, HR Strategy

[Figure 3-2] is an extension of the basic model of human resource management shown in Chapter 1. In the basic model, it was confirmed that human resource management is to achieve the purpose of the business pursued by the organization through improvement of individual performance. The figure shows the basic model plus mission/vision and business strategy. In addition to this, HR Strategy and HR Planning are expressed in a form that affects human resource management activities.

As we looked at the missions of various companies in Chapter 1, mission refers to the fundamental purpose for which an organization exists. And it is a vision that expresses the purpose of these projects as concrete goals. Merck's mission, a

Figure 3-2 **Human Resource Management Extension Model**

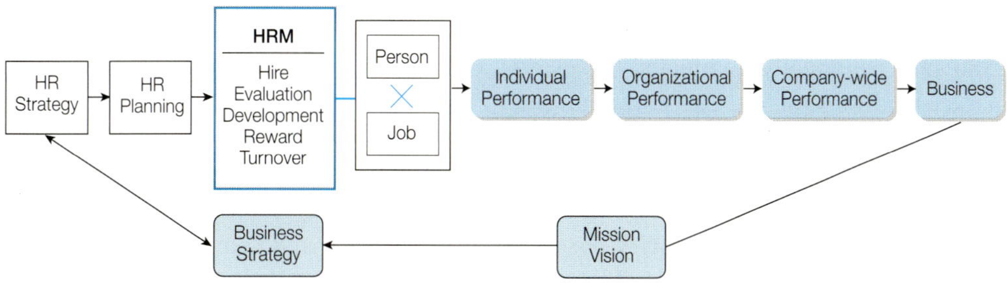

multinational pharmaceutical company, was "to preserve and improve human life through the pharmaceutical business." Merck's vision, embodying this, is as follows. "Making a difference in human life through innovative pharmaceuticals, vaccines and health products for animals worldwide. We want to be the best research-intensive biopharmaceutical company. We contribute to presenting leading innovation and solutions for the present and future of mankind."[2)]

Vision is the wish of the organization and its members to reach the future. Resources are needed to realize the vision, that is, to achieve the purpose of the organization. Strategy is a specific plan for efficient and effective use of resources. Strategy started originally from military terminology and is widely used in business administration. The strategy is to establish a mid- to long-term plan for how the organization will use its resources to win over competitors in the market and how to allocate resources. Strategies include corporate strategy and business strategy. Functionally, there are financial strategy, marketing strategy, production strategy, R&D strategy, and so on, and there are HR strategies for the efficient and effective use of human resources that we deal with in this textbook.

2.2 HR Strategy

HR strategy refers to mid- to long-term plans for efficient and effective use of human resources to achieve business objectives in the organization. The HR strategy informs the overall direction of how the organization will specifically acquire talent and how to use it to achieve the vision it aims for the next 5 to 10 years. For example, as shown in [Figure 3-3], a company in the IT industry set its HR strategy to 'optimize manpower structure and operation and secure core competencies to have competitiveness in an environment where industry competition is intensifying'. This company considers that human resources account for an absolute proportion of the input factor due to the characteristics of the IT service industry, and team work is carried out on a project basis. However, in addition to the labor cost competition, which was the traditional source of competition in the IT industry, the need to establish a new HR strategy emerged at a time when the competence of professional manpower became important. The company's HR strategy was set in the direction of ① cost reduction through optimization of HR structure and operation and ② improvement of productivity through reinforcement of core competencies of professional personnel.[3)]

HR strategies can vary depending on the company's philosophy and strategy, even in the same industry. For example, Coca-Cola and Pepsi-Cola, which have long divided the global beverage industry, are pursuing very different HR strategies. Founded in 1886 and traditionally dominated the market, Coca-Cola has consistently maintained its market-leading strategy. The corporate brand image has also emphasized conservative and traditional values. In addition, it has been demanding loyalty and organizational commitment while providing long-term employment for internal members. For this reason, Coca-Cola's HR strategy has maintained a base pay system that emphasizes internal promotion and seniority based on lifelong work and family balance. Also, incentive pay has been determined based on groups, not individuals. On the other hand,

Figure 3-3 An Example of an IT Company's HR Strategy

HR Characteristics

IT Service Industry Structure Characteristics

- Manpower takes the absolute weight of the input and it is an important factor in determining productivity
- Project unit business
  - It is important to predict whether an order will be received as it is an order base project
  - The teamwork of the project team is important

HR Characteristics of IT Service Industry

- Professional Specialty as well as Managerial Setting of Traditional HR is important
  - Professional manpower drives productivity
- Skills are diverse, and individuals can possess multiple skills
- Managers such as PMs are of great importance
- Timely input is a key factor in cost reduction
  - It is difficult to predict the size and timing of manpower input based on the order base
  - The search cost of manpower is high and the lead time for timely input is long

HR Strategy

- Optimizing HR structure/operation and obtaining core competencies to secure competitiveness in an environment where competition in the industry is intensifying

HR Structure/Operation Optimization

- Contributing to cost reduction and profit maximization through optimal manpower operation in terms of quantity
  - HR structure systematization
  - Adjustment of demand/supply of manpower flexible to business strategy

Strengthening Core Competencies

- Improving productivity by enhancing the quality of manpower (Securing/developing professional competencies)
  - Securing core competencies at the Global level
  - Securing/developing professional and hot skills
  - Core talent management

Pepsi-Cola, founded in 1902 following Coca-Cola, pursued a market-following strategy and aggressive marketing strategy. In advertisements, the brand image that emphasizes youth has also been emphasized. Employees have been demanding a spirit of challenge and adventure like a venture company and quick response to the new environment. The HR strategy of Pepsi-Cola has been based on strong performance-oriented HR management, and it has introduced the incentive system based on the recruitment of competent external talents and individual achievements rather than internal promotion, It also introduced a stock option system for all employees for the first time in the industry. The difference in HR strategy between Coca-Cola and Pepsi-Cola is also noticeable in the CEO's decision. In the case of Coca-Cola, the CEO has been selected from among the talents who have traditionally joined as new employees, including Ahmet Muhtar Kent, who have grown inside Coca-Cola.[4] On the other hand, PepsiCo's former CEO Indra Nooyi, a woman from India, was scouted from a consulting firm. Ramon Laguarta, who became the current CEO following Indra Nooyi, was also recruited from outside and became the first Spanish CEO of a large American multinational company.[5]

2.3 HR Strategy and Strategic HR

HR strategy depends on the vision and mission the organization pursues and the strategy to achieve it. Therefore, HR strategies will be varied according to the organization. The process of establishing a HR strategy is called strategic HR. Since the HR strategy is the mid-to long-term use plan of human resources, strategic HR can be said to be the process of deciding how to establish the mid- to long-term use plan of human resources. The criteria for establishing HR strategies are the organization's goals and objectives expressed in the organization's mission and vision. In strategic HR, it is important to define talent that fits the goals and objectives of the organization. This is called the talent image (image of right people: In-Jae-Sang), and the talent image serves as an indicator of what kind of talented people are equipped with the competencies, qualities, and attitudes necessary for the organization. HR management is a general

Table 3-1 **Strategic HR Choice Options**

HR AREA	STRATEGIC DECISION-MAKING CRITERIA	AVAILABLE OPTIONS
Hire	Recruitment method	internal recruitment, external recruitment, new employee focus, focused on experienced employees
	Selection decision	line manager decision, line manager participation, centralized decision
	Selection tool	document screening, structured interview, aptitude test, assessment center
Evaluation	Evaluation methods	relative evaluation, absolute evaluation
	Purpose of evaluation	development purpose, control purpose, personnel decision
	Evaluation subject	direct supervisor, multi-rater evaluation, peer evaluation
Development	Training method	individual training, group training, OJT
	Training content	reinforcement of job expertise, reinforcement of organizational culture, reinforcement of global competency
	Career development	development-oriented, market-oriented
Reward	Wage level	lead policy, matching policy, lag policy
	Wage composition	base pay, allowance, performance-based pay, welfare benefits
	Base pay	seniority, job, role, skill
Turnover	Employment adjustment policy	retirement guarantee, early retirement, permanent restructuring
	Turnover management	inducing voluntary turnover, utilizing involuntary turnover

activity that discovers, develops, and motivates these talents. When the talent required for the organization is defined through strategic HR, it is decided which HR management method to use accordingly.

For strategic HR to be successful, managers need to know what options are available for human resource management. Managers need to understand how to use these options. It can be said that the human resource management that we want to learn in this textbook is to learn what options are available and which options are most desirable in certain situations.[6)]

<Table 3-1> gives examples of the options available for each HR functions.

3. Utilization of Strategic Human Resource Management

What we want to deal with in strategic human resource management is how to strategically use human resource management in an organization to increase performance and ultimately achieve the purpose of the business. In the 2000s, such discussions have been more active. In particular, technological advances comparable to those of the 4th industrial revolution such as artificial intelligence, 3D printing, and big data technology are taking place in recent years. In such an environment, there are deepening concerns about how companies can maintain or secure a competitive advantage in human resource management amid these changes.

There is no disagreement that human resource management should be approached strategically. However, in order for strategic human resource management to specifically have a positive impact on performance, several conditions are required. This can be divided into external fit and internal fit.[7)] HR strategies can contribute to improving corporate performance when the following five conditions are met.[8)]

① The more the HR strategy is suited to the organization's strategy, the higher the business performance. (External fit)
② The more the HR strategy is suited to the business environment in which the organization is located, the higher the business performance. (External fit)
③ The more the HR strategy is suited to the organizational characteristics, the higher the business performance. (External fit)
④ The better the HR strategy can utilize the capabilities of the organization, the higher the business performance. (External fit)
⑤ The more consistent the activities of recruitment, evaluation, development, compensation, and separation, which constitute the HR system (HR strategy), the higher the business performance. (Internal fit)

3.1 Fit with Organizational Strategy

Organizational strategy refers to the short- and long-term plans for a company to use limited resources to achieve its goals. Strategies can be divided into corporate strategy, which is carried out at the corporate level, and business unit strategy, at the business unit level.[9)]

Corporate strategies are divided into an evolutionary business strategy, in which companies actively participate in new businesses and diversify their current business portfolio, and a steady-state strategy that tries to keep the current business steadily and maintain market share rather than rapid growth.

The evolutionary business strategy requires an entrepreneurial spirit to take risks and create new business opportunities from its members. For this, the HR strategy seeks to actively recruit talented people from outside rather than promotion from inside. And high-performing employees need a corresponding incentive system. On the other hand, in the case of a steady-state strategy, as shown in the case of Coca-Cola, they want talented people who can grow their business steadily and stably while maintaining a strong market share. Therefore, rather than taking risks, an HR strategy suitable for teamwork among members and a stable organizational culture is needed. They select talents that fit the company's culture and policies as new employees. In addition, there is a need for a HR system that can grow into a CEO through career management and continuous education and training.

The typical classification of business strategy can be divided into cost advantage and differentiation advantage, depending on where to find the competitive advantage.[10)] Using this, Professor Michael Porter classifies the strategy into a differentiation strategy, a cost advantage strategy, and a focus strategy focused on only one area.[11)] Another popular type of business strategy is the classification by Miles and Snow, which distinguishes between the defender and the prospector and the analyzer.[12)] The classification of each type is somewhat different in specific content, but in order to understand the HR strategy according to the business strategy to be explained in this textbook, it is intended to be simplified and classified into cost advantage and differentiated advantage.

[Figure 3-4] explains the connection between the two types of business strategies and HR strategies. There is a critical success factor (CSF) between business strategy and HR strategy. The CSF refers to the factors that are essential to the successful implementation of the strategy. In order for the strategy established by the company to succeed, a critical success factor is needed, which is linked to the HR strategy. Differentiation advantage strategy is a strategy to secure a competitive advantage through innovative ideas, and it is important to quickly launch differentiated products or new products. The key success factors for this are mass customization, continuous innovation, and shortened production cycles in production while reflecting the needs of customers and enabling mass customization. The HR strategy for this should select active, risk-taking, innovative and creative talents, and provide education and training programs to help them reach their potential. There is also a need to provide incentives for innovative ideas and product or process innovation.

The cost advantage strategy is a strategy to secure a competitive advantage through low prices, and cost reduction through efficient operation is important. The critical success factor for this is the excellence of operation through the elimination of unnecessary processes and the efficiency that can maximize the effect of the minimum cost. The HR strategy for this requires a human resource plan that can utilize as few

Figure 3-4 Linking Business Strategy and HR Strategy

Business Strategy	Critical Success Factor, CSF	HR Strategy
Differentiation advantage • Through innovative ideas competitive advantage • Differentiated products, rapid launch of new products	Mass customization and innovation Shorter cycle time	• Active and risk-taking fun, innovative and creative selection and nurturing of human resources • Performance based pay on innovative ideas and products, and process innovation
Cost advantage • Competitiveness through low prices • Cost reduction through efficient operation	Operational excellence Cost-effectiveness	• Efficient manpower management • High productivity with less manpower • Focus on the labor costs of competitors • Cost control • Minimize welfare benefits

human resources as possible. The wage level of a market-following strategy that can have an advantage over competitors in labor costs is required, and welfare benefits should also be minimized. In evaluation, it is necessary to control the behavior of members through relative evaluation.

If we look at actual examples of the two strategies in the automotive industry, automobile companies of high-end brands such as Porsche, Mercedes-Benz, and BMW will use the differentiated advantage strategy and the HR strategy accordingly. On the other hand, France's Renault, India's Tata, or China's Shanghai Automobile Group will use cost advantage strategies. Even within a company, it can vary depending on the brand of the car. For example, Hyundai's Genesis may use a differentiation strategy and Avante may use a cost advantage strategy.

3.2 Fit with Business Environment

The business environment depends on the characteristics of the market in which a company provides products or services. Whether corporate competition is limited to the domestic market or expands to the global market is also an important factor. In addition, each industry has its own characteristics, so the business environment varies depending on the industry the organization belongs to. For example, the traditional manufacturing industries such as textiles, shoes, or food and beverage processing industries have different skills required for human resources than those related to computers, information and communications, or artificial intelligence, which belong to the cutting-edge industries, which can lead to different HR strategies.

In order to examine the relationship between the business environment and HR strategy, it is necessary to examine what environmental factors exist. Environmental factors can take into account the degree of uncertainty, the volatility of the environment, the magnitude of environmental change, and the complexity of the environment.[13) The degree of uncertainty depends on how accurate information is given in analyzing the business environment. Lack of information makes it difficult to make appropriate decisions related to management. The volatility of the environment is how often the business environment surrounding an organization changes. The greater the environmental change, the higher the environmental volatility. The magnitude of change in the environment depends on whether the amplitude of the change in the business environment is large or not. Even if changes in the environment do not occur often, if a large change occurs once it changes, the magnitude of environmental change is large. On the other hand, even if environmental changes occur frequently, but the amplitude is not large, the magnitude of environmental changes can be said to be small. The complexity of the environment is how many variables must be considered in predicting the business environment. The more variables to consider, the more complex the business environment. These four factors are related to each other, but they are not always highly correlated. For example, even if the uncertainty of the environment is high, it may not be complicated. Or, the volatility of the environment is small, but the magnitude of the change is large once it changes.

<Table 3-2> explains how the four factors of the business environment described above are related to the HR strategy. For example, if the uncertainty of the environment is low, a human resource plan can be established in detail, and since the content of the job does not change well, it is easy to provide specialized training for the job. On the other hand, when environmental uncertainty is high, it is difficult to establish a specific human resource plan. Therefore, it is necessary to establish a human resource plan that can respond flexibly to changes. In addition, since the content of the required job is highly likely to change depending on the environment, education and training to strengthen general competencies applied to various jobs such as problem-solving skill and creative thinking are necessary.

3.3 Fit with Organizational Characteristics

If the business environment factor is a judgment on the outside of the organization, the organizational characteristics are judgment on the inside of the organization. HR strategy should take into account not only external factors but also internal factors of the organization. This includes production process, market share, management philosophy, organizational structure, and organizational culture.[14)]

The production process is what processes go through to deliver a product or service to a customer. As a typical example, there are companies that repeatedly produce products according to a well-planned production procedure, while others have to produce new results from time to time according to customer needs. Examples of the former would be factories that produce automobiles, electronics, and steel. Examples of the latter might be advertising companies, consulting companies, or research institutes that need to continuously create new products. However, it should not be overlooked

Table 3-2 **Business Environment and HR Strategy**

ENVIRONMENTAL FACTORS	EXAMPLE OF HR STRATEGY WHEN LOW	EXAMPLE OF HR STRATEGY WHEN HIGH
Degree of uncertainty	• Specific human resource planning • Job-specific training • Fixed pay • Evaluation by supervisor	• General human resource planning • General competency training • Variable pay • Multi-rater evaluation
Environmental volatility	• Control-based evaluation • Job-specific training • Fixed pay	• Flexible evaluation • General competency training • Variable pay
Magnitude of environmental change	• Clear job description • Formal recruitment and socialization • Make employment strategy • Similar evaluation procedure	• General job description • Informal recruitment • Buy employment strategy • Differentiated evaluation procedure
The complexity of the environment	• Control-based evaluation • Internal promotion • Centralization of wage determination • Evaluation by supervisor	• Flexible evaluation • Recruitment of external experienced employees • Decentralization of wage determination • Multi-rater evaluation

that even companies in the same industry may have different production processes. HR strategy required in the repetitive production process would be appropriate with specific job descriptions, education and training and evaluation, and compensation centered on fixed pay. On the other hand, HR strategies in organizations that require creativity, such as advertising companies and consulting, will be appropriate with flexible job descriptions, training and evaluation for general competencies, and compensation centered on performance pay.

As for the market posture, as shown in the case of Coca-Cola and Pepsi-Cola, the HR strategy will be different between the market leading company and the company trying to follow and lead. Market leading companies will need HR strategies that pursue stability to maintain the market, while latecomers need HR strategies that pursue innovation and strong sense of achievement to secure aggressive markets.

Managerial philosophy also influences HR strategy. Depending on what management philosophy the founder or CEO of a company has, the required behavior of the members varies. For example, in the case of a company that has a strong risk aversion tendency and an authoritative management philosophy, it is more likely that the CEO has an HR strategy such as fixed pay-oriented compensation, centralized decision-making, and control-oriented evaluation system. On the other hand, if you have a strong risk preference, encourage members' participation, and have an egalitarian management philosophy, you may have HR strategies such as performance based compensation, decentralized decision making, development oriented evaluation system, and 360 degree evaluation.

Organizational structure can be divided into two. First, there are companies with a formal organizational structure that have a long decision-making stage and well differentiated functions. Second, there are companies that have a concise decision-making stage, a flat organizational hierarchy, and a less formalized structure. Each HR strategy is different. In the former case, a specific job description, centralized compensation decision, and control-centered evaluation system are predominant, whereas in the latter case, a general job description, decentralized compensation decision, and development-oriented evaluation system will be needed.

Organizational culture is also an important factor to consider in establishing HR strategy. If the organizational culture pursued by the organization is proactive and energetic, and expects performance-oriented entrepreneurship, an HR strategy appropriate to this is required. On the other hand, if you have a corporate culture that is traditional, conservative, and demands loyalty from its members, and the organization provides a corresponding long-term employment relationship, a different HR strategy is needed.

3.4 Fit with Organizational Capabilities

Organizational competency refers to a distinctive core competence that differentiates a company from other competitors in order to have a competitive advantage. Organizational competency is a concept that is distinct from the individual competence of each member and means providing a competitive advantage at the level of the entire organization.

For example, in the case of 3M, which is famous for post-it, organizational competency, is the creative R&D ability to create products with adhesion that cannot be provided to other companies. On the other hand, in recent years, although most of the delivery companies are following, the organizational capability of Domino's Pizza, which once dominated the delivery pizza industry, was the delivery speed. The organizational capability of Southwest Airline, can be said to be the passion of members who can provide fun to customers and the organizational culture that provides it. As such, organizational competencies are diverse. HR strategies should be able to maintain and strengthen these organizational competencies. Southwest Airlines' HR strategy, for example, uses a strictly structured interview method to select new employees who thoroughly match the organizational culture. Also, applicants who have already encountered the organizational culture of other airlines are excluded. It uses a variety of non-monetary compensation methods to motivate and pride its members, and employs an employee stock ownership plan (ESOP) so that all members can hold their own shares.

3.5 Congruence among HR Functions

If the suitability of the HR strategy and the four factors, such as organizational strategy, business environment, organizational capabilities, and organizational capabilities, as discussed above is called external fit, the other is considered to be an internal fit to create strategic HR. It is necessary to have mutual coherence between various HR areas. Previously, in <Table 3-2>, HR areas were divided into recruitment, evaluation, development, compensation, and separation. However, they are not separate from each other, but must function complementarily to improve the organization's performance. For example, if you are actively hiring experienced employees from outside, and if they come inside the company and do not provide an opportunity to maximize their capabilities through evaluation or compensation, the strategy for hiring excellent talent will be useless. As another example, in order to motivate members, a company tries to pursue an HR strategy to reinforce individual incentives, but the evaluation system is performing absolute evaluation, and if there is an leniency error in the evaluation practices of managers, then individual differentiation may not be achieved and new HR strategy cannot be succeeded.

4. Strategic Human Resource Planning

Previously, in [Figure 3-2], an extension model of human resource management was presented, and HR strategies were explained in detail. Looking again at [Figure 3-2], it can be seen that human resource planning (HRP) is the link between HR strategy and specific HR functions. In Chapter 5, the specific activities of human resource planning will be described again, and in this chapter, strategic human resource planning (strategic HRP) will be briefly discussed.

First of all, human resource planning can be defined as an activity for specifying strategies and transferring them to execution of HR management. In other words, strategic HRP means an activity to strategically determine the quantity and quality of human resources required to achieve the vision and mission of the organization. While HRP, which has been practiced by many organizations in the past, has been limited to simply collecting necessary personnel at a functional level to maintain the status quo, strategic HRP is an active concept of human resources required from a company-wide perspective to achieve strategic goals. In other words, strategic HRP is an essential activity in order to utilize human resources as a source of competitiveness.

Strategic HRP plays a very important role in setting and implementing an organization's strategy. In addition, by grasping the situation of available human resources through strategic HRP, it makes it possible to judge whether the organization's strategy is realistically feasible, and furthermore, it affects the revision of the strategy. In other words, strategy and HRP are not in a one-sided relationship in which the HR strategy is influenced by the HRP, and the HR strategy again has an influence on the organizational strategy. For example, recently, many companies are making efforts to find new business opportunities according to the technological revolution in the face of the 4th industrial revolution (industry 4.0). Let's say that a company has set its organizational strategy to create new products using artificial intelligence (AI) according to the Fourth Industrial Revolution. In order to successfully execute these organizational strategies, artificial intelligence experts are absolutely necessary, and HR strategies to recruit or develop them have been established. Accordingly, strategic HRP was implemented to analyze the supply and demand of artificial intelligence experts, and to establish an HR action plan. However, it was concluded that the practical constraints were too large to be found through the human resource plan, and that the cost burden was too high to recruit AI experts from the outside, and that more time was required to nurture them inside. If so, it will be impossible to execute the organizational strategy as it is, and a new and revised organizational strategy will be needed.

HRP strategically predicts the demand for human resources necessary to achieve the strategic objectives of the organization and predicts the supply of human resources available to the organization; and it includes an activity to establish an action plan to resolve the difference between the predicted demand and supply of human resources.

The action plan is related to specific human resource management activities such as recruitment, evaluation, compensation, and separation management. The linking of HR strategy and HR management activities is the final stage of HR planning, the action plan. The action plan simply does not mean reducing the difference between supply and demand in terms of quantity. Action plans should be consistent with the strategic direction of human resource management. Therefore, it is necessary to first establish a HR strategy before establishing a specific action plan. For example, the following HR strategy is possible.[15)]

- Senior managers consist of 75% from internal promotion and 25% from external recruitment.
- Focus on fostering and recruiting core jobs that currently show competitive advantage.
- Use contract workers, for jobs that require special skills.
- If surplus manpower occurs in one sector, training is given as soon as possible and relocated to another sector.
- Reorganize work to make good use of talent.
- Operate internship programs with nearby high schools to secure certified engineers in advance.

Ending Case

POSCO's HR Strategy

POSCO (Pohang Iron and Steel Co., Ltd) was founded in April 1968 as a steel company. With the strong leadership of Taejun Park, the first chairman of POSCO, it has grown into a world-class steel company in the short span of 25 years. POSCO was ranked first for 11 consecutive years in the "World's Most Competitive Steel Company" from 2010 to 2020.

With the inauguration of Chairman Jeong-woo Choi in 2018, POSCO declared 'With Posco' as a new vision. Three strategies to achieve 'With POSCO' are presented: Business With POSCO that pursues value with business partners such as customers, suppliers, and business partners, Society With POSCO that creates a better society together, trust and creativity, People With POSCO that creates corporate culture together. The emphasis is on "Coporate Citizenship," which is not simply a profit-generating company, but a social responsibility.[16)]

Chairman Jeong-woo Choi emphasized the following strategic directions in his recent New Year's address.[17)] "As a business strategy, we will firmly maintain the gap in the competitiveness of the steel business, but at the same time we need to accelerate the creation of performance in the group business, and focus on fostering next-generation businesses. The Smart Factory, which was previously promoted, goes beyond the optimization of unit processes and promotes overall optimization through process integration. Through this, we will evolve and develop into Smart Factory 2.0, which improves productivity and error rate, and dramatically improves cost competitiveness of the entire value chain such as quality, logistics, facilities, safety, and energy. The secondary battery material business, which is being fostered as a core business of the group, strengthens the value chain from raw materials such as lithium, nickel, and graphite to cathode materials and anode materials, and continues to expand production capacity to become a global top tier."

Chairman Choi also emphasizes the innovation of organizational culture in his New Year's speech. "Organizational culture innovation is needed to think creatively and challenge boldly on the basis of trust and harmony. Using the Design Thinking methodology, it is necessary to discover the problems that have been excessive in practice and promote business innovation that fundamentally solves them. In addition, we are not afraid of challenges, lead change, and seek new growth opportunities. We will actively cultivate New Collar talents who possess the innovative mindset of 3C (Challenge, Change, Chance)."

To put these visions and strategies into action, POSCO changed the official name of the HR department to HR Cultural Office.[18)] As the department name implies, POSCO HR is now more focused on improving the organizational culture than ever. Although the proportion of millennials in POSCO is 36% in 2019, it is expected to reach 60% by 2024. To date, the number of baby boomers is the most at 48%, but after 5 years it will decrease to 26%. Therefore, how to work with a new generation and a new organizational culture are a big concern. POSCO is operating a separate coaching school through the Human Resource Creation Center to improve leadership. External professional coaches are assigned to provide professional counseling, or programs such as leadership diagnosis, feedback, and meditation are conducted. In addition, feedback is provided through diagnosis by department, and a two-day empathy plus workshop for the entire department is operated to improve the organizational culture.

The HR department is reinforcing performance and competency-based fair and field-oriented HR, and strategic fostering of next-generation leaders. In order to renew the atmosphere of the organization and enhance the vitality of the organization, long-term positions are replaced, and people with excellent performance and competency are promoted to executives regardless of the seniority. POSCO develops "playing coach-type" leaders, rather than 'managing' leaders, who run directly and support the work of members. The playing coach assigns tasks according to the capabilities of the employees, and supports the employees to complete their own tasks from start to finish. POSCO is operating a POSCO-type agile organization by introducing a cell organization in the new growth area. It is a form that can freely open and close the organization as a unit of work. If there are 3 or more members, a cell organization can be created, and anyone can become a cell leader regardless of the rank. It is attempting to transform the organization according to the problem that needs to be solved by breaking away from the existing practices that have set up an organization and pursued work.

POSCO first introduced MBO in 2000. The MBO's annual process is determined through a one-on-one interview with the supervisor after establishing organizational goals according to the company-wide strategic direction and specific action plan at the beginning of the year, connecting individual goals with organizational goals. It is common to set 4-5 individual goals, and performance evaluation is conducted twice a year, divided into the first and second half. In particular, prior to making the final evaluation, the objective and acceptability of the evaluation are enhanced by sharing and agreeing on the degree of goal achievement through a one-on-one interview between the evaluator and the subordinate.

"When you think about the way we work, it's not alone, but organizations work together. So, even if you've excelled in your work, the contribution of the person in charge may be another matter. The person in charge did not perform well, but the project performance may have been good because the boss was good. Considering these points, it is recommended to give feedback immediately when the work is done. In this case, most of them accept the results. However, if you go to the end of the year and talk at once, there may be a backlash." (Posco CHRO Yang Byung-Moo)

In fact, POSCO has introduced a regular performance management system in the past. Although the work performance was evaluated on a monthly basis and feedback was made at all times, the work load increased due to the evaluation, so it returned to the existing system. It was meaningful that coaching was done in a timely manner by checking the performance at all times and by checking the target achievement rate, but the operation was not easy. Although POSCO has such experience, opinions are gathered that the evaluation method, which is determined according to the relative evaluation distribution rate, should be changed due to changes in the workforce and the influx of millennials. CHRO Yang expressed his expectation that POSCO's relative evaluation method would be sufficiently improved. In the process of deriving the optimal improvement plan, POSCO plans to collect the opinions of employees from various levels. In addition, joint research with the POSCO Institute of Management and benchmarking of other companies will be conducted in parallel to improve fairness of evaluation and employee acceptance at the same time.

Discussion Questions

1. POSCO is a steel company that is a traditional manufacturing industry, but has been making a lot of efforts to diversify its business recently. How are these diversification efforts affecting POSCO's HR strategy?
2. Recently what is the most important point in POSCO's HR strategy?
3. Like other Korean companies, POSCO's workforce structure is changing rapidly. How will the HR strategy change according to this change in the workforce structure?
4. POSCO maintains a relative evaluation system. What if the evaluation system needs to be changed in light of POSCO's vision and strategy?

CHAPTER 4

Person and Job

Learning Objectives

1. Explain the meaning and importance of individual differences in human resource management.
2. Explain the meaning and types of competencies and motivations.
3. Understand the definition and characteristics of the job.
4. Explain the type of job design.
5. Explain the purpose and procedure of job analysis.
6. Explain the point method among job evaluation methods.

Introductory Case

Roh Hwan-ju is the head of S Chemical's Cheongju plant. Company S originally made cassette tapes and videotapes. From the beginning, S Company's core competency was to manufacture and supply films that meet the diverse needs of B2B customers. Cassettes and videos were no longer supplied to the market and faced a crisis, but demand for film exploded as televisions were replaced by flat panel displays from CRT(cathoe-ray tube) TVs. Due to this, the factory's profit rate is not so high, but it is operating a stable business.

Plant manager Roh Hwan-ju joined as an engineer in this company and has long experience in the film manufacturing process. The employees in the field who have worked with the plant manager Roh for a long time are very skilled. The needs of B2B customers are very diverse and detailed. For example, film thickness, size, color, surface treatment, etc. Nevertheless, so far, it has responded smoothly to the needs of such diverse customers with the high skill of the field staff. Until now, customer satisfaction has been very high. Employees in the field understand and handle even the sensitive parts of the machine through a long experience, so they are well accommodating to delicate customer needs. In addition, the fact that the employees have a high basic understanding of chemical products and a considerable sense of design was the reason why the product became the top-notch.

But one day, when the CEO called the plant manager Roh Hwan-ju, his thoughts began. The CEO's argument is that with the current manual method, it has reached its limit to meet all the demands of customers that are changing day by day. In addition, although it is currently well suited to the needs of B2B companies, it was expected that the demands of corporate customers would be stronger in order to satisfy the ever-changing needs of consumers. At the current manufacturing process speed, it is difficult to respond to the new needs of customers. In fact, the plant manager Noh was well aware that indirect complaints have been increasing recently due to the delivery date problem.

The CEO's idea is that only smart factories that can receive information on product specifications requested by customers and process them directly through artificial intelligence (AI) can overcome this crisis. So, he was asked to create a 4th industry TF in the company and find an implementation plan with the headquarter computer center. Plant manager Roh Hwan-ju's mind is complicated. When it becomes a smart factory, what happens to the work process, how should the jobs of existing employees change, and what are the necessary competencies for the smart factory? The plant manager felt like a pile of tasks to be solved.

Discussion Questions

1. How is the company's production strategy changing?
2. How is the change in technology according to the production strategy predicted to have an effect on the job?
3. What is the difference between the competencies existing employees have and the competencies that are newly needed?
4. If you were the plant manager, how would you approach this problem?
5. What are the new and disappearing jobs due to the 4th Industrial Revolution?

In Chapter 1, we presented the basic model of human resource management in [Figure 4-1] to explain the relationship between human resource management and performance. This model emphasized that the ultimate goal of human resource management is to successfully support the business, the goal pursued by the enterprise. A business is affected by the performance of the entire company, and in turn, the performance of the company is affected by the performance of the unit. And the performance of the unit depends on the performance of the members of the organization. In order to improve the performance of these members, people and jobs should be properly managed, and the activity to manage them is HR management. In this chapter, before understanding each function of human resource management (recruitment, evaluation, development, compensation, turnover), which will be dealt with in detail from the next chapter, we would like to explain what is needed to improve the performance of each member.

1. Extension of the Basic Model of Human Resource Management

[Figure 4-1] is an enlarged view of factors affecting performance among the basic human resource management models examined in Chapter 1 using a magnifying glass. As explained in Chapter 1, in order to achieve a goal, that is, performance, an individual

Figure 4-1 Extension of the Basic Model of Human Resource Management

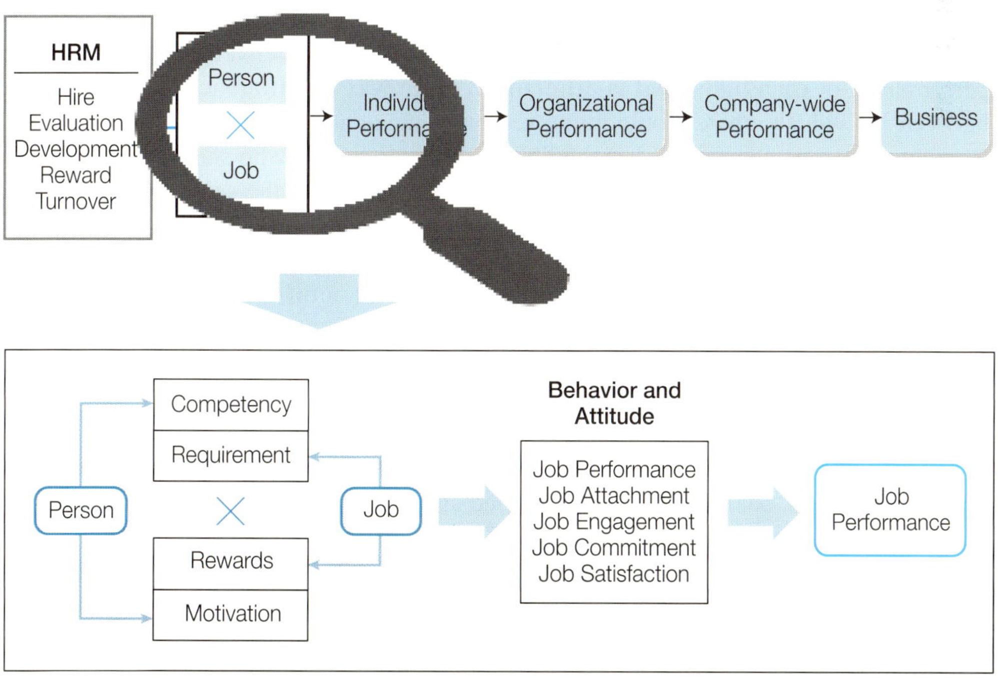

in an organization must take actions and have an attitude that can positively affect performance. For example, if you have to put your job into action through actual work (job performance), have passion (job engagement) and affection (job attachment), and immerse yourself in your job (job commitment), performance will be improved. It also increases one's own satisfaction (job satisfaction). When the level of satisfaction increases, a virtuous cycle is created in which one can work with more passion and affection in the work they are doing.

Human resource management not only improves organizational performance by creating such a virtuous cycle, but also ensures that employees are satisfied and rewarded in their work life. So, what is needed to make these individuals develop positive behaviors and attitudes? This can be achieved only when the person and the job are properly harmonized, as has been emphasized repeatedly. However, standards are needed for the proper match between the individual and the job. These are factors that affect performance. First, the factors influencing performance are possessed by an individual and are determined by competency and motivation. And the competency that an individual should have is determined according to the job requirements required for the job. On the other hand, in order to motivate people, rewards must be made.

2. Person

2.1 Difference in Person

2.1.1 HRM and Difference in Person

The reason why human resource management is necessary is because the performance of each individual is different. If there was no difference in performance between individuals, there would be no reason to make any effort or evaluation. There is no doubt that people are fundamentally equal human beings who should all be treated equally, but at the same time we know that not all people are the same. We also know that not everyone can excel in every way, except in very exceptional cases. They differ in many ways, such as appearance, personality, physique, physical strength, abilities, and the environment in which they were raised. Without these differences, human identity would be lost. However, what we are interested in the human resource management that we deal with in this textbook is not the difference in all aspects that people show, but the individual differences that affect performance.

On the other hand, reflecting individual differences in human resource management may cause discrimination. Both differences and discrimination presuppose that each person is different, but differences are justified and discrimination is not. Discrimination is not treating a person as an equal person. Discrimination is also strictly prohibited by law. For example, what the law typically prohibits is discrimination based on gender, disability, age, religion, etc.

The human resource management has the premise that the competencies required for different jobs are different and the interests of individuals are different. This difference is important because it appears as a difference in performance in performing a specific job. It is the result of long-term research that those who have the appropriate competency for the job and the will to perform the job perform higher than those who do not, and feel greater satisfaction and reward.

2.1.2 Factors that Affect Performance

Factors that affect performance are very diverse and depend on the kind of work you do. For example, in basketball, the taller you are, the more likely you are to throw the ball into the hoop. On the other hand, in the case of horse racing, taller is disadvantageous. Rather, shorter and lighter weight puts less strain on the horse and increases the chances that the horse will reach the finish line sooner. However, if a typical company hires people because they are tall or short, you will think it is strange enough to be covered in the TV's "Oh my God" section. The factors that increase performance like this depend on what kind of work you are doing. For this reason, it is important to find the factors that lead to performance in the job through job analysis.

Although there are many factors that determine performance, scholars have summarized them as competencies and motives that induce individuals to perform performance-enhancing behaviors through research. Competency here means the ability to do something. Competency is the aggregate of knowledge, skill, and ability. KSA is an acronym for knowledge, skill, and ability. The KSA is representative as a key element of competency, but it also includes many other elements. Motive is the will to do something. Other expressions of motive include passion, effort, and enthusiasm. What causes you to have motive is called motivation.

In the lower part of [Figure 4-1], it is indicated that competency and motivation are multiplied and affect behavior, attitude, and performance. It is important to note that competency and motivation influence performance by multiplication and not addition. For example, if competency is 5 and motivation is 5, multiplication becomes 25 and addition equals 10. On the other hand, if the competency is 7 and the motivation is 3, the addition is still 10, but the multiplication is 21. In other words, when using addition, the two cases are the same, but when using multiplication, the case of 5 and 5 has a better effect on performance than the case of 7 and 3, respectively. The meaning of the multiplicative relationship between competency and motivation for performance is as follows. First, it is the synergy effect between the two factors of competency and motivation. The two factors have a synergistic effect with each other, and the higher both factors increase, the greater the effect on performance. Second, both factors are important. When only one factor is good, the effect on performance is not large. Moreover, if one factor is zero, the performance is zero, no matter how high the other factor is. Third, the balance between competency and motivation is important. When one factor is properly balanced, the effect on performance is greater than when one factor is higher than the other. In the following, we take a closer look at competencies and motivations.

2.2 Competency

2.2.1 Definition of Competency

Competency is a concept that is almost similar to ability, but recently many companies are using competency instead of ability. The reason for this is as follows. First, it is to distinguish among potential abilities that can be actually exercised and have a direct impact on performance. In other words, in order for competency to affect performance, it must be manifested in actions and attitudes. No matter how high a potential ability is, it is useless if it is not manifested in actions and attitudes to affect performance. Competency is a concept created to focus more on potential abilities that directly affect performance. Second, competency is used to identify what makes the difference between ordinary people and high performers. There may be no insignificant abilities, but for management purposes it is not efficient to cover all of them. For example, arithmetic skills such as addition, subtraction, multiplication, and division are important as basic skills. However, there is no doubt that those who have graduated from universities in Korea have some basic abilities. If so, arithmetic skills will not need to be dealt with in human resource management. On the other hand, negotiation competency cannot be said to be high just because you graduated from college. For example, if the competency common to high-performing consultants in a company specializing in M&A is the negotiation competency, this will be an important factor to be dealt with in each human resource management function of recruitment, evaluation, training, and compensation.

However, theoretically and practically, the definition and scope of competency are very broad, so it is not easy to organize them into one. In the background of the frequent confusion in the corporate field, competency is sometimes defined as the aggregate of KSA that has been traditionally used in human resource management, and in other cases, competency is used as a separate concept distinct from KSA. The latter tends to be used mainly in the field of human resource development. In this case, in order to define competency as a differentiated concept from KSA, it is necessary to find new competency. To this end, it often goes through a complex and time-consuming process called competency modeling. On the other hand, in the case where competency is defined as a traditional KSA aggregate like the former, it is sufficient through job analysis without a separate process for deriving competency. There is controversy over how to define competency, but considering that this textbook is for managers rather than HR experts, it was judged that it is more appropriate to define competency in the traditional KSA rather than a complex competency model. Therefore, in this textbook, competency is defined as the aggregate of KSA.[2)] However, in order to differentiate it from general KSA, competency is defined as KSA that directly affects job performance.

In order to understand competency based on this definition, additional understanding of knowledge, skills and abilities(KSA) is required.[3)] For reference, a general definition of KSA and examples of each of KSA are presented here. What the company uses for human resource management is to select the necessary KSA among them. As described above, the selection criteria will be what is required to achieve high performance in the job.

1) Knowledge

Knowledge is a set of information that is directly related to the performance of a job. Information includes concepts, facts, procedures, etc. In general, knowledge used in human resource management is specific to a job, occupation, or industry. O*NET (Occupational Information Network) of the US Department of Labor provides examples of types of knowledge that can be used in various jobs. As shown in <Table 4-1>, it is classified into business management, manufacturing and production, engineering, mathematics, science, medical care, education, art, law, communication, and transportation.

2) Skills

Skills are observable competencies that can use or apply knowledge to perform

Table 4-1 Example of Knowledge

<table>
<tr><td rowspan="6">Business management</td><td>Administration and management</td><td rowspan="2">Medical service</td><td>Medicine and dentistry</td></tr>
<tr><td>Administrative</td><td>Therapy and counseling</td></tr>
<tr><td>Economics and accounting</td><td>Education and training</td><td>Education and training</td></tr>
<tr><td>Sales and marketing</td><td rowspan="5">Arts and humanities</td><td>English language</td></tr>
<tr><td>Customer and personal service</td><td>Foreign language</td></tr>
<tr><td>Personnel and human resources</td><td>Fine arts</td></tr>
<tr><td rowspan="2">Manufacturing production</td><td>Production and processing</td><td>History and archeology</td></tr>
<tr><td>Food production</td><td>Philosophy and theology</td></tr>
<tr><td rowspan="5">Engineering and technology</td><td>Computer and electronics</td><td rowspan="2">Law and public security</td><td>Public safety and security</td></tr>
<tr><td>Engineering and technology</td><td>Law and government</td></tr>
<tr><td>Design</td><td rowspan="2">Communication</td><td>Telecommunications</td></tr>
<tr><td>Building and constuction</td><td>Communications and media</td></tr>
<tr><td>Mechanical</td><td>Transportation</td><td>Transportation</td></tr>
<tr><td rowspan="7">Math and science</td><td>Mathematics</td><td></td><td></td></tr>
<tr><td>Physics</td><td></td><td></td></tr>
<tr><td>Chemistry</td><td></td><td></td></tr>
<tr><td>Biology</td><td></td><td></td></tr>
<tr><td>Psychology</td><td></td><td></td></tr>
<tr><td>Sociology and Anthropology</td><td></td><td></td></tr>
<tr><td>Geography</td><td></td><td></td></tr>
</table>

Source: https://www.onetcenter.org/content.html

specific jobs. Determining what skills are needed to perform a job is possible through direct observation. Because a skill is acquired through repeated learning and effort, it is sometimes expressed as proficiency. Skill also functions as a link between knowledge and ability while performing a job. The most directly effective factor for job performance is ability, but it is not easy to acquire in a short period of time because the ability is formed over a long period of time. On the other hand, knowledge can be acquired in a short period of time through learning, but having knowledge does not mean that it can be directly applied to a job. Therefore, companies tend to invest in education and training to improve skills as a way to increase job performance in a short period of time. As shown in <Table 4-2>, skills are largely divided into basic skills and cross-functional skills. Basic skills include content such as reading, listening, and writing, and process ones such as critical thinking and active learning. Cross-functional skills include social

Table 4-2 Example of Skills

BASIC SKILLS					
Content	Reading comprehension	**Process**	Critical thinking		
	Active listening		Active learning		
	Writing		Learning strategies		
	Speaking		Monitoring		
	Mathematics				
	Science				
CROSS-FUNCTIONAL SKILLS					
Social skills	Social perceptiveness	**Technical skills**	Operations analysis	**Resource management skills**	Time management
	Coordination		Technology design		Management of financial resources
	Persuasion		Equipment selection		Management of material resources
	Negotiation		Installation		Management of personnel resources
	Instructing		Programming	**System skills**	Judgment and decision making
	Service orientation		Operation monitoring		Systems analysis
Complex problem solving skills	Complex problem solving		Equipment maintenance		System evaluation
			Troubleshooting		
			Repairing		
			Quality control analysis		

Source: https://www.onetcenter.org/content.html

skills, complex problem solving skills, technical skills, resource management skills, and systems skills.

3) Abilites

Abilities refer to the intrinsic property of an individual to perform a variety of different tasks. In practice, skills and abilities are sometimes used without distinction, but the difference between skills and abilities is that abilities do not change well because they are formed for a long time and can be applied to various jobs with different contents. Aptitude is often used in conjunction with ability, and aptitude is a type of ability. Most of Korea's leading companies conduct aptitude tests as recruitment tests (Global Samsung Aptitude Test: GSAT),[4)] LG Aptitude Test, Hyundai Motor Group Aptitude Test (HMAT), SK Comprehensive Competency Test (SKCT), etc.). This aptitude test is to verify common abilities required to perform various jobs. As shown in <Table 4-3>, abilities include cognitive ability, psychomotor ability, physical ability, and sensory ability.

2.2.2 Types of Competencies

We have defined competency as the aggregate of KSA in this textbook. Here we look at the types of competencies. There are many different competencies that companies use. These can be broadly classified into four types of competency.

1) Common Competency

Common competencies refer to basic competencies that all members of an organization must possess. Most companies create a talent image and present it on their website, so you can find it easily. In some cases, the company's official website presents the common competencies along with the talent image separately. For example, Sempio Foods, one of the representative companies in the food industry, presents three types of talent: a humble person, a selfless person, and a person with passion. In addition, challenge, teamwork, professionalism, customer orientation, and ethical awareness are presented as common competencies. In Sempio Foods, ethical awareness is presented as a common competency, and challenge, teamwork, professionalism, and customer orientation are divided into basic competencies.[5)] Sempio Foods is also famous for conducting unique cooking interviews to measure these common competencies during the hiring process. The cooking interview consists of a team of 4 to 5 applicants, using the ingredients given to decide a cooking theme and menu, and creating and presenting dishes based on teamwork. What the company wants to see through the cooking interview is not the taste of food, but rather the determination of whether the applicant meets the company's talent in the process of cooking.[6)]

2) Leadership Competency

Leadership competency refers to the competencies that leaders in a position to lead the members of an organization should have. In the hierarchy of the organization, from the CEO to the team leader at the forefront of management, leadership is required

Table 4-3 Example of Abilities

COGNITIVE ABILITIES		PSYCHOMOTOR ABILITIES		SENSORY ABILITIES	
Verbal abilities	Oral comprehension	Fine manipulative ability	Arm-hand steadiness	Visual abilities	Near vision
	Written comprehension		Manual dexterity		Far vision
	Oral expression		Finger dexterity		Visual color discrimination
	Written expression	Control movement abilities	Control provision		Night vision
Idea generation and reasoning abilities	Fluence of ideas		Multilimb coordination		Peripheral vision
	Originality		Response orientation		Depth perception
	Problem sensitivity		Rate control		Glare sensitivity
	Deductive reasoning	Reaction time and speed abilities	Reaction time	Auditory and speech abilities	Hearing sensitivity
	Inductive reasoning		Wrist-finger speed		Auditory attention
	Formation ordering		Speed of limb movement		Sound localilzation
	Category flexibility	**PHYSICAL ABILITIES**			Speech recognition
Quantitative abilities	Mathematical reasoning	Physical strength abilities	Static strength		Speech clarity
	Number facility		Explosive strength		
Memory	Memorization		Dynamic strength		
Perceptual abilities	Speed of closure		Trunk strength		
	Flexibility of closure	Endurance	Stamina		
	Perceptual speed	Flexibility, Balance, and Coordination	Extent flexibility		
Spatial abilities	Spatial organization		Dynamic flexibility		
	Visualization		Gross Body coordination		
Attentiveness	Selection attention		Gross body equilibrium		
	Time sharing				

Source: https://www.onetcenter.org/content.html

for each stage of the organization. Examples of competencies that are widely used as leadership competencies include visioning, strategic thinking, change management, talent development, decision-making, and networking, performance management, interpersonal skills, employee motivation, communication, self-management, etc. Human resource management, which is covered in this textbook, can be considered to be included in the leadership competencies that a leader should have.

3) Professional Competency

Professional competency refers to the competencies commonly required for each major professional function of an organization. For example, since the competencies required for each specialized field are different, such as marketing, finance, human resources, purchasing, information technology, production, and R&D, the competencies suitable for each field are derived and used in all human resource management activities such as recruitment, evaluation, and nurturing. do. For example, <Table 4-4> shows a specific example of the marketing expertise of a domestic electronic company.[7)]

4) Job Competency

Job competency is a competency that is applicable to all members and is a competency required to perform a specific job. It is an essential competency to enhance the performance of the job, which is confirmed by job analysis and recorded in the job description. Job competency is related to professional competency. If professional competency is a competency that is commonly required for all jobs in a particular field of expertise, job competency is a competency required for a specific job in a specialized field. In the previous case, professional competency in the marketing field was a competency required for all jobs in this field. On the other hand, if there is a domestic B2B marketing job among marketing, this job requires job competency that is not required for other jobs in the marketing field. Of course, there are cases where separate job competencies are required for each specific job, and some companies manage only general competencies in a broadly defined specialized field rather than specific job specific competencies. Specific examples of job competency will be discussed in job analysis and job description.

2.3 Motive

2.3.1 Definition of Motive

A motive can be defined as "the internal force that provokes, directs, and sustains a behavior".[8)] A motive is the desire to do something, and it means being able to put it into practice. What causes you to have motive is called motivation. Motivation in human resource management is important because, no matter how talented you are, you cannot achieve good results if you do not have the will to do your best. A company should be able to motivate its employees to improve job performance through human resource management. Psychologists have long studied why and how people are motivated. The discipline of 'organizational behavior', a subject offered at most business schools, is also

Table 4-4 **Specific Examples of Professional Competencies**

COMPETENCY NAME	COMPETENCY DEFINITION	COMPETENCY-RELATED KNOWLEDGE/SKILLS/ABILITIES
Internet business understanding	Technical knowledge of internet business, ability to grasp trends, and understanding of business structure (cost, major sales factors, etc.)	IP and N/W basic knowledge, accounting principles, cost accounting
Marketing strategy establishment ability	Ability to select a target market based on the 4Ps, confirm the concept and positioning, develop marketing activities accordingly, and establish a detailed implementation plan	Advanced skills in business administration and marketing
Market analysis ability	Ability to predict market characteristics, competitive situation, and market size, analyze future market demands and competitive scenarios, and reflect them in business	market research theory, statistics, excel
Ability to understand customer needs	Ability to evaluate customer satisfaction, discover customer dissatisfaction factors and future needs (price, product development factors, service upgrade factors, etc.) and reflect them in marketing	consumer behavior theory, price theory, marketing
Data processing and analytics	Ability to systematize and categorize customer information based on customer information to discover implications and utilize them for marketing activities (CRM)	DB marketing, CRM strategy
Ability to improve marketing processes	Ability to improve and process all processes necessary for marketing activities such as billing, cost, purchase, and system	Ability to improve all marketing processes (billing, purchase, opening, promotion)
Sales channel management ability	Ability to devise and implement training for efficiency measures for salespeople and distribution network channels, and to reflect the requirements of sales channels in marketing	Sales channel management ability (statistics and performance management), ability to collect sales requirements, communication ability
Business consultation ability	Ability to achieve negotiation goals in internal and external negotiation, with the government, and the necessary negotiation skills	Ability to improve negotiation skills
Promotional ability	Ability to develop ideas and efficiently perform necessary events/publicity/advertisement/promotional events to maximize the effect	marketing promotion strategy, advertising strategy, luxury brand strategy
Proposal writing and presentation skills	Ability to identify customer needs, provide appropriate solutions, discover service differentiation points, and propose the most efficient communication to customers	presentation skills, PowerPoint usage skills

an academic field that arose from the accumulation of research on motivation. Since the details of motivation are dealt with in the organizational behavior course, here we will look at six motivational theories that are directly related to human resource management.

2.3.2. Motivation Theory

1) Maslow's Hierarchy of Needs

Abraham Maslow asserts that there are five levels of human needs. As shown in <Table 4-5>, it starts with physiological needs, which is the lowest need, and leads to security needs, social needs, esteem needs, and the last step, self-actualization needs. Among them, physiological needs and safety needs are low-level needs, which are mainly caused by deficiency. Therefore, once the needs are satisfied, people do not seek these needs any more. On the other hand, the other three needs are higher-order needs, and when the lower-level needs are satisfied, people will increasingly pursue higher-order needs and ultimately want self-actualization. The need for self-actualization does not arise from lack. Therefore, being satisfied does not mean that you stop seeking this need, and the more it is satisfied, the more you want to pursue it.

The implications of Maslow's hierarchy of needs theory for human resource management are that humans have basic needs like animals, like physiological needs and safety needs. However, when this is satisfied, humans, unlike animals, want to pursue higher-order needs. People work in companies not just to solve the problem of making a living. People go to work to satisfy their desire to socialize and be recognized by others. Furthermore, ultimately, they have a desire to grow in an organization, to use their capabilities to the fullest, and to become the best in their field of expertise. As the economy develops and society becomes more prosperous, higher-order needs become more important than lower-level needs.

2) Herzberg's Two-Factor Theory

Herzberg explains human needs by dividing them into motivators and hygiene factors. Similar to Maslow, motivating factors correspond to higher-order needs and hygiene factors correspond to lower-order needs. For example, motivating factors

Table 4-5 **Maslow's 5 Levels of Needs**[9]

STAGE OF DESIRE		CONTENTS
Higher-order needs	Self-actualization	The need to realize one's potential, to grow, to be creative, and to accomplish
	Esteem	The need for respect and recognition from others
	Social	The need to belong, to interact with others, to have friends, and to love and be loved
Low-order needs	Security	The need for safety, family stability, and economic security
	Physiological needs	The need for food, sleep, water, air, and sex

include responsibility for work, sense of achievement, challenge, and recognition from others, and hygiene factors include salary, benefits, working conditions, and relationship with supervisors. The difference between Herzberg's two-factor theory and the hierarchy of needs theory is that these needs are viewed as two separate dimensions, rather than as one dimension. In other words, the motivating factor becomes a satisfaction factor, and the hygiene factor becomes a dissatisfaction factor. If the hygiene factor is not satisfied as a dissatisfaction factor, the level of dissatisfaction increases. On the other hand, as the motivating factor is a satisfaction factor, the satisfaction increases the more it is satisfied. However, dissatisfaction does not increase just because the motivating factors are not met.

The implication of Herzberg's two-factor theory for human resource management is that both motivators and hygiene factors are important and require separate management. If the working environment, salary level, welfare, etc. are poor, the satisfaction of organizational members will greatly decrease, and the will to work cannot be increased. However, this does not mean that these factors alone should not be regarded as important. Resolving hygiene factors does not automatically increase motivation to work. Rather, the more the organization emphasizes hygiene factors, the more the members become obsessed with hygiene factors only. One of the reasons Hyundai Motor's labor union is criticized is that it is demanding an excessively high wage increase while already receiving a high salary. This attribute of the union deserves to be criticized, but on the other hand, it is necessary to look at whether it is because the company has overemphasized only the hygiene factor. Motivational factors are possible only if you feel meaning and reward from work itself rather than salary or welfare benefits. In order to increase the motivation level of members in an organization, it is necessary to allow them to find a sense of responsibility, achievement, and a sense of challenge.

3) Hackman and Oldham's Job Characteristics Model

Hackman and Oldham's job characteristics model shows that people have different motivations for work depending on how they design their jobs. In the job characteristics model, when a job has five characteristics: skill variety, task identity, task significance, autonomy, and feedback, job performers realize the meaning of work. And when this happens, people feel responsible for the results and have a desire to continue learning. These results bring about improvement in internal satisfaction, quality improvement in job performance, increase in job satisfaction, and low turnover and absenteeism rates. Of course, this process does not apply equally to everyone. The effect varies according to individual differences. Individual differences appear in the knowledge and skills that an individual possesses, the strength of the desire to grow, and the satisfaction with the current situation. For example, a person with a strong desire to grow can reorganize his or her job to have five core job characteristics. On the other hand, those who have a weak desire to grow weaken these relationships. Here are five key job characteristics that are important to motivation, as highlighted by Hackman and Oldham:

① **Skill variety:** How diverse are the types of skills required to perform a job. Jobs

Figure 4-2 **Hackman and Oldham's Job Characteristics Model**[10)]

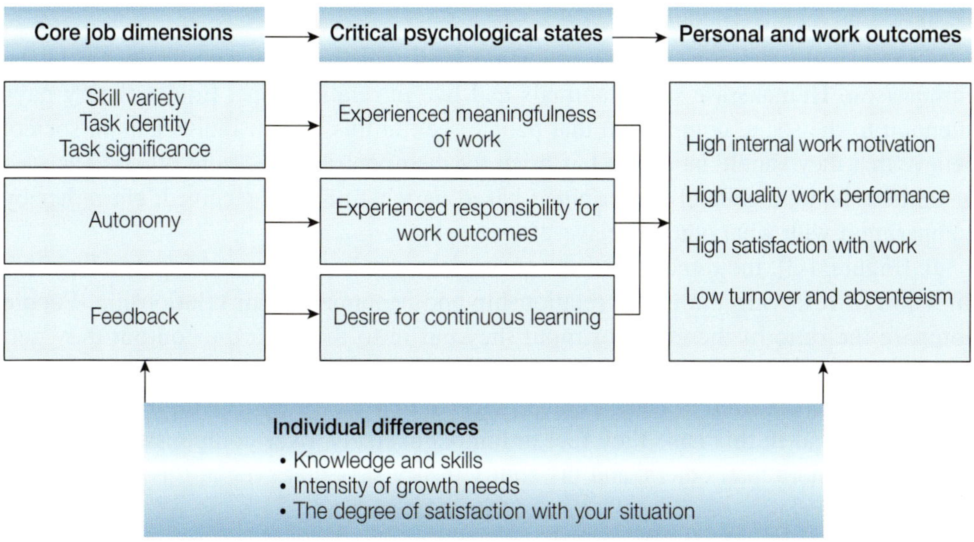

Source: Hackman & Oldham, 1976.

with high skill variety broaden the range of jobs performed by individuals.

② **Task identity:** It refers to the degree to which an individual knows that his/her job is connected to the entire organization. Individuals with high task identity jobs can see how their jobs are linked to the performance of the organization as a whole.

③ **Task significance:** How important an individual's job is to the lives and work of others within or outside the organization. Jobs with high task significance can have a significant impact on other people or the entire organization when done wrong.

④ **Autonomy:** It refers to the degree of personal responsibility that an individual feels about his or her job. The higher the level of discretion in independent judgment or decision-making, the higher the autonomy.

⑤ **Feedback:** It refers to how well an individual knows about the results of the work performed. Jobs that receive feedback well are those where you can immediately learn about the results of your work.

The primary implication that job characteristics theory gives to human resource management is that the motivation of organizational members varies according to how the job is designed. But what goes one step further is how leaders create the organizational environment, even if they perform the same job. Alternatively, the level of motivation may vary depending on how the members are assigned tasks and given meaning. For example, when setting goals in the performance evaluation process, reminding them of the meaning and letting members know what level they have reached through continuous feedback is important for motivation.

4) Adams' Equity Theory

Adams' equity theory, unlike other motivational theories, emphasizes relative comparison. Humans are social animals and live in relationships. Equity theory pays attention to the social comparison that people seek in this aspect. Individuals in society believe that they should be paid a fair price for their contributions from others. The idea of fairness is not absolutely determined based on what one has received, but rather by comparing it with what others receive.[11)]

In [Figure 4-3], the direction of motivation is people's actions, and it proceeds in the direction of resolving the unfair relationship and becoming a fair relationship. People compare the ratio of the effort or input they put in to the reward or output they get, and the ratio of the effort or contribution others put in and the reward or result they get. Undercompensation is when people perceive that they are receiving relatively less than others, and in this case they feel unfair. Conversely, over-compensation is when one receives more than others, and the equity theory says that even at this time, it feels unfair.

The implications of the equity theory for human resource management are particularly closely related to compensation. If you feel that the reward you are receiving is small compared to the amount of effort or contribution you put in, your motivation to work decreases. This is true for both people and job aspects. First, if you are doing the same job and someone other than you is getting a high reward for an unfair reason, your dissatisfaction will increase. Fairness varies according to the times. In the past, it was natural to accept high wages if you were older or have a high tenure even if you did the same job according to seniority, but the new generation is increasingly not. Second, in terms of job, you feel that it is unfair if you are performing a valuable job that is difficult and has a high contribution to the organization compared to other people, but

Figure 4-3 Equity Theory

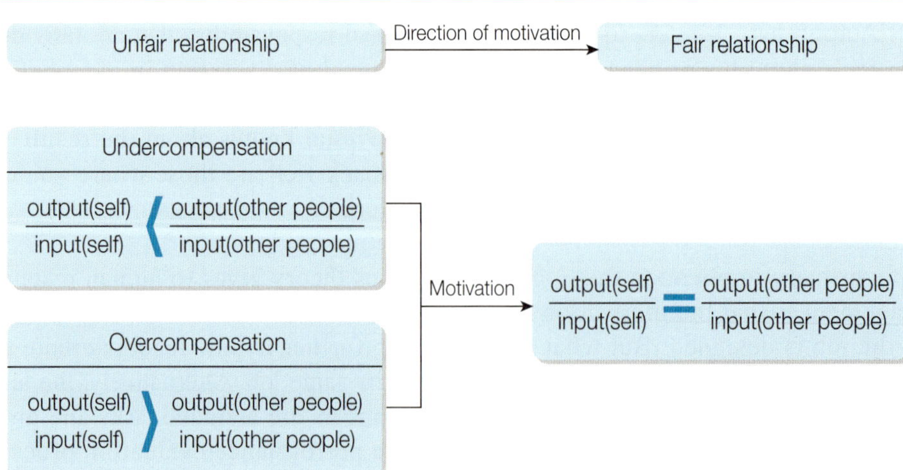

the compensation is the same.

5) Vroom's Expectancy Theory

Vroom's expectancy theory focuses on the process by which motivation is created. Expectancy theory consists of three elements: expectancy, instrumentality, and valence. The expectancy is the expectation that hard work can lead to results. If effort cannot be translated into results, there will be no expectations. Instrumentality is the possibility that, if there is an outcome, this can lead to some tangible result. For example, if incentive is provided when performance is high, instrumentality will increase. The last is valence, which is whether the degree of reward is meaningful. If the reward is worthwhile, it is value, and if it is not and the reward is mediocre, it is less value. These three factors are closely related. In other words, when there is an expectancy that when an effort is made, that effort can lead to results, people strive. But this alone is not enough. When effort leads to performance, there should be a reward for performance. Of course, compensation is not just about monetary compensation. A sense of accomplishment, pleasure, and fun are also important rewards. But this is still not enough. Finally, the reward must be worthwhile. If the value of a reward felt by an individual is not large, its meaning as a reward is lost. Expectancy theory contributed to a better understanding of people's motivation. In particular, it was emphasized that all three conditions must be satisfied in order for repetitive motivation to be possible.[12)]

The implications of expectancy theory for human resource management can be found in all three elements of the theory. First, in terms of expectancy, in order to induce the efforts of organizational members, the efforts must lead to performance. This may vary depending on individual capabilities. When assigning tasks to individuals, it is necessary to entrust tasks suitable for each individual's capabilities to raise expectations for the results of their efforts. Second, in terms of instrumentality, appropriate rewards should follow when members work hard and get results. In particular, the relationship of trust between the organization and its members is important, and if you promise that the results of your efforts will lead to rewards such as promotions or bonuses, if you don't keep them, people's motivation to work hard will be lost. Third, in terms of valence, the reward should be what members feel meaningful. It can vary from person to person, and it can also vary from generation to generation. Maslow's Hierarchy of Needs theory, discussed earlier, can be used here.

6) Locke's Goal-setting Theory

Locke's goal-setting theory emphasizes the setting of appropriate goals as the most important factor in motivation. A goal can be said to be a desirable future outcome pursued by an individual, group, or organization. According to goal setting theory, when members set goals, they are more motivated than when they do not set goals. However, not all goals are motivating. Scholars have revealed through various studies which goals are motivating.[13)] In summary, goals should be challenging and specific. What challenging and specific means is not an abstract and ambiguous goals like 'I will work hard', 'I will achieve high performance', and 'I will do my best'. It means a goal that is specific, not too difficult, but not too easy, and achievable with effort, such as "I will find and improve the errors of the information and communication system that are continuously occurring within three months."

Goal setting theory is closely related to human resource management, and the representative one is the management by objectives (MBO) system, which is used by many companies in performance evaluation. The MBO is an evaluation system that directly utilizes the goal setting theory. It allows members to set their own goals and evaluates them according to whether they have been achieved. It was first devised by Peter Drucker, an American business scholar, and argued that organizational performance is maximized when all members, from the CEO to front-line managers, set consistent goals. Therefore, goal setting is carried out in stages for each level of the organization. For example, the goal of the team leader is linked to the goal of the headquarters or division, which is a higher level department. The goals of the team members are in turn linked to the goals of the team organization. All goal setting processes are achieved through mutual participation. The goal of a team member is not just given by the team leader, but is set through prior consultation between the team leader and team members. The MBO does not end with setting goals, but carries out an intermediate process of continuously checking and giving feedback in the process of carrying out goals. And evaluation is made on the basis of whether or not the finally set goal has been achieved. This is a continuous process that is reflected in the goal setting for the next fiscal year.

3. Job

3.1 Understanding Job

3.1.1 Definition of Job

In order for an organization to carry out its business successfully, it needs resources, and the most important resource among them is human resources. Human resources are needed because there is a demand from customers. In order for an organization to offer a product or service to its customers, it needs the people—that is human resources—who create it, deliver it, advertise it, and sell it. By customer demand, we mean the activities necessary to satisfy the customer's demand. Demand for human resources means not only a person in need, but also an activity necessary to meet customer needs. Necessary activities are the work that people in the organization have to do. The unit for systematically managing the work is a job.

The job in english is used in many ways in everyday life. It is often used to say that there is a shortage of jobs because our economy is struggling. Or, among friends, it is also used when asking such questions, "Did you get a job?" In this way, job is used as a term such as employment or occupation. However, the job used in human resource management is somewhat different from this.

Jobs are tasks assigned to individuals by organizations to achieve business objectives. All members of an organization are assigned roles and responsibilities according to their respective positions in the organization. The roles and responsibilities assigned to each are called positions. The positions of members within the organization, that is, positions, can be identified through the organization chart. The organizational chart indicates the position of each member in the vertical hierarchy and horizontal relationship.

A job is a grouping of positions with similar roles and responsibilities and classified for the purpose of management. The relationship between jobs and positions varies from organization to organization. For example, Kim Chul-soo who works at a rather large company in Seoul is in charge of recruiting new college graduates in the HR department. Because the company is large, there are two more people besides Kim Chul-soo who are responsible for recruiting new college graduates every year. In this way, three people are performing the job of recruiting new college graduates. That is, in this company, one job includes three positions (employees). On the other hand, when Kim Cheol-soo moved to a small venture company, he had only the head of the department and himself in the personnel department. Kim Chul-soo had to be in charge of the HR department, not only in hiring but also in salaries and welfare benefits. Because this company is small, there are no other employees except for Kim Chul-soo, who is in charge of HR. That is, in this company, there is only one position (employee) per job.

3.1.2 Similar Terms Related to the Job

The following are terms related to jobs that are mainly used in large corporations. As shown in <Table 4-6>, there are terms that describe the concept composed of jobs gathered together above the job, and the concept composed by dividing jobs into small units below. Classification of concepts related to jobs is somewhat different depending on the size of the company or the characteristics of the industry.

<Table 4-7> presents examples of how the concepts related to the job described in <Table 4-7> are used in actual companies.

Table 4-6 **Understanding of Job-related Terms**

CONCEPT	EXPLANATION
Job Group(Family)	• A set of tasks with different content but similar functions
Job Series	• A group of jobs that have different scope of responsibility in the hierarchy of an organization but have similar task contents
Job	• Set of tasks with similar duties and responsibilities • A collection of tasks, duties, and responsibilities performed by one person • Group of positions with similar duties and responsibilities
Position	• A set of duties and responsibilities assigned to be performed by a person within an organization • Position in the hierarchy within the organization (number of members = number of positions)
Duty(Role) & responsibility	• A set of tasks that serve a similar purpose
Task	• Work activities to perform a specific purpose in performing a job

Table 4-7 **Examples of Use of Job-Related Terms**

CONCEPT	EXAMPLES
Job group	(Korea electronics) **Support job group**, production job group, sales job group, R&D job group
Job series	(Support group) **Human resources**, finance, legal, purchasing
Job	(HR job series) **Recruitment**, evaluation, compensation, training, labor and management
Position	(3 people in charge of recruitment) Chul-su Kim, Su-yong Lee, Han-yi Park
Duty & responsibility	(Recruitment job) Prediction of manpower demand for university graduates, **announcement of recruitment**, review of application documents, selection screening, notification of successful applicants
Task	(Announcement of recruitment) Selection of fields of recruitment, writing text for recruitment advertisements, and contact with media outlets to advertise recruitment notices

① **Job group**(or job family): A criterion for categorizing jobs with similar functions, although the contents of the tasks are different. Because different functions are performed within the organization, human resource management is often applied differently. Examples of the job group include a production job group, a support job group, a sales job group, and an R&D job group.

② **Job series:** A set of jobs that have similar tasks but different scopes of responsibilities in the hierarchy of an organization. For example, within support job group, there are human resources, finance, legal, purchasing, etc.

③ **Job:** A set of tasks with similar duties and responsibilities. For example, within the human resources job series, there are recruitment, evaluation, compensation, training, and labor-management jos.

④ **Position:** A set of duties and responsibilities assigned to be performed by a person within an organization. It means the position in the hierarchy within the organization, and the number of members and the number of positions in the organization are the same. All members have duties and responsibilities to fulfill for the success of the business. For example, Kim Chul-soo, who is in charge of recruitment, is responsible for several activities related to the recruitment of outstanding college graduates.

⑤ **Duty & responsibility:** A set of tasks that perform a similar purpose. Tasks assigned to individuals in an organization that must be performed in the performance of their duties. Duties and responsibilities are sometimes referred to as roles and responsibilities in other terms. For example, in order to hire college graduates, Kim Chul-soo needs to predict the manpower demand of college graduates, post a recruitment notice, receive applicants, review documents and conduct selection screening, and notify successful applicants of acceptance.

⑥ **Task:** A work activity to accomplish a specific purpose in performing a job. It means specific tasks required to perform a job, and several similar tasks are gathered to become one duty and responsibility. For example, in order to hire a college graduate and to fulfill the duties and responsibilities of posting a recruitment notice, Cheol-su Kim must select a recruitment field, write a text for the recruitment notice, and contact the media that will advertise the recruitment notice.

3.2 Job Design and Job Redesign

Jobs arise and disappear naturally as organizations grow and develop. Job design is the process of finding and assigning jobs to people that are most suitable for the purpose pursued by the organization. Deciding how to allocate small units of tasks to people determines how the entire organization is structured. This is called organization design. The result of organizational design is an organization chart. If you look at the organizational chart, you can see at a glance what industry the organization belongs to, what kind of business it is in, and what kind of jobs it performs in what hierarchy.

There are various tasks that an organization must perform in order to achieve its business goals. In order to manage these tasks efficiently and effectively, they should be separated into appropriate units and assigned to individual members. This is called job design.

On the other hand, job redesign is a way to break away from the monotony caused by overly subdivided task performance and to increase interest and motivation in the job performance process. As the term redesign suggests, it has the meaning of designing the existing job design in a different direction.

3.2.1 Job Simplification

With the development of capitalism, job simplification is a primitive form of job design in organizations in the modern sense. Job simplification is a job design method that divides and allocates processes in a way that minimizes the tasks that people have to be responsible for. Because it is a simplified job, anyone can easily learn the contents of the task without much skill or experience. In addition, since the simplified task is repeatedly performed, mastery is improved, and specialization is obtained in the field. The principle of division of labor suggested by A. Smith in his book 『The Wealth of Nations』 shows the extreme efficiency of job simplification. If a worker makes pins from wire at a pin manufacturing plant, an average of 20 pins can be produced per day. The process of making a pin consists of 18 tasks, including taking, straightening, cutting, and bending the wire. If the division of labor is divided into several processes by applying job simplification, one person can focus on only one or two processes. Adam Smith said that if 10 people split the pin process, he could produce 48,000 pieces per day. One person could produce about 20 pieces, but through job simplification, one person can produce 4,800 pieces a day. This is a 240-fold increase in productivity.[14)]

In this way, job simplification made it possible to maximize productivity, and based on this, the mass production system was completed. However, job simplification increases the likelihood of job stress and loss of motivation as the monotonous task is repeatedly performed. The psychological harm that job simplification can bring to people is well illustrated in "Modern Times," played by Charlie Chaplin. As a result, job simplification can lead to side effects such as an increase in the defect rate and a decrease in worker productivity over time.

3.2.2 Job Enlargement

A representative of the early job redesign was job enlargement. Expanding the scope of an individual's task by simplifying the process into several steps and assigning them to an individual is called job enlargement.

3.2.3 Job Enrichment

While job enlargement is the horizontal expansion of the job scope, job enrichment is a job redesign that expands the job scope vertically as well. As it is not enough to relieve the sense of alienation or stress felt by workers just by giving the individual a wide range of tasks horizontally, an attempt to expand the scope of responsibility as an alternative to this is called job enrichment.

3.2.4 Job Rotation

Job rotation is also a method of job redesign, in which the jobs performed by an individual are exchanged at regular intervals. In this way, workers can experience a variety of jobs, free from the monotony of repeatedly performing only one job.

3.3 Job Analysis

Job analysis means systematically collecting and organizing information about job.

3.3.1 Purpose of Job Analysis

Job analysis is a necessary process for understanding the job. When an organization is first created, tasks are assigned and organized to carry out the purpose of its business. At the beginning of the organization, the contents of the job are clear, so it is not difficult to understand. However, as the business environment and technology change over time, changes in job contents are inevitable. In addition, as an organization grows, develops or declines, new jobs are created or existing jobs are eliminated.

For human resource management, it is necessary to reflect these situations in which job contents change or new jobs are created or disappeared. Job analysis is performed periodically in order to take into account these changes in the environment. For this reason, job analysis is essential in all areas of human resource management, such as recruitment, evaluation, training, compensation, and turnover management. For example, in order to hire new or experienced employees from outside for a certain job field, it is necessary to know well the competencies and qualifications required in that field.

However, if the required competency and qualification requirements change due to changes in the contents of the job field, this should be reflected in the hiring process. Otherwise, hiring errors will occur. In order to conduct performance evaluation for employees, it is necessary to clarify the contents of the job performed by the employee and the required level of competency and to set the evaluation criteria. In the case of compensation, when determining the basic salary, it is necessary to know the contents of the job to determine the value of the job. In addition, basic information about the job must be provided through job analysis for human resource management activities such as training or turnover.

3.3.2 Procedures for Job Analysis[15)]

The process of collecting job information, which is the basis of human resource management, must be systematic. Job analysis is generally performed through six steps as shown in [Figure 4-4].

1) Confirm the Purpose of Job Analysis

Depending on the purpose of the job analysis, the information to be obtained through job analysis varies, and the job analysis method also varies. Therefore, the first thing to be done in the job analysis process is to clarify for what purpose the job analysis is performed. For example, if you want to perform job analysis to improve the overall human resource management system, it is necessary to collect general information about the job. A suitable job analysis method would be to directly interview a job incumbent or a subject matter expert (SME). On the other hand, if job analysis is to be conducted to develop an evaluation tool based on deriving the competencies required by the job based on the behavior, it would be appropriate to use the critical incident technique (CIT). The job analysis method will be described later.

Figure 4-4 Job Analysis Procedure

① Confirm the purpose of job analysis	• The contents and method of job analysis vary depending on the purpose of job analysis
② Review background information	• Review background information such as organization chart, process chart, and existing job description
③ Selection of representative jobs	• Selection of the representative job or representative position among the jobs subject to job analysis
④ Conduct job analysis	• Collecting job information using job analysis methods
⑤ Verification of Job analysis content	• Verification of the accuracy of the job analysis through a manager or subject matter expert
⑥ Writing job description	• Organize the contents and results of the final job analysis in the job description

2) Review Background Information

A task that must be done before performing job analysis is a review of background information. In order to understand the job, first, it is necessary to understand how the jobs are arranged through the organizational chart and the inter-relation between the jobs. How work is done in detail can be reviewed through a process chart. Also, in the case of a company that has performed job analysis in the past, there is a job description, so it should be checked in advance.

3) Selection of Representative Job

In the case of a small company, since the number of jobs is not large, a complete job analysis is possible. On the other hand, if the company is large, it takes a lot of time and money to analyze all jobs. Therefore, it is a way to select and analyze representative jobs rather than analyzing all jobs except in cases where it is absolutely necessary. Also, if there are many people in charge of performing the same job, it is not necessary to analyze everyone's job. In this case, it is desirable to analyze the job through the representative person in charge. For example, if there are 100 employees in domestic sales, it is not necessary to know the job descriptions of all of them. Among them, job analysis is conducted through several representatives.

4) Conduct Job Analysis

This is the stage in which the planned job analysis is actually carried out. After selecting the target job by referring to the previous information reviewed above, job information is collected through a pre-planned job analysis method. Job information can be broadly divided into information about the job itself and information required for the person in charge of performing the job. Information on the job itself includes job title, job overview, job responsibilities, duties, and tasks. It also includes information about relationships with other jobs and the environment in which the job is performed. The information required for the person in charge of performing the job includes the minimum qualifications required to perform the job, such as academic background, skill qualifications, or experience, and job competency including knowledge, skills, and abilities required to perform the job.

5) Verification of Job Analysis Contents

This is a step to check whether the job-related information collected through job analysis is correct and whether there are any errors. It is verified by the direct supervisor of the person in charge of the relevant job or by a job content expert (SME) who knows the details of the job well. The verification process not only determines whether the job description is accurate, but it is also a necessary process to increase the acceptability of organizational members.

6) Writing Job Description

The final result of job analysis is a job description that summarizes the contents of job analysis in a certain format. In the past, it was often the case that job content was organized in the job description, and information required for the person in charge of performing the job was separately arranged in the job specification. However, recently, it is a general trend to organize them all in one job description. Therefore, job specifications are not used, but job descriptions are used throughout this textbook.

3.3.3 Job Analysis of Unit Organizations by Managers

Job analysis is performed for various purposes. Job analysis conducted from a company-wide perspective is mostly done by the HR department, which is an internal HR expert, or by requesting an external expert such as a consultant. Even if this is done by experts, the specific details of the job are known to the person in charge or manager, so their active participation is essential.

On the other hand, even if job analysis is not carried out company-wide, managers can also conduct it for organizational management purposes at the unit level. In the process of setting goals at the beginning of the year, job analysis can also be done in the process of reviewing the contents of the employees' jobs once again. In this case, job analysis can be easily performed as follows.[16)]

① After gathering members in the meeting room, briefly explain the purpose of job analysis.
② Inspect the basic contents of each individual's duties (individual interviews are conducted if necessary, such as when the contents of the job are changed).
③ When the basic contents of the job are agreed upon, the duties and responsibilities necessary for the performance of the job are checked.
④ When the duties and responsibilities are agreed upon, the tasks to be performed by each duty and responsibility area are checked.
⑤ When agreement is reached on the outline of the job, duties and responsibilities, and tasks to be performed, edit the job description finally.

3.3.4 How to Collect Job Information

The purpose of job analysis is to systematically collect job information and use it as basic data for human resource management activities. There are many ways to collect information. The information collection method should be selected in accordance with the object or purpose of the job analysis. If necessary, multiple information collection methods may be used. The following is a brief description of representative methods for collecting job information.[17)]

1) Observation

Observation is a method of understanding the job and collecting job information by directly observing the job performance process. When a job incumbent performs his/her job, the job analyst observes and records it. The observation is used as a method to increase the understanding of the job when the job analyst does not understand the job well. Observation is suitable for jobs that are primarily physically active. On the other hand, in the case of a job that mainly involves mental activity, it is not appropriate because it is difficult to observe the job performance process. The observation method was used a lot in the early days of industrialization, but it has not been widely used recently. However, it is still being used in industrial engineering and educational technology.

2) Questionnaire

The questionnaire method collects job contents or job-related information through a job incumbent or job expert using a standardized questionnaire in advance. The questionnaire developed in developed countries such as the United States and widely used are PAQ (position analysis questionnaire), JEM (job element method), MPDQ (management position description questionnaire), and FJA (functional job analysis).[18] In addition, in some cases, a questionnaire developed by a management consulting company is used. The questionnaire method is widely used in large-scale manufacturing where many people are engaged in one job.

3) Diary

A diary is a way to ask the person in charge of job performance to record the progress of the job every day. Recently, there are cases in which recording is facilitated using a computer or the Internet. The job analyst organizes the recorded job information and collects job information.

4) Interview

The interview is a method in which the job analyst conducts a face-to-face investigation of the person in charge of job performance using a pre-structured questionnaire. In some cases, information is collected by surveying multiple job incumbents or by dividing job incumbents into several groups in the form of a workshop, conducted by job analysts. Due to time and space constraints, it is difficult to interview all the people in charge of the job, and it is common to select a representative.

5) Critical Incident Technique(CIT)

The critical incident technique collects information focusing on important events related to job performance rather than taking all the details of the job. The critical incident technique is a method that pays attention to the actions of the person in charge of performing duties, and collects and organizes information on the characteristically considered efficient and inefficient actions. The results of the critical incident technique are used in behavior-related evaluation methods (eg, behaviorally anchored rating scales (BARS)) or are often used as the content of education and training. The critical incident technique is mainly used in department stores, police, schools, banks, and administrative agencies that deal with customers and civil servants a lot. CIT can be used together with the various job analysis methods mentioned above, such as observation, questionnaire, diary, and interview.

3.3.5 Preparation of Job Description

A job description is a document that systematically organizes job information collected through job analysis. As described above, in the past, job descriptions were divided into job descriptions and job specifications, but most companies included them all in one job description. The format of the job description varies from organization to organization. As shown in <Table 4-8>, this description focuses on the contents generally included in the job description. <Table 4-9> is an example of job description used in the national competency standard (NCS) promoted by the Korean government.

Table 4-8 Job Description Example

Job Title: Auto Sales **Job Code:** 000A3
Belong: Automobile Finance Division **Department:** Auto Finance Division 1
Occupation: Marketing Sales **Serial:** Sales Planning
Reporting System: Auto Finance Team Leader
Date: 20××year ○month ○ day **Writer:** Kim Su-ro **Verifier:** Jang Dong-hee

Job Overview: Establish a sales planning to achieve the target and performance (profitability) of handling domestic new car and rental car products. Analyze and manage performance, operate rental car maintenance, and support other automobile sales management tasks.

Duties and Responsibilities

1. Operate domestic new car installment products. (30%)
   - Establish mid-to long-term and annual plans for domestic new car installments.
   - Conduct market research and competitor status research on installment payments for new domestic cars, and establish an operation plan based on this.
   - Manage the price of installment products for new domestic cars.
   - Negotiate product development and other tasks with affiliates such as credit card companies.
2. Operate rental car products. (30%)
   - Establish mid-to long-term and annual plans for rental car.
   - Conduct market research and competitor status research on rental car installments, and establish an operation plan based on this.
   - Manage rental car product prices.
   - Directly manage rental car sales channels.
   - Carry out customer consultation, review, and execution related to rental car.
3. Operate rental car maintenance services. (20%)
   - Establish rental car maintenance and insurance costs.
   - Carry out business registration of rental car and business related to government offices.
   - Operate insurance products related to rental car maintenance, such as damage adjustment.
4. Support other automobile business management tasks. (20%)
   - Establish operating standards for sales channels.
   - Support for special sales contract and delivery work.
   - Support operation, management, and planning of additional services.

Job Competencies

MS-Office usage ability, basic knowledge related to loan agreement system, market trend monitoring, knowledge about finance and financial products in general, problem solving process understanding, credit legal knowledge, planning ability, communication ability, logical expression of opinion, situation analysis and judgment

Minimum Qualification

At least 1 year of experience working in a branch office, at least 2 years of college graduation (regardless of major), level 3 English proficiency

Table 4-9 **NCS Case (recruitment)**

Classification Unit: 0202020203_16v2

Competency Unit Name(job name): Human Resources Recruitment

Definition of Competency Unit(job overview)
Recruitment is the ability to establish a plan, recruit, select, and perform follow-up management after hiring in order to secure human resources suitable for the organization.

Competency Unit Elements(duties and responsibilities)

1. Establish a recruitment plan
   - According to the organization's mid- to long-term business strategy and annual business plan, it is possible to grasp the manpower requirement plan for the year.
   - It is possible to analyze the manpower that can be recruited within the organization considering the retirement, transfer, and promotion of organizational members.
   - By analyzing the identified demand and supply manpower, it is possible to plan the size of the recruitment.
   - Recruitment plans can be established in consideration of the required fields, the size of the recruitment, and the timing of recruitment.
2. Recruitment of prospective recruits
   - The labor market environment can be analyzed to secure the necessary manpower.
   - You can plan an efficient recruitment method according to the established recruitment plan.
   - Recruitment information can be explained to applicants in order to secure the necessary manpower.
3. Selecting prospective recruits
   - Based on the applicant's application form, document screening for each job position may be conducted.
   - Interviews can be conducted for those who pass the document screening.
   - Candidates can be selected based on the results of the interview screening process.
4. Post-recruitment management
   - Pre-training can be conducted for prospective employees before joining the company.
   - Department placement can be decided based on the aptitude and ability of prospective employees.
   - In order to retain the selected excellent manpower, the organizational culture can be spread to prospective employees and their families.

[Knowledge]
Organizational vision system establishment method, mid- to long-term business strategy establishment method, recruitment technique, interview technique, personality test technique, labor law, organization understanding, use of publicity media, employment rules, case study of follow-up management of prospective hires.

[Skills]
Document writing technology, spread sheet usage ability, manpower management plan establishment ability, presentation technology, communication technology, cost effectiveness analysis technology, statistical processing ability.

[Attitude]
Open communication, strategic thinking, sociable attitude, positive attitude, analytical thinking, positive opinion listening attitude.

1) General Information about the Job (job identification)

First, the job description includes general information about the job to know what the job is. Since the structure and system of each organization is different, it is necessary to provide information suitable for the characteristics of each organization.

- Job title: A unique title given to a job
- Job code: A serial number assigned to a job for management purposes.
- Division: The upper division to which the job belongs. division or headquarters unit
- Department: The unit department or team to which the job belongs
- Job family: The job family to which the job belongs
- Job series: The series to which the job belongs.
- Report to: Direct supervisor reported by the person in charge performing the job
- Date: The date of writing the job description
- Job analyst: The person in charge of the job or job analysis expert who wrote the job description
- Verifier: The direct supervisor or content expert who reviewed the contents of the job description

2) Job Summary

Summarize the core contents of the job or the most important duties and responsibilities in one or two sentences.

3) Duties & Responsibilities

This is the core content of the job description. Here, it describles what the job does (what is done), how the job is performed (how is done), and why the job is performed and what the result of performing the job is (why is done). The specific tasks of the job are written as duties and responsibilities, and the specific activities to be performed are described as tasks. In general, about 5 duties and responsibilities are described, and about 5 tasks are described for each duty and responsibility. In total, there are about 25 tasks essential to performing the job. Also,.in some cases, the weight of each duty and responsibility in the job is indicated. In this case, when the total amount of work is 100, the weight of each duty and responsibility is taken into consideration.

The job performance method describes the work tools, machines, or materials required to perform the job. The result of performing the job summarizes the goal or final result to be performed by the person in charge of the job. The method of performing the job and the results of performing the job shall be described only when necessary.

4) Job Competencies

It describes the competencies required of the person in charge of performing the job in order to successfully perform the job. Competency can be said to be a key factor in achieving performance. Job competency includes all knowledge, skills, and abilities that are highly related to the performance of the job. When describing the competency, the basic common competencies necessary to perform most of the duties are excluded. In addition, competencies that may differ between individuals in charge of job performance are excluded. Only fill in the competencies necessary to perform the job.

5) Minimum Qualification

The minimum qualification refers to the qualifications required for the person in charge of performing the relevant job. These are the minimum qualifications that must be checked in the process of selecting applicants to perform the relevant job. Examples are mainly academic background, major field, or prior work experience.

3.4 Job Evaluation

3.4.1 Definition and Characteristics of Job Evaluation

Job evaluation is to evaluate the relative value of a job. In other words, it is to rank the jobs within the organization based on their relative values. The relative value of a job is an indispensable process when human resource management is conducted centered on the job, especially when job-based pay is introduced.

Job evaluation has the following characteristics.[19)]

First, job evaluation evaluates the value of the job itself, not the person performing the job. In Chapter 1, we defined HR management as the harmonization of people and work/jobs to achieve the organization's goals. Therefore, when it comes to evaluation in personnel management, there are evaluations of people and evaluations of work (jobs). Generally speaking, evaluation in companies means evaluation of people. However, job evaluation refers to evaluating the value of a job independently of people.

Second, every job has value. However, their relative importance is different. Even in the evaluation of a person, the company's evaluation is not intended to judge the dignity of the person. However, it is intended to determine whether the person is performing well in its assigned role and performance. As such, the relative value in job evaluation is intended to determine the relative importance, not to judge whether the value is 'have' or 'not'. It should be clearly understood that job evaluation is evaluating the relative value, not the absolute value of the job.

Third, job evaluation is a process of making a subjective judgment on the value of a job based on an objective standard. What makes job evaluation difficult is that the evaluator is a person, not a machine. The criteria for job evaluation can be objectified, but the subjective judgment of the job evaluator must follow when the criteria are actually applied to evaluation. In this respect, the success of job evaluation depends on the fairness and reliability of the evaluators who evaluate the job.

3.4.2 Job Evaluation Method

Job evaluation methods are broadly divided into relative evaluation methods and absolute evaluation methods. For relative evaluation, there are ranking and classification methods, and for absolute evaluation, there is a point method. Among them, the point method is the most used recently.

1) Ranking Method

The ranking method is a method of determining the order of jobs based on criteria such as the complexity of the job or the importance of the job. This is based on job-to-job comparison and is the easiest and fastest way to evaluate a job. In particular, the ranking method is useful when the size of the organization is small and the number of jobs is small. The biggest advantage of the ranking method is that it is simple to use. On the other hand, it is possible to check the hierarchy between jobs, but it is not possible to know how much the relative value between the jobs differs. For example, if the ranks of the three jobs in ABC are 1st, 2nd, and 3rd, the sequence of the three jobs can be known, but the difference between jobs A and B or between jobs B and C cannot be known. At this time, if the difference in value between the A and B jobs is large but there is little difference in value between the B and C jobs, in reality, the B and C jobs must belong to the same grade, but this cannot be determined by the ranking method.

2) Classification Method

The classification method is a more advanced method of ranking, in which a rating table is made in advance to properly judge each job and classify it into the appropriate grade. The classification method is similar to the ranking method, but it is distinguished in that it sets the grading criteria in advance. The advantage of classification method is that it is relatively easy to perform and inexpensive. However, it is not easy to make a grade in advance. In addition, there are cases where it is necessary to forcibly assign a specific job even though it is not suitable for the level.

3) Point Method

In the point method, the factors for evaluating a job are determined in advance. Then, after assigning a number according to the importance of each factor, the total score is calculated to evaluate the value of each job. <Table 4-10> is a job evaluation tool in the steel industry as an example of applying the point method. The point method evaluates individual jobs with evaluation factors. Evaluation factors are divided into several levels (levels or scales) and explanations for the corresponding levels are provided. The evaluator evaluates the relevant job for each factor based on the explanation of each level of these evaluation elements and assigns a score. As in the example of <Table 4-10>, job evaluation factors are largely composed of skill, effort, responsibility, and working conditions, and each is further subdivided into job evaluation factors. In the example of the steel industry, 10 sub-evaluation factors are presented. Each sub-item has a different level for each item. From a 3-point scale to a 5-point scale, the scale varies according to the characteristics of the factors. Also, since the weights are different, the score given to each factor is different even on the same 1-point scale. The point method compensates for the weaknesses of the various job evaluation methods mentioned above, and can be viewed as a method that can secure objective results. However, it is not easy to select a factor that is a criterion for evaluation by reflecting the characteristics of various jobs, and it is also difficult to determine the weight for each factor.

Table 4-10 **Job Evaluation Tool Using the Scoring Method**

JOB EVALUATION FACTORS	SUB-ITEMS	MEASURE				
		1	2	3	4	5
Skill(32%)	Job processing and manipulation(5%)	31	37	43	50	
	Experience(12%)	63	74	87	102	120
	Problem solving and judgment(15%)	79	93	109	128	150
Effort(21%)	Mental effort(10%)	52	61	72	85	100
	Concentration(11%)	58	68	80	94	110
Responsibility (27%)	Responsibility for safety management(14%)	73	86	101	119	140
	Responsibility for people management(13%)	68	80	94	111	130
Working conditions (20%)	Working hours(4%)	29	34	40		
	Work environment(5%)	37	43	50		
	Risk(11%)	80	94	110		

Ending Case

Hana Tour: Introduction of Flexible Working System[20)]

Established in 1993, Hana Tour is the largest travel company in Korea and has 23 affiliates and 35 global networks around the world. Based on economies of scale, Hana Tour has contributed to the qualitative and quantitative growth of the travel industry by providing competitive prices, sales through various distribution channels, and travel services through a direct network. In 2000, it was listed on the KOSDAQ for the first time in the industry, and in 2011, it was transferred and listed as a stock exchange. In 2006, it was listed on the London Stock Exchange. Hana Tour has a vision to grow into the 'global NO.1 cultural tourism distribution group'.

Unlike the manufacturing industry, the travel industry does not require separate factory facilities. It is a knowledge industry that is not limited by time and space in planning, production, sales, and travel service provision in order to distribute the intangible product called "travel". In the travel industry, individual creative thinking is important to provide various values to customers, and for this, an environment where members can enjoy self-development and leisure is needed. Since 2011, Hana Tour has introduced a flexible working system to change working methods and work environments, encouraging employees to induce their own creative thoughts and values.

Hana Tour is introducing a variety of flexible working systems in line with the management goal of 'balanced growth through smart working'. In general, the flexible working system increases productivity by providing flexibility with respect to working hours and places of work. However, many companies are reluctant to introduce it due to a workplace culture centered on face-to-face work, the absence of a job suitable for the flexible working system, and the CEO's lack of will. In the early stage of introduction, Hana Tour, like other companies, had a low use rate of the flexible working system due to lack of awareness. However, in order to prepare for the changing market environment along with the strong will of the CEO, in 2012, through thorough preliminary job surveys, company-wide employee interviews, and linkage of the rate of use of flexible working systems to key performance indicators (KPIs) of officers, etc. The environment was created in which the flexible working system could be applied from 2010.

In addition to systemic changes, the HR department also conducted various organizational culture improvement campaigns so that employees themselves could break away from their existing work methods in a new work environment and improve them with new work methods and create new ideas.

Hana Tour's flexible working system is divided into flexible commuting system, telecommuting system, smart sales and smart work center. The flexible commuting system allows employees to set their own commuting time for 3 reasons (8:00-17:00, 9:00-18:00, 10:00-19:00) is a system in which employees select one of the options to work. Telecommuting is a system in which work is performed from home for at least one month for reasons such as long-distance commuting, childcare, and work efficiency. For efficient work, the company provides office equipment for travel-related tasks such as laptops and Internet phones. Smart Sales is a flexible working system for efficient time management of salespeople. Salespeople can freely visit on-site business partners, etc. directly from their home, regardless of business hours or locations, and freely commute to and from work. As of April 2017, 657 of Hana Tour's 2,500 employees (211 flexible commuting, 144 telecommuting, 302 smart sales) were using the flexible working system.

Meanwhile, the Smart Work Center is to implement the base work system by renting offices to 11 bases in Seoul/Gyeonggi area for employees who take too long to commute. In the smart work center, workers are not line workers in the existing organization, but different jobs and departments are gathered. Therefore, it was designed to work in a flexible seat type except for some special jobs. A video conferencing system was established to facilitate communication between the Smart Work Center and the head office, and for tasks requiring collaboration, a seat management system was introduced to cooperate with relevant departments, and a computerized system was installed to check the status of seat use in real time. Through this, it was possible to find out where colleagues in departments that require collaboration work in.

After the introduction of the flexible working system, the response of employees was positive. Since the introduction of the flexible working system, sales have been steadily increasing, and in particular, the employee turnover rate is showing a decreasing trend. The turnover rate decreased from 9.3% in 2011 to 5.8% in 2015. Due to the nature of the travel industry, which shows a high turnover rate, it can be said that the reduction in the turnover rate is a big effect of the flexible working system. In terms of employee satisfaction, 78.3% of all employees were satisfied. With the introduction of the Smart Work Center, the average commute time was reduced by an average of 1 hour and 10 minutes, from about 2 hours (44km) round trip to 58 minutes (10km). Through this, time was secured for employees' leisure life and an environment for work-life balance was prepared. In particular, it has been possible to prevent career interruptions for working mothers who have childcare and work at the same time and to continue working. After the introduction of the system, the postpartum return rate of working mothers was found to be 90%.

However, it cannot be said that the flexible working system has been fully established yet. The tasks of the flexible working system that Hana Tour has are as follows. First, it is the accumulation of stress and fatigue of the manager (person in charge). One of the biggest difficulties after the introduction of the flexible working system was the burden of having to achieve the two goals of performance management and employee management at the same time. In terms of management, as team members opt for flexible working hours, the tasks managers need to pay attention to in terms of management have increased. Second, there is the issue of efficiency due to the non-face-to-face business process. In the reality of having to perform common tasks through collaboration, the question of whether there is a work vacancy due to non-face-to-face is still ongoing among members. Third, there is a difficulty in communication between team members. In addition to the basic aspects of goal setting for performance creation, task division, and achievement of work goals through collaboration, emotional exchange and social activities among members are also important. After the implementation of the flexible working system, more and more employees are complaining about feelings of alienation, loneliness, and individualism. This is a factor that can negatively affect the overall organizational culture in the long run. Fourth, complaints about alternative reverse discrimination remain among headquarters employees who are classified as exceptions to the flexible working system due to the characteristics of their residence and security issues. It is one of the challenges to be solved in the future. Lastly, although it is a problem for a small number of employees, as the control of the position manager has been loosened due to remote work, there have been some cases where the flexible working system such as negligence or refusal to work overtime has been abused to cause damage to the organization.

Discussion Question

1. What are the characteristics of Hana Tour's flexible working system?
2. Is Hana Tour's flexible working system the type of job redesign covered in the textbook or is it another organizational management method?
3. What effect is expected of Hana Tour's flexible working system in light of the basic model of human resource management, and is such an effect expected to occur?

CHAPTER

5

Staffing

1. Importance of Staffing
2. Human Resource Planning
3. Recruitment
4. Selection
5. Staffing and Role of Managers

Learning Objectives

1. Understand the importance of staffing.
2. Understand obectives and tools of human resource planning.
3. Identify and compare diverse recruiting sources.
4. Analyze recuiting activities based on customer perspective.
5. Choose appropriate selection tools according to validity and reliability.

Introductory Case

Young Wave (virtual name), which produces and supplies mid-to-low-priced fashion clothing targeting young people, has been grown rapidly by accurately predicting the tastes of young customers and choosing a strategy to supply a variety of products quickly on and off line at low prices. In particular, due to the recent explosive growth in the Chinese market, there is a large shortage of people. In order to secure necessary manpower, the HR team posted job offer in newspapers and online, and received resume and letter fo self-introduction from many applicants. And today, for the applicants who passed the first document review, HR team leader and line team leaders under whom the hired has to work gathered to conduct an interview.

Kang, the head of the domestic sales team, also participated in the interview as a interviewer, and is already interviewing 15 people just in one day. There are many applicants, but no one who seems to be well qualified, so the day is long and boring to him. One of the applicants who stood out among them has a lot of sales experience and excellent sales performance. He also showed strong confidence and enthusiasm, saying that he applied for a new growth opportunity during the interview process. Kang's heart is focused on this applicant, while Park, HR team leader, is showing a somewhat reserved position. The reason for this is that although his performance and motivation are high, he is not considerate of other employees and this may interfere with cooperation among them.

During the interview, the applicant emphasized that salesman must accomplish own performance at all cost, and shows little respect for cooperation and lack of understanding for the vision and the culture of the company. However, Team leader Kang is not sure if salesman should understand the vision or be cooperative. He never see a salesman not promoted because of that kind of problem. On the contrary, no one can get promotion without excellent performance. In addition, Kang is skeptical about how to evaluate vision and personality through interviews. To him, it is more rational to select people with objective things such as sales experience and performance, rather than personality or fit with culture.

Discussion Questions

1. Which of the opinions of Team Leader Kang and Team Leader Park is correct? What makes you think so?
2. Why should applicants have a good understanding of the vision or culture of the company they want to join?
3. Is an interview an appropriate selection tool to judge teamwork, cooperation, and consideration? If not, what is the alternative tool?

1. Importance of Staffing

Staffing is the starting point for human resource management. Human resource management consists of a process that starts with staffing and connects to evaluation, compensation, training and education, and turnover management. Hiring is also a moment when an individual seeking a job meets an organization. Staffing is also accepting human resources that a company needs as an input from the environment. In order for a company as an open system to survive and grow, it needs a cycle of continuously accepting new workforces and sending out existing workforces. When human resources with new perspectives and skills are no longer supplied, the organization's metabolism is blocked and the organization is bound to stagnate.

Staffing is important because, above all, recruiting excellent talent determines the productivity and competitiveness of a company. It is so crucial to the point that people are saying "1% of genius feeds the remaining 99%". That's why most advanced companies make all their efforts to secure core talents. Developing competencies after hiring people is also an important strategy, but as the environment or business changes quickly, it is becoming more important to acquire the appropriate people the company needs from the start. This is because development takes a lot of time and money, and there are many competencies that are difficult to develop through education such as basic personality, character, and attitude.

Staffing refers to all activities to secure the human resources required by the organization in the labor market. Staffing is again divided into recruitment and selection. Recruitment refers to various activities that make the qualified manpower to apply to the company, and selection is an activity that selects the best among the applicants. In order for staffing to be successful, recruitment must be conducted effectively, and selection must be done fairly and accurately. Finally the human resource secured through the recruitment and selection process need to be well adapted to and settled in the company. If not, they may quit the company. For this, the organizational socialization of newly joined is also important.

2. Human Resource Planning

2.1 Necessity for Human Resource Planning

Before recruiting and selecting, it is necessary to first review how much more manpower will be needed or remaining in the future from a company-wide perspective, and then respond according to the forecasted situation. Human resource planning refers to a series of plans for a company to secure or maintain the appropriate manpower necessary to achieve its business purpose in the future. The reason why such a plan is important is that manpower is different from products in nature, and it is difficult to purchase and use immediately if necessary. When the labor market is short of manpower supply, it is not easy to immediately find the manpower that the company needs. In addition, it is virtually impossible in Korea to cut immediately an excess of workforce due to labor law regulations. Therefore, it is important to predict the situation in advance and implement necessary countermeasures step by step.

As the business environment changes very rapidly in recent years, there is also a critical view that it is unnecessary to prepare and respond to human resource plans in advance as in the past. However, human resource planning is still necessary even if the environment changes quickly. Acquiring and retaining personnel without any preparation is difficult and very risky. This is because it is almost impossible to secure excellent manpower without any plan. The problem becomes even bigger if the quickly acquired manpower turn out not to have the necessary competencies or if they do not fit with the value of the company. In addition, if the manpower is cut without sufficient planning, the companies could face fierce opposition or resistance from employees, and this could bring about a very negative impact on the company's performance or image. Because the environment changes rapidly, it is necessary to establish a human resource plan from a short- to mid-term perspective of less than two years, and prepare various scenarios considering environmental changes. In general, human resource planning is prepared by the HR department or, in some cases, the strategic planning department. However, the framework or perspective of human resource planning is also very important to line department managers. because it is not possible to determine necessary manpower without it. They have to review how the work of the department will change in the future and examine the size of the required manpower accordingly. If the work of the department will be reduced, they should take necessary training or measures in advance for how to discover new businesses or to transfer to another department.

2.2 Planning and Implementing Human Resources

The following [Figure 5-1] shows the human resource planning process. A company establishes a business plan based on the sales forecast for the products or services it supplies. At this time, technological changes that have a significant impact on the supply of products or services are also closely reviewed. Basically, the demand for manpower is determined by the demand for products or services. Therefore, the size of manpower to successfully carry out such a project is determined according to the contents of the business plan. If you are planning to expand your business, you will need more manpower than current level. If your products enters mature market, it is mostly probable that you don't need new workforce. However, even such companies will need new personnel if business investments are made to find new growth engines. If a company tries to explore new opportunities to cope with shirinking market, it needs to reduce and hire people at the same time. As a result, the total amount of manpower required is the same size as the current manpower, but there may be many changes in the required manpower's skill or job.

Figure 5-1 Flow of Human Resource Planning

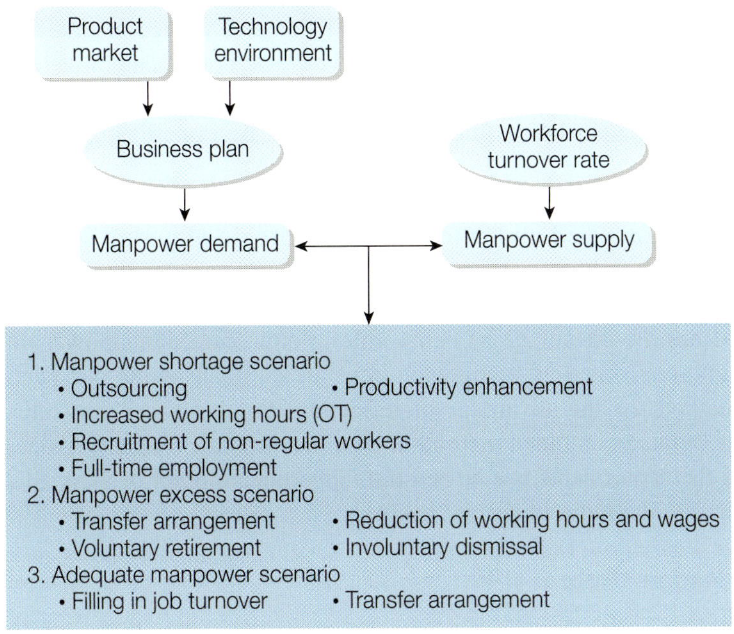

2.2.1 Methods to Predict Manpower Demand

There are quantitative and qualitative methods for predicting the size of the workforce required by a company if we classify them by the characteristics of forecasting techniques. And top-down and bottom-up methods exist when distinguishing the methods from the perspective of the process of making predictions. Quantitative method is a method of grasping necessary manpower demand based on quantative measures such as sales volume or growth rate. In this approach, sophisticated statistical analysis methods such as regression analysis or trend analysis are used for accurate prediction. In the case of the qualitative method, experts consisting of business and HR managers judge and decide the demand for manpower in consideration of future market prospects and the company's business performance prospects. The quantitative estimation method has the advantage that it can be estimated by substituting various conditions or situation variables in the process of predicting manpower demand. For example, it is possible to estimate manpower demand by gradually changing sales or growth rate.

However, the quantitative estimation method is basically estimating the future using data from the past, so it is premised that the same phenomenon or pattern as the past will continue in the future. Therefore, there is a disadvantage in that accuracy is inferior in a situation completely different from the past regarding competition pressure, new technology, and labor productivity. It is the qualitative estimation method that can compensate for these shortcomings. This is because in this method, it is possible to estimate the required manpower demand in consideration of various rapidly changing environmental factors. However, there is a disadvantage in qualitative metnod that it is difficult to simulate the required manpower demand while varying environmental conditions. The realistic and effective solution is to use both quantitative and qualitative estimates in parallel. It can be said that it is a balanced approach making an estimate based on past empirical data and then adjusting it by considering the judgment of experts.

With respect to the top-down and bottom-up method, the former is a method of estimating the required manpower by the strategic planning office and the HR department, while the latter is a method demanding each department to request the necessary manpower and aggregates them to calculate the new manpower. The top-down method has the advantage of being able to concentrate manpower on businesses or departments requiring new manpower from the company-wide perspective, and the bottom-up method has the advantage of reflecting the manpower demands required in the field. In general, a combined method is used in which the manpower size aggregating all request of the departments is adjusted through strategic point of view allocating more human resource to the more important business.

2.2.2 Managers' Role in HRP

The most basic role of a manager in predicting manpower demand is to determine whether there is actually a need for new hands in the department he is in charge. This is because the manager is the one who can grasp this most accurately. Sometimes companies survey the workload to determine the demand for new personnel, but such a survey alone is not enough to accurately determine the number of new personnel needed. When the workload of the departemtn is excessive, it can be temporary or permanent. Or, by changing or adjusting the work method, manager can make works done without hiring new people. Therefore, managers should not simply play a passive role in determining whether a new manpower is needed by accurately grasping the amount of work, but have to take an active role in finding ways to handle the work without increasing manpower through various innovative measures.

2.3 Solution to Different Scenarios

The results of the human resource planning are largely divided into three situations. The first is when there is a shortage of future manpower, the second is when there are redundant workforce, and the third is when there is no significant change. It is necessary to respond appropriately to these different situations keeping in mind that each scenario need different action.

1) Shortage of Manpower Scenario

When it is expected that there will be a shortage of manpower in the future, various solutions can be used. In a business environment where competition is becoming fiercer and uncertainty is ever increasing, rather than hiring full-time personnel, it would be wise to extend working hours or improve productivity. In particular, such a response is essential when there is insufficient confidence in whether manpower is constantly needed. If necessary workforce is concentrated in a specific function or department, it is also necessary to consider outsourcing the work.

2) Surplus Manpower Scenario

It is very important to plan ahead and respond in advance when surplus manpower is expected to occur. The first thing that needs to be reviewed is the transfer of workforce. Depending on the department, there may be places where manpower is needed, so it is possible to avoid a situation in which manpower is sent out against their will. However, it should be noted that if a trasnferd person does not have the right skills or competencies, it can reduce the productivity of individuals and organizations. It is also necessary to freeze the hiring to reduce the scale of manpower adjustment because there is a risk that it may be regarded as neglecting efforts to avoid layoffs prescribed in the Labor Standards Act. In cases where it is difficult to resolve the surplus manpower only by hiring freeze or internal transfer, the manpower must be reduced through voluntary retirement or layoff. In the case of layoffs, Korean law stipulate that the financial difficulty must be very serious, and the company has to make an effort to avoid it.

3) Adequate Manpower Scenario

Even if there is no significant change in the size of the workforce overall, it is necessary to take some adjustments. This is because even if there is no major change, there may be departments that require manpower while others may need to reduce it. Or, although the size of the manpower is appropriate, there are areas where new knowledge, skills, and competencies are required. Therefore, efforts should be made to ensure that human resources can be effectively utilized at the right place while appropriately performing human resource management activities such as recruitment, transfer, and education and training.

3. Recruitment

In practice, there are many cases where recruitment and selection are not necessarily distinguished. In terms of securing the necessary manpower in the labor market, there is no need to distinguish between the two. However, the reason for the distinction between recruitment and selection is that the major issues arising from recruitment and selection are significantly different. In the case of recruitment, it is important to make talented people to apply cost-efficiently, while in the case of selection, it is important to accurately identify and select the talented person having required competencies.

3.1 Managing Recruiting Sources

Regarding recruitment, the most important issue is which recruiting source to use. HR managers have to determine through which channels the company will recruit the necessary personnel. Depending on the sources, the cost or effect can vary greatly. However, since most companies use almost the same recruiting source as other companies, it is often overlooked that analysis of recruiting sources is important. For this reason, when a person with technical expertise in a specific field is required, posting an announcement in a newspaper without much thought is done. In this case, applicants will come, but it is difficult to expect to see a person with the high level of professional knowledge and experience that the company needs. Rather it would be more wise to find a magazine that experts read or a site they connect to each other and posting an announcement there. In the following, let's take a look at various recruiting sources that companies can use.

1) Current Employees

Recruitment is generally conducted for human resources in the external labor market, but there are cases where recruitment is done for employees currently working in companies. The job posting system is to notify members of a vacancy or new job opening within a company and allow internal members to apply. It is important in that it provides opportunities for new career development to members while securing applicants with whom companies have accurate information on attitudes and competencies. Because of such positive effects, advanced companies often use internal job offerings.

2) Referral from Incumbents

It is a kind of recruiting manpower by using recommendations from employees. This has been mainly used as a convenient way for SMEs to secure manpower without incurring recruitment costs, but recently, it has been actively used in IT companies to search for technical talent. This method has the advantage of being able to accurately capture and recruit excellent talent whose skills have been verified in the market through the network of members. It is frequently used when there is a job shortage in the professional manpower market. Another advantage of this method is that the employees can help the people they recommend to adapt to the new organization. In general, when the recommended person is confirmed for hiring, a certain incentive is given to the employees who had recommend him.

3) Print Advertisement

In the past, the most familiar recruitment method for Korean companies was to post recruitment announcements in major daily newspapers. In the employment season, it was important for the whole family to read the job ofter in the newspaper, cut and scrap them. In recent years, as recruitment through the internet has spread greatly, the role of recruitment through printed pages has been significantly reduced. However, some companies still use the internet and newspaper pages in parallel. In the case of institutions or companies belonging to the public sector, it is mandatory to publish a notice in the newspaper to show that hiring is fairly administered.

4) Internet Recruiting

Online recruitment is becoming a new norm. Job portals, such as Job Korea and

Spreading Referral from Incumbents

According to a survey for 208 personnel in charge of the personnel, it was found that more than half of companies are implementing the "referral from incumbents," in which applicants are recommended by current emplyees and selected. It was also confirmed that 51.9% of companies are implementing this practice. The reason for implementing it was because the applicants can be reliable (50% response). Subsequently, because it could reduce hiring time' (21.3% response), 'because it could reduce the turnover rate' (18.5% response). The satisfaction of HR managers for the job performance of employees who joined by this practice was 'normal' (40.7%), 'somewhat satisfied' (38.9%), 'somewhat dissatisfied' (9.3%), and 'very satisfied' (8.3%), 'very dissatisfied' (2.8%). On the other hand, when asked if they would continue to maintain the referral from employees in the future, 86.1% answered 'yes', which shows that this practice is becoming a very important recruiting metnod. (Source: Nocut News, 12th Jyne 2013)

Saram-In are playing an important role in recruitment. There are worknets operated by the government, but they are known to be low in practical use. And it is also becoming more common for companies to post recruitment announcements directly on their website. In particular, in the case of famous companies, there are many cases where it is not necessary to use the online recruiting service portals because people interested voluntarily visit and carry announcements. The advantage of recruiting through the website is that it can be an opportunity for visitors to increase their understanding of the company. However, it is important to note that if managers are only recruiting among the people who visit the website, they may miss out on the people your company really needs.

5) Employment Agencies

It is also possible to recruit using an employment agencies called often headhunting firm. This is a suitable recruitment method when a company wants to quickly secure a small number of necessary professionals without being known outside. If you use them, you can save the cost and time of having to review a large number of applicants, but instead, the commission is quite high. The agencies generally recommends multiple candidates it deems suitable, and the firm interviews them to make a final decision. This method is usually used to scout key people or talents who are currently working for other companies.

6) Social Recruiting

With the advent of social media such as Facebook, Twitter, and LinkedIn, more and more cases are used for recruitment, which is called social recruiting. Companies may directly post recruitment announcements on social media or identify necessary personnel information through it. Social Recruiting not only can significantly reduce costs, but also has the advantage of being able to quickly perform recruitment activities globally beyond the country. In addition, it is also an advantage that interactive communication is possible. However, it also has a limitation that it is difficult to access people who do not use social media. Social recruiting is spreading rapidly, mainly among US companies. According to a research agency in the U.S., the proportion of companies that are recruiting or plan to recruit through social media is steadily increasing. Companies that have an intention or plan to use SNS for recruitment have already exceeded 90%, and the proportion of companies that have actually hired human resources through social media is also approaching 80%.[1)] And a survey done in U.K. shows that 94% of recruiters use social media.[2)] The mostly used media are LinkedIn, Facebook, Twitter and Instagram in the order of frequencies. Social recruiting is already becoming a common practice in the job market.

3.2 Customer-Driven Recruitment

Often, HR managers proudly say that recruitment is well done if it succeeds in attracting a large number of applicants. Was it really good? If the competition rate is 100 to 1, 99% of applicants will not be able to be hired, and there is a high probability that they will have negative feelings toward the company. No matter how politely you notify their failure, it is difficult for the party to have positive feelings toward the company for at least a certain period of time. Considering that they are our potential customers in the marketplace, we can never boast of high competition rate. This problem is a side effect of losing the view that applicants are our potential customers.

When it comes to recruitment, taking the customer's perspective means that the recruitment activities are conducted while always keeping in mind that applicants are customers of the company. From a customer's point of view, it is more desirable to visit the applicant's space or network directly than to make applicants visit the website to obtain information. Social recruiting or campus recruiting is a example of customer-oriented recruiting activity. From a customer's point of view, what is important is an understanding of the needs and motivations of applicants applying for the company. It is important for the company to determine the talents it needs and make sure that the right people apply for it. However, if managers do not understand the expectations of the applicants, unilateral hiring will be inevitable, resulting in higher turnover rates. If managers accurately grasp the expectations and needs of applicants and engage in recruiting activities, they are more likely to increase the possibility of recruiting excellent talent. In particular, the effect of recruitment is greater when an employee value proposition is made by focusing on the applicant's expectations or needs during the recruitment process. The employee value proposition(EVP) includes all of the satisfaction, rewards, work environment, leadership, and relationships with colleagues that employees can experience while working as a member of the organization. In other words, it means how well company can satisfy a future employee after hiring. Well-prepared EVP attracts great talent and empowers employees to engage with passion and commitment to work and company.

3.3 From Periodical to Need-Based Recruitment

An important feature of Korean companies in the recruitment was recruitment, conducted periodically on a regular schedule. It was a unique hiring practice in Korea that differed greatly from US and European companies. They regularly conduct recruitment in March and September when graduates enter job markets after schools. Korean companies prefer to recruit people who meet the vision or values that the company aims to secure for the future. This hiring method was possible because the manpower management of Korean companies was not specialized in job. Instead, the newly recruited was nurtured while allowing them to experience various jobs.

However, the regular employment is gradually being replaced by need-based recruitment consisting of staffing only when there are job vacancies or they need specific talent for use. Large companies representing Korean economy such as Hyundai Motor Company, LG Group, KT, and SK have abolished regular recruitment, and this change is expected to have a significant impact on other companies as well. It is known that Samsung will continue to implement regular recruitment for the time being. This change results from the fact that it becomes more and more inefficient to acquire talent in advance under the unpredictable environment. This change also come from the fact that companies are more concerned with the cost and profitability than in the past. In the low-growth era, investing a lot in human resources in advance inevitably puts a burden on corporate profitability.

This kind of just-in-time hiring from the standpoint of a company is cost elficient in that it can secure and utilize the necessary manpower when it is needed. From the standpoint of applicants, it is also a positive change in that they can apply to the companies when they want to work without having to wait for the certain period of time. However, it is important to understand that need-based recruiting means more than just hiring people at the moment. Companies need to notify jobs to be filled, and therefore, unlike in the past, hiring is based on the job. This can move Korean human resource management more to the job-based one. On the other hand, As regular recruitment give place to need-based recruitment, networks and close communication formed between the newly hired who joined the company at the same time are expected to disappear.

4. Selection

When applicants are found through recruitment activities, it is important to select the talent the company wants among them. In selection, the starting point is to clearly identify the characteristics or qualities that the company is searching for. These characteristics is a common competency that must be considered in all selections. In Korea it is called by the name of "talent image", while in America and Europe it is discussed under the title of organizational fit of the applicants. And there are competencies required for each job group or job. Selection criteria result from these two kinds of characteristics. After the selection criteria have been determined, it is necessary to check and verify if the applicants have such characteristics by using reliable and valid selection tools.

4.1 Company's Talent Image

The first thing that must be clarified for selection is the talent image that the company is searching for. The talent image is a big picture of what kind of the people the company wants to hire. In the absence of talent image, it is difficult to recruit the talent the company needs, especially because there is no clear guideline on what competence the company has to focus on. Without it, the probability of selection errors could be very high in that each manager participating in the selection process evaluates talents with his own criteria. Since the talent image is based on the company's management philosophy, mission and vision, and corporate culture, it should be considered important not only in the recruitment stage, but also in competency development. The talent image of a company differs from company to company, but there are some common aspects. According to a survey of the top 100 companies by the Korean Chamber of Commerce,[3)] most companies cited "communication and cooperation" as the competency that talented people should have. Subsequently, it was found that companies value competencies in the order of 'professionalism', 'principles and trust', 'challenge spirit', 'ownership', and 'creativity'. Compared to the same survey done five years ago, the importance of communication and cooperation increased significantly, while the spirit of challenge, which was most important in the past, fell to fourth place.

4.2 Selection Process and Tools

In the recruitment stage, it is important to make sure that excellent talents with the competencies required by the company apply for the company. When the recruitment phase is over, the selection process begins after that. In the selection process, it is necessary to accurately identify and select the talents the company needs without errors. If an error occurs in the selection process, the company cannot secure the desired talent, resulting in unfortunate situations for both individuals and organizations. In addition, all the expenses and efforts the company has invested in the recruitment stage so far would be lost. Therefore, the importance of accurate selection cannot be overemphasized. Of course, even the wrongly selected personnel can improve their skills to some extent through development effort. However, although knowledge can be easily improved, competencies such as character, attitude, passion, and creativity are difficult to develop. And it is these capabilities that companies today desperately need to realize performance and strengthen their competitiveness. Therefore, companies should make efforts to develop effective selection tools by investing money and time.

All companies go through the selection process using a variety of methods and tools to select the talent they want. There is no single most desirable selection procedure or method. However, in reality, the selection procedures and methods used by most companies are similar. [Figure 5-2] shows the selection process and tools that are mainly used by large Korean companies.

Figure 5-2 **Selection Process**

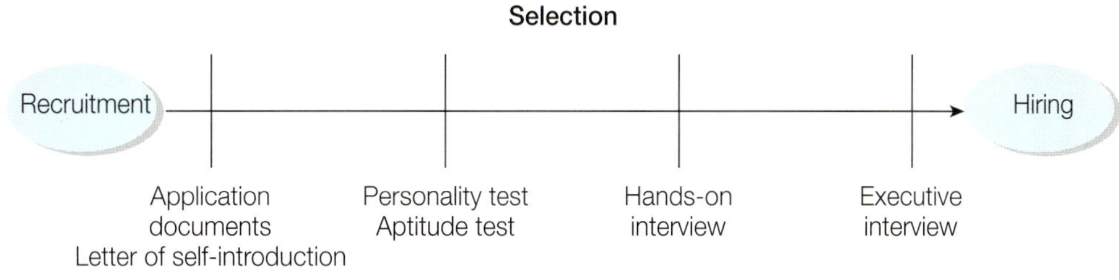

4.2.1 Application Documents Review

Most of the selection process starts from document screening. At this time, the documents for review are a job application form and a letter of self-introduction. The information companies want to know about the applicant through the application form are their major, academic background, career, certification, and special activities or experiences. In the case of hiring new graduates, they are required to fill in their majors and academic grades, and extracurricular activities except working experience. When companies classify and evaluate job applications, the most important considerations are majors, academic background, and academic grades such as GPA.

The application form asks for formal and objective information. The disadvantage is that it is difficult to understand the applicant in-depth because it contains only information that can be objectively grasped. In particular, it is difficult to identify talented individuals with a spirit of challenge, a propensity to accomplishment, and creativity. In order to compensate for this, most companies require the applicants to submit a letter of self-introduction. The characteristics, qualities, and attitudes of applicants shown in the self-introduction are identified and used in the selection process. Requesting a self-introduction letter already existed for a long time, but it is showing a significant change in that it has become an important means by which personnel in charge read carefully and reflect it in hiring decisions.

Traditionally, the biggest dissatisfaction that applicants feel during the hiring process is that the company filter applicants based on the information such as the school they graduated from rather than competency or skills. And demanding excessive personal information such as gender, age, religion, height, weight, education, parents' education and property, etc. on the job application form is likely to infringe on equality rights and human rights. In this regard, in 2003, the National Human Rights Commission of Korea recommended firms for ending the practice of asking to the applicants region of origin, family's education and position, property, religion, etc. In the public sector, this kind of unreasonable practice have been abolished. However, there are many cases in private sector where companies still use job applications that require excessive personal information. Since the practice of requesting excessive personal information in the application form may be considered discrimination as stipulated in the law, it is necessary to reduce the demand for personal information irrelevant to the competency or

Figure 5-3 **Example of Application Form**

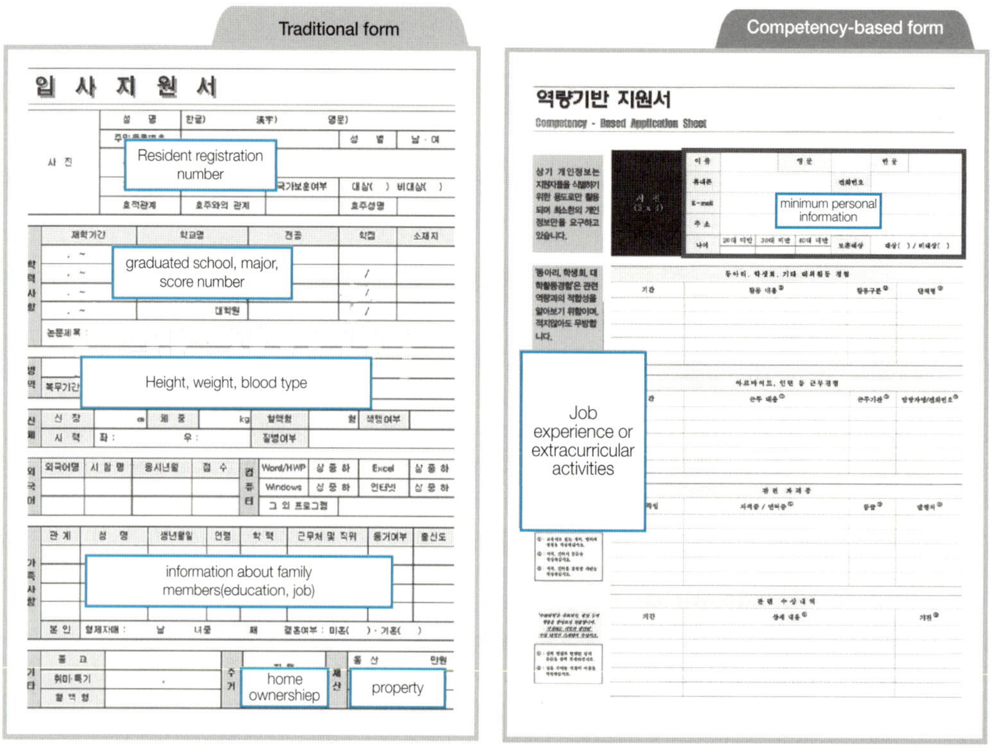

job performance.

In this regard, the Ministry of Employment and Labor released a standard resume form in 2013 with the elimination of the information about school, height, and weight, etc., and induces companies to make improvement efforts. The difference from the conventional job application forms is that it requires minimal personal information while intensively requiring information related to the individual's experience to help identify competency.

4.2.2 Personality and Aptitude Test

There was a time when it was common to take the written test after the document screening, but now most companies use the personality and aptitude test instead of the written test. The reason is that test scores have no significant correlation with organizational adaptation or work performance after entrance. The written test is basically a tool to measure knowledge, and the knowledge measured at this time is far from the knowledge required to achieve work performance in the field. Therefore, selection through written examination gradually disappeared, except for some cases where the objectivity of selection is very important, such as hiring public officials. The Samsung Job Aptitude Test (GSAT), which is the most representative example of

Korean aptitude test, was introduced in 1995 for open recruitment based on applicants' abilities rather than applicants' specifications or educational background, and has been successfully in operation until now.

Usually personality and aptitude test are done in one package in Korea, and applicants often do not make difference between them. However, they are two different tests. First, if we look at the personality test, there are two types of personality test, and they are used individually or in parallel. One is a personality test to screen out applicants with personality problems. At this time, the personality test has the purpose of identifying and filtering people with characteristics that may negatively affect performance. For example, this is to exclude people with extreme tendencies, such as making it very easy to lie or breaking morals or rules. This is because if such a person enters the company, he or she can commit corruption or cause great damage to the organization.

On the other hand, there is another personality test to measure the competency level. At this time, the personality test judges the score based on the characteristics that have a positive effect on the performance of the job, and is measured based on the Big 5 model or the competency model developed by the company. The Big 5 personality refers to five personality types that are highly related to behavior within an organization. These include conscientiousness, agreeableness, emotional stability(neuroticism), extroversion, and openness to experience. Whether you use the Big 5 model or a model developed based on the company's talent requirements, concienciousness, innovation, and challenge are almost always factors that appear in the personality test. It needs to keep in mind that conscientiousness refers to achievement-oriented, autonomy, responsibility, and self-competence, rather than measuring the degree of honesty and diligence. Therefore, the higher the conscientiousness, the higher the probability of work performance, and based on this, personality factors such as conscientiousness are highly considered in the selection.[4)]

Hidden Function of Personality Test

The personality and aptitude test aims to select a person who is expected to produce good results after entering the company by judging the personality, learning ability, adaptability, etc. However, the most immediate positive effect that Korean companies experienced after introducing these tests was that they were able to exclude personnel requests. In fact, recruitment requests from people with power or strong influence come to the HR managers even the number is significantly decreasing nowadays. The reality is that it is difficult to openly refuse when high-ranking people ask for personnel. At this time, companies that use the personality and aptitude test respond to postpone the talk after passing the tests. HR managers' experience tells that not many people who are recommended for solicitation pass the personality test. Therefore, the request for personnel is automatically excluded. If that person passes the tests, then it is not a solicitation, but a talent recommendation, so there is nothing bad from the company's standpoint.

The personality test score does not increase even if someone study hard for the test. This is because the personality itself is very stable and has characteristics that are difficult to change easily. This is why the personality test is highly reliable and valid. However, criticism may arise as to whether it is appropriate to use factors that are difficult for individuals to control or change as a means of selection. Given that a company is an organization built for business performance, considering the selection of personality factors that can affect performance is not a legal issue. However, whether personality factors actually have predictive power for work performance becomes an important issue, and in order to secure this, it will be necessary to analyze the predictive validity in the personality test during its development process.

The aptitude test is a test for predicting the ability to successfully carry out activities related to education or occupation in a specific field. In general, the aptitude test can be used as a means of predicting performance after employment, or it can also be used for the purpose of grasping a career or job that suits for young people. Whereas the aptitude test in the educational field is mainly for grasping the career path, the aptitude test conducted by companies focuses on the aspect of selecting and predicting performance in advance. The measurement contents of the test are generally composed of verbal reasoning ability, numerical ability, abstract reasoning ability, spatial perception ability, mechanical comprehension, perceptual speed and accuracy.[5)] In general, in the case of aptitude test, about 50% of the items measure intelligence and the rest consists of measuring the ability to understand, acquire, and adapt within the company. Most large corporations in Korea are using their own aptitude tests.

4.2.3 Interview

Interview is a very important selection tool that has never been omitted in the selection process from the past to the present. It is not an exaggeration to say that not only in Korea, but in all countries around the world, there are no cases where hiring is decided without interviews. However, there have been many changes in the purpose, content, and method of the interview in Korea. If past interviews were the last step to confirming those who have already been hired, the purpose of verifying the competence of applicants through interviews has recently become stronger, and various methods are being tried for this.

There are various types of interview, and they can be classified into structured and unstructured interview. A structured one is an interview in which the duration of the interview, the content of the question, and the desired answer to be expected are determined in advance, whereas the unstructured one is freely interviewed without such a predetermined framework. In the case of an unstructured interview, it is difficult to make a consistent evaluation because the content of the interview and the response of the applicant vary greatly depending on the interviewer.

And unprepared interviewers often make the applicants complain about being asked wrong questions. Questions such as whether 'Are you married?', 'You look younger than your age!', and 'What do your parents do?' are some of these examples. Structured interview is known to be more reliable and valid than unstructured interview. There are

Blind Hiring

In order to eliminate discrimination in the hiring process and ensure fair hiring, the government mandated blind hiring in the public sector in 2017. Because of the wrong name, there is a misunderstanding of hiring people without seeing anything. However, the essential point is that discriminatory factors such as educational background, place of origin, physical condition, etc. should not be recorded in the resume, and the hiring decision should be made by judging whether they have the necessary competencies for the job performance during the interview process. Meanwhile, the revised Recruitment Procedure Act, which took effect in July 2019, also prohibits requesting unnecessary personal information for work, so blind hiring is likely to spread in the private sector as well. There is still a objection to that idea and banning to require the school, major, and score is excessively restricting for hiring decisions. According to the results of a survey on the effectiveness of blind hiring[6)], it was found that the job competency and organizational adaptation of employees who joined through blind hiring were generally similar to or somewhat higher than before. HR managers responded that the diversity of human resources was significantly increased by blind hiring compared to the past, and that it contributed significantly to the fairness of the hiring process, while responding that the time and cost of the hiring process increased more than in the past.

generally three types of questions in structured interviews. First, there are questions about job knowledge to confirm the expertise of the job field to be applied for. Scond, there are situational questions to confirm the ability to respond to in a virtual situation which would most likely to occur in that job field. Finally, there are behavioral questions having aim to identify what experiences the applicants have had.

Interviews are generally conducted in two with different natures and purposes. The first interview is called by a wide variety of names, such as personality interview, presentation (PT) interview, competency interview, discussion interview, in-depth interview, etc., depending on the company, and the actual contents are different. However, they have a common point in that the team leader conduct interviews, and that the focus is on evaluating the competencies of applicants. In the first interview, the applicant's values, personality, presentation ability and confidence are identified and evaluated through various questions. In general, the first interview is conducted in an in-depth interview method in which sufficient time is given to the interview and the basis for the applicant's response is tracked and understood through additional questions.

In the case of an in-depth interview, by asking a leading or main question and then observing the applicant's response, interviewers judge whether the applicant's answer is an embodied content based on his or her own experience, or just a improvised answers without concrete experience or solution. For example, as is shown in <Table 5-1>, by asking various questions about the process and method of how to find an solution in the face of an unfamiliar situation or task, not only can interviewer filter out false answers, but also it is possible to judge how much the applicants have experience of creative problem solving and whether he will be able to effectively solve problems in similar

Table 5-1 **Example Questions of In-depth Interview**

EVALUATION CAPABILITY	CREATIVE PROBLEM SOLVING
Leading question	Please let us know if you have experience in unexpected work or if you have been assigned to a project and performed new tasks you are not familiar with.
Probing question	• What was the first activity you performed after receiving that task? • What methods and procedures have you used to understand the situation? • How have you overcome lack in work knowledge or experience? • How did you resolve conflicts with other people or colleagues in the process? • Have you received help from others to compensate for your lack of experience or knowledge? And how? • What advice would you give if you had a colleague in the same case as you? • How would you respond if you face a similar situation again?

situations in the future.

PT interview, discussion interview, competency interview, etc. are all interviews to evaluate competency, and these are basically based on the assessment center method. The assessment center method is a method of evaluating the competence of the applicant by presenting various tasks or roles related to the job situation that the applicant will take on in the future and observing the response behavior of the applicant. Various tasks such as presentation (PT), group discussion, in-basket, and role playing are used. What Korean companies call PT interviews and discussion interviews is named after the assignments used in the assessment center. Since it is costly to use all of the different exercises of assessment center, only one or two exercieses are used to assess the applicant's competence. In the case of competency evaluation based on the assessment center method, an appropriate task must be developed reflecting the job situation, while the competency and role of the assessor are very important.[7)]

The second interview is called an executive interview and is the final step in the selection process. After selecting two or three times of the number of people expected to be hired, the leaders at the executive level meet the applicants in person, interview them, and make the final decision. At this stage, in most cases, the focus is on personality or suitability with the company culture rather than on competence itself. This is because the competency has already been sufficiently filtered out in the previous stage.

4.2.4 Intership Linked to Hiring

Originally, interns were used to enhance students' experience of the world of work during vacations and to increase their organizational adaptation in the case of future employment. However, recently, a hiring-type internship practice is rapidly spreading, in which, after hiring as an intern, assignments are given for several months, and then the job is evaluated and finally hired. This practice, which was introduced and utilized by large private companies, is now spreading to public companies. Almost all large companies are recruiting interns for hiring purposes, and some companies, such as NHN, hire all new graduates through internships.

There are many reasons for the spread of hiring interns, but it is largely due to the limitations of the selection tools that companies use. Despite the active use of various selection tools we just reviewed above, the performance of the newly hired after entering the company are often disappointing. Therefore, rather than selecting applicants based on past experiences or hypothetical situations, it would be more wise to use intership which can minimizes selection errors by directly observing and evaluating the attitudes, behaviors, and competencies of the applicants. This is the most important purpose of the internship program in Korean companies.

It is clear that this approach contributes to reducing selection errors. However, it is important to understand that there are a number of side effects that may occur if the HR department or line managers use it inappropriately. First of all, the internship should not be too long. This is because those who cannot be hired after internships can have great difficulty finding new employment opportunities in the labor market. In addition, psychological wounds or betrayal can be felt if it cannot lead to employment. In particular, it should be noted that complaints about fairness will increase when roles or tasks performed by interns are not carefully structured and evaluated fairly.

4.2.5 Artificial Intelligence-Based Selection

With the advancement of technology called the Fourth Industrial Revolution or digital transformation, the method of using artificial intelligence in selection is rapidly spreading. A pioneering example is Pymetrics which provides a program that identifies applicants' capabilities through games and uses them for selection. The company allows applicants to play a variety of games through a computer, and in the process, understands the applicant's capabilities. In addition, Japanese SoftBank's artificial intelligence robot Pepper also conducts interviews with applicants to determine whether they are qualified for the job. The artificial intelligence created by Midas IT in Korea also determines the propensity, competence, and suitability for recruitment by observing not only the content of the answers but also the body reactions such as voice, facial expression, and tension. Midas IT is providing artificial intelligence recruitment services to domestic companies under the name Midas InAir.

Artificial intelligence recruitment is gradually spreading among Korean companies. Companies mainly use artificial intelligence in the process of hiring new employees. According to a survey on the new recruitment plan of major companies by the Korea Economic Research Institute,[8)] 11.4% of companies are already using artificial intelligence for new recruitment, and 10.7% of companies have plans to use artificial intelligence in the future. Compared to the previous year, the number of both companies using AI recruitment and those with plans to use AI has increased, indicating that AI recruitment is on the rise. Companies using artificial intelligence mainly use artificial intelligence in document screening and interviews. An important reason for companies to adopt artificial intelligence is to improve work efficiency and fairness in the selection process. Examining documents or conducting interviews takes a lot of time and effort. By using artificial intelligence, the time required can be greatly reduced. In addition, if

HR Manager's Gaze on Hiring Artificial Intelligence

Although artificial intelligence technology is rapidly developing, most of Korean companies are still cautious about introducing artificial intelligence recruitment in earnest. According to a 2018 survey by Job portal company Incruit,[10)] 81.5% of respondents answered that they have no intention of introducing AI hiring. In addition, large companies tended to use artificial hiring compared to SMEs. 33.4% of large companies said they have already or are willing to introduce them, while 94.5% of SMEs said they have no plans to introduce them. Meanwhile, according to this survey, HR managers also appear to be cautious about using artificial intelligence. Seven out of 10 HR managers (72.2%) oppose AI hiring, and the main reason was 'because there is a concern that job seekers with various personalities will be evaluated by only one criterion'(33.6%). It is said that introducing AI recruitment for fairness and convenience may rather bury the diverse personality of job seekers. In addition, the reasons for the opposition were 'It will be limited to show-on (recruitment) marketing'(24.8%) and 'It is difficult to accurately evaluate the atmosphere or personality of thc applicant that can only be grasped face-to-face'(16.8%). On the other hand, the 1st place in the approval opinion was 'It is possible to effectively verify whether applicants have been plagiarized or cheated at the self-introduction or interview stage'(48.1%).

artificial intelligence is used, it is possible to make a fairer selection in that it can reduce the discriminatory words and actions of the interviewers that often occur during the interview process.

However, it is worth noting that the validity of artificial intelligence based selection is not necessarily high. There are no studies that directly compare the validity of the existing selection tools and artificial intelligence methods, but some companies have abandoned the artificial intelligence recruitment method because the validity of the artificial intelligence method is very low.[9)] Meanwhile, in terms of customer-oriented staffing, the perception or reaction of applicants to artificial intelligence is also very important. It should be taken into account that if applicants do not trust the judgment of artificial intelligence, the antipathy for dropout can be very high. Also, artificial intelligence is not free from discrimination. Existing discriminatory practices can be transferred to artificial intelligence in the process of learning data. That's why Amazon decided not to use artificial intelligence biased on the preference for men. Therefore, it is reasonable to recognize that there are still certain limitations in artificial intelligence based selection, and appropriately combine and use artificial hiring and existing selection tools.

4.3 Validity and Reliability of the Selection Tools

It is very important to identify and hire the talent the company needs. Therefore, the effectiveness of the selection is determined by how accurate the tools used for selection are. This is because if the company uses the wrong means to select, it does not select the talent that the company needs, but rather select a person who do not fit with the company. Among the many conditions that a selection tool must have, the most important are reliability and validity.

Reliability means that the results of multiple tests are consistently displayed without any significant difference (across time reliability), or it can mean that the results appear consistently regardless of who the evaluator is (across raters reliability). In the case of lack of reliability, it is difficult to be sure that the score shown by the applicant at a specific point in time actually accurately reflects his or her competency level. From the standpoint of a company that needs to acquire talent, it is impossible to use such unstable tools to select. In addition, if a selection tool with low reliability is used, it is difficult for a company to defend against criticism or lawsuits claiming that the selection decision is discriminatory.

On the other hand, validity means whether or not the selection tool is measuring the content originally intended to be measured. For example, let's say that the global competency is considered a very important competency in light of the business environment in which the business is becoming global. When it comes to selection, the challenge is how to measure global competency. In most companies, global competency is often replaced with English test scores such as TOEIC or TOEFL. If so, does the English score accurately represent global competence? It is clear that English is an important means of communication in the international arena, but it is difficult to say that it represents global competence. This is because the sensitivity or understanding of other cultures, the perspective of understanding and viewing business globally, and the experience of working effectively in teams with people from different cultural backgrounds can be more important. Therefore, it is difficult to say that the English score, which measures global competence, is highly valid.

As for validity, there are content validity and empirical validity. Content validity is whether the content that the selection tool wants to measure is related to actual job that the applicants would do. For example, in the case of an interview, there is no content validity to ask about the appearance or the family that has nothing to do with work. There may be various empirical validity, such as simultaneous validity, discriminatory validity, and predictive validity, but predictive validity is an important factor in selection. The predictive validity is the degree to which the future is predicted, and how well the tool used for the current selection predicts the job performance after the applicant is hired. Since the purpose of hiring is to secure talented people who can perform well, predictive validity is very important when developing a selection tool. It is the most accurate to verify the predictive validity of the selection tools based on the actual data of the company, and even when developing a personality test, verifying the predictive validity based on actual personnel data is a basic procedure.

When the selection tool is classified based on two factors, reliability and validity, it can be summarized as one of the following four cases as shown in [Figure 5-4]. Although the English test scores are highly reliable, they cannot be said to be highly valid. This is because there are jobs where English plays an important role in job performance, and some jobs do not. In the case of interviews, the validity is high, but there are many cases of low reliability. This is because the results can vary greatly

Figure 5-4 **Diverse Combination of Reliability and Validity**

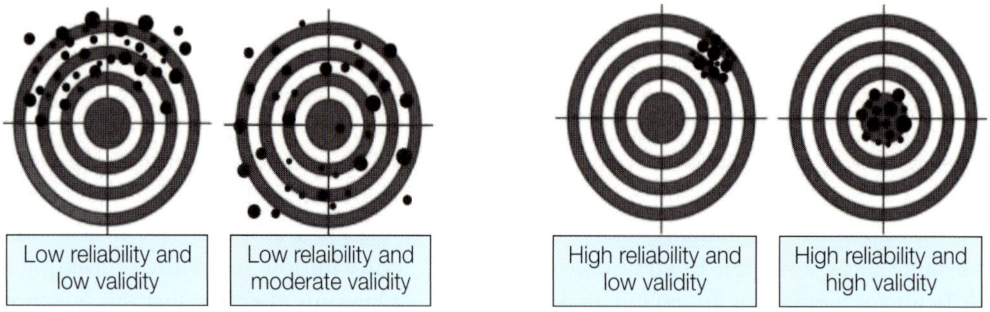

depending on who the interviewer is. The most ideal selection tool is to have both high reliability and high validity. However, it is not easy to have both. Nevertheless, it is necessary for managers and personnel in charge to make continuous efforts to increase the reliability and validity of the selection tools. If either of them is insufficient, it will result in missing precious talent.

When chossing a selection tool, it is ideal to use a selection tool that has both reliability and validity, but costs must be considered. For example, in the case of the assessment center method, it is known that both reliability and validity are high, but it has the disadvantage that it takes a lot of time and cost. For that reason, in interviews for new employees, only some types of tasks such as group discussions or presentations are selectively used among the general modules used in the assessment center.

4.4 Hiring and Organizational Socialization

There are many cases in which the newly hired after going through a selection process leave the company soon after joining. Why are applicants leaving the company in less than a year, despite the fact that they succeeded in finding a job in the company they wanted to work for? The circumstances are not different in Korean leading companies that always rank first in the employment preferences of enrolled students. They are also struggling with the high turnover rate, which occurs intensively in less than a year after joining. Although many companies are making efforts, the high turnover rate of new employees is not easily reduced. This phenomenon does not appear only in the case of new employees. Even for experienced employees hired from outside, there are many cases where they do not adjust well to the new company and move back to other company. Why is the turnover rate after hiring so high? There can be several reasons. After joining the company, unexpected personal circumstances may occur. However, it is difficult to say that personal affairs occur intensively only after entering the company. This phenomenon needs to be understood from the perspective of organizational socialization. Organizational socialization is a process in which an individual who joins a new organization understands and adapts to the organization's culture, values, and norms, thereby naturally feeling himself as a member of the

Lies in the Job Interview

Job-seekers who want to get a job often lie unintentionally during the job interview process. However, the price is very high. Companies are aware of the lies of applicants during the hiring process, which has a significant impact on hiring or not. As a result of a survey of 'the applicant's lies' among 927 member companies in 2020 conducted by a job portal SaramIn in 2020, 83.8% of the interviewers said they experienced a situation where the applicant lied in the job interview.[12)] And 97.6% of interviewers said they penalized for such lies. In particular, 73.6% of the interviewers said, 'There is an experience in which the applicant was eliminated because it was judged to be lying.' Personnel managers cited the most obvious lie as 'The salary is not important.'. Next, 'I have a lot of work-related experience', 'I can do everything I am asked for', and 'I think this company is the first and last one I want to work for.'

organization. Through organizational socialization, individuals can not only understand their expected role, but also build cooperative relationships and trust with various people in the organization.[11)]

The high turnover rate after hiring is likely to result form problems in the organizational socialization process. So, what kind of effort should the HR department or line managers do to solve this problem? First of all, it is important to provide accurate information about the job and the company so that applicants can precisely understand their job duties and the company's culture. This is called a realistic job preview, and it has the effect of promoting organizational socialization by making realistic judgments and expectations about work and organization before joining. This is also very important in terms of customer-oriented recruitment management. The company does not unilaterally select people, but introduces the job and the company to the applicant so that he or she can make judgments and make decisions. Therefore, organizational adaptation is greatly promoted.

Next, orientation is important after entering the company. Orientation is an activity that makes new employees understand and familiarize themselves with the organization's culture and values, policies, rules and procedures. If the realistic job preview focuses on what the applicant will do after joining the company, then the orientation is more about understanding the organization than the individual's job. Korean companies put more time and effort into orientation than Western companies. In fact, it is not difficult to find an orientation held by large Korean companies for new employees for about four weeks. As such, it can be said that Korean companies try to closely connect the attitudes of their members with the organizational culture.

Finally, mentoring is necessary for adaptation and organizational socialization after joining. Organizational socialization is an ongoing process and does not end with a single orientation. In particular, the role of a mentor who can help new recruits solve various difficulties or problems that they face in the process of carrying out their work, and teach the organization's culture and work process is very important. As competition intensifies in Korean companies as well, it makes manpower management tight, so unlike in the past, the culture of helping and teaching junior employees is rapidly disappearing. In this situation, the role of a mentor become more important. It is also necessary to establish and operate a mentor-mentee relationship systematically, and to establish a culture and system in which people in need can always receive help by making the culture of the entire department or organization open and cooperative.

5. Staffing and Role of Managers

Hiring is the starting point for human resource management. It cannot be overemphasized of accurately identifying and hiring talented people needed for the company. Securing excellent talent has a significant impact on a company's competitiveness. That's why advanced companies put more effort into recruiting and selecting talented people. In the case of Google, it is famous for having a lot of interviews before it makes a final hiring decision. The human resource plan must be reviewed before hiring begins. It is impatient and risky to start hiring just because you need the workforce right now. It is necessary to judge whether manpower demand is continuous or temporary, and the overall flow of manpower supply and demand must be reviewed. It is necessary to be able to predict the demand for manpower through forecasting future business prospects, and to simultaneously review the supply of manpower including turnover rate. When it is determined that manpower is constantly needed, then recruitment is carried out and the good applicants are selected.

Recruitment is an activity that makes the excellent personnel required by the company apply for the company, and recruiting source is an important issue. Recruiting source is very diverse, such as employees, employee referrals, internet, paper advertisements, and manpower intermediaries. Recently, social recruiting through social media such as LinkedIn, Facebook, Twitter has emerged and extensively used. In recruitment activities, a customer-oriented perspective is important. It is not always good to have many applicants. It is more desirable to have the right number of applicants. Keep in mind that all applicants are potential customers of the company, and try not to have any complaints or negative images of the company during the recruitment and selection process.

In selection, it is important to use a selection tool with reliability and validity. In general, the selection process of Korean companies consists of document screening based on self-introduction and application form, personality test, first interview, and second interview. Selection based on competency, not specifications, is important. Companies and managers should make efforts so that selection should be based on individual competency, experiences, values. It is also necessary to increase reliability and validity through structured interviews, while utilizing various tasks based on the assessment center method. There should be no discrimination based on gender, race, or age in hiring. Various laws, including the Constitution, strictly prohibit discrimination in hiring. Nevertheless, discrimination still exists in the real world. Attempts are being made to take social responsibility by taking a step further from non-discrimination to open employment opportunities for relatively marginalized minorities. The most basic and important countermeasure to avoid discrimination is to establish hiring standards and requirements in connection with the job or job characteristics. Managers should pay special attention and effort to avoid discrimination in the hiring process.

Ending Case

NCS(National Competency Standards)-based Hiring at HRDK[13)]

Since 2015, the National Competency Standard (NCS) has been introduced into public institutions, and many of them currently making hiring decisions by evaluating competencies of the applicants. National Competency Standards (NCS) refers to "knowledge, skill, aptitude, etc. required for the performance of occupational duties at industrial sites, which are systemized by the State by industrial sector and level" (Framework Act on Qualifications, Article 2 Subparagraph 2).

The government's policy to use NCS in public institutions is to ensure that hiring decisions are made according to the competencies required to perform the actual job, not the specifications. In Korea, the specifications means a kind of accomplishments the applicants have such as graduated school, overseas study, English score. There had been a strong competition among students to make good specifications and it bring about keen criticism against it because these specifications are not much related to the job competency in most cases. The policy of government was to create a competency-based society instead of specifications-based one by selecting the national job competency standard that standardizes and presents the knowledge, skills, and attitudes required for a specific job at the national level, and presents basic vocational competencies such as organizational comprehension and communication skills. When used appropriately as a selection tool, it can be an alternative that can improve both person-job fit and person-organization fit.

Until 2012, Human Resources Development Service of Korea (hereinafter referred to as HRDK) hired employees using a process such as 'document screening-written test- interview-career record check-hiring. In the application form, the name, resident number, telephone number, military service information, veteran status, disability status, address, etc. are required. In the form, specifications include hobbies and specialties, family information, educational level, foreign language level, certificates. And applicants have to submit career history and self-introduction. Document screening was conducted for applicants who were primarily filtered according to specifications such as language scores. In the written test, Korean history and knowledge of current affaires were presented as common subjects, and law, administration, business administration, economics, education, and computer science were presented as major subjects.

From 2013 to 2014, HRDK has improved hiring system in the direction of implementing competency-based hiring. At that time, the Ministry of Employment and Labor proposed a core job competency evaluation model as a part of improving hiring

[Figure 1] NCS-Based Hiring Process at HRDK

Step	Process	Tasks	Activities	In charge
1	Needs identification	Identification of workforce needs	Analyze need for the workforce based on job NCS classification	HR and Line dept.
			⇩	
2	Vocational competency	Identification of vocational competency	Analyze vocational competency for the job	HR and Line dept.
			⇩	
3	Recruitment announce	Identification of job competency(KSA)	Define KSA based on the job description	HR and Line dept.
			⇩	
4	Application acceptance	NCS-based Application form	Develop questions to identify vocational competency	HR dept.
			⇩	
5	Written test	Test of vocational basic competency	Develop test items to identify communication and organizational understanding competency	HR dept. Expert agency
			⇩	
6	Job interview	Competency-based job interview	Job interview based on job competency	HR and Line dept.
			⇩	
7	Hiring decision		Comprehensive and final decision	

practices to prevent excessive competition to accumulate specifications, and recommended the practice of competency-based hiring to public institutions. During this period, the entire job application was improved, and job competency evaluation was introduced, and the interview test method improved. For the job application, the specification field was completely deleted and the application form based on job competency was newly designed. In addition, replacing written major tests, a job competency test was introduced, and competency interviews and in-depth personality interviews were introduced to increase reliability and validity.

Meanwhile, in accordance with the government policy of implementing a competency-based society in 2015, HRDK further began to improve the hiring process and introduced a new hiring system using NCS in earnest. Although major improvements were made earlier in terms of competency-based hiring, the need to specify the evaluation of job competency emerged. In order to solve the problem, HRDK decided to use the 'Vocational Basic Skills Module' and 'National Competency Standards (NCS)

Application Package' developed by HRDK itself. This NCS-based hiring process is composed of 7 steps. With regard to NCS, the most important step is the step 4 of submitting an NCS-based application, and the step 5 of competency evaluation.

As for the outcome, it is clear that there have been some positive results. First, thanks to the NCS-based hiring system, it was possible to select talents with high job and organizational fit. The newly hired showed high organizational understanding and organizational adaptability. In addition, the dropout rate was lowered from 9% to 2% compared to the previous year, reducing the cost for human resource management at the institution's standpoint. Second, the new system provided equal employment opportunities to job seekers. The NCS-based hiring process was focused to identify vocational and job competency of the applicants without seeing academic background and scores at all, offering an opportunity to the applicants who should not have had the job interview in the past. This NCS-based hiring system is expected to contribute to enhancing the image of HRDK as a public institution that fulfills its social responsibilities. Third, the NCS-based recruitment system showed that the so-called specifications had little effect on the hiring decision. HRDK conducted a survey on NCS-based hiring for those who were hired by the this system. According to the survey, most respondents thought that specifications such as TOEIC score and certifications were not helpful unless they were related to the job.

Discussion Questions

1. In the past, HRDK required applicants to take written examinations for common subjects and major subjects. What are the strengths and weaknesses of the written test method?
2. Since 2015, with the emphasis on fair hiring based on competency, NCS-base hiring has spread rapidly among public institutions. Why are governments and public institutions working to introduce it?
3. HRDK does not consider academic background including graduated school, or academic grades in the hiring process, but is employing competency-based approach. Is it right not to consider education background or grades?
4. What is the most necessary thing for hiring to ensure validity and fairness as a selection practice?

CHAPTER

6

Performance Evaluation and Performance Management

1. Strategic Approach to Performance Evaluation and Performance Management
2. Performance Evaluation
3. Performance Management
4. Manager's Role

Learning Objectives

1. Can explain the difference between performance evaluation and performance management.
2. Two purposes of performance evaluation can be explained.
3. Can present the pros and cons of relative and absolute evaluation.
4. Can explain the difference between the behavior standard scale method and the management by objectives.
5. Can explain what SMART goals are.
6. Understand the psychological differences between managers and members about the causes of performance problems.
7. Understand managers' efforts to avoid rating errors.

Introductory Case

Kim Chul-su is a researcher at the Korea Economic Research Institute. After earning his master's degree in economics, he worked at the institute for about 10 years. For the past 10 years, the department where he worked has not had a formal evaluation system. However, Kim Chul-su has been informally evaluated as a good researcher. Following the restructuring last year, Kim Chul-su moved to a new research planning office. Other employees of that department have also been transferred from various departments following the restructuring. A new CEO was also appointed, and as soon as he took office, he instructed the heads of all departments to formally evaluate the performance of employees. A new evaluation form was also provided. The new evaluation system includes peer evaluation and self-evaluation to reflect recent trends. Accordingly, the head of the new department, Director Lee Hoe-taek of the Research Planning Department, instructed the employees, including Kim Chul-su, to complete self-evaluation and peer evaluation. Based on these results, Director Lee Hoe-taek completed the evaluation of all employees and submitted them to the HR department. Before sending to the HR department, Director Lee Hoe-taek met with the employees individually and explained the purpose of the performance evaluation and the results of the individual evaluation. However, about a week after submitting the results of the evaluation, the CEO gave an order to re-evaluate all of them. In fact, all department heads were given these instructions. The CEO saw that none of the employees received a "C" or "D" as a result of the department heads' evaluation, and almost all employees received an "A" rating. Director Lee Hoe-taek explained these details to the employees and asked them to conduct peer-evaluation and self-evaluation more objectively this time. After re-evaluation, Kim Chul-su discovered that his boss, Lee Hoe-taek, gave him a lower evaluation in all areas. On the other hand, Choi Dong-tak, another co-worker, received an "A" grade. Like Kim Chul-su, Choi Dong-tak had a master's degree in economics, but he had been working at the institute for less than two years. Before coming to the newly reorganized department last year, he had worked as an employee under Director Lee Hoe-taek, and it was known that the two were quite close. After the evaluation was conducted, a decision to increase the salary was made. According to the results of the evaluation, Kim Chul-su was informed that next year's salary had been frozen without an increase. It was also explained that the most important reason for the freeze of the salary was that he did not receive an "A" grade. After this series of events, Kim Chul-su did not personally speak with Lee Hoe-taek, and tried to do official work through e-mail if possible. Kim Chul-su gradually lost his motivation and complained badly to his colleagues about the evaluation. On the surface, it seemed that Kim Chul-su went to work at 8 am every day and stayed in his office until 5, but was found to spend most of his working time reading a book or newspaper.

Discussion Question

1. Why do you think this institute conducted performance evaluation?
2. What was the result of introducing evaluation?
3. What is the reason for the decline in Kim Chul-su performance in the case?
4. What are the ways to improve Kim Chul-su performance?
5. What would you do if you were Director Lee Hoe-taek?

Human resource management is a management method to achieve the vision, mission, and goal pursued by the organization. In addition, human resource management should support the members of the organization so that they can fully use their capabilities and potentials and lead a motivating and satisfying work life. Performance evaluation within the organization is also not different from the basic purpose of human resource management. However, in reality, it is often seen that the focus is only on the outcome of the evaluation rather than the aspect of using the evaluation well. In particular, from the HR department's point of view, evaluation should be conducted fairly and objectively to minimize the dissatisfaction of members, which is also an important purpose of evaluation. However, it is important for managers in charge of organizational performance to motivate members and actively perform their assigned tasks through evaluation. In doing so, it is necessary to achieve the objectives of the responsible organization and fulfill the given mission. But the reality is unfortunately not. According to a survey by the Korea Chamber of Commerce and Industry in 2017, 7 out of 10 Korean workers said they did not trust the company's evaluation system.[1)] The following are negative reactions to the evaluation of managers and members of the organization.

- "Evaluation is a pain in the ass. It is a painful task to have to formally criticize subordinates' usual work performance and attitude."
- "This is a subjective evaluation. The evaluation is inaccurate and biased towards honesty."
- "Will the evaluation really change the person?"
- "Evaluation is impossible. Do managers really deserve to evaluate?"
- "It's not my fault. It is to blame the members for the company's faults. The system as a whole is wrong."

This is why managers understand the importance of evaluation, but at the same time it is the most troublesome to them. Moreover, recently, the results of evaluation have to be used for promotion, compensation, and development, and even reflected in decision-making regarding dismissal, and this should be given to members as feedback. This makes the evaluation more difficult for managers.

However, evaluation cannot be avoided. As Peter Drucker, who is called the father of modern management, said, management without evaluation is impossible. Recently, as the function of human resource management has been strengthened and the strategic role has been emphasized, companies also want to deal with evaluation from a strategic perspective. This is also the reason why companies use the term performance management more often in place of personnel evaluation. Performance management is more comprehensive than other similar terms, and it is common to include evaluation as one of the performance management processes. This chapter examines the difference between performance evaluation and performance management and explains how managers should utilize performance management after understanding the basic framework of evaluation.

1. Strategic Approach to Performance Evaluation and Performance Management

There are two types of evaluation in human resource management: job evaluation and person evaluation. In Chapter 4, we looked at job evaluation. This chapter discusses the evaluation of people. Several similar terms have been used together for the evaluation of people in companies. For example, performance evaluation, performance appraisal, personnel rating, performance rating, and people evaluation are frequently used. Although the terms used by each company are different and the contents are slightly different depending on the terms, the difference in the essential meaning is not large, so it is okay to use them interchangeably. Here, we will use it in a unified way for performance evaluation.

Traditionally, performance evaluation has been defined as the systematic evaluation of current and potential usefulness possessed by members in an organization. This characteristic of the definition of the traditional performance evaluation shows the past-oriented aspect that the manager observes and judges the performance of the members that have already occurred. On the other hand, recently, it has been defined as "the process of identifying factors to increase organizational performance, measuring the performance of employees according to this standard, and managing them to improve performance."[2] The difference between the current definition and the past is that the performance of the members has not already occurred and can be improved according to the efforts of managers and members, and the ultimate purpose of the evaluation is to improve the performance, not the evaluation itself.

This is also related to the shift in human resource management to a strategic approach. Similar to other human resource management, the approach to the evaluation system has shifted from the perspective of simply measuring the performance of members (this is called the measurement perspective) to the perspective of viewing it as a holistic system that manages the performance of members in order to achieve strategic goals (this called management perspective).[3] As shown in <Table 6-1>, from the measurement point of view, evaluation is aimed at accurately measuring the performance that has already occurred. On the other hand, from the management point of view, it is regarded as a communication process in which managers, who are leaders, and members, who are subordinates, jointly set goals and communicate information to improve performance. Today, all global companies use performance evaluation as an important tool for active human resource management to develop employee capabilities and improve performance to achieve organizational goals.

Performance management emerged in this context. This is also the reason why companies are using the term performance management more instead of performance evaluation. For example, IBM Korea defines performance management as follows. "Performance management allows employees to know what each of them must do, how to do it, and how to improve the way they work to achieve the company's business goals. Based on the evaluation results, managers can use it as a basic tool in determining the salaries and promotions of employees. It is used as a means for mutual communication

Table 6-1 **Approach to Personnel Evaluation: Measurement vs. Management**

	MEASUREMENT APPROACH	MANAGEMENT APPROACH
Basic assumptions	A member's performance has already occurred and can be accurately measured.	The performance of the members is not fixed and depends on the leadership of the manager.
Definition of evaluation system	Evaluation is an accurate measure of the performance of members that have already occurred.	Evaluation is a process for achieving goals and a means for managing performance.
Objectives of the evaluation system	Accuracy, reliability, consistency	Usefulness, effectiveness, and achievement of organizational goals
Operation center	HR department that designs evaluation systems, evaluation tables, evaluation standards, and evaluation tools	Manager responsible for performance management, employee development, coaching and feedback
Evaluator's role	Passive role in executing evaluation according to given evaluation criteria	Responsible for the competency development of members and an active role in improving performance
Evaluatee's role	Subject of observation	An active participant in improving performance
Relationship between manager and member	Independent roles as evaluators and evaluatees	An interactive relationship that sets goals together and continuously communicates to improve performance.

between managers and employees about the career development of each employee."[4)]

If performance evaluation is focused on the evaluation itself, performance management can be seen as focusing on improving performance through evaluation. In this sense, performance evaluation and performance management are not very different, but if strictly defined, performance evaluation can be said to be one element of performance management. What you see in [Figure 6-1] is a typical example of a company introducing performance management from a strategic point of view. It depicts the connection between the company-wide vision, mission, and goals with the goals of each department or work unit, and then with the goals of individual members. In the figure, the circle includes three elements of performance management, and it can be seen that one of them is performance evaluation.

The reason why companies are actively introducing performance management is because it has a positive effect on performance improvement. As can be seen in [Figure 6-2], looking at the results of recent empirical studies, it can be seen that the companies that introduced performance management improved their productivity compared to the companies that did not, and thus the company's financial performance was good. It shows that companies that have introduced performance management have higher sales per capita and per capita profit than those that do not, and their ROE and ROA are about twice as high.[5)] If, after conducting the performance evaluation, the morale of

Figure 6-1 **Strategic Performance Management**

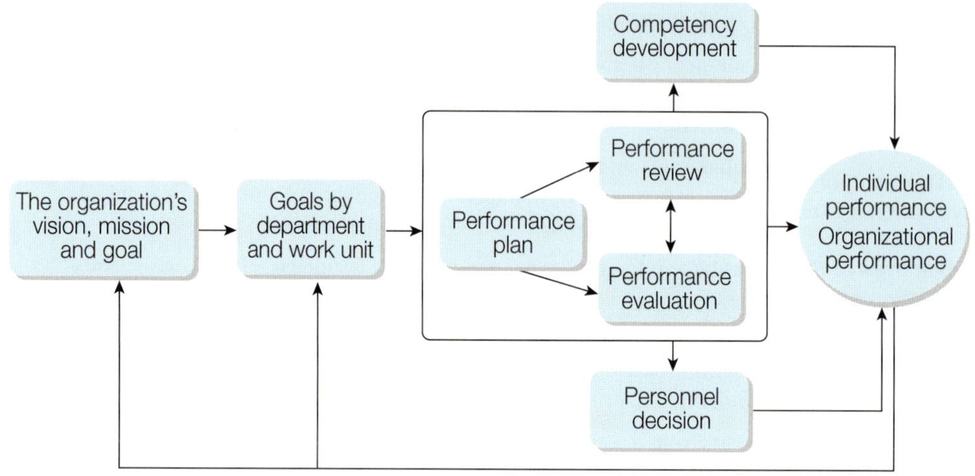

Figure 6-2 **Effect of Performance Management**

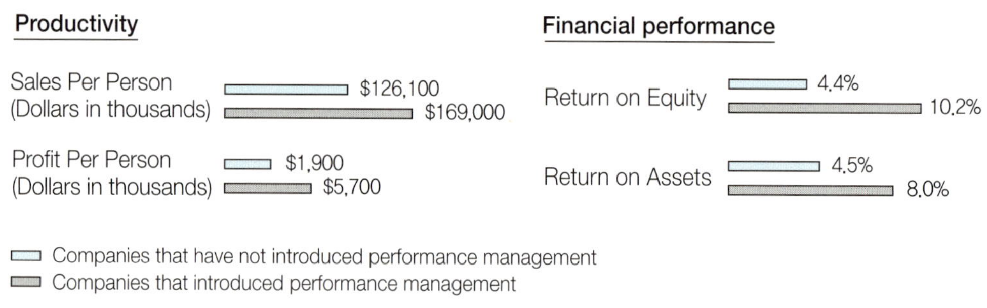

the members has deteriorated and performance has deteriorated, there is no reason to make a complicated and difficult evaluation. Regardless of the term used, it should not be forgotten that the final purpose of evaluation is to increase the performance of the company by motivating the members to do their work.

2. Performance Evaluation

In order for managers to make good evaluations, they must first have an understanding of the overall performance evaluation system. The elements constituting the evaluation system are rather complex. To make them easier to understand, the seven elements are summarized as 6W1H as shown in [Figure 6-3]. This method, which is frequently used by Japanese scholars, facilitates the understanding of the evaluation system.

Figure 6-3 **Understanding the Personnel Evaluation System**

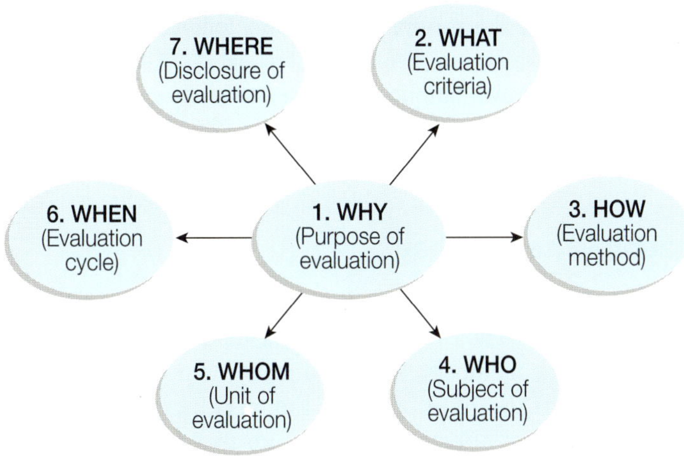

2.1 Purpose of Evaluation (why)

First, what is the purpose of performance evaluation? Earlier, it was explained that the ultimate purpose of performance evaluation is to contribute to the improvement of competitiveness and performance of a company as a component of human resource management. In order to achieve this macroscopic goal, the purpose of performance evaluation can be divided into two main categories.

1) Basic Data for Administrative Decision

The evaluation results secure fairness in human resource management and become objective data for rational personnel decisions. Based on this data, promotion decisions are made for excellent performers or members with high competency, and conversely, it is used for disciplinary action or dismissal decisions for low-performing members or members with problems. The courts and the Labor Relations Commission also place importance on the performance evaluation through a reasonable procedure in determining the disciplinary action or dismissal of the employees conducted by the company. If performance evaluation is not conducted fairly, there is a high possibility that it will be judged as unfair disciplinary action or unfair dismissal. In addition, the evaluation result becomes a standard for determining the amount of salary increase or determining performance pay or incentives.

2) Basic Data for Development Purpose

Without evaluation, it is difficult for members to identify which areas are strengths and which areas are weaknesses. Therefore, the evaluation results are used as basic data to identify individual strengths and weaknesses in order to develop the shortcomings of employees. In order for an organization to continuously pursue performance improvement, it is essential to improve the capabilities of its employees. A clear judgment and analysis of the current level is required to improve the competency of employees, and performance evaluation plays such a role. Managers are coaches who are responsible for improving their employees' competencies, and can guide subordinates based on the results of evaluation. From the perspective of the organization as a whole, the results of performance evaluation can be used to analyze the causes of the difference between high-performing and average employees. Through this, change management and development direction of the entire organization can be set.

2.2 Evaluation Criteria (what)

Here, issue is what criteria the members will be evaluated. In other terms, this is called an evaluation factor. The evaluation criteria should be directly or indirectly related to the performance of the members. What is directly related to performance is the output (or achievement) that is the final result of the work performed by the members. An indirect one is a factor that affects the process up to the final result and can be called an input. The reason for evaluating not only the final product but also the process is for continuous improvement of performance. <Table 6-2> is the performance evaluation

Table 6-2 Traditional Personnel Evaluation Table of Korean Companies

PERFORMANCE EVALUATION SHEET

AFFILI-ATION	POSITION	NAME	BIRTH DATE	DATE OF ENTRY	CURRENT PAY GRADE	LAST PROMOTION DATE
Evaluation period	From to:	~				

ELEMENT	ITEMS	CONTENTS	POINTS	EVALU-ATION
Compe-tencies	Business knowledge	Possession of general and professional knowledge and experience required for job performance and the degree of use from a company-wide perspective	8	
	Planning creativity	Ability to devise and plan new ways to improve work processing methods and solve problems with a problem awareness	8	
	Persuasive skills	Ability to successfully perform one's duties and solve problems with an amicable and sincere interpersonal relationship and negotiation attitude	8	
	Leadership skills	Accurately grasping subordinates' qualities and providing smooth guidance, leading them to contribute to the achievement of the organization's goals, and the degree to which they are trusted	8	

ELEMENT	ITEMS	CONTENTS	POINTS	EVALU-ATION
	Analytical judgment	Ability to accurately identify and analyze the core of the planned and ordered tasks, predict related and future matters, and take appropriate countermeasures	8	
		Subtotal	40	
Attitude	Accounta-bility	Recognizing one's role within the organization, faithfully performing assigned duties, and taking responsibility for the results	5	
	Positiveness	Proactive attitude to actively and voluntarily perform work with a developmental and ambitious attitude and to actively improve the status quo	5	
	Cooperation	The degree to which efforts are made to improve communication between upper and lower co-workers by promoting organic cooperation among other departments and other employees with the interests of the entire company in mind	5	
	Cost awareness	Attitude to use manpower, materials, equipment, time and expenses economically and efficiently	5	
	Self-development	Degree of effort to improve self-qualification and growth for the improvement and development of work ability	5	
	Management conscious-ness	Having a firm belief in the company's ideology and goals, the attitude of mind to support the company's policy and the degree to which others understand the policy	5	
		Subtotal	30	
Perfor-mance Outcomes	Achievement level	The degree to which one has contributed to the achievement of goals by efficiently, reliably, and efficiently performing tasks in accordance with the management policy without errors and errors.	15	
	Contents of outcomes	The degree to which tasks are planned without waste of time and effort by accurately grasping the contents and problems of the task, and the task is handled quickly within the designated period	15	
		subtotal	30	
		Total	100	
Evaluator's opinion		Evaluator position	Name	Sign

table used by mid-sized companies in Korea. In this company, competency and attitude as input and performance as output are for the evaluation criteria. Examples of each standard used by companies are as follows.

① Competency: knowledge, skills, and abilities required for job performance (KSA)
- Basic skills (judgment, comprehension, etc.)
- Work-related abilities (professional knowledge, planning ability, etc.)
- Interpersonal skills (leadership, persuasion, etc.)

② Attitude: Consistent tendency to feel and respond to an object in an organization
- Attitude towards work (responsibility, activeness, spontaneity, etc.)
- Attitude towards people (fairness, trust, cooperation, etc.)
- Attitude towards the organization (loyalty, discipline, management consciousness, etc.)

③ Achievement: Final result
- Amount of work
- Quality of work

On the other hand, as performance management was recently introduced into companies, the traditional evaluation factors were criticized as being too general regardless of the competitiveness of the company, and the concept of competency was introduced as an alternative. As we saw in Chapter 4, competency is similar to ability and attitude, which are input factors, but among them, it can be defined as a combination of specific knowledge, skills, and abilities (KSA) that make members achieve high performance in the process of job performance. Competency consists of factors that are highly related to performance, observable through behavior, and that can be improved through development. In Chapter 4, we also looked at how competencies are divided into common competencies, leadership competencies, job competencies, and professional competencies. <Table 6-3> shows examples of common competencies and leadership competencies among the competency evaluations conducted by a mid-sized company in Korea. The company presents the evaluation criteria for each competency in detail, and evaluates them on a 5-point scale based on this. It is also noteworthy that there is an item called performance management among leadership competencies.

Table 6-3 Cases of Competency Evaluation of Korean Mid-sized Company

CLASSIFICATION	COMPETENCY NAME	COMPETENCY DEFINITION	EVALUATION STANDARD	EVALUATION
Common competencies	Ethics	Comply with company regulations and policies with a strong professional/ personal ethics, and act properly according to moral judgments that are consistent with the values of the organization.	Follow the standards of the organization and company regardless of personal interests, and share/report management and work-related data honestly without distortion. Earn trust by consistently delivering on our promises to our co-workers, bosses, and customers.	

CLASSIFICATION	COMPETENCY NAME	COMPETENCY DEFINITION	EVALUATION STANDARD	EVALUATION
	Creation	By breaking away from stereotypes and demonstrating imagination and insight, continuously provide value to stakeholders.	Approach from a variety of perspectives beyond facts and experiences, use imagination and insight to conceive and propose ideas.	
			Create an atmosphere where creativity and new challenges are respected.	
	Passion	Constantly challenge ourselves to create results based on strong commitment to work and execution.	To accomplish one's job, focus and mobilize all resources, take risks and try before others.	
			By taking the lead in everything and actively supporting members of the organization, become role models for members.	
	Innovation	Have a problem-conscious awareness of existing processes and systems and strive to improve them, and strengthen organizational capabilities through continuous interest in the external business environment and capture of change opportunities.	Propose directions and ideas to innovatively improve existing processes, work methods, and systems, and try to change them.	
			Actively accept the innovative proposals and ideas of other members and reflect them in work.	
Leader competencies	Talent development	Stimulate, promote, and strengthen organizational members so that they can maximize their capabilities and grow into competitive talents.	Identify the potential strengths of our members and give them tasks and opportunities to actually grow them.	
			Provide specific directions and guides to members and provide honest and constructive feedback on performance continuously.	
			Appropriate compensation is provided for the performance of the members, and morale is boosted by praising the hard work and effort shown in the process of achieving the goal.	

<table>
<tr><th>CLASSIFICATION</th><th>COMPETENCY NAME</th><th>COMPETENCY DEFINITION</th><th>EVALUATION STANDARD</th><th>EVALUATION</th></tr>
<tr><td rowspan="9">Leader competencies</td><td rowspan="3">Business insight</td><td rowspan="3">Continuously develop potential growth areas and seize new business opportunities based on broad knowledge and skills in the industrial environment and the relevant work.</td><td>Pay attention to meaningful changes or risks/opportunities in the market and collect/analyze relevant information.</td><td></td></tr>
<tr><td>Identify potential growth areas and develop revenue models.</td><td></td></tr>
<tr><td>Find and implement ways to create new markets.</td><td></td></tr>
<tr><td rowspan="3">Vision and direction</td><td rowspan="3">Establish the organization's vision and strategy, and clearly present specific directions to the members to induce consensus and participation.</td><td>Leaders themselves have a clear vision and share the vision and goals of the organization as a whole.</td><td></td></tr>
<tr><td>In order to achieve the vision, the implementation plan is divided by unit organization and presented, and the core goal to be focused on is set.</td><td></td></tr>
<tr><td>By providing continuous feedback on whether or not the vision/strategy has been realized or the results are provided to members, the ability to execute the vision is strengthened.</td><td></td></tr>
<tr><td rowspan="3">Performance management</td><td rowspan="3">Maximize organizational and individual performance by linking the goals of the organization with the goals of the members, performing continuous management to achieve the plan, and evaluating performance accurately and fairly.</td><td>Clearly set individual goals and responsibilities for achieving organizational goals (team or department, headquarters), and recognize the link between individual performance and organizational performance.</td><td></td></tr>
<tr><td>Remove obstacles by continuously monitoring the work process and performance of organizational members and provide methods necessary to achieve performance goals.</td><td></td></tr>
<tr><td>The performance is evaluated accurately and fairly according to the degree of contribution of the members of the organization to the achievement of the goals of the organization and department and the level of difficulty of the goal level.</td><td></td></tr>
</table>

2.3 Evaluation Method (how)

As modern companies emerged after the Industrial Revolution, evaluation methods have been developed in various ways. Evaluation methods can be broadly classified into relative evaluation and absolute evaluation. The difference between the two evaluation methods lies in the standard of comparison. Relative evaluation is a method of determining superiority through comparison between evaluation subjects. Absolute evaluation, on the other hand, is a method of determining how close an evaluation target is to the evaluation criteria compared to the pre-set absolute evaluation criteria.

There has been constant debate over whether the relative evaluation is better or the absolute evaluation is better. In the case of Merck, a multinational pharmaceutical company that was founded more than 100 years ago, it started with a relative evaluation, but was changed to an absolute evaluation due to side effects, and then changed to a relative evaluation due to the side effect of the absolute evaluation. This process is repeated several times. As such, both methods have their pros and cons, and it is impossible to conclude which one is better. Ultimately, it is the best way to decide depending on where the company puts the philosophy and policy of human resource management, and it can be said that it is more important what kind of attitude managers evaluate regardless of which system is introduced. <Table 6-4> compares and analyzes the advantages and disadvantages and suitable situations of relative and absolute evaluation.

2.3.1 Relative Evaluation

Relative evaluation is the oldest evaluation method in human history, and is the simplest and easiest to understand. On the other hand, it also has several problems. Representative relative evaluation methods include the ranking method, paired comparison method, and forced distribution method.

1) Ranking Method

The ranking method is a method in which the manager compares the subjects to be evaluated and determines the order from the best employee to the last. In some cases, the criteria for comparison are set in advance. For example, in the case of an R&D department, it could be based on their contribution to the development of a new product. On the other hand, without these specific criteria, managers can subjectively judge and rank the overall behavior or attitude. There are simple ranking methods and alternate ranking methods. The straight simple ranking method is used when the number of subjects to be evaluated is small, and it starts with the best employee and immediately determines the next ranking. On the other hand, if the number of evaluators is large, it is not easy to simply rank them. In this case, an alternate ranking method is used, in which the best employee is selected first and then the worst employee is selected from among the remaining employees.

Table 6-4 **Relative Evaluation vs. Absolute Evaluation**

	RELATIVE EVALUATION	ABSOLUTE EVALUATION
Type of evaluation system	Raking, paired comparison method, forced distribution	Rating scale, behavior anchored scales, MBO
Advantages	• Appropriate for personnel decisions such as promotion, dismissal, and performance pay • Clear distinction between low performers and high performers • Prevent leniency tendencies	• Focus on process rather than outcome • Feedback on performance and improvement are possible • Avoid excessive competition and facilitate collaboration
Disadvantages	• Make people too obsessed with results • Induce excessive competition and make collaboration difficult • Decreased morale of middle talent, who make up the majority	• There is a lot of room for evaluation errors such as leniency • There is a high possibility that the evaluation system will become unpopular
Suitable situation	• When it is necessary to establish performance-based HR practices • When motivation is needed through interpersonal competition • When it is necessary to distinguish between excellent and low performers • When the leaders' management and evaluation competencies are insufficient	• When cooperation between members is needed rather than competition • When it is necessary to increase the competency and morale of members • When the classification of talent is ambiguous or meaningless • When the leaders' management and evaluation competencies are high

2) Paired Comparison Method

The paired comparison method can be said to be a modified form of the ranking method. As the term suggests, the paired comparison method is a method of determining who is superior by comparing all members of an organization to evaluate with each other. For example, if the finance team leader evaluates six team members, all six members compare each other to determine which of the two is superior, giving the best employee 1 point and the other employee 0 points. In <Table 6-5>, in the comparison between Eunha Lee and Dongju Park, Eunha Lee was judged to be excellent, and one point was given to Eunha Lee. After all comparisons are made, the assigned score is calculated and the ranking is determined from the highest score. As shown in the table, Cheol-soo Lee received the highest score of 4 points and took 1st place, and Kyung-jun Choi received the lowest score of 1 point and placed 6th.

3) Forced Distribution Method

There is no problem with the ranking method and the paired comparison method when the number of subjects to be evaluated is small, but it is not easy to compare them when the number of subjects is large. For example, there are 60 students in a human

Table 6-5 **Example of Paired Comparison Method**

Evaluatees	Eunha Lee	Park Dong-ju	Kyung-Jun Choi	Chul-soo Lee	Kim Ha-nam	Eunkyung Jang
Eunha Lee	-	0	0	0	1	1
Park Dong-ju	1	-	0	1	1	0
Kyung-Jun Choi	1	1	-	1	0	1
Chul-soo Lee	1	0	0	-	0	0
Kim Ha-nam	0	0	1	1	-	0
Eunkyung Jang	0	1	0	1	1	-
Total score	3	2	1	4	3	2

resource management class taught by authors at a university, and it is very difficult to compare and rank them all. The evaluation method used when the number of evaluation subjects is large is the forced distribution method. The forced distribution method is a method in which a grade is determined in advance and a certain ratio of subjects to be evaluated is assigned to each grade. For example, a large Korean company uses four grades (E (excellent), G (good), S (satisfactory), and I (improvement)) at the rate of 15%, 35%, 35%, and 5%, respectively. The forced distribution method is difficult to use when the number of evaluation subjects is too small. In addition, side effects occur when there is a large difference in performance by department or when there is a significant difference in competency among members. Therefore, there are companies that apply the grade ratio differentially between departments by reflecting the performance of each department. For example, as shown in the case of Merck in <Table 6-6>, when the business division's performance is good, the ratio of high grades increases, and in the opposite case, the ratio of low grades increases. If a business unit's performance received EX (exceptional), the ratio of TF (top 5%) was originally 5%, but that division is allocated up to 8%. On the other hand, if the division's performance received NA (not acceptable), the TF ratio drops to 1% and the LF (lower 5%) ratio increases from 5% to 10%. Merck has been operating the evaluation system for a long time and has experienced the advantages and disadvantages of absolute and relative evaluations. Through this experience, both relative and absolute evaluations are used together. The top 5% (TF), 15% (TQ), and bottom 5% (LF) use the relative evaluation of the forced distribution method, but the absolute evaluation is reflected for the majority of the members of the middle 75%. There are three grades (OU, VG, GD) in the 75% section, but the manager of the unit department decides which grade to give.

2.3.2 Absolute Evaluation

Unlike relative evaluation, absolute evaluation is a method in which an absolute performance standard is set in advance, and a score is assigned by evaluating how close the subject is to this criterion. Scores can be given on a 100-point scale like school test scores, or can be evaluated on a 3-point, 5-point, 7-point, 10-point scale. The

Table 6-6 **Individual Evaluation/Organizational Evaluation, Relative Evaluation/Absolute Evaluation Mixed Case(Merck company)**

		EVALUATION GRADE ALLOCATION RATIO BASED ON BUSINESS DIVISION PERFORMANCE				
Evaluation grade according to individual performance	Evaluation Methods	Performance of business units				
		EX (Exceptional)	WD (With Distinction)	HS (High Standard)	RI (Room of Improvement)	NA (Not Acceptable)
TF(Top 5%)	Relative	8%	6%	5%	2%	1%
TQ(Top Quintile)	Relative	20%	17%	15%	12%	10%
OU(Outstanding) VG(Very Good) GD(Good)	Absolute	71%	75%	75%	78%	79%
LF(Lower 5%) NA(Not Acceptable)	Relative Absolute	1%	2%	5%	8%	10%
PR(Progressing)		Not Applicable				

absolute evaluation method allows managers to more easily determine the strengths and weaknesses of members in the process of performing tasks and develop their competencies. For example, relative evaluation only provides information that Lee Cheol-soo is first and Choi Kyung-Jun is sixth. On the other hand, in the absolute evaluation, if Lee Chul-soo is excellent in responsibility and sincerity but creativity is average, Choi is evaluated as having insufficient responsibility and integrity but excellent creativity. Therefore, Lee Cheol-soo is generally excellent, but his creativity is inferior compared to other areas, so this part needs to be supplemented. On the other hand, it is desirable for Choi Kyung-Jun to be entrusted with a job in a field where creativity can be utilized well. Although the absolute evaluation method has advantages over relative evaluation, it is also a method that causes rating errors such as leniency error, central tendency, or halo effect.

1) Rating Scales

The rating scale method was developed to evaluate the attributes, traits, or competencies inherent in people. It is a traditional evaluation tool that has been used since the emergence of a modern company, and it is one of the most used even today. The rating scale method collectively refers to all methods that use scales. As a similar term, it is also called graphic rating scale or trait rating scale. In this method, the evaluation factors to be measured in the organization are presented in advance and the evaluator gives a score according to a certain scale. A five-point scale is the most common, and a three-point or seven-point scale is sometimes used. The traditional performance evaluation table in <Table 6-2> seen earlier is an example of a typical rating scale method. In this case, a 5-point scale, an 8-point scale, and a 15-point scale are used for each item. When managers evaluate scales, they sometimes think that if the number of scales is reduced or increased, it will be evaluated better. However, the results of the empirical study showed that there was no correlation between the number of scales and the accuracy of evaluation. Scholars emphasize that, rather than the number of scales, managers' attitudes toward evaluation, organizational culture, or environment are the most important factors influencing evaluation results.[6)]

The rating scale method is the most used evaluation tool because it is easy to design by HR departments and not difficult for managers to evaluate. However, it is also the method with the highest risk of rating errors because managers use their intuition to evaluate them according to their own subjective criteria. Behavioral anchored rating scales (BARS), which will be explained next, has emerged as an alternative.

2) Behavioral Anchored Rating Scales (BARS)

Attributes are literally traits inherent in people, so they cannot be observed. What we can observe is the language and gestures that people express outwardly, that is, their behavior. Measuring behavior as an evaluation tool is what managers make to evaluate based on the externally observable behaviors of the people. For example, whether a person is responsible is an intrinsic property. Because this is not observable, managers evaluate them by taking into account how they felt while working with their subordinates. An evaluation method based on the observable behavior of members is the behavioral anchored rating scales (BARS).

The BARS is similar to the rating scale method in that it uses a scale. The difference, however, is that managers focus on observable behaviors rather than on attributes inherent in people. Therefore, in order to develop a BARS, it is necessary to first confirm what the observable behavior is. For example, if there is an evaluation standard called customer mindset, the rating scale method can evaluate whether or not there is a customer mindset on a scale of 1 point 'not at all' to 5 points, 'very much'. However, it is not specific here what the difference between 1 and 5 points is, and because of this, evaluators subjectively evaluate according to their own standards. That is, the possibility of an error in evaluation increases. If the customer mindset is evaluated using the BARS, specific behavior is suggested. For example, when evaluating call center employees, a score of '1' is undesirable and increases customer dissatisfaction by impatiently dealing with customer complaints. '5 points' helps dissatisfied customers and understands their complaints by listening to the situation in detail and kindly explaining the parts that the company can handle and the parts that cannot be handled. [Figure 6-4] is an example of an evaluation table using the BARS for a bank's credit transaction job.[7)] In order to design the BARS, there must be specific examples of behavior for each job. As we saw in Chapter 4, job analysis is essential for this, and the job analysis method used at this time is the critical incident technique.

3) Management by Objectives (MBO)

If the rating scale method or the BARS evaluates the input in the process until the result is made, the management by objectives (MBO) evaluates the final output. The MBO is known as a management technique first proposed by Peter Drucker, and is

Figure 6-4 Example of the Behavior Standards Scale Act

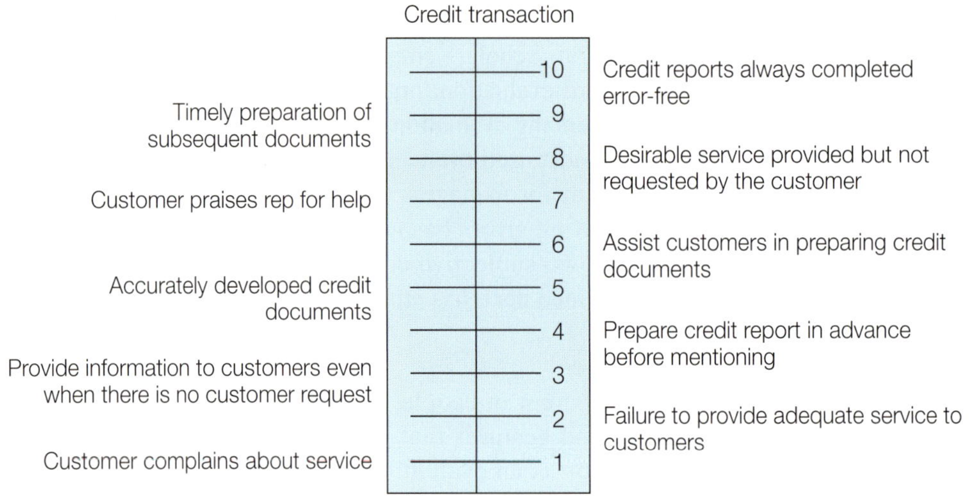

a method in which employees set goals in advance and evaluate them according to whether these have been achieved. In general, managers and subordinates together plan the work to be done during the evaluation period (usually every year), set specific performance goals, and decide how to evaluate them. The MBO is based on one of the motivational theories, the goal-setting theory. Goal setting theory is the theory that when people set goals for what they want to do, they are motivated to strive to achieve them.[9)] When people set goals compared to when they don't set any goals, they set the direction of their actions and generate a desire to achieve them. The goal at this time should be

OKR (Objectives & Key Results) Method

Recently, the OKR (Objectives & Key Results) method is being discussed in companies. It was developed by Intel and Google and received attention. In Korea, it is reported in the media that IT companies such as Naver and Carrot Market and financial institutions such as NH Securities and Hanwha Life are introducing it. There are criticisms of MBOs behind the discussion of OKRs. Since MBO sets goals for each year and evaluates them only at the end of the year, it has disadvantages in that it is slow to respond to rapid changes in the environment and it is difficult to provide real-time feedback. On the other hand, Google, which is a representative example of introducing OKR, follows the 3·3·3 rule. Short cycle of 3 months, focus through 3 goals, and boost momentum by utilizing 3 Key results per goal. However, it has not yet been generalized not only to Korean companies but also to global companies. On the other hand, John Door, a leading proponent of OKR, does not recommend using OKR directly for evaluation.[8)] It remains to be seen how the OKR will be linked to the evaluation system in the future.

set as challenging as possible but achievable. If it becomes a goal that can be achieved without much effort or impossible to achieve even if you do everything you can, you lose motivation. <Table 6-7> is an example of the MBO evaluation conducted by a foreign-invested company operating in Korea. As shown in the example, the objective is completed after the subordinate has a goal setting interview with the boss. The subordinate establishes a specific action plan to achieve this goal. Finally, the evaluation is judged according to whether the goal has been achieved.

2.4 Who is Responsible for the Evaluation (who)

It is a matter of who will evaluate. A good evaluation should be made by someone well positioned to fulfill both roles. First, it must be evaluated by a supervisor with management authority. It has the authority to promote the subordinate, to allocate and distribute wages, and must have the authority and responsibility to directly control the behavior of the subordinate. Second, it should be evaluated by a person who can closely observe the behavior of the person being evaluated. A proper evaluation can be made only when evaluator is able to observe and judge the normal work process and results. In traditional organizations, direct managers are well positioned to fulfill these two roles. Therefore, in most companies, the direct supervisor becomes the primary evaluator. In some cases, the direct supervisor of the primary evaluator becomes the secondary evaluator to correct errors that may occur in the primary evaluation.

In a traditional organization, the immediate supervisor also has management authority, and the subject of evaluation does not become an issue in the position where he or she can observe. However, due to the recent change in the organizational environment, the immediate supervisor has limitations in observing the performance or behavior of the subordinates. For example, with the introduction of the team system, the scope of the manager's control has been greatly expanded. With the absence of middle managers, it is not uncommon for a team leader to have to evaluate more than 30 to 40 team members. Organizational management and culture have also changed. Considering the needs of customers, many decision-making rights have been given to the person in the field who is directly in charge of these customers. Also, due to technological change, moving up to the top of the organization does not lead to having more technical knowledge. Rather, in terms of professionalism, field workers have more new knowledge and skills than managers. All of these changes are making it difficult for managers to evaluate their subordinates.

As a result, people who can understand the behavior of the person being evaluated, other than their direct supervisor, participate in the evaluation, and multi-rator evaluation or 360-degree feedback is actively being introduced to companies. As shown in [Figure 6-5], 360-degree feedback includes self-evaluation, peer evaluation by team members, subordinate evaluation by subordinates, and customer evaluation, in addition to traditional supervisor evaluation. Multi-rator evaluation and 360-degree feedback are used as similar terms. However, multi-rator evaluation includes the meaning of actively reflecting the evaluation results in personnel decisions. On the other hand, in the case of 360-degree feedback, the term "feedback" is used in the sense that it is a variety

Table 6-7 Management by Objectives (MBO) Case of Korean Company

◈ **Objective** The performance goals of the evaluated are recorded in relation to the business plans of the company and affiliated units. First, the evaluated sets the items and then supplements and confirms them through a goal setting interview with the evaluator. Based on the SMART principle, it is expressed in specific and clear terms, and the target level for each item must be included.

◈ **Weight** Allocate weights for each target item set so that the total is 100%. At this time, the evaluator must check whether the weights set when considering the business plans of the company and the unit organization are properly reflecting the priority and importance of each target item.

◈ **Detailed Action** Record what activities the evaluated will do to achieve the set goals. As much as possible, subdivide and describe tasks in detail so that the schedule for each activity, what the results are, and what criteria can be evaluated in the future are clearly expressed. It also describes what obstacles are expected and what kind of support is needed to overcome them.

◈ **Rating** First, the evaluated reviews the work progress results so far and determines the evaluation grade of Outstanding (OS), Meet Expectation (ME), NI (Need Improvement), and MR (Marginal) for each target item. The evaluator determines the evaluation grade for each item by checking the review notes and the final work performance results. Remember that the evaluated conducts self-evaluation, but the final judgment is made by the manager, and the manager is responsible for the legitimacy of the evaluation result.

◈ **Result** The evaluator provides specific reasons why the rating was given. Provide specific opinions as much as possible so that the evaluated can accept the evaluation results and help improve work performance.

OBJECTIVE	WEIGHT	DETAILED ACTION	RATING		RESULT
			SELF	MANAGER	
By building the Mobile Office System by September, the indirect cost of 100 million won was saved from October to December.	50%	• Establish a specific business plan to build the Mobile Office System by the end of January • Development of organizational operation plan to build Mobile Office System by the end of June • By February 10, business consultation with the purchasing team to improve the office environment, purchase necessary equipment, receive quotations, compare and review, and select a company • Pilot test conducted until the end of August to verify the new system • Conduct training for team leaders on new system construction by the end of September • Evaluation of indirect cost savings after system introduction • Development and implementation of questionnaires to evaluate member satisfaction with the new system	ME	OS	√ Prepare a specific master plan according to the business plan and carry out the work according to the schedule √ Reengineering business processes for system design work √ A relatively inexpensive company is selected through price competition comparison according to the company's quotation √ As a result of the satisfaction survey, 90% of respondents indicated that they were very satisfied with the Mobile Office System √ In the fourth quarter, the target of 100 million won in indirect cost reduction was not achieved, but 50 million won of cost was saved √ Training on the system prevents members from experiencing confusion in adapting to a new system

Figure 6-5 Traditional Supervisory Evaluation and 360 Degree Multi-Rator Evaluation

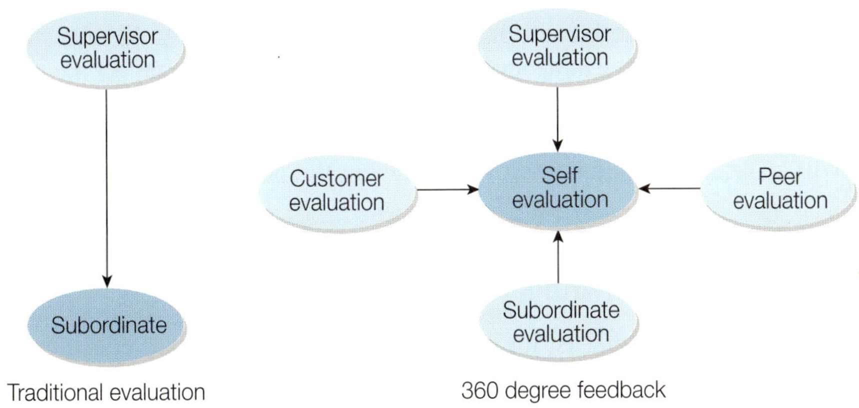

of information that supervisors use to refer to their subordinates' evaluations. Many companies are systematically introducing 360-degree feedback. However, even if there is no formal multi-rator system, managers need to use 360-degree feedback informally to make more desirable evaluations and demonstrate leadership.

2.5 Unit of Evaluation (whom)

The evaluation unit refers to the evaluation range that can be evaluated by one evaluator, that is, the span of control that the evaluator can manage. As we saw earlier, in traditional organizations, the span of control was narrow, about 5 to 8 people, but in today's organizations, the span of control is widened to 30 to 40 people, and in the case of production departments, there are even more than 100 people. In general, if the scope of the evaluation is out of about 15 people, the evaluation becomes difficult.

There are two important operational issues that may arise from the unit of evaluation. The first is the difficulty of comparison within organizations. In a traditional organization, it is easy to compare and evaluate because the characteristics of the tasks performed by the members of the evaluation unit are similar. On the other hand, it is not easy to directly compare with each other because members who perform different tasks are often working together within one organization. This adds to the difficulty for managers to evaluate.

The second issue is the difficulty of comparison among members of organizations. In particular, it becomes more difficult in the case of relative evaluation. For example, as in Korean companies, when evaluation results are reflected in promotion, they are not used only within the unit organization, but are expanded to the company or business unit level. In the case of Western companies, where managers are given personnel authority, the evaluation results become personnel decisions because the units of comparison between members to be reflected in wage or promotion decisions or the units of evaluation evaluated by managers are not different. On the other hand, in the case of Korean companies, where the decision-making authority for human resource management is concentrated in the HR department, all evaluation results conducted by each department are collected for personnel decision-making. At this time, since each manager has different evaluation tendencies, it is not easy to reflect the evaluation results of each unit department as it is, so various adjustment methods are used. If the evaluation unit and comparison unit are different, there is a high possibility that fairness issues will arise, and the side effect of increasing the political behavior of managers occurs.

2.6 Evaluation Cycle (when)

The evaluation cycle, that is, the number of evaluations, should consider both the accuracy of evaluation and the complexity of management. As the number of evaluations increases, the accuracy of evaluation may increase. However, as the burden on the evaluators increases, the possibility of biasing toward formal evaluations increases. In addition, the complexity of management increases the cost of management. However, if the number of evaluations is too small, that is, if the evaluation period is too long, various errors including a recency error that consider only recent actions and achievements occur due to the limitations of the evaluators' memory. As a way to solve this dilemma, companies limit formal evaluations to once or twice a year, but have managers give feedback to subordinates on a quarterly basis.

2.7 Disclosure of Evaluation Results (where)

Disclosure of evaluation results refers to providing feedback to members with the specific details and scores of evaluation. Depending on the degree of disclosure, this could range from making all scores publicly available to all employees to providing no information at all. In the past, Korean companies had a practice of not disclosing information at all, but recently many companies are providing information.

Disclosure of evaluation information to members has advantages and disadvantages. As an advantage, members can identify their strengths and weaknesses along with the evaluation results and use them to improve future performance or develop capabilities. In addition, the acceptance of the evaluation can be increased as the evaluation result is fed back. When the evaluation results are disclosed, evaluators also become more cautious in their evaluation and try to maintain objectivity and fairness. On the other hand, as a disadvantage, there is always the possibility of errors in evaluation, and disclosing the evaluation results can cause conflicts between leaders and subordinates. If the evaluation result is good, satisfaction and acceptance are high, but if it is not, dissatisfaction may accumulate and deteriorate the atmosphere of the organization. When the evaluation results are disclosed, managers become more cautious about evaluation, and consequently, evaluators adopt a conservative attitude, which may increase the tendency to centralize or leniency effect. In companies where the disclosure of evaluation results is common, supervisors are required to provide feedback on evaluation results to subordinates and sign the evaluation form at the same time. Employees who do not agree with the outcome may express their dissatisfaction through the grievance process. In terms of performance management, it is desirable to disclose the evaluation results to improve the performance of employees.

3. Performance Management

Performance management is a strategic and integrated process for the organization to achieve sustainable performance through individual performance improvement and competency development.[10] It is also an ongoing communication process based on partnerships between managers and subordinates to clearly set and achieve goals. The process of performance management uses the plan-do-see, which is the general process of management. As seen in [Figure 6-1] Strategic Performance Management, it leads to performance planning-performance check-performance evaluation.

3.1 Performance Planning

Performance planning is the process of setting performance goals. This is a process in which managers and subordinates set goals for the work the employee needs to perform over a set period of time (typically one year) and plan how to achieve them. Previously, we looked at the management by objective(MBO) as a method of absolute evaluation. In performance management, the performance planning utilizes the MBO. As explained above, a well established goal, based on goal-setting theory, induces desirable behavior and produces desirable results through motivation. What is discussed in the goal setting process is not only the goal and the achievement plan, but also how the goal has been achieved, what obstacles may occur in the goal achievement process, what kind of effort is needed to overcome them, and what kind of support is provided by the leader. Just as performance management itself is a communication process between leaders and subordinates, the goal setting process is not a unilateral goal assignment by the leader, but a communication process for exchanging opinions to derive more desirable results.

3.1.1 SMART Goals

Setting goals is not an easy task and should be considered as a task of overcoming trial and error through repeated learning. If performance management is not something that ends in one year, but is continuous, to increase the competencies and motivation of the members and ultimately to increase the performance of the organization, it is not desirable to expect perfection from the beginning. Many studies have been conducted on which goals are desirable. As a result of studies, it has been concluded that there is no single correct answer, but rather a criterion of a goal to be achieved. This is referred to as the SMART goal, after the first letter of the English language as a standard of desirable goals. First, are the goals specific? Second, is it measurable? Third, are the goals challenging and Achievable if the members work hard? Fourth, is the goal properly achieved (Relevant) because it was well connected with higher-level goals such as company-wide or departmental? Sometimes it is expressed as Realistic. Since realistic is similar to achievable, it is used here as relevant in this textbook. Fifth, is a deadline set (Time-bounded) to achieve the final goal? The SMART goal setting method is used in various ways. For example, it is also used in the Manifesto movement to audit whether the promises of candidates are appropriate in the elections of the National Assembly or local government. SMART is used as a criterion for voters to determine whether a candidate's promise is a temporary promise for an election or a feasible promise.

3.1.2 Key Performance Indicators (KPIs)

Key performance indicators are frequently used to check and evaluate whether goals have been achieved. The key performance indicators serve as a criterion for judging whether the set goals have been properly achieved.[11)] For example, if the HR department sets the goal of raising the morale of its members, evaluation is possible only if there is a standard to determine whether the morale of the members has increased. Key performance indicators that can be used at this time are the turnover rate, attendance rate, and employee satisfaction. It is not always necessary to use key performance indicators when setting goals. The evaluator can subjectively judge whether the goal has been achieved. However, in this case, various fairness or evaluation accuracy problems may arise. For this reason, not only private and public corporations but also government agencies are using the key performance indicators a lot.

KPIs are important as indicators to determine whether or not performance has been achieved, but more importantly KPIs serve as a guide for employees' behaviors. Before KPIs are established, there is tacit agreement within the organization what behavior is desirable. Because they are sometimes implicit, conflicts arise between leaders and subordinates when problems arise. KPIs have the advantage of clearly indicating which behavior is desirable by making it clear. However, at the same time, KPIs can be a double-edged sword because they serve as guidelines to guide employees' behaviors. The case of the police department above is a good example of this. If KPIs are used well, they can be of great help in improving organizational performance by mobilizing members in one direction. KPIs serve as indicators for judging whether performance

Table 6-8 SMART Goals

STANDARD	CHECK POINT
Specific	• Are the goals specifically expressed? • Are the goals focused on the end result?
Measurable	• Are there any criteria to measure whether the goal has been achieved?
Achievable	• Are the goals challenging and achievable with hard work? • Is it realistic compared to past performance or the average of the comparison group?
Relevant	• Are the goals properly linked to the goals of higher-level organizations, such as company-wide or departmental?
Time-bounded	• Is there a final deadline for achieving the goal?

National Police Agency in Korea KPI Case

Many organizations tend to think of KPIs as easy. KPIs can be disastrous if misused. Let's take the example of the police department in Korea. A few years ago, there was a time when the whole country was noisy over child molestation cases. In the midst of this, there was a case in Kyunggi province where a former convict of raping a minor tried to kidnap an elementary school student and failed. The problem arose when the police tried to cover up the incident. At first, the police tried to treat the attempted kidnapping of an elementary school student as a simple assault. Perhaps the sexual assault case would have been buried had it not been for public attention, but it was caught in the antennas of journalists, and the police were smitten by the media. The police's negligence has come to the fore, but the question is why this behavior occurred. The reason was the setting of the KPI. When the National Police Agency introduced performance management, the crime rate and arrest rate were set as KPIs. The crime rate should be lowered to get a good score and the arrest rate should be raised. It was especially important to lower the violent crime rate. As a result, the police changed violent crimes to simple crimes and reported them. In addition, since the arrest rate must be increased, efforts have been made to increase the arrest rate for even small crimes. It is for this reason that the rate of misdemeanor crimes among ordinary citizens has risen significantly. Due to the wrong KPI, the original duty of the police is disappearing all over the place.[12)]

has been achieved and at the same time providing guidelines on how members should act. Leaders need to think carefully about how an organization's KPIs can affect their members. Conversely, KPIs should be set so that they can induce desirable behaviors required of members in the organization.

As one of the KPIs, a balanced score card (BSC) is widely used by companies recently. Balanced performance indicators are presented as a way to solve problems that arise in long-term sustainable management when a company only targets financial indicators. BSC establishes KPIs from four perspectives: finance, customer, internal process, and learning and growth. <Table 6-9> shows examples of KPIs based on balanced performance indicators. Leaders who adopt BSC in their organization need to understand BSC, determine where their organization's mission and vision contribute to the company's BSC, and set KPIs.

3.2 Performance Review

Performance review is a step that managers use to improve the performance of organizational members. Everyone wonders if their work is going well and what other people think of their work. People are afraid of critical feedback, but they also look forward to it. It is similar to when students take an exam and then wonder whether they did well on the exam or not. On the other hand, managers also want to give genuine feedback to their subordinates. Judging from his own experience, the problems of subordinates who are juniors at work are also clearly visible. Leaders expect members

Table 6-9 **KPI by Balanced Score Card (BSC)**

Finance	• Per capita sales • Profit excluding labor cost (net profit per person - labor cost) • Net income per capita • Contribution of labor cost (amount) • Year-over-year sales growth • Net profit growth compared to the previous year
Customer	• Sales target achievement rate by service • Service extension rate (renewal retainer fee/ existing fee) • Sales target achievement rate by industry • Growth rate of number of clients by industry • Customer retention rate • Customer satisfaction
Internal process	• Productivity • Working hours per person • Ratio of support personnel labor cost to sales • Ratio of sales force to total workforce • Customer development success rate (number of contracts/number of proposals)
Learning and growing	• Job satisfaction • Turnover rate • Job fatigue (job stress) • Contribution to knowledge management (quantitative and qualitative evaluation) • Participation in education and training (percentage) • Attendance • Education and training cost per person • Acquisition rate of completed credits by qualification • Language credits

to improve the performance a little bit more. Leaders also want their members not to go through the trial and error they experienced. Performance review is the application of this universal psychology to performance management process. The performance review consists of an analysis of the performance conducted by the members and an interview process in which the analyzed contents are fed back to the members.

3.2.1 Analysis of Performance

The first thing a manager should do for a performance review is to clearly analyze the results of the work performed by subordinates so far. Performance analysis is to determine whether the results of employees' work are desirable or not meeting expectations. Analysis of performance should also include analysis of the causes of results. If a desirable result is obtained, what is the cause, and conversely, if an undesirable result is obtained, the cause should be clearly analyzed. Broadly speaking, the causes of performance results shown by members can be divided into two categories. The first is a personal cause. Personal causes are internal factors that are attributable to the performer herself or himself. Personal causes are divided into competency and motivation, as emphasized several times in this textbook. Second, it is a situational cause. Situational causes refer to external environmental factors that members have no control over and are not responsible for, but that can influence members' behavior.

What managers should be aware of when analyzing performance is that there is a psychological difference in the causes of problems between leaders and subordinates. When a problem occurs, different psychological mechanisms are activated for leaders and subordinates. Leaders are more likely to commit the fundamental attribution error. Attribution refers to the tendency to infer the cause of a behavior, especially when subordinates' performance is low, to attribute the cause of the problem to the individual responsibility of the actor while underestimating the situation. In other words, when there is a problem in the performance of subordinates, managers tend to find the root cause in personal factors (competency and motivation) rather than situational factors. On the other hand, subordinates are more likely to commit a self-serving bias. Self-serving bias refers to the tendency to seek external causes in case of failure and seek internal factors in case of success. It is consistent with the Korean proverb, "If it goes well, it's my credit, if it's bad, it's the fault of my ancestors." As a result, when subordinates have performance problems, they tend to look for the cause of the problem in external situational factors rather than looking for the cause of the problem internally (ie, lack of motivation or lack of competency).

Managers should understand the psychology of superiors and subordinates well in the performance management process. The most desirable solution is for the manager to open up all possible causes of the problem and analyze it closely. It is also a good way to make and use a situational factor checklist. The following are examples of questions to check the situation.

- Is work coordination and work arrangement between employees appropriate?
- Are the necessary information or instructions for performing work appropriate?
- Is the equipment or other support needed to perform the job adequate?
- Is the supply of raw materials, parts and other necessary materials smooth?
- Were the financial support necessary for the performance of the job adequately provided?
- Is teamwork active among team members?
- Were the education or training necessary for the job adequately provided?
- Have employees been given sufficient time to complete their tasks?
- Did the work environment interfere with the work performance of the members?
- Was the interest and support of colleagues adequately provided? (especially when a new employee or an experienced employee from outside)

3.2.2 Feedback Interview

After the performance analysis has been done, in order to give feedback to the members based on this, an interview with the members is required. Of course, feedback may be provided through e-mail or on-line. However, the most commonly used and most effective method is a face-to-face one-on-one interview. Interviews are one of the activities that Korean company managers lack the most and feel uncomfortable with when compared to global company managers. Managers in Korea think that it is unnecessary to conduct separate interviews because they have a strong collectivistic culture and there are many places to eat lunch or have a dinner together. However, it is important to avoid discussing personal matters in a group or at a dinner party. Interviewing is one of the leadership competencies that managers must be familiar with, and it is a skill that can be developed through training.

For a feedback interview to be successful, there are a few things that must be kept in mind. The first condition for the success of the feedback interview is how much the manager values feedback and prepares thoroughly in advance. Pre-preparation includes checking the personnel records and observation records of performance of the subordinates. In addition, it is good to prepare subordinates as well, and it is desirable to inform them of the schedule and purpose of the interview in advance. By doing this, leaders can eliminate the anxiety that subordinates will experience during the interview process in advance and change the passive attitude of defending herself or himself.

Second, it is clear that the purpose of the interview is to improve performance. One of the most common mistakes managers make is dealing with subordinates with emotional outbursts. The purpose of the interview is not to hold employees accountable for what happened or to relieve your anger. It is also undesirable to criticize the individual, discuss the past, or attempt to induce guilt in subordinates during the interview process. <Table 6-10> gives examples of common mistakes managers make during feedback interviews. Third, in order for a feedback interview to be successful, communication skills must be used well, and questions and listening are particularly important. Giving feedback doesn't necessarily mean that leaders drive every conversation. Rather, listening is more effective than leading conversation. In addition, it is necessary to encourage subordinates to understand the cause of the problem and think of a solution on their own through active questioning along with listening.

Table 6-10 Manager's Common Mistakes in Feedback Interview Process

- Accusations against individuals
  - Are you listening to me?
  - You don't even know what you're talking about, do you?
- Discussion focused on the past
  - What the hell have you done in the last five years?
  - If you had collected coins every time you were late, you would have already been rich.
- Attempts to induce guilt
  - If you were thinking of our company, you wouldn't have done this.
  - Do you know how much I care for you?
- Unsolicited advice and instructions
  - Is this the only way to solve the problem?
  - Don't say nonsense, finish work by tonight and go to my desk with the results.
- Aggressive questions
  - How the hell did you come to that conclusion?
  - Can't you keep your posture straight when giving your opinion?
- Expression of disbelief
  - I think I said that last time.
  - Can you really finish it on time?

3.3 Performance Evaluation

Systematic aspects such as standards and methods of personnel evaluation were discussed earlier. Here, we will mainly discuss the role of managers. When a manager evaluates from a fair and objective point of view, in itself, it increases the acceptability of evaluation results, but it also improves organizational performance by improving the performance of employees.

3.3.1 Rater Error in Evaluation

The most important thing managers should pay attention to in the evaluation process is that they should try not to make a rater error. Errors occur due to various causes in decision-making about people. Managers must always be vigilant because errors can also occur when managers evaluate their subordinates. Leaders need to be aware of what errors can occur and what efforts are needed to reduce them. It is impossible to completely eliminate errors. If a manager thinks he's not making any mistakes, he's mistaken. Rather, the evaluation may not be made more fairly due to the mindset that there is no error. The first step in reducing error is acknowledging that you can make mistakes. According to the research results so far, the errors that managers make in the process of performing the evaluation are diverse: halo error, horn error, recency error, and similar-to-me error, contrast error, restriction of range error, etc. The definition for this is shown in <Table 6-11>. In what situations evaluation errors occur and what countermeasures are available, we will look at the following.

Table 6-11 Evaluator Errors

Halo Error	An error in which the evaluator applies some criteria to all others, or makes an evaluation based on the evaluator's comprehensive impressions.
Horn error	It is similar to the halo error, but it means an error of evaluating in a negative direction.
Recency error	An error in which the evaluation is influenced more by recent events than the past or overall performance or behavior of the person being evaluated.
Similar-to-me error	The error in which the evaluator evaluates people more favorably of the person who is similar to him or her.
Contrast error	An error that occurs when an evaluator evaluates in comparison to others rather than by given objective criteria.
Restriction of range	An error in which the evaluator evaluates the subjects and evaluates them within a limited score without appropriately distributing them in the form of a normal distribution. There are three types: leniency, which values too high, central, which focuses on the medium, and severity, which values too low.

Figure 6-6 The Evaluator's Evaluation Process

3.3.2 Causes of Evaluation Errors and Countermeasures

An evaluation error means that the evaluator assigns a score different from the true score for the subordinate's performance with prejudice or intention. The behavior evaluated by the manager proceeds in the process of observation-perception-judgment-evaluation as shown in [Figure 6-6]. Errors in evaluation may occur throughout the evaluation process.

1) Observation

In order for the evaluation to take place, it is necessary to be able to sufficiently observe the process and results of the work performed by the subject of evaluation. However, observations may not be made for various reasons, such as subordinates working outside the company. Alternatively, since observation is made but evaluation is performed only once or twice a year, a recency error may occur in which past events are not remembered and only recent results are remembered. In order to prevent this, the manager should make an effort to observe sufficiently, and make a note of observation and keep it as a document. Many companies are providing evaluation diaries to help managers or making them available online. If you are physically in a position where observation is difficult, you should make an effort to listen to the opinions of others. 360-degree evaluation can also be used in this case.

2) Perception

People do not perceive all the information that comes through their eyes. If you're thinking of a different person while sitting opposite each other, you may not be able to remember the person's actions or words. Even if observation has been made in the evaluation process, selective perception can be achieved in which only the desired part is perceived. In particular, serious errors occur when the evaluator perceives and evaluates with a bias toward a specific group based on past specific experiences or erroneous information. For example, if a perception is based on a particular region, a particular school, or prejudice against men or women, the evaluation will be distorted. If you like something, you don't perceive the bad parts and try to perceive only the good parts. The opposite is also true. To reduce this, it is important for managers to acknowledge that they may be biased. If you rely only on your own memory, there is a high possibility of errors in the perception process. Therefore, it is necessary to observe objective events, take notes, and keep them in the record. In order to prevent such errors, the company allows the second-ranking person who is the manager of the manager to adjust the results of the manager's evaluation.

3) Judgment

In order to evaluate, it is necessary to determine whether the subordinates' behavior perceived by the manager is desirable or undesirable. Errors can also occur here. For example, the halo error, which sees only one good thing and evaluates everything as positive, or the horn error, which sees one thing wrong and evaluates everything negatively, may occur. Errors in the judging process occur while comparing the subject of evaluation with others without seeing them as they are. There is a similar-to-me error where you want to give a higher score just because subordinates have similar hobbies, values, religious or political positions, or even because you and your subordinates are close to home. Alternatively, the contrast error of managers judging the rest of their employees against very good subordinates often occurs. As before, clear observation and recording are essential for managers to reduce errors that occur in the judgment process. In a company, as one of the efforts of managers to reduce errors that occur in the decision-making process, training for evaluators is provided. There are various training methods, but the most effective is to adjust the comparability of the evaluation standards that exist among the evaluators, and the representative training method is frame-of-reference training.[13)] Frame-of-reference training is a training method that allows managers to unify their eye level through case studies, simulations, or role play with the standards presented by the company rather than their own standards.

4) Rating

As the final process of the evaluation, it is left to give the final score to the subject to be evaluated, but errors may occur even at this time. In particular, when absolute evaluation is carried out, it is caused by managers intentionally limiting the use of only a part of the evaluation scale. Collectively, this is called restriction or range error. Using only high scores is called leniency, using only low scores is called severity, and using only moderate scores is called central tendency. The area used may differ depending on the characteristics of the manager, but the cause is mostly the same. This occurs because you are not sure about the difference between your subordinates or you are afraid of backlash from your subordinates, so you can't confidently give a score. When the observation, perception, and judgment of the evaluation process described above are not properly performed, the manager is tempted to limit the scope. In order to reduce such errors, companies conduct relative evaluations or forced distribution methods to be adjusted by department. However, since these methods also have limitations, side effects may follow. Therefore, it is most important and fundamental for managers to have a fair and objective mind and to make an effort to evaluate based on clear observations and records.

4. Manager's Role

Performance evaluation and performance management should be used as tools to increase organizational performance and stimulate the motivation of members. To this end, the HR department must make continuous efforts to improve the system so that it can be designed fairly. However, no matter how well designed the system is, if it is not operated properly in the field, it becomes useless. Therefore, in order for performance evaluation and performance management to be successful, the role of managers who directly deal with employees in the field is important. The manager's role can be divided into two categories. First, the manager must act as a fair judge. The evaluation should be fair. In order to achieve a fair evaluation, the manager must play the role of a judge who can observe the performance of the members from an objective point of view. Second, managers should act as coaches. Managers should provide advice and feedback on what problems the members have in their performance and how to improve them. Here, you have to go beyond the role of a simple observer and play the role of a coach who directly leads the members and pays attention to each member.[14)] Sometimes, the role of a judge and the role of a coach are at odds. A good manager should be able to balance these two roles.

Ending Case

LG Display's Performance Evaluation and Performance Management[15)]

LG Display is the number one company in the global display market share and currently has about 50,000 employees. LG Display produces all the displays we encounter in our daily life, such as TVs, laptops, and smartphones, and is changing its product lineup from existing LCDs to OLEDs that enable high-definition and innovative designs. As a global company, LG Display operates 7 production subsidiaries, 7 sales subsidiaries, and 11 branch offices around the world, and strives to recruit and nurture talents with passion, expertise, and teamwork.

LG Display is seeking HRM to practice the "LG Way", the management philosophy of the LG Group, and the "meritocracy" of management that respects human beings. The purpose of performance evaluation is to improve individual performance to increase organizational performance and further link to company performance. However, the over-emphasis on meritocracy can lead to individualism that harms teamwork due to internal competition. In addition, there are various operational issues, such as intentional distortion of the evaluation results, which have a great influence on promotion. The evaluation system was initially created with good intentions, but unexpected issues arise during its operation.

LG Display strives to establish the evaluation system as a performance management process to improve performance beyond the evaluation of individual results. To this end, performance is evaluated by dividing it into achievements and capabilities. The 'achievement' evaluation result is used as a criterion for compensation differential, and the 'competency' evaluation result is used for development and promotion purpose.

The achievement evaluation consists of a 'KPI' evaluation and a 'contribution' evaluation. KPI evaluation measures the degree of achievement of performance goals assigned to individuals in connection with company-wide goals. Contribution evaluation is an item that recognizes the part that is difficult to measure with KPI alone, or that silently performs tasks that are not revealed for the performance of the organization. In addition to the goals given to individuals, the company evaluates the contribution to organizational performance and gives additional points. It accounts for about 20% of the overall achievement evaluation score. Achievement evaluation is ranked relative to each position. The evaluation grade is divided into five stages, S, A, B, C, and D, and strict relative evaluation is carried out. S and A grades are around 30%, and low performance C and D grades average about 10%.

Competency evaluation includes an annual competency review for all employees and a regular competency evaluation for promotion targets. The competency review is conducted at the end of every year along with the achievement evaluation, and the strengths and points of improvement of the employees are described in descriptive form. Competency review is used only for the purpose of providing feedback to the subordinates. It is used purely for the purpose of development. The regular competency evaluation is conducted only for candidates for promotion in the corresponding year. In the regular competency evaluation, absolute evaluation is first conducted for each individual, and then relative ranking is performed at the overall organizational level. In the case of regular competency evaluation, multiple superiors, including senior managers, conduct evaluations in addition to direct superiors to enhance fairness. Regular competency evaluation uses a 3-point scale of 'exceed expectation', 'meet expectation', and 'need improvement' by using 9 competency items according to LG Display's talent image.

LG Display is emphasizing four points for continuous performance management.

First, the line of sight (alignment) is strengthened. Personal goals and evaluation items are set in connection with the organizational goals. Make sure employees have a clear understanding of the organization's strategy and mission so that they can know what they need to do for organizational success through individual performance goals.

Second, clarify the link between performance and reward. Clearly present criteria in advance of what kind of reward can be obtained when organizational and individual goals are achieved. It also clearly defines what the performance goals are and what competencies are needed to achieve them. Performance goals are set at a challenging but feasible level to match the individual's competency level.

Third, it induces individual performance improvement and competency development through continuous monitoring and coaching so that evaluation can become a continuous performance management process centered on development.

Fourth, try to strengthen the evaluator's leadership. Emphasizes the role of managers to improve member performance. In particular, it encourages them to become coaches, mentors, and counselors, rather than staying in the role of a judge (police, judge) that determines superiority and inferiority among subordinates. To this end, leadership training is being strengthened.

LG Display is contemplating how to change the performance evaluation and performance management system in the future. The trend of changes in the evaluation system of global companies is also having an impact. This is because domestically, in the face of low growth, it is necessary to respond in terms of performance evaluation and performance management in line with issues related to overall human resource management, such as higher ranks due to organizational stagnation and the aging of the population. In addition, the company considers constantly about whether the current performance evaluation and performance management have a positive effect on the motivation of employees and have a positive effect on the present and future performance improvement.

Recently, global companies are moving away from the framework of relative evaluation through annual evaluations. There is also a report that, after the formal evaluation interview, which was held once a year, was eliminated altogether, the conversations about performance between managers and employees increased significantly. This also means that the burden of evaluation has been reduced and the focus has been on the discussion of performance itself. Companies that used to represent strong meritocracy in the past, such as GE and Microsoft, are now changing, judging that the old methods are no longer valid. Although these changes cannot be said to be suitable for all companies, LG Display is also studying the recent trend of changes in evaluations of global companies and researching whether changes are necessary.

The link between evaluation and compensation is also contemplating what changes are needed in the future. Currently, LG Display, like other Korean companies, is moving in the direction of giving organizational leaders the right to directly differentiate compensation for employees, but it is still in the early stages of implementation. In order to give leaders the authority to link evaluation and compensation in the future, the capabilities of the leaders of the organization in charge of evaluation should be increased, and this will take time.

Recently, there are many arguments for shifting to job-based HR. It is also true that the operation of job-based HR has many advantages. However, in order to apply job-based HR to actual companies, an appropriate environment must be prepared. At LG Display, internally, there is a sufficient consensus among its members about 'performance(meritocracy) based HR', which is the basis of performance evaluation and performance management. However, it is difficult to see whether the performance-based implementation method should be 'job-based' at a stage where employees can fully understand and accept it. However, from a long-term perspective, job-based HR and job-based performance evaluation and performance management are being carefully considered as one of the most appropriate response directions to adapt to the changing environment in the future.

Discussion Question

1. Wouldn't it be fair if we didn't take this into account when the relative evaluation by job position may have difficult or high uncertainties depending on the characteristics of the job or the characteristics of the organization?
2. As more global companies such as GE and MS have recently abandoned relative evaluation and introduced absolute evaluation, LG Display is also considering the introduction of absolute evaluation. Which evaluation method is preferable?
3. What changes can be expected in the performance evaluation and performance management systems of Korean companies in the future?

CHAPTER 7

Human Resources Development and Training

1. The Meaning and Importance of Human Resources Development
2. Competency Development Process
3. Education and Training
4. Evaluation of the Effectiveness of the Program

Learning Objectives

1. Understand that the importance of developing human resources is growing more and more recently in companies.
2. Three areas of human resource development can be explained.
3. Can explain the difference between a career in a traditional perspective and a new protein career.
4. Understand each stage of the competency development process.
5. Understand the different types of education and training.
6. Understand the four methods of evaluating the effectiveness of a development program.

Introductory Case

Manager Lee Sang-hwa was a researcher in charge of design at an auto parts company. As a woman, she was a leader in the company, and she wanted to be a role model for her juniors, too. Balancing home and work was not an easy task for her, but fortunately her spouse actively helped with the household chores and understood her career so that she was able to focus on her work. Manager Lee had sufficient capacity to contribute to the company and was also contributing greatly to the organization's performance. The parts designed by her were original and were well received by customers in terms of practicality. Through these efforts, she was selected as a key talent in the company.

However, due to the recent reorganization, she has been seriously thinking about whether or not to move to other company. Team leader Yoon Byung-hee, who worked with Manager Lee before the reorganization, understood the situation of manager Lee well and was aware of the manager Lee's work life and career goals. They talked a lot from time to time and Yoon sincerely tried to listen to her grievances. While working under leader Yoon, manager Lee felt that she was growing a lot and was able to have a stable work life. However, with the reorganization, a new team leader Kim Ki-jae was appointed. The newly appointed team leader, Kim, had no interest in Lee's working situations or personal circumstances. In particular, team leader Kim felt dissatisfied that employees put their personal time into competency development. He made it a habit to say that a workplace is not a school, and would not allow employees to participate in training programs conducted by outside institutions. Manager Lee seriously considered changing jobs. At the same time, she received an unofficial offer from a competitor to pay her a higher salary than her current salary. Despite indirectly expressing this intention to the team leader with passing words at a dinner party, Kim did not pay any attention to her. In the end, she regretted breaking up with her co-workers, but decided to move to another job. In particular, the most heartbreaking thing for manager Lee was that she did not show success in this job to the younger female employees who used her as a role model until the end.

Discussion Questions

1. What made Lee Sang-hwa decide to change job?
2. What does competency development mean for employees?
3. How did the actions of team leader Kim Ki-jae affect the members?
4. Does the glass ceiling phenomenon that women feel at work actually exist?
5. What would you do if you were Kim Ki-jae?

It has traditionally been customary in Korean companies (especially large corporations) to become executives after entering the company through a promotion ladder that leads to employee(Sawon)-assistant manager(Daeree)-deputy manager(Guajang)-manager(Bujang). Or, even if she or he did not become an executive, she or he could work until the retirement age. Even if it is not explicitly stated in the employment contract, it is a psychological contract that both the company and its members implicitly agree to. In a psychological contract relationship that presupposes lifelong employment, once you join the company, the company takes care of all career management and competency development. Individuals did what they were instructed to do according to the designed training program. Upon joining the company as a new employee, they received orientation while staying in company dormitory for a long time (sometimes 1 year). After the orientation, they were assigned to departments and jobs regardless of their intentions. When they were assigned to a department, they received on-the-job training (OJT), As time passed and they were promoted according to their seniority, training for the position manager was provided for each stage of promotion. The same program was applied to all members, and both managers and members had to follow the plan of the HR department without any special concerns.

However, this psychological contract changed significantly in the wake of the IMF crisis in the late 1990s. The company is no longer guaranteeing employment until retirement age. From the perspective of employees, if better working conditions and compensation are given, they are ready to change the company. A new psychological contract was made. In the new psychological contractual relationship, career management and competency development is working differently than in the past. First, there will be a scramble for excellent talent, the so-called war for talent. Since the level of talent becomes the level of competitiveness of the company, companies make efforts like a war to secure excellent talent. Second, the better the talent, the more interested in how the company will help them, how they will develop their capabilities, and whether their market value will increase. In other words, nurturing talents and improving their competencies has become very important to not only increase a company's competitiveness, but also to retain and motivate talented people. In particular, with the advent of the MZ generation, this phenomenon is becoming common.[1)]

In this chapter, the meaning and importance of human resource development, and specifically, what kind of process should be taken for competency development and education and training of human resources will be dealt with. In this process, managers are given responsibility and authority for nurturing and developing talent. As with other human resource management, managers and human resources departments should act as strategic partners to work together to enhance the competitiveness of the company by improving the competencies of its members.

1. The Meaning and Importance of Human Resources Development

1.1 Human Resources Development

Human resource development (HRD) refers to all activities that an organization supports so that its members can acquire the necessary competencies to achieve current and future goals. It includes three HRD components: individual development, career development, and organizational development.[2)]

First, individual development or education & training is an activity to improve the knowledge and skills that each member lacks. Education is mainly conducted in the classroom to improve knowledge, and training is mainly conducted in the field to improve the skills of members. Individual development is very diverse, from socialization or orientation for new employees, OJT, manager education, internal/external MBA, promotion education, position education, executive education, and education for retirees in preparation for retirement.

Second, career development is an activity to match each member's individual career desires with the goals pursued by the organization. Career development includes career planning and career management. Career planning means that each member plans the activities necessary for his/her career from a long-term perspective in consideration of his/her interests, values, and competency level. Career management means to support and manage the career plan established in this way at the organizational level so that it can be accomplished as intended. Career development is a combination of individual effort and organizational effort, and with this meaning, the term career development planning (CDP) is often used in the corporate field.

Third, organizational development is carried out at the organizational level and refers to intentional activities to increase organizational effectiveness and the welfare and satisfaction of members. Organizational development activities include employee surveys, change management, company-wide quality management, various improvement activities such as Six Sigma or employee suggestion system, sports competitions, and foundation anniversary events.

The details of human resource development are beyond the scope of this textbook. Many universities are offering human resource development courses separately from human resource management. Courses are also offered in the Department of Educational Engineering, Industrial Psychology, or Education. It is a required subject for students who want to become professional in the human resources field. This chapter mainly deals with talent nurturing, competency development, and education and training necessary for human resource management from the perspective of managers and members.

1.2 Meaning of Career and Recent Trends

A career refers to the set of experiences and competencies that a person acquires in relation to a job or work during one's lifetime. As shown in [Figure 7-1], a career traditionally proceeds through five stages of growth, exploration, settlement,

Figure 7-1 Career from a Traditional Perspective

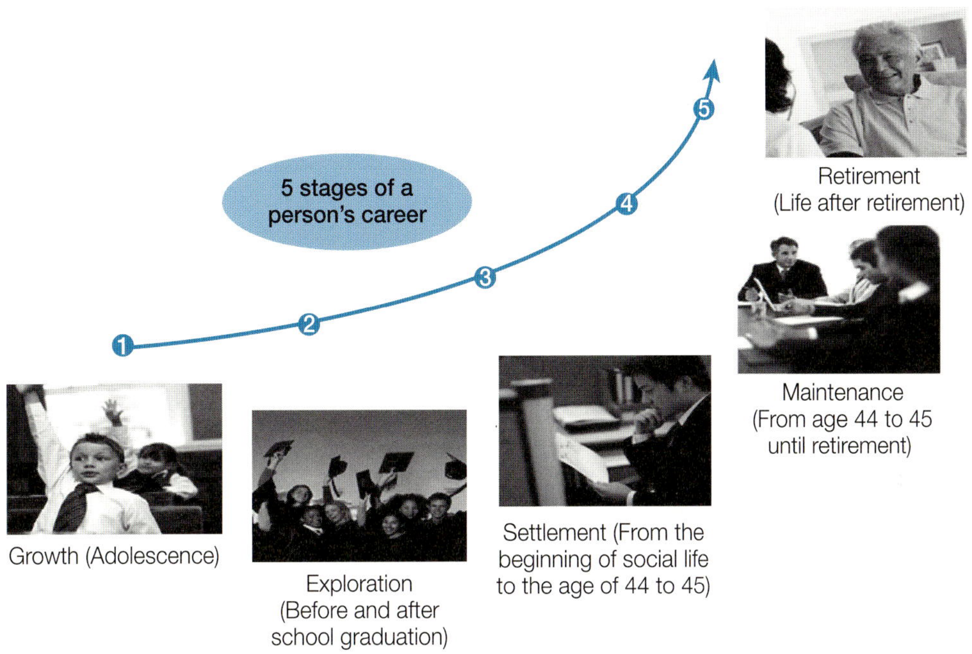

Figure 7-2 From the Traditional Ladder Model to the Protein Model

maintenance, and retirement during a person's lifetime. However, these traditional careers are gradually disappearing. The era of traditional careers that were guaranteed a lifetime employment with a higher rank, wage, authority, and stability over time at one job is gone, and a new era has come in which one has to choose and take responsibility for one's own career. Consequently, the individual ultimately takes responsibility for designing and developing a successful career. However, as long as they are members of the organization, managers should be interested in their careers. In an environment where the practice of lifelong employment is collapsing recently, what kind of career development opportunities can be provided by the organization is becoming an important criterion for selecting and maintaining a job.[3)]

The traditional career model is the promotion ladder model. It is a model in which a new employee joins the company and goes through the stages of his/her career, moving up the promotion ladder to the upper levels of the organization. In the traditional promotion ladder model, promotion is an important motivator. However, the new career model is the so-called protein career model.[4)] The protein career was given by Professor Douglas T. Hall, was derived from Proteus, the freely transformable sea god in Greek mythology. The new protein career model does not develop a career by using the promotion ladder, but increases one's own value through the improvement of competency. The recent tendency of many large Korean companies to reduce their ranks also reflects this new career model.[5)] For example, Samsung Electronics decided to reduce the existing 7-level position to 4 stages, discard the position title, and unify the title with 'Nim' or 'Pro'. In addition, LG Electronics reduced the rank from 5th level to 3rd level. The employee position (Sawon) left as it was, and assistant manager position(Daree) and deputy manager positions (Guajang) were reduced to 'Sunim', and manage positions were reduced to 'Chaegim'.

What the new career model requires is a career with the ability to freely change and adapt in a rapidly changing environment, that is, to increase employability. If office workers do not adapt to the new protein model, their careers will stagnate. As a result, when anxiety and stress in life increase, they cannot adapt to the organization and eventually become a problem employee. In order to overcome this, the individual needs constant development of competencies. Organizations and managers should also support individuals to continuously develop their own competencies through career management.

1.3 Key Talent Management

GE, called the Talent Academy, is famous for investing more in training than hiring. Unlike Google and Microsoft, GE prefers graduates from US state universities such as Michigan and Wisconsin rather than graduates from famous private universities such as Stanford, Harvard or Yale.[6)] GE implemented a policy to discover talents with high potential rather than those already outstanding and develop them into excellent talents. The concept developed by GE to nurture talented people into leaders is the leadership pipeline.[7)] To help them grow by defining the competencies required for each stage of leadership, leading to working-level managers - beginner managers - middle managers - area managers - business general managers - group managers - corporate managers (CEOs), and giving them trials and challenges. These leaders are now serving as CEOs not only at GE, but also at other companies. Korean companies are also investing in nurturing talent by benchmarking GE's leadership pipeline model. [Figure 7-3] shows the leadership pipeline model of Korean conglomerates.

Figure 7-3 **Leadership Pipeline Model of a Large Conglomerate in Korea**

1.4 Subjects and Responsibilities for Competency Development

1.4.1 Human Resources Department

The HR department and HR manager design and implement the competency enhancement of employees from a macroscopic and long-term perspective of the organization. They explore training programs to achieve organizational goals from a company-wide perspective, establish a formal competency development system, and provide specific programs. They also play a role in identifying the needs of individual members of an organization for competency development and supporting members to recognize the need for competency development on their own, and cooperate with managers in this regard. Also, after the competency development program is provided, its effectiveness is evaluated and improvement plans are established.

1.4.2 Manager

If the HR department sets the need and goals for competency development from a company-wide point of view, the managers who lead the unit determine the need for competency development needed by each individual together with their organizational members. And managers encourage subordinates to actively participate in competency development programs. In addition, in many competency development programs, such as OJT, coaching, mentoring, job rotation, and succession planning, managers directly participate and play a role in strengthening the competency of members. In particular, in recent years, managers have been increasingly emphasizing the responsibility for developing their members' competencies.

1.4.3 Individual

The ultimate responsibility for competency development rests with the individual members. Individuals must set their own career visions and goals and understand for themselves what competencies are needed to achieve them. Individuals need to know what a career is, why they are responsible for their own career management, where they can receive support for competency development, from whom they should receive support, and when appropriate competency development is needed in their career stages. In addition, it is necessary to familiarize themselves with all aspects of career management and competency development, such as how to develop competency. HR departments and managers can support individuals, but it must be individuals who must act.

2. Competency Development Process

The need for competency development arises from the difference between the members' current competency level and expected competency level. Through competency development, it aims to promote learning and improve the performance of its members, ultimately strengthening the competitiveness of the organization. A variety of competency development processes are suggested by scholars, but here, the four-step competency development process is used from the manager's point of view. First, the assessment stage confirms the need for competency development, and needs analysis at the organizational, task, and individual level is performed. The second stage is the direction setting stage, in which the goal of fostering and capacity development is set. This is the stage in which members understand the growth potential within the organization and set a career vision. Third, as the development stage, it is the process of implementing a specific program to improve the competency of members by narrowing the gap between the current level and the expected level. There are various development programs used by companies, and examples of companies using them are also introduced here. In the fourth evaluation stage, it is identified whether the goal of the competency development effort has been achieved, which parts are insufficient, and what is needed for improvement. The evaluation phase is dealt with at the end of this chapter.

2.1 Assessment Stage

The assessment is a stage to grasp the current competency level of the members as a starting point for nurturing talent and developing competency. Most managers have an intuitive sense of what competencies their subordinates lack. For example, the accounting team leader knows that the new employee is not familiar with basic accounting books. The head of the R&D department feels the need for team members to acquire knowledge about new technology trends. However, it is not desirable to judge the need for competency development solely based on intuition. Depending on the manager's preference or interest, it may be biased toward a specific area, which prevents systematic competency development. Also, competency development has no effect if it is determined only by the unilateral needs of the organization. The career needs of each member should also be taken into account. It is important to ensure that the needs of the organization and the needs of the members are in harmony. In the assessment stage, the current competency level (as-is) of the members should be measured to identify the difference between the desired competency level (to-be), which is the next stage.

2.1.1 Organizational Analysis

Organizational analysis refers to a review of factors throughout the organization that will affect competency development activities. Organizational analysis is an activity to determine what the capabilities required to achieve the goals pursued by the organization are and how close the current organizational competency level is to the required competency level. Developing and nurturing the competencies of employees is an essential process for improving organizational performance, which is the basic starting point for human resource management. Organizational performance is related to the vision, mission, and strategy pursued by the organization. Therefore, the competency development of members comes from the organization's vision, mission, and strategy. Organizational diagnosis from a company-wide perspective is mainly carried out by the HR department or the education and training department.

On the other hand, organizational diagnosis conducted at the level of individual unit organizations should be carried out under the responsibility of the department head of the unit organization. Many companies are setting up competency models for each department or job group in order to select new employees and develop and evaluate the competencies of members. For example, Eli Lilly, a multinational pharmaceutical company, has created and utilized a competency model in which the competency of the HR department is defined in detail by classifying skills, knowledge, and other characteristics.[8)] As shown in [Figure 7-4], Eli Lilly's HR department selected six competencies, including creative problem-solving, customer focus, resource utilization, HR technical expertise, influence, and effective communication, and skill, knowledge, and others (beliefs, motives, traits, values).

2.1.2 Task Analysis

Task analysis is the process of confirming tasks necessary for individual job performance and knowledge, skills, and behaviors required for task performance. Task analysis is mainly performed through job analysis and is summarized and arranged in the job description. In Chapter 4, job analysis and job description were discussed. In the example of the job description presented in Chapter 4, we saw that the competency required for the job was presented. As such, companies describe in detail the KSA required for the job in the job description. Occasionally, the job description includes an

Figure 7-4 **Eli Lilly's HR Manager Competency Model**

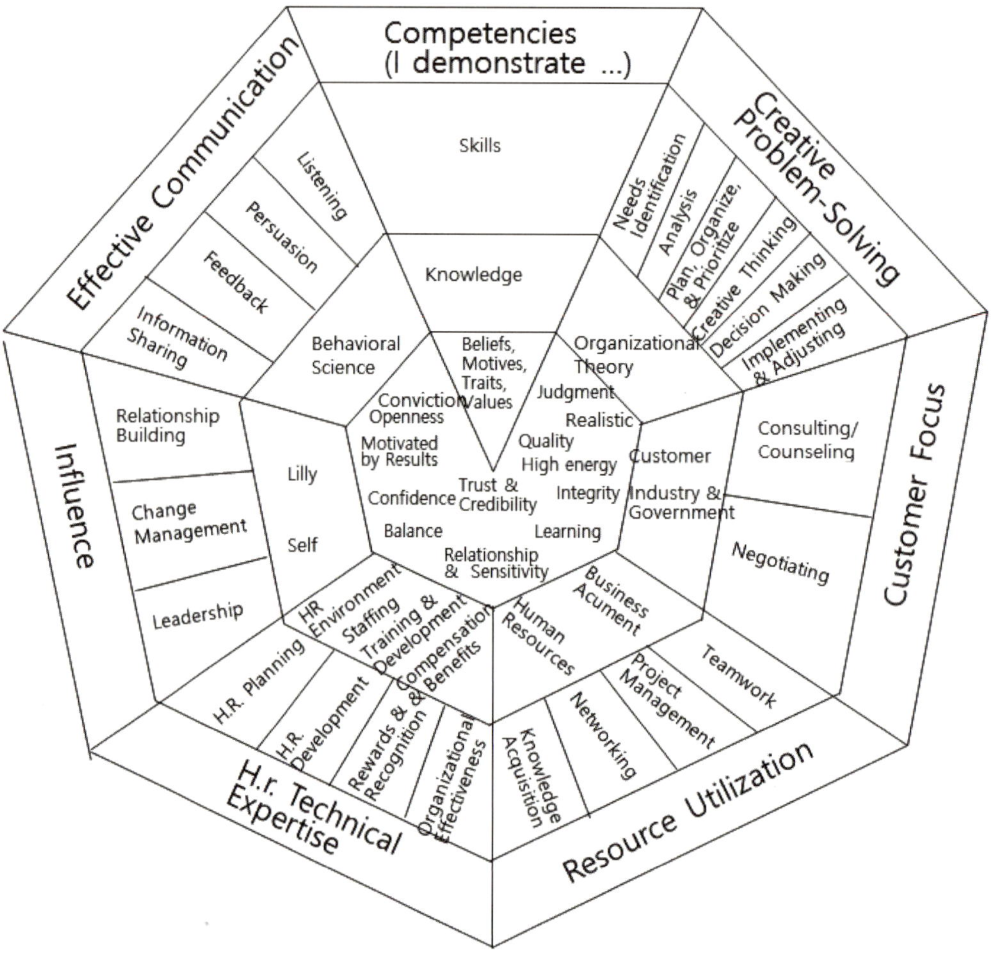

overview of the job, main activities and skills, knowledge, and competency necessary for job performance, as well as the contents of education and training required to develop the competencies required to perform the job.

As such, task analysis aims to understand the job itself, not the person in charge of performing the job. Confirmation of necessary competency through task analysis is made through the following steps.

- Job analysis for each job
- Write job description for each job
- Confirmation of tasks to be performed at the job
- Check the KSA required to perform the task
- Confirmation of KSA that can be developed through HRD programs
- Priority selection of KSA that can be developed

2.1.3 Individual Analysis

Organizational analysis and task analysis are the processes of judging areas requiring development at the organizational level, whereas individual analysis is the process of determining areas requiring development at the individual level. It is the process of determining where individuals who perform various jobs are lacking in the areas that need development in their current job performance or the competencies required to achieve future career goals. In individual analysis, there are many self-assessment tools that each individual can judge for himself or herself. Members can use these tools to determine their strengths, weaknesses, and areas of interest. In addition, managers of human resources departments or unit organizations can analyze each individual's competency level from an objective point of view. Next, we will look at the methods of individual analysis that are frequently used by companies.

1) Personality Test

For personality tests, MBTI and DiSC are well known in addition to the Big 5 personality test tools discussed in Chapter 5. MBTI (Myers-Briggs Type Indicator) is a personality type indicator designed to be used in daily life based on Jung's theory of psychological types.[9] Through self-report items, each person's preference is found when recognizing and judging such as extroversion/introversion, sensing/intuition, thinking/feeling, judging/perceiving, and combining four preference indicators to classify 16 personality types. [Figure 7-5] shows the 16 personality types of MBTI. DiSC classifies people into four types according to how they perceive their environment and their power in the environment: Dominance, Influence, Steadiness, and Conscientiousness. Personality doesn't change often, so it's very difficult to change through development. However, understanding your personality helps you understand yourself. In addition, since there are characteristics suitable for each job, it is necessary for managers to understand the personality characteristics of members for future job assignments or career development.

Figure 7-5 **MBTI**

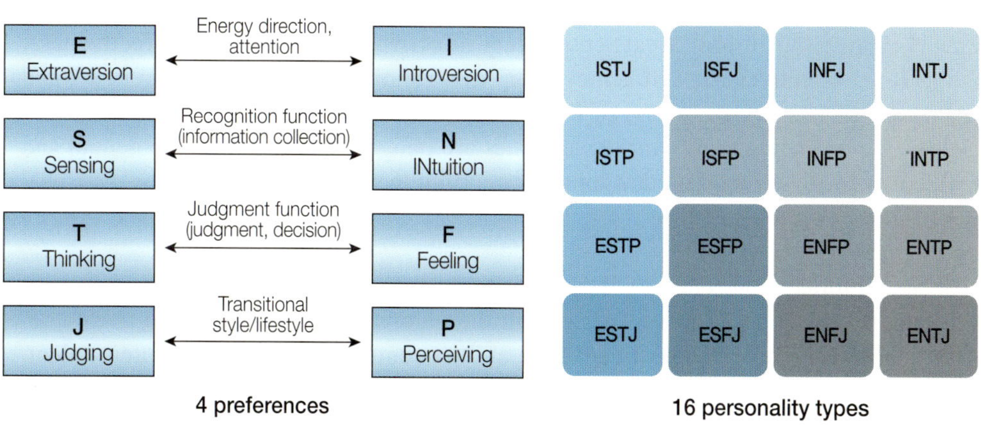

2) Competency Diagnosis

Competency diagnosis is a method for determining the level of competency that members need now or in the future. Competency diagnosis can be judged by the members themselves or by the manager. <Table 7-1> shows an example of a competency diagnosis checklist. In the example, the diagnosis proceeds according to two criteria. First, the need for development determines whether the competency is necessary for performing the current job or for the future career. On a three-point scale, the higher the score, the more urgently needed competency. Second, the current level is whether the member currently possesses the corresponding competency. On a three-point scale, the higher the score, the higher the degree of lack of competency. The total score is calculated by multiplying the two criteria. Competencies corresponding to a score of 9 are those that employees need immediately to perform their current job or for future careers, and urgently need to be developed.

3) Performance Evaluation

The results of performance evaluation and performance management discussed in chapter 6 are also used as data for personal analysis. In particular, performance management, which checks employees' performance improvement and develops them through coaching, is closely related to talent development and competency development. However, since performance evaluation measures the current job performance process, there is a limit to nurturing and developing talents from a future-oriented perspective. In order to compensate for this, many companies conduct the following potential evaluation in parallel.

4) Potential Evaluation

Potential evaluation(or appraisal) is also called promotionability forecasts. If performance evaluation mainly focuses on current job performance, potential evaluation focuses on the growth potential of employees. In particular, companies continuously evaluate the potential of talented people who can grow into core leaders, and if there are any shortcomings, companies try to supplement them through development. Multinational company Philips, for example, conducts a potential evaluation of key leader candidates every three years.[10)] In Philips, potential evaluation of various items is carried out in four areas: conceptual effectiveness, operational effectiveness, interpersonal effectiveness, and achievement motivation. In addition, the strengths and weaknesses of a leader are analyzed in a narrative form. Managers in Philips who have key leadership candidates as their subordinates are obliged to evaluate their potential and provide them with appropriate development opportunities.

5) Succession Planning

Succession planning refers to selecting and nurturing successors in advance in case a vacancy occurs in an important position in the organization. This serves to prevent an unexpected leadership vacuum in advance and prevent the leakage of excellent talent. In this respect, succession planning functions as an in-house selection process, which is why it is often equated with replacement planning. However, the succession plan goes

Table 7-1 Competency Diagnosis Checklist

Competency Diagnosis Checklist

- Check your own competency level based on the following criteria. The competencies presented here are examples. In fact, you will be able to find out what your job-related competencies are.

◈ Instruction

- **Development Needs**: Whether the competency is necessary for the job or future career
  1. Development is not urgent.
  2. Development will be necessary in a near future.
  3. It is the competency required to perform the job immediately.

- **Current level**: To what extent do you have the relevant job competency?
  1. It has reached a considerable level even now.
  2. It is equipped to some extent now, but more effort is needed.
  3. It is not enough to interfere with the immediate performance of the job.

- **Score = need for development × current level**

  1-3 points: Areas of competency excluded from the focus of development

  4-6 points: Competency areas that are not urgently needed but are needed in the future

  9 points: Competency areas that urgently need to be the focus of development

COMPETENCY TYPE	ABILITY	DEVELOPMENT NEED	CURRENT LEVEL	SCORE
Basic capacity	Foreign language			
	Database			
	Data analysis technique			
	Utilization of software			
	Information gathering			
	Presentation skills			
Knowledge	Change of management environment			
	Understanding the industry			
	Understanding competition companies			
	Customer's disposition			
	Responsible work expertise			
	Related business knowledge			
	Ethics code			
	Company business issues			
	Company regulations			
	Organizational operation and procedures			
	Organization management			

COMPETENCY TYPE	ABILITY	DEVELOPMENT NEED	CURRENT LEVEL	SCORE
Knowledge	HR management			
	Market research method			
	Six sigma			
Inter-personal skills	Peer relationship			
	Understanding of others			
	Relationship with boss			
	Conversation			
	Memo			
	Persuasion			
	Interview skills			
System skills	Coordination			
	Build teamwork			
	Negotiation skills			
	Systemic thinking			
	Prediction for the future			
	Logical thinking			
Management skills	Reasoning			
	Strategic thinking			
	Situational adjustment			
	Experimentation			
	How to generate ideas			
	Customer consultation			
	Project management			
	Time management			
	Business process/value chain			
Problem solving skills	Stress management			
	Crisis management			
	Problem-solving			
	Document writing			
	Planning			
	Decision-making			
	Schedule management			

beyond the meaning of a contingency plan in case of a vacancy. This is an activity to enhance the competitiveness of a company by discovering and nurturing outstanding talents who will be leaders in the future, and improving their competencies.[11] Managers in leadership positions have to think about how to nurture key talents beyond simply selecting their own successors. For example, GE's succession plan is famous. Legendary CEO Jack Welch announced that he would implement a succession plan ten years before he left office. He has since encouraged to develop the potential of young talent through competition among potential leaders. In the end, Jeffrey Immelt was selected as the next CEO out of about 100 candidates. Korean companies have also been institutionalizing succession planning recently. <Table 7-2> is an example of succession planning implemented by a Korean conglomerate. For each organization's leader position, the 1st to 3rd positions are selected in advance, and for each candidate, the development results of the past two years are recorded and a development plan for the next two years is established.

6) Assessment Center

The assessment center or competency assessment center is a method in which a multi assessors evaluate the behavior of the person being assessed in various multi-situation using various multi-methods. The assessment center is widely used in global companies as a method to determine the capabilities of key leaders or executives who are eligible for promotion. It is also used by the Korean government to select candidates for high-ranking civil servants. Unlike traditional performance evaluation in which superiors evaluate from a subjective point of view, the assessment center has high reliability and validity because a large number of trained evaluators objectively evaluate it through

Table 7-2 **Succession Plan Example**

1st place	Personal Information	Name	Belong	Tier/Level
		Age	School/ Major	Language/ Certificate
	Development results over the past two years		Development plan for the next two years	
2st place	Personal Information	Name	Belong	Tier/Level
		Age	School/ Major	Language/ Certificate
	Development results over the past two years		Development plan for the next two years	
3st place	Personal Information	Name	Belong	Tier/Level
		Age	School/ Major	Language/ Certificate
	Development results over the past two years		Development plan for the next two years	

Table 7-3 Competency Techniques Matrix of Evaluation Center

Division	Case analysis	Oral presen-tation	Group discussion	Role play	In-basket technique	Oral fact search	Leader group task	Business game
Problem solving	●		●	●	●	●	●	●
Decision	●	●	●	●	●	●		●
Leadership			●	●	●		●	●
Empathy				●	●			
Administrative skills				●	●			
Empowerment				●	●			
Planning and organizing	●				●			●
Perseverance		●				●		
Teamwork			●					●
Oral communication		●	●	●		●	●	●
Written communication	●				●			

pre-made simulation tasks.[12)] As shown in <Table 7-3>, various evaluation techniques such as case analysis, oral presentation, group discussion, role play, and in-basket are used in the assessment center. Each technique evaluates the appropriate competencies. For example, case analysis assesses problem-solving, decision-making, planning and organization, and written communication skills, whereas oral presentation assesses decision-making, perseverance, and oral communication skills. In this way, it is possible to judge various aspects of members through various evaluation techniques.

2.2 Direction Stage

In the direction setting stage, the member understands the career vision in which he or she can grow within the organization and sets goals. This stage is closely related to the assessment stage because the setting of future career goals must be realistic and take into account the current competency level. It is up to each member to set the direction for competency development. However, the manager plays the role of supporting and coaching, and the HR department provides various types of information or professional consulting. In particular, the manager of a unit department should be able to understand the career needs and goals of the members in his/her department well, check the level of competency development through periodic interviews, and provide counseling for future career directions.

1) Career Path

The career path means providing information about the stages of promotion and career opportunities where individuals can grow within the organization. It is common to use a chart so that members can see the entire career path at a glance. In the case of Korean companies, the concept of career path is not well developed because there is the rank system and the rotation between jobs is active. This system is helpful in nurturing a generalist by allowing them to experience various fields, but it is an obstacle to growing as an expert in the field of work. On the other hand, companies with well-developed jobs have a job grade system centered on their jobs, so career paths for each job are clearly set. If you set your field of specialization in this organization, you can find out the career path as an expert that suits you. Recently, as Korean companies have introduced job-oriented HR management, more and more companies are providing career paths for job experts. [Figure 7-6] shows the career paths of financial experts in a large Korean company that have introduced job-oriented HR management.

2) Dual Career Ladder

The dual career ladder, also called the multiple career ladder, is mainly used by professional groups such as researchers in the R&D department. The dual career system offers members multiple career paths. The manager path is for those who want to grow as managers, just like in a general organization, and the expert path provides a way to grow as a professional even if you are not in a manager's position in a specific area of expertise. Due to the slimming of the organization and the introduction of downsizing

Figure 7-6 **Examples of Career Paths for Financial Experts at Large Corporations**

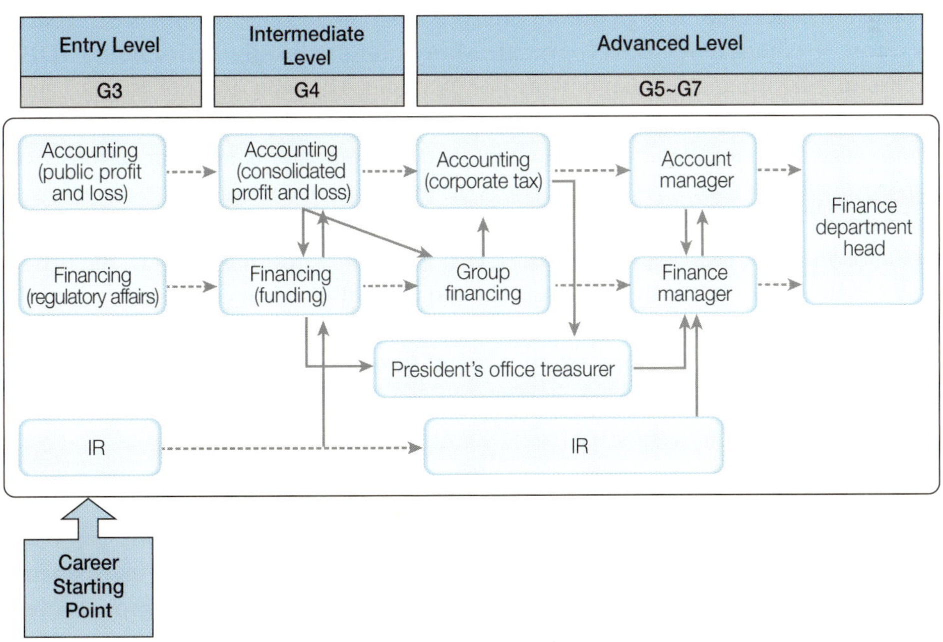

or the team system, the positions of managers are decreasing, and the role of managers is being replaced by the development of IT technology. Under these circumstances, the perception that promotion as a manager is the only way to survive in an organization is undesirable for both the organization and its members. For example, British Petroleum (BP), a multinational oil and gas producer, has created a dual career system so that its R&D and technical personnel can use their capabilities to the fullest, even if they are not in managerial positions.[13)] BP's dual career system maintains the existing rank system and designed a professional career path separately. By presenting the expert's competency step by step, employees can understand and prepare for their current competency level and the competencies needed to grow into experts in the future.

3) Job Posting Systems

Job posting systems are also treated as a type of internal recruitment in Chapter 5. When a vacancy occurs in an organization, it is to provide an opportunity to apply to internal members first before recruiting from outside. The reason why the internal Job posting system can play a role in setting the direction in the competency development process is that it presents in detail the competency or qualification conditions required for the job. It not only motivates employees who applied for the job posting competition, but also creates career goals for those who cannot apply right now, but who have the desire to enter the position when the opportunity arises in the future. In addition, even if you applied but were rejected, you will understand what aspects were lacking that led to your rejection, and through this, you will be able to set the direction for competency development.

4) Individual Development Planning

Individual development planning (IDP) is also an activity to set career goals and direction of competency development. Many companies are introducing IDP as a process of performance management. For example, Hanwha and the Korea Chamber of Commerce and Industry are introducing the IDP system. All members set goals for performance and competency improvement, and the company is opening various training courses to support them.[14)] <Table 7-4> is an example of individual development plans implemented by a large Korea company. Each member establishes a short-term and mid- to long-term career development plan (CDP) together with the manager, identifies the competencies required for this, and sets the target level for each competency. In order to achieve the competency development goals set in this way, specific detailed action plans are also established. In this process, if a member needs support from the company, the manager requests it to the HR department.

2.3 Development Stage

In the development stage, specific activities are executed to reduce the gap between the current level of competency (as-is) identified through the previous assessment and the target competency level (to-be) set through direction setting. In this process, the role of the manager of the unit organization and the role of the HR department in establishing

Table 7-4 Examples of Individual Development Plans of a Large Corporation in Korea

• CDP plan establishment

DIVISION	GOAL (DETAILED JOB DESCRIPTION)	DESIRED MOVE DEPARTMENT	MOVING HOPE TEAM
Short term (within 3 years)	Resource Development Specialist	CIC across □ CIC within □ CIC across □ CIC within □	Resource Marketing Team
Mid/long term (3 years~)		CIC across □ CIC within □ CIC across □ CIC within □	

• Competency and development plan

BIZ/JOB DEVELOP-MENT AREA	TARGET LEVEL	REQUIRED DEVELOPMENT SPECIFIC COMPETENCIES	DETAILED ACTION PLAN	
				ENTERPRISE SUPPORT NEEDS
Car	A0 level		• Field trip/structured training/education (in-house/external)/certificate/self-development	• External training/dispatch that requires the support of warriors • Coaching/mentoring of specific department managers/executives, etc.

the human resource development system are important. Managers should support their subordinates to improve their competency while performing their work in the field. This is done through coaching, mentoring, OJT, etc. The HR department provides support through a job rotation system that allows for systematically diverse job experiences and education and training programs that take place outside of work.

1) OJT

OJT (on-the-job training) is a learning process through experience in job performance. There is no better way to learn than experience. Official OJT conducted at the company level is mainly provided to new employees in a systematic way. There are existing employees in charge of OJT, and there are often manuals for training methods. Yuhan-Kimberly established in 1970 as a joint venture between Yuhan corporation in Korea and Kimberly-Clark in US, for example, first hires new employees as interns, then goes through a week's orientation before placing them on the job site.[15] After being assigned to the field, they undergo an official OJT and evaluation process for about three months. A senior employee is assigned to each new employee and gives training on how to operate the machine and how to respond in case of a problem. In addition to the official program for new employees, OJT is an essential way to continuously improve the competencies of members and prepare for the future of the organization.[16] In addition to participating in various projects and assigning new and challenging tasks, it can provide opportunities for members to learn through various activities. Providing these various opportunities is an important role for managers. OJT has the advantage of being able to save time and money for education and training besides that it is provided in a variety and flexibly on-site. In addition, through this process, OJT can make members understand the goals and strategic direction of the business and play a positive role in motivating them.

2) Coaching

Coaching plays a role in helping members to strive for competency improvement on their own. Chapter 6 also emphasized the manager's role as a coach. Unlike teaching, coaching is not a leader who decides what the members should do and directs and controls them to follow it, but rather helps members to understand their potential and to bring it out. Managers also need considerable competencies to be successful in coaching.[17] The leader who showed the best coaching leadership in Korea is coach Guus Hiddink, who was loved by the people by placing Korea in the semifinals of the 2002 World Cup. He not only improved the performance of the Korean soccer team, but also helped each player grow to become a world-class soccer player. As such, managers should pay attention not only to improving the performance of members through coaching, but also to improving the competencies of members. The basic philosophy of coaching is to motivate members through higher needs, such as self-esteem and self-actualization, rather than the lower needs in Maslow's hierarchy of needs, which we studied in Chapter 4.

3) Mentoring

Mentoring means that a senior (mentor) shares his/her experience and competency with a junior (mentee) and supports the junior to maximize his or her potential. Mentoring is sometimes operated as a formal program by the organization, and there is also informal mentoring that occurs naturally between a boss and a subordinate or a senior and a junior. Recently, many Korean companies such as Doosan, KT, POSCO, Amorepacific, Dongbu Electronics, Hyundai E&C, and SK E&C are introducing an official mentoring system. In the case of POSData, the turnover rate of new employees was very high due to the characteristics of the IT industry. After introducing formal mentoring for new employees in 2001, the turnover rate decreased by 7-8%.

In general, mentoring has three functions. First, social and psychological support

Table 7-5 **Classification of Mentoring, Coaching, and OJT**

	MENTORING	COACHING	OJT
Purpose	Support for learning and personal growth for future organizational life as well as current organizational work for junior employees	Improving performance by correcting inappropriate behavior and improving capacity to take on new responsibilities	Improving productivity through quick acquisition of current tasks
Focus	Learning and career development from a current as well as a long-term perspective	Resolving current and future organizational tasks and improving competency	Improving the competencies required to perform current duties
Subject	Seniors and juniors regardless of department	Leaders within the same department (usually direct boss)	Senior employee within the same department
Relation	Relationships that are not related to work	Formal hierarchical relationship based on work	Work-oriented vertical relationship
Place	No location restrictions	Office	Work site

function to help junior employees who are having difficulties in adjusting to organizational life. Second, to set career goals so that they can have a successful work life, and to improve interpersonal skills and networking necessary for organizational life. Finally there is a learning support function that enables continuous learning by providing information and feedback related to opportunities to learn inside and outside the organization.[18] Mentoring is similar to coaching and OJT, but it can handle a variety of topics that are not related to work, and it can be smoothed out by supporting the mentee to solve problems on his own (Refer to <Talbe 7-5> for the difference between mentoring, coaching, and OJT).

4) Job Rotation

Job rotation is a system traditionally designed to prevent boredom and loss of motivation for simple repetitive tasks in manufacturing plants, but in modern times, it is also actively used to improve competency and motivate office employees. Recently, through job rotation, not only can the individual members improve their competency and motivate them, but organizations can acquire more accurate information about their jobs and individuals and learn to improve their performance.[19] For example, job rotation can provide information about which employees are suitable for the job. In addition, when job rotation occurs, it is possible to determine whether the difference in productivity is caused by the job or individual differences. In Korea, there are criticisms that excessive job rotation hinders professional development, but it is essential for human resource management to nurture new employees or core talent, and many companies officially operate a job rotation system. Global companies have been actively using job rotation to develop the capabilities of key talents from an early age. For example, Philips

Electronics conducts job rotation in order to induce core talents in the early stages of their careers to have various experiences. Philips' core talent job rotation principle provides a systematic device for young talents aged 30-35 to grow through core jobs (Phillips calls these jobs breeding ground jobs).[20] This core job is limited to jobs that can take responsibility for important budgets, manage managers, and report directly to the CEO. GE's leadership development program goes through a similar process, and Jeffrey Immelt, who was CEO of GE, was also provided with opportunities to develop competency and verify his competency through various job experiences.

5) Action Learning

Action learning is a development method that is mainly used for management candidates. Action learning is literally a compound word of action and learning, which allows learning to occur naturally in the process of performing tasks. Learning through action learning is mainly done in teams. The team is given a real organizational problem as a task. In this process, trainees learn both the content aspect and the process aspect of the task with the help of a facilitator.[21] Action learning was designed by a British scientist to effectively educate low-income youth, and has since spread as global companies such as GE began to introduce it as a manager education method. In Korea, companies in various industries such as Samsung, Hyundai Motors, CJ, and Daelim Industrial are introducing action learning, and recently, it is spreading to general educational institutions such as universities and high schools. The effect of action learning is that learners not only acquire new knowledge in the process of solving problems on their own, but also learn from the heart by continuously looking at themselves.

6) Various Internal and External Training Programs

Education and training programs provided by the human resources department or human resource development department actually help members of the organization acquire knowledge and skills in various fields. Most of Korea's leading companies are meeting the demand for education and training by operating their own training institutes. Samsung Human Resources Development Center of Samsung Group, LG Human Resources Center of LG Group, SK Academy of SK Group, and Hyundai Human Resources Development Center of Hyundai Motor Group are representative training institutes. Education and training programs vary in content and delivery methods. Recently, with the development of ICT technology, online learning, e-learning, and massive open online course (MOOC) are being actively conducted, and blended learning or flipped learning that combines the advantages of online and offline is also emerging. <Table 7-6> is an example of online education provided by a Korean conglomerate. As shown in the table, a wide variety of educational programs such as job requirements, position requirements, corporate values, general management, professional jobs, foreign languages, etc. are provided to various employees and managers. Various training methods and contents will be dealt with in detail in the next section.

7) Advanced Management Program (AMP)

The advanced management program (AMP) is a competency development program

Table 7-6 **Examples of Online Training for a Large Corporation in Korea**

JOB TITLE REQUIRED	OFFICER	CORPORATE VALUE	GENERAL MANAGEMENT	PROFESSIONAL JOB	FOREIGN LANGUAGE
Senior manager Prospective manager Required rank I Required rank II Required rank III Experienced employee New recruits	Business manager MBA	Corporate culture Ethical management Value management Shared growth Corporate brand	Management/ Economics Strategy/ Innovation Leadership Business skills Business general	R&D Purchase Production Sales/Service Marketing Finance Accounting Human resources Information technology	English Japanese Chinese Spanish Arabic

that mainly targets executives, including the CEO, to acquire the latest management techniques in connection with the university. AMP has several advantages besides being able to learn the latest management techniques. In the AMP process, not only executives of large corporations, but also leaders from various backgrounds such as SMEs, public corporations, government agencies, judicial institutions, and legislative institutions gather. Due to this, various information can be acquired through networking and mutual learning can be achieved. In addition to management techniques, in the AMP course, participants can broaden their thinking by listening to lectures on topics that are not normally encountered, such as humanities, history, art, literature, and health.

3. Education and Training

Education and training is one element of human resource development. As described in section 1, the first of the three HRD components is individual development, which is used synonymously with education and training. On the other hand, development and training are sometimes distinguished from each other. Development is mainly preparing for future jobs from a long-term perspective, whereas training means acquiring direct knowledge or skills needed to perform current jobs. In this respect, education and training can be said to be a concept that encompasses short-term and long-term perspectives, as well as various programs for current and future jobs. These activities are sometimes divided into upskilling to improve the competencies required for the current job and reskilling to develop the potential for future growth.[22)]

3.1 Training Methods

Companies operate the program using various methods once the subjects and contents of the training are selected. The most representative method is a method in which the instructor directly transfers knowledge to the target audience in the classroom, but various other participatory education methods are being developed. In particular, in recent years, various technological advances have been applied to education and training methods.

Unlike traditional lecture-style education and training, in which the instructor communicates the learning contents, the participatory method refers to a method in which the instructor promotes the inquiry activities of the learners through various methods and the learners participate in the learning process proactively.[23)] The participatory methods can be expected to promote information sharing and teamwork through learners' interaction. In recent years, both university education and corporate education have promoted participatory training methods and are becoming increasingly common. However, participation is not without its merits. It takes a lot of time compared to the lecture method, and the number of trainees is inevitably limited. In addition, the participatory methods also require the teaching skills of the instructors, and there is a risk of lowering the learning effect compared to the lecture method if conducted without appropriate feedback. Therefore, in order for the participation methods to be effective, both instructors and learners need an active will to participate with appropriate skills.

1) Nominal Group Technique (NGT)

Nominal group technique (NGT) was developed as one of the collective decision-making methods, and applied to education and training. Nominal group technique (NGT) literally means a nominal group, and it is an educational method that induces all learners to participate by restraining discussion. It mainly uses post-it notes or paper, and have participants write their thoughts first without discussion. In addition, by honestly expressing one's opinion regardless of the opinions of others, it increases participation and induces mutual communication. By having all learners take turns expressing their opinions, it ensures that all learners participate without being marginalized. Recently, electronic devices are used to communicate in NGT process.

2) Brainstorming

Brainstorming was also developed as a collective decision-making method and applied to education and training. As a way to induce creative ideas, all participants freely present their thoughts with one topic. In this teaching method, participants do not criticize each other and present all ideas, including nonsensical ones, without the concept of good or bad. This is an educational method that encourages people to create new ideas by combining their own thoughts with those of others.

3) Visual Thinking

Visual thinking is an educational method that allows the learning content to be created and expressed as an image. After a core topic is decided, participants create visual language related to the topic through various images such as symbols, speech bubbles, and arrows to express and share their opinions and thoughts.

4) Role Play

Role play is an educational method in which learning takes place by setting a virtual situation in real life and assigning a role to the learner to experience it through acting. The role-playing method is a diverse and widely used educational method. For example, role-playing is also used in mock interviews conducted for job-seeking students at universities.

Case of Role-Playing Education and Training in a Private Telecommunication Company in Korea (competencies to be developed: performance evaluation, subordinate nurturing, teamwork formation, communication)

You are Heechan Kim, Team Leader of the Next-Generation Communication Service Team at the R&D Headquarters. You would like to meet Kyung-Hyun Jeong, senior member of the Next Generation Communication Service Team, and have a 30-minute interview about his work performance and organizational life. Kyung-Hyun Jeong has been working at the R&D Headquarters for 12 years and is in charge of developing services that are expected to play an important role in the growth of UB-Telecom in the future. These days, Kyung-hyun is immersed in self-awareness about growth within the organization and interpersonal relationships, and thinks that he has no vision for development at the R&D headquarters. He is planning to go to a doctoral program for a breakthrough self-change, and he is in a situation where he can go to college at any time if he decides on his own. If you try to stop him from going to a doctoral program, he has the extreme idea that he might leave the company. Kyung-Hyun Jeong has shown excellent performance since joining the company, but his performance has been very poor recently. There may be various reasons, but above all, the work so far has mainly required individual ability, whereas the recent work has mainly been the work that has to be carried out through collaboration with co-workers or distribution of roles with subordinates. However, in interpersonal relationships, Jeong Kyung-hyun is evaluated by colleagues within the organization as showing a selfish appearance that only prioritizes his own work. His subordinates also say that he has an egotistical mindset, expressing dissatisfaction with their work performance attitudes and results that they are not meeting the level they require. As a result, he has been receiving poor feedback in performance evaluation.

You should provide coaching and mentoring about work and interpersonal relationships through interviews about the recent slump of Kyung-hyun Jeong due to the lack of a vision within the organization and the work stress caused by uncomfortable relationships with colleagues and subordinates. Attached here are the basic background of the recent appointment of Kyung-Hyeon Jeong, data on performance evaluation, results of tasks performed, and data related to activities within the organization, such as indirect testimonies from colleagues. You will have 30 minutes to review the attached materials and prepare for the interview. After 30 minutes, Jeong Kyung-hyun will arrive at the office, and you will have a 30-minute interview with him.

5) Problem-based Learning

Problem-based learning(PBL), which has been widely used as an education and training method for doctors in medical schools, is also applied to the business field.[24) In PBL, the instructor presents the task derived from the case to the learners and the learners learn in the interactive process of team work in the process of solving it. PBL requires learners to learn independently before entering into team work. Unlike task force (TF) teams that are formed to solve problems in an organization, PBL uses problems to improve competency.

3.2 Contents of Education and Training

Companies provide various contents for education and training according to the target of education and training.[25)]

1) Skill Training

Skill training is the most common education and training. Skill training is conducted in various fields required by the organization, from basic skills to specialized skills. In particular, changes in technology require new knowledge and skills directly necessary for members to perform their duties. For example, LG Electronics is demanding not only engineers but also general office workers with the data analysis capabilities necessary to solve problems in the field due to advances in artificial intelligence (AI) and big data technologies. To this end, the company is conducting training programs for various competencies from AI technology or algorithm utilization ability or data collection to analysis.

2) Retraining

Retraining is training for a new job rather than an existing job. It is implemented to support employees in adapting to a new work environment when existing job contents are changed or job disappears due to reorganization of the industrial structure or the advent of new technology. Amazon, the world's largest e-commerce company, has announced that it is retraining its approximately 100,000 employees, a third of its workforce.[26)] Amazon's retraining, which will last through 2025, aims to help employees find new jobs, either by moving to another job within the company, or by moving to another company altogether. For example, the company helps employees who were in charge of logistics obtain certifications in high-demand fields, such as nursing or aircraft maintenance, if they want.

3) Creativity Training

Creativity training is conducted on the premise that creativity can be learned through training. Rather than acquiring new creativity, it can be said that the focus is on bringing out the potential of creativity inherent in everyone. Among the methods of education and training, the nominal group technique, brainstorming, or visual thinking are frequently used for creativity training. For example, mind map is a creativity training program developed using visual thinking.

Table 7-7 **Five Major Legal Compulsory Education in Korea**

TITLE	OBLIGATORY	TRAINING HOURS	RELATED LAWS	FINE FOR NEGLIGENCE	RESPONSIBLE AGENCY
Education to improve awareness of the disabled in the workplace	Employers and all workers	1 hour or more once a year	The Employment Promotion and Vocational Rehabilitation Act for the Disabled	A fine of not more than 3 million won	Korea Employment Agency for the Disabled
Occupational safety and health education	Businesses with 5 or more employees (except for some industries)	6 hours or more every quarter	Occupational Safety and Health Act	A fine of not more than 5 million won	Korea Occupational Safety and Health Agency
Sexual harassment prevention education in the workplace	Any business that employs workers	More than once a year	Act on Gender Equality in Employment and Support for Work-Family Balance	A fine of not more than 5 million won	Ministry of Employment and Labor
Personal information protection education	Person who processes personal information	1-2 times a year	Personal Information Protection Act	A fine of not more than 500 million won in case of an accident or incident	Korea Internet &Security Agency
Retirement pension education	Retirement pension plan subscribers	More than once a year	Employee Retirement Benefit Security Act	A fine of not more than 10 million won	Korea Labor Welfare Corporation

4) Diversity Training

Diversity training is training to understand cultural and demographic diversity in the workplace and to actively utilize them for creativity. In a passive sense, it is to prevent discrimination in culture or sex through diversity awareness, but in an active sense, it is to more effectively solve the problems of an organization by utilizing various perspectives through diversity management. For effective diversity management, many global companies have a chief diversity officer(CDO). According to Wikipedia, about 20% of Fortune 500 companies have a CDO.

5) Statutory Compulsory Education

In addition to education and training based on voluntary needs of companies, there is also education and training stipulated by law as a policy regulation of the government. Currently, in Korea, as shown in <Table 7-7>, there are five statutory compulsory educations such as education on awareness improvement of persons with disabilities, education on occupational safety, education on prevention of sexual harassment, education on personal information protection, and education on retirement pension.

4. Evaluation of the Effectiveness of the Program

The final process, evaluation and feedback, is to determine whether various competency development and education and training programs have been carried out as intended and whether they are cost effective. Here, it is identified whether the goal of competency development and education and training efforts has been achieved, which parts are insufficient, and what is needed for improvement. In the final stage, the HR department improves the system through systematic evaluation, and managers provide feedback to members. The evaluation of the company-wide education and training program provided by the HR department will be formally conducted. On the other hand, the managers of the unit organization should also evaluate the various employee competency development efforts made in their own organization. The 4-level model suggested by Kirkpatrick is the most used for competency development and evaluation of education and training programs.[27] As shown in [Figure 7-7], the 4-level is divided into reaction, learning, behavior, and results based on the degree of ease of measurement and value to the organization. Reaction is easy to measure while having the lowest value to the organization, whereas results have high value to the organization while being

Figure 7-7 4-Level Competency Development Evaluation Model

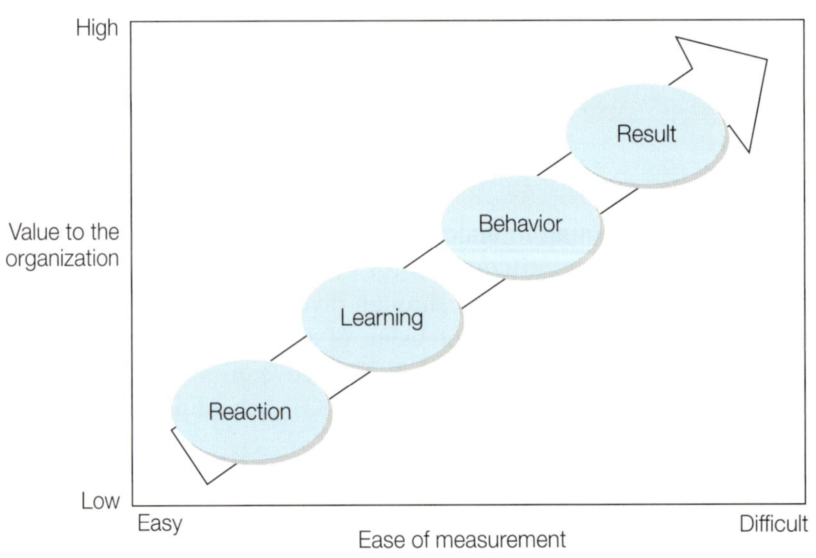

difficult to measure.

4.1 Reaction

Reaction refers to the members' reaction to competency development and education and training programs. For classroom education, lecture evaluation of instructors or curriculum is the most common method. The satisfaction of education and the degree of delivery of content are mainly evaluated through surveys.

4.2 Learning

If the goal of competency development and education and training programs is for members to acquire new knowledge or skills and use them in the process of job performance, the evaluation of learning is to evaluate the extent to which these new knowledge or skills have been learned. The easiest example is taking a test, but in most cases this is not enough.

4.3 Behavior

If the evaluation of learning is based on how much new knowledge and skills have been acquired, the evaluation of behavior is how much is reflected in practice. In other words, it determines how much the effects of competency development and education and training programs are applied to the actual field beyond what is inherent in the members.

4.4 Results

Results evaluate how much competency development and training programs have contributed to organizational performance. You can use the return on investment (ROI) method, which measures the contribution to actual performance versus the cost of your program. In addition, there are various methods for evaluating results, ranging from direct measurement methods such as cost reduction, productivity increase, production time reduction, creative idea suggestion, and interpersonal improvement, to indirect measurement that managers make subjective judgement through observation.

Ending Case

Renault Samsung Motors' Talent Development Strategy[28)]

Renault Samsung Motors was established in September 2000 when Renault Group, a French global automobile company, took over Samsung Motors, which was founded in 1995 and applied for court management in 1999. At the time of its inception, about 2,000 Samsung Motors employees were hired and succeeded, and now there are about 4,000 employees, double the number at that time. Sales are also showing a fivefold growth from about 1 trillion won in 2001 to 5 trillion won in 2015. Renault Samsung Motors' business sites are composed of the Busan plant, the Kiheung central research center, thc Scoul office, and regional sales offices. Renault Samsung Motors has three management policies: 'Customer First', 'Optimal Efficiency', and 'Global Localization' centering on the vision of 'Pursuing the highest customer satisfaction based on profitable growth as a member of the Renault Nissan Alliance'. In the meantime, there have been difficulties in various business environments, and there have been pains such as reduction of staff through voluntary retirement, but overcoming these difficulties and launching new car models, the SM6 and QM5, is entering its second heyday.

Renault Samsung Motors' human resource development principle can be said to be talent management based on in-depth discussion and sufficient verification through the HR committee. The HR committee is a body that decides all matters related to talent management, such as performance evaluation and salary determination, promotion, career development, and rewards and punishments. The HR committee is composed of three levels: the company-wide HR committee, the headquarters HR committee, and the department HR committee.

The most important purpose of operating an HR committee is to secure objectivity in decision-making and to increase employee acceptability of decisions. Rather than the head of a department under direct control decides on HR issues for employees, the relevant department heads through the HR committee try to make decisions as rationally as possible through sufficient verification. Also, since it is a decision made by many department heads in a meeting called the HR committee, department heads have the advantage of being able to deliver feedback to members more efficiently. The HR committee deals with HR issues such as evaluation of members, salaries, career development, and rewards and punishments. In addition, in particular, High Performance & Potential (HPP) and Succession Plan (SP) are discussed.

In Renault Group, core talents or high performers (HPP) are classified into three types as shown in <Table 1>: Emerging High Performance Potential (EHPP), High

Performance Potential (HPP) and Corporate High Performance Potential (CHPP). Among them, each country manages EHPP like Renault Samsung Motors. At Renault Samsung Motors, EHPP manpower is verified and recommended by the HR committee at the headquarters, and the final decision is made by the CEO after consultation with the HR department. For HPP and CHPP, the CEO of Renault Samsung Motors recommends top-ranking manpower among EHPPs to regions and groups, and the final decision is made by the group.

<Table 1> Core Talent Classification of Human Resources

TYPE	CONTENTS
Corporate High Performance Potential(CHPP)	• Excellent manpower managed at the group level • Qualifications: Work experience in two or more countries + in Local/Region/Group Executive committee member
High Performance Potential(HPP)	• Excellent manpower managed at the region level • Qualifications: Work experience in at least two countries
Emerging High Performance Potential(EHPP)	• Excellent human resources managed at the local level • Qualifications: Experience in at least two local positions

If selected as an HPP manpower, you must complete the core business class and intensive business class, which are internal training within the company. In addition, they will have the opportunity to broaden their business insight through various educational programs such as attending forums hosted by domestic educational institutions. Some of the HPP manpower will complete the group MBA course held annually by the Renault-Nissan Group overseas to enhance their global capabilities. Through this education, HPPs around the world can interact with each other, and these talents will be provided with the opportunity to experience the global market and develop their global business acumen. Also, for HPP, the Renault Leadership Assessment (RLA), an assessment center hosted by the Renault Group, is being run. Through this evaluation, the management ability, organizational management and leadership style, and crisis and conflict management ability of key talents are systematically evaluated and analyzed, and the results are received from experts and reflected in the individual competency improvement plan. Currently, about 80 HPP talents selected by Renault Samsung Motors are dispatched overseas to Europe, China, Japan, and India.

Succession planning (SP) is also one of the important issues that the HR committee deals with. Each year, succession plans are established and decided for important positions above the team leader. Succession planning discusses selecting candidates for succession and how to nurture them. Candidates are classified and managed into three types in terms of organizational status and short-term, mid-to-long term: Emergency candidate, Ideal candidate, and Further candidate (refer to <Table 2>). In general, only one emergency candidate, who should be put in immediately when a vacancy occurs, is selected, and at least three candidates are selected for the other two types of candidates.

<Table 2> Classification of Candidates for Succession Planning

Emergency Candidate	Candidates who can work immediately when an unexpected position vacancy occurs
Ideal Candidate	Candidates suitable for the position in consideration of the overall organizational situation and individual competency
Further Candidate	Candidates who can be promoted to the relevant position in the mid-to long-term

Ideal candidates and Further candidates are important to nurture, so the head of the relevant department shares the relevant details with the candidates. In addition, through personal interviews, a competency development plan necessary for leadership is established and implemented. Through the succession plan, healthy competition among members is made possible, and this process is to induce the competency of Renault Samsung Motors members to level up.

Discussion Question

1. What are the characteristics of Renault Samsung Motors' talent development strategy, and is this talent development strategy suitable for Renault Samsung Motors' mission, vision, and business strategy?
2. If, like Renault Samsung Motors, the department head does not directly make HR-related decisions, but instead goes through the HR committee, doesn't the leadership's HR authority weaken?
3. What are the characteristics of Renault Samsung Motors' succession plan?

CHAPTER 8

Compensation Management and Pay Structure

Learning Objectives

1. Understand the importance of pay from the perspective of the company and employees.
2. Understand and utilize various types of rewards from the perspective of total rewards.
3. Understand the conceptual framework for managing pay.
4. Understand pay policies compared to the market pay.
5. Understand the basic factors for pays structure such as job, role, ability, and seniority.

Introductory Case

When thinking about the future, Director Kim is upset. This is because, in the next few years, he will be subject to the wage peak system, and his pay will be reduced by 10% every year. He knows that the business environment is difficult and it is natural to give up a certain amount of pay in order to maintain employment until the retirement age. But it is true that he feels a little down. When he joined the company, there was a salary system for each position, and even if he was not promoted, the basic salary increased every year, and other allowances linked to the basic salary increased. At that time, employees trust the company and burn their passion, and the company is responsible for the rest, so there was not much interest in how the pay system was designed and operated. All of the colleagues joined the company at the same time received almost the same pay, and promotion was a far more important concern than pay.

Then, after the sudden IMF economic crisis, the pay system was overhauled in full swing. Even in the same position, the wage increase varies depending on the performance, which bring on an atmosphere in which everyone takes care of his own achievements. At that time, he was worried that the new pay system might rather do harm to the organization, even he did not openly object to it. Now again, the story of the reform of the pay system is being heard. If the company needs it, the system can be changed, but he thinks that it is still necessary to listen to the opinions of the employees. Management begins to emphasize the need to reorganize the pay system suitable for an aging of the employees along with the eventual extension of the retirement age. There are also stories of going to the job-based or role-based pay. While asking himself why it is so difficult to pay decently to make work hard, he is on his way to work for today.

Discussion Questions

1. The pay peak system reduces the labor cost burden on the company. If so, what are the downsides effects?
2. What are the rewards the company can provides to its employees?
3. What is the difference between monetary compensation and promotion in terms of cost and effectiveness?
4. What are the advantages and disadvantages of pay differentials based on performance?
5. Why do Korean companies need to reorganize the pay system and what are the desirable directions for it?

It is the basic principle of human resource management that the organization pays the corresponding rewards in return for the labor the employees provide for the organization. When pay management is understood as such a principle, it may seem very simple, but it is quite complex and difficult in reality. This is because pay is not the only compensation paid for work. The rewards that organizations can give to individuals vary widely, including not only wages, but opportunities for promotion, career development, and learning opportunities. It is difficult to effectively manage pay without a comprehensive understanding of the various means of compensation provided by companies.

When focusing on pay, it is important to decide to take a clear policy compared to the market pay level. Also, pay is not a single form, but is often divided into basic salaries, allowances, and incentives. This types of pay and how to combine them is to be considered for the effective compensation management. How to increase the basic salary according to what criteria is also another important task in pay management. The decisions that companies make in the process of designing and operating a compensation system not only have a significant impact on the motivation and commitment of the employees, but also have a significant impact on the company's labor costs and competitiveness.

1. Total Compensation

In order for managers or employees to accurately understand compensation management, they must first understand the concept of total compensation. Total compensation in a narrow sense refers to all types of financial compensation and convenience that employees receive from the company on the premise of an employment relationship.[1)] On the other hand, in a broad sense, total rewards include, in addition to the aforementioned rewards, recognition and status from the organization, employment security, challenging jobs, and learning and development opportunities.

When it comes to compensation, the first thing we come to mind is the monthly salary paid in cash, which is the most basic component of compensation. In many cases, basic salary and some allowance are included in monthly salary but basic salary represents the most large and the most important portion. In European and American companies, the form of pay is simple, so the basic pay is a monthly pay without various extra allowances which is not the case for Korean companies.

Cash compensation is not just a salary. Cash is paid in the name of bonuses once every few months or around Lunar New Year's Day and Chuseok. The amount of these bonuses is set in advance, but there are also variable incentives in which the payment amount is determined according to the performance of an individual, team, or company. From the point of view that pay is income for a living, cash benefits are of great importance, especially for employees with low pay is.

However, cash is not the only rewards the organization provides to its members. Welfare benefits are not cash compensation, but provide a variety of necessary benefits to members. Examples of such things as financial aid and health insurance are typical

Figure 8-1 Total Compensation

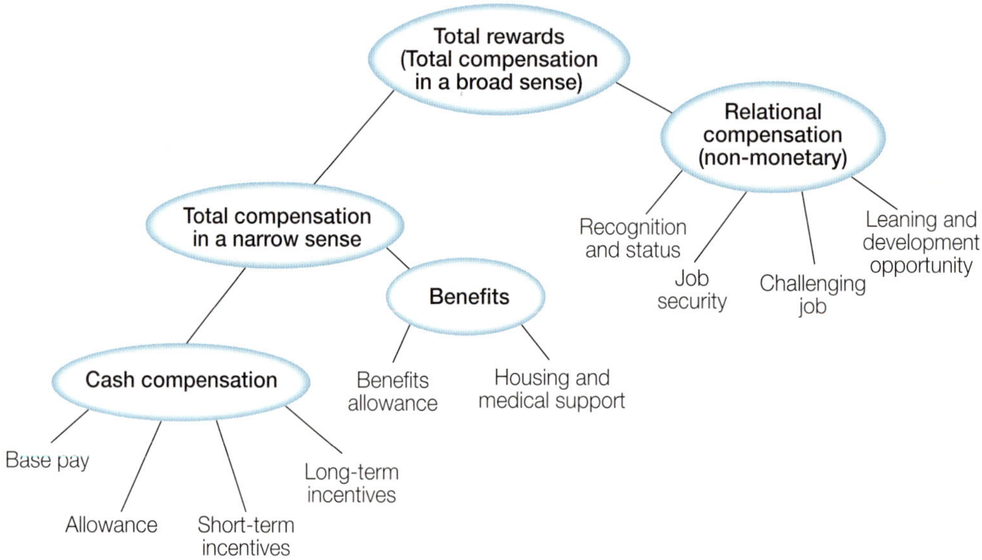

Source: Adapted by authors from Newman, Gerhart and Milkovich(2017, 12th)

examples. Company could pay cash which allow employees to choose benefits by themselves, but in this case, it is difficult to take advantage of discount benefits resulting from collective purchase of insurance services, and there is no guarantee that the cash paid to individuals will be used for benefits. Companies with well-equipped welfare benefits have merit to attract excellent talent, even if their pay level is similar or slightly lower than those of other companies.

Traditionally, the most basic consideration for job seekers when deciding which company to choose is the level of cash pay and benefits described above. However, companies have various additional means of compensation in addition to pay and welfare benefits. Whether the job at the company is interesting or challenging, whether the organizational culture or atmosphere of the company recognizes and nurtures its members, whether it is a company that does not let people out well even if the company becomes difficult, etc. cannot be quantified financially but it is a very important condition for the choice. In the recent rankings of companies that college students want to work for, the fact that Kakao surpassed Samsung Electronics and ranked first shows this well.[2)] Students prefer Kakao for the growth and vision. The same is true of the reason talent leaves the company. Talented employees resign when they feel that their work is not interesting, or that they cannot grow through their work.[3)]

The total compensation perspective is very important to job seekers, employees, and companies alike. From the point of view of job seekers and incumbents, a place to devote their passion is a place where they can grow. Of course, it is necessary that the level of monetary compensation be maintained at a competitive level, but that is not a

Students Seeking for a Iron Rice Bowl

Technological and economic environments are changing rapidly, and companies are hunger for innovation. On the contrary, the tendency of students to find a stable job is getting stronger, immersing themselves in the civil service examination. In Noryangjin, where private academies are concentrated, the streets are crowded with people who are preparing for the exam. Some are turning their criticism to the students who only want stability and the education system that produces them. But are the students really wrong? From the standpoint of job seekers who have to choose a job, it is natural to find companies with high wages and good working conditions. For them, it is an economically reasonable decision-making. Rather, is it not a problem that many Korean companies are failing to provide attractive rewards or opportunities for growth to invest for the youth. This is why it is important to develop an organizational culture, personnel system, and leadership of managers that can stimulate passion and creativity.

sufficient condition. If we could translate the recognition and growth opportunity into monetary value, it must be a very large amount. Therefore, it is important to consider non-monetary compensation as well as monetary compensation when considering which company to work for. Especially for those who are early in their careers, this point of view is even more important.

The total compensation perspective is important for companies as well. All companies try to keep pay competitive in the labor market. If not, it is difficult to secure excellent talent. However, for a large number of companies, it may be practically difficult to pay market wages. Startups and SMEs are representative examples. For them, inducing or motivating members with non-monetary compensation can be an effective compensation strategy. On the other hand, even for a large company, it is not easy to always maintain the best monetary rewards. In addition, talented people who

War for Talent between Google and Facebook[4)]

With Facebook's rapid growth, there is a war over talent as well as competition over business. Already, a significant number of Google's core personnel have moved to Facebook, and as a result, there is a great sense of crisis that Google may lose technology, know-how, and innovative ideas to competitors. To protect its talent, Google is trying to make a massive salary increase and bonus payments. The power of Facebook to attract talent is known as an organizational culture that guarantees autonomy and creativity, a founder who presents a vision, and a high reward and growth opportunity. However, no company always wins the talent war. In the past, Google was a black hole that attracted talent from all over the world. The war of IT companies over talent shows that financial compensation is important, but organizational culture, leadership of management, and growth opportunities are just as or more important.

come to the company only expecting financial compensation may have less immersion or loyalty to the company than those who have seen the company's mission or vision. Considering these points, strengthening non-monetary compensation can also benefit large corporations. However, reinforcing non-monetary rewards is not as easy as you might think. This is because the CEO, HR department, and managers must all share a vision, participate in, and work together.

2. Importance of Compensation

The importance of non-monetary compensation was emphasized while explaining the total compensation earlier. However, pay in cash is the most basic rewards from the past to the present and even in the future. This is because if a certain amount of pay is not provided, it is difficult to secure excellent talent and make it difficult to make them work hard, no matter how good the non-monetary compensation is. Pay is very important to both employees and the company for the following reasons.

2.1 Importance of Compensation for the Employees

Pay is very important to the employees of the company for the following reasons. First, pay is income for workers' livelihoods. Employees of the company are wage workers. In other words, pay provided by companies is their only source of income. Therefore, how much pay is provided is a factor that determines the level of livelihood. The nature of pay as a source of livelihood is of particular importance to employees who work in low-wage occupations or are in the early stages of their careers. This is because they have to make a living with the pay they received. Employees of large corporations are not threatened with their livelihood due to the low pay level, but there are still 3,110,000 workers in Korea who fall below the minimum wage, which is 15.5% of the total workers as of 2018.[5)]

Second, pay speaks of individual' social status. Therefore, pay is still important for those who receive well above the market wage. Pay is an important signal that summarizes and conveys an individual's social status in our capitalist society. Popular occupations, such as lawyers and doctors, are no longer able to enjoy the same high pay and corresponding positions as in the past as the labor supply has increased recently. It can be said that it is a representative example of how the level of compensation for a given job affects social status.

Third, pay affects the self-esteem that employees feel about themselves. It cannot be said that the pay level mechanically determines an individual's self-esteem, but it is clear that it has an important effect. This is because it is difficult to feel self-confidence or self-esteem while receiving low pay in a capitalist society. In particular, it is difficult to have a positive attitude toward oneself if one is paid lower wages than his friends working at other companies. Pay is another expression of trust or recognition that an organization sends to the individual.

2.2 Importance of Compensation for the Companies

Pay is also very important from the management perspective for the following reasons. First, pay is an critical cost for companies. Although the labor costs incurred by hiring people vary greatly depending on the industries, it is known that they represent approximately 5% of their sales in large Korean manufacturing companies. In the case of the chemical industry, this ratio is very low, and that of small and medium service industry is very high. In addition, the importance of labor costs is relatively small during a growth period when sales increase rapidly, but it become very important when growth is stagnant or sales decline. This is because if management reduce expenses, including labor costs, the profit will be improved accordingly. That's why many companies try to cut their workforce when the economy gets tough. Therefore, controlling labor costs to an appropriate level becomes a very important task for management and HR departments.

Second, pay has a significant impact on securing, utilizing and maintaining the necessary manpower. If the pay level is low, it is difficult to secure excellent workforce. In particular, it is very difficult to bring in career talent from labour market unless a sufficiently competitive pay is provided. In addition, the hard-earned talent will soon leave the company if appropriate pay is not paid. That's why some companies pay a retention bonus for those who are in charge of important projects to keep them from leaving.

Third, pay has an great influence on the utilization and motivation of manpower. If pay is determined by the number of years of service each year, the motivation to work hard may weaken because pay rises even if they do not produce results. If management raise pay for those who have done well in consideration of the results of their work, it will be likely to increase motivation for those who have worked hard. The annual salary system, Yeonbongje, which has spread rapidly in Korea after the IMF economic crisis, is the pay system introduced for that purpose.

3. Framework for Compensation Management

In order to design and operate a pay system, it is necessary to understand the pay management framework. This framework consists of pay level, pay form, and pay structure. First, managing the pay level is a question of at what level the company's average pay is set and managed compared to other companies in the same industry. In this case, it becomes a very important task to maintain the competitiveness of pay compared to other companies and to set an appropriate level of pay taking into account the financial situation of the company. The form of pay is the types of pay given to employees, and the timing of payment. In the form of pay, the rational composition of different types of pay are emphasized. The pay structure is a question of what principle the pay is to be differentiated among employees. That principle must be convincing and fair to employees. The pay principle is the determining logic of basic pay, and it includes seniority-based pay, competence-based pay, job-based pay, and role-based pay.

Figure 8-2 Framework for Pay Management

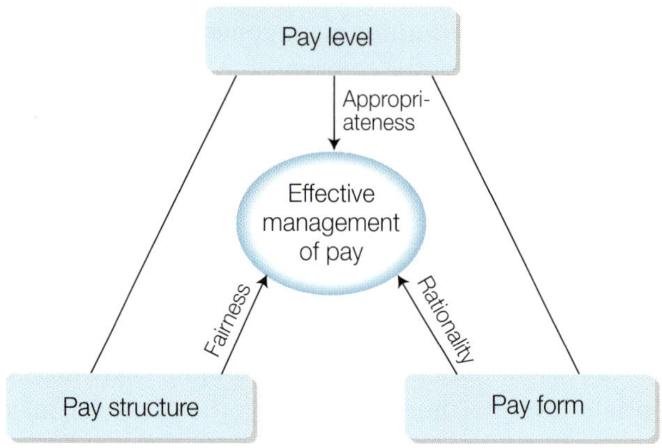

Source: Kim, Sikhyun, 1991, *Human Resource Management*.

3.1 Management of Pay Level

The first thing that is needed to manage pay level is to determine to which level the company's average pay will be taken compared to its competitors. Job seekers and employees compare the company's pay level with the pay offered by other competitors. If it is too low compared to the market level, it is difficult to secure talented workforce. Therefore, the pay should be set at a level that is competitive in the labor market. This is called the competitiveness of pay, and it is also expressed as external equity of pay in terms of whether it is fair compared to other competitors outside the company.

When it comes to pay level, companies have to choose their own pay policy compared to market pay. The lower limit of pay is the minimum wage promulgated by the government. All companies doing business in Korea are obligated to pay same or more than the minimum wage. Meanwhile, the upper limit is determined by the financial capabilities of the company. This is because pay level that exceed their ability to pay cannot be maintained continuously. Within that range, companies can strategically choose a level of pay they think appropriate. There are three types of pay level policies that companies can adopt.

3.1.1 Lead Policy

It is a policy to secure and retain excellent talent by paying higher pay compared to market wage. It is called a lead policy in the sense of leading the pay ahead of the high level. In many cases, dominant companies in the market take lead policies to secure talent. This includes companies such as Naver, Kakao, Samsung Electronics, SK Telecom, and Hyundai Motor Company that Korean university graduates prefer. Among European and American companies, the dominant companies often stipulate that their pay have to maintain competitive wage levels that is in the top 5% to 10% of the market

Figure 8-3 Strategic Choice of Pay Level

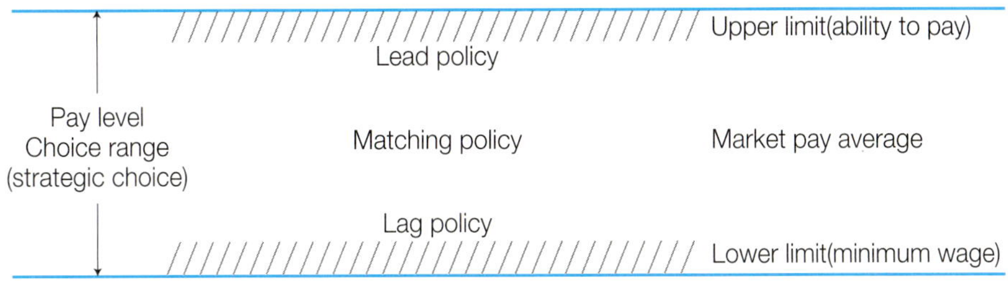

wage. If management take this policy, it can expect the effect of favoring company's image or brand as an employer. However, since labor costs are high, sales or profits must be able to fully support this.

3.1.2 Matching Policy

The matching policy is to pay the market's average level. Since the average level is paid, there is no special penalty for hiring or retaining human resources, but it is difficult to expect differentiated benefits in terms of securing excellent talent. It is called a matching policy in the sense that pay is determined by matching the market average. This is the pay policy of most companies. It may be difficult to regard it as an active strategic choice or policy because it is following the pay level of the market as it is. Some companies intentionally pay only market-level even though their financial ability allows the lead policy. Their intention is to acquire people who relate to the company's vision, core values, and business instead of people who prefer high wages. This case can be said to be a clear strategic choice. In addition, if it is possible to secure talent without having to pay high pay because of the company's reputation or opportunities for career development, it may be effective to choose a matching policy.

3.1.3 Lag Policy

This is called a lag policy, meaning that pay is lagging behind the market average. Most small and medium-sized enterprises(SMEs) with poor financial capacity have adopted this policy. However, in the case of SMEs, it is difficult to say that all SMEs adopt this policy because comparisons over pay are made between SMEs. In the case of a company that is forced to take a lag policy, it is difficult to secure the necessary manpower. The shortage of manpower in SMEs is a prime example. Since it is difficult to find people who want to work under this policy, there are many cases of relying on foreign workers under the form of industrial trainees. Companies adopting this policy need to actively seek ways to utilize non-monetary compensation other than pay. An example is the wide range of discretion of the work, challenging and meaningful work and work-family balance.

Light and Shadow of the Minimum Wage Act

Most countries regulate the minimum wage that must be paid to workers by law. The minimum wage is a device that allows workers to maintain a minimum survival or living, and is generally determined by hourly wages. In Korea, the minimum wage is fixed by the Minimum Wage Commission, and the hourly wage of the minimum wage in 2021 is 8,720 won. This is 1,822,480 won when converted into a single worker's monthly wage. The minimum wage is newly determined every year. In the process, the labor unions always demands a high increase, while the employers argues for a freeze or a slight increase. If the minimum wage is too low, the number of workers who are not protected increases, and legal protection becomes ineffective. But if the minimum wage is too high, there will be a risk of reducing employment by increasing the labor cost burden on companies. Recently, some countries, such as the United States, Japan and Korea, have shown a movement to raise the minimum wage to revitalize the economy.

Source: home page of Minimum Wage Commission (www.minimumwage.go.kr)

3.2 Management of Pay Form

Pay form is often understood as a method of calculating and paying wages, and classified into hourly, monthly and annual wage. However, the hourly wage is actually paid in the form of a monthly wage, and the annual wage is calculated on an annual basis but are paid monthly. In this point of view, the distinction between hourly wage, salary or annual salary does not require in-depth conceptual discussion or explanation. It is therefore more meaningful to approach the form of pay by the distinction between basic pay, allowances and incentives, because each form has different logic and use.

A company may pay only basic salary to its employees, or pay allowances and incentives in addition to the basic salary. For example, in the case of European and American companies, wages are generally paid in two simple components, that is a basic salary and an incentive. Paying wages like this has the advantage of being simple, easy to understand and manage. However, in the case of Korean companies, wages have traditionally been provided in various ways such as basic pay, various allowances, fixed bonuses, and incentives. Historically, it is clear that there are reasons and roles for each form of wage, but as time goes by, the role of allowances and fixed bonuses is disappearing. For example, by the introduction of the annual salary pay, Yeonbonje, many allowances and fixed bonus are integrated into basic salary. In the case of production workers in large companies, there are still many allowances and fixed bonuses in addition to the basic salary.

Meanwhile, wage forms can be classified into fixed pay and variable pay. In the fixed pay the amount of money to be given to employees is determined in advance, while in the variable pay, it is decided ex post according to performances. The basic salary, allowances, and regular bonuses correspond to fixed pay. Originally, the word bonus means extra money paid as a reward ex post, so it has a variable character. But in Korea,

Figure 8-4 Forms of Pay

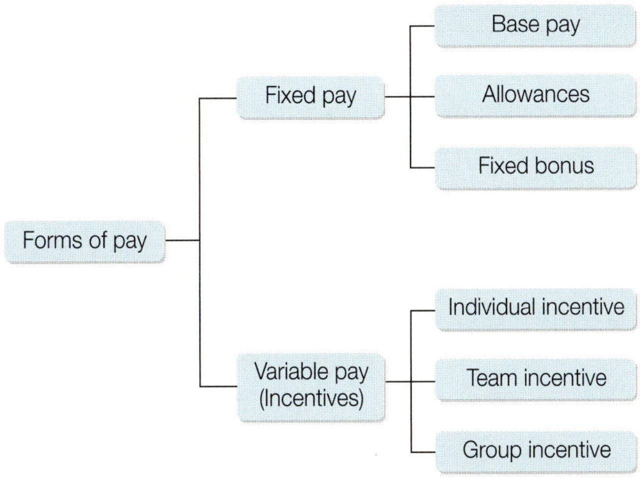

as can be seen in expressions such as '600% of the basic pay', the bonus was used as a fixed compensation. Although the term "fixed" is a term that cannot be used with bonuses that have a variable meaning, the system of "fixed bonuses" has been used in

Regular bonus is ordinary wage

On December 18, 2013, the Supreme Court declared that regular bonuses paid regularly, uniformly, and fixedly are included in ordinary wages through a ruling by the all-in-one consensus. The "ordinary wage" means hourly wage, daily wage, weekly wage, monthly wage, or contract amount to be paid to an employee for a specifically agreed work or entire work on a regular and flat basis(Enforcement decree of the labor standard act, article 6). The ordinary wage is the legal base used for calculating the overtime allowance that must be paid when overtime work is performed. The Labor Standards Act and the Enforcement Decree does not stipulate whether or not a regular bonus is a ordinary wage. An administrative interpretation made in 1988 considers that regular bonus is not ordinary wage. However, workers at Gabeul Autotech filed a law suit against company demanding unpaid wages insisting that regular fixed bonus must be counted as ordinary wages. In 2012, the Supreme Court ruled that regular bonuses be regarded as ordinary wages. Faced with strong demand from business worrying its serious impact of the ordinary wage lawsuit on the economy, the principle was reaffirmed exceptionally through the ruling of the all-in-one consensus. The Supreme Court forbided, however, to claim additional wages for this ruling because both the labor and management parties were aware of and respecting the administrative interpretation at the time. Due to this ruling, the form of wages of Korean companies changed significantly, such as regular bonuses being included in basic pay or changed into variable incentives.

practice longtime. However, as these regular bonuses were regarded as ordinary wages by the Supreme Court decision in 2013, the fixed bonuses are gradually disappearing.

3.2.1 Base Pay

Base pay is a wage paid by a company in exchange for performing work at the company without any special conditions after establishing an employment relationship with its employees. From a employee's point of view, the total amount of wages they receive counts, but the level of base pay is of utmost important for the following reasons. First, the base pay reflects the internal rank of workers, and second, it is used as the basis for calculating fixed bonuses and allowances. Third, the base pay represents the degree of stability of workers' wage income. Therefore, how much base pay is paid and what criteria is used to determine it influence greatly the internal equity of pay that employees feel.

In order to design a base pay structure that can be applied to all employees, management must arrange the ranks of individual employees or their work according to some principles. It is possible to consider using market wages as base pay without any specific principle. But, in this case, managing the wage difference rationally and fairly becomes very difficult. Each time when the market wage for a specific job changes, management is obliged to review the entire pay structure to maintain the pay differential between positions or jobs within the company, which is almost impossible.

The criteria determining the rank related to wages can be based on different principles. Seniority pay put a big emphasis on the service period while competence pay considers the knowledge and ability as the most important factor. These are person-based principle in that personal characteristics determine pay grade and pay level. On the other hand, in job-based pay, base pay is determined by the job characteristics. In role-based pay, it is set by the role size. Both are a kind of job-based pay in that pay is established on the value and the role of the job. We will take a close look into it in more detail later in this chapter.

To be exact, it is important to understand the level of the base pay and its increase separately. This is because the decision logic of the base pay and the logic of its increase do not always coincide. In general, the increase of base pay tends to be determined based on the principle of the pay structure. For example, in the case of the seniority pay, the increase of the basic salary is determined according to the service year. In the case of the job-based pay, the pay is increased basically through the promotion to the upper level job. In the competence pay, pay will be increased as the level of job competency rises. However, the increase in base salary is not necessarily made in that way. Regardless of what the pay structure is, it is not unusual to see a base-up in which pays are uniformly increased to all members every year through bargaining between labor and management. Even in the case of job-based pay, pay increase can be done in consideration of performance over a precedent period of time.

3.2.2 Allowances

If the base pay is a basic salary that must be paid to everyone in an employment relationship, an allowance is a compensation that is paid in principle only when certain reasons or conditions exist. For example, overtime pay, which is a very important part of the pay for workers, is paid only when they work in excess of the working hours prescribed by law or collective agreement. The reason why companies need to use allowances is that there are times when it is difficult to compensate adequately and effectively with base pay alone. Let's take an example. If company wants to pay additional compensation for certain employees doing particularly difficult or dangerous work, it would be no wise to raise the base salary. There is no guarantee that the person currently in charge of the job will continue to take on the job in the future. In particular, in the case of Korean companies that have been flexibly transfering manpower, the allowances were the most appropriate tool to meet this kind of temporary need for compensation. On the contrary, in European and American companies, there is no need to operate such an allowance because the nature of this difficulty of the job is already considered in the process of job analysis and evaluation, and consequently in the pay.

Depending on the purposes, allowances are classified into job-related allowances, subsidy allowances, adjustment allowances, and legal allowances.[6)] Job-related allowances are compensation for specific aspects of the job. Typical examples are the risk allowance paid to employees who do dangerous work, the post allowance paid for the responsible managerial position, and the qualification allowance for certification. The subsidy allowance refers to the family allowance, inflation allowance, housing allowance, and commuting allowance, etc., which are paid to subsidize living cost because it can be difficult to live with basic salary alone. These allowances varies depending on the number of families, or is paid differently depending on the existence of a self-owned house or commuting distance. Adjustment allowances are provisional allowances paid to adjust for temporary disparities in wages caused by reorganization of the pay system, merger and actuisition, and change of workers' assignments. Lastly, legal allowances are allowances that must be paid in accordance with the Labor Standards Act when a reason for payment occurs. The overtime work allowances, night-time and holiday work allowances, and dismissal notice allowances are typical.

Traditionally, Korean companies have operated many types of allowances. The companies prefer to use allowances because the increase of the base pay raises other allowances and regular bonuses. In addition, the labor union also needed to highlight the bargaining outcomes that were differentially obtained in the year during bargaining process. In particular, in the period when the government implemented a policy to control the pay increase rate of private companies, allowances were often used as a means to avoid the control. As a result of the accumulation of the allowances, the type of allowances increased significantly, while the proportion of the allowances compared to the basic salary showed a figure reaching 40-50% to certain Korean firms. However, there has been a trend of consolidating many allowances into base pay. This is because for white collar employees, the form of pay has been greatly simplified to base pay through the introduction of an annual salary system. However, it is true that production workers who work in companies with strong labour union influence still have many allowances.

3.2.3 Fixed Bonus

When Korean employees describe their pay level, there are many cases where they explain that the total cash pay consists of the annual base salary and the fixed bonus. The term bonus is not logically appropriate in that bonus imply a variable compensation depending on a good deed or performance while it is used as a fixed pay determined in advance. European and American companies do not operate a fixed pay in the form of a bonus. The characteristics of bonuses in Korean companies are that they are set in advance, and that its size is not small. The bonus is usually set at several hundred percent of the montly base pay and is paid twice a year around great national holidays, Seolnal and Chuseok. The fixed bonuses have been actively utilized because they were excluded from the base for calculating legal allowances such as overtime allowance. However, since fixed bonuses were included as ordinary wages by the Supreme Court's decision in 2013, the need for companies to maintain bonuse is greatly reduced.

3.2.4 Incentive

Incentives are a form of pay in which the amount to be paid is not determined in advance but is determined afterwards according to the performance. Although it is determined ex post, the size or range of incentives paid is usually stipulated in advance, so that members can predict the amount of incentives they can receive to some extent. Incentives are representative of the pay-for-performance because they are basically based on the performance of individuals, teams, or organizations. Details on incentives, motivation, and types of incentives are covered in Chapter 9, which deals with entirely performance pay.

Incentives are a method that has traditionally not been used well in Korean companies. In the case of special occupations such as sales, it is natural that sales incentives are used, but it is rare to pay incentives to all members based on the performance of individuals, teams, or companies as a whole. The principal reason was that the management style of Korean companies was not friendly with short-term performance. In fact, they tended to pursue long-term performance, and they were more familiar with a collective HR philosophy and system. It was therefore difficult for them to establish an incentive differed according to performance between individuals and teams. However, after the Aisan financial crisis of 1997, incentives are actively being utilized as Korean companies have changed their management style and human resource system as a whole towards performance oriented one.

When it comes to incentives, companies have to decide how much to take the ratio of fixed and variable pay. It is possible to construct a pay form with only a fixed pay without variable part, but there is a disadvantage that the stimulus to make efforts for performance is weakened. However, incentives alone cannot constitute total pay because basic life of employees becomes unstable. Most companies make an effort to manage the percentage of incentives within the range of 10-20% of total cash pay. On the other hand, the ratio of incentives can be applied differently for each position and job group. In general, the higher the pay level, the higher the incentive ratio should be. And it is reasonable to say that the proportion of incentives for the sales group is high while the proportion of incentives for the support group is low.

4. Management of Pay Structure

There are many people in the company doing different works. It is difficult to imagine a company paying the same money for all employees. The pay that employees receive in return for their work tend to be different. It is because the education level and the content of the work are different, and because the rank within the company is not same. The pay structure mean to be a rule or principle for determining pay. This rule may be the number of years you have worked at the company, your educational level, the importance or value of the work, or the size of the responsibilities and roles.

In the seniority-based pay, the number of years of service at the company is used as an important criterion for determining the base pay. In the skill or competence-based pay, base pay is anchored on the skills or competence required to perform the job. In the job-ability based pay originally developed in Japan, the base pay is related to the ability of employees to perform work. In job-based pay, the base pay is set by the content or value of the job. When the base pay is determined by the role expected from each grades across-the-board, it is called role-based pay. On the other hand, it is impossible to set a base salary solely on the performance. In the exceptional case of piece-rate pay, the entire pay is determined by the performance, but it is difficult to regard it as a base pay because it is not a fixed pay set in advance. Therefore, it is common to use performance as a base for paying incentives or pay raise.

Pay structure is largely divided into a structure based on people and a structure based on work. The seniority-based pay and job ability pay are based on people, and job or role-based pay are based on work. Japanese and Korean companies have traditionally used people-based structure, but are now faced with a strong need to shift to work-based one.

To figure out pay structure in Korean companies, we have to understand employees grade system. In the past, Korean companies operated a pay system in which the individual's base pay was determined by the grades and service year. Specifically, each company had a pay table where grades are predetermined by the positions set across-the-

Figure 8-5 Tow Different Approaches between Person and Work

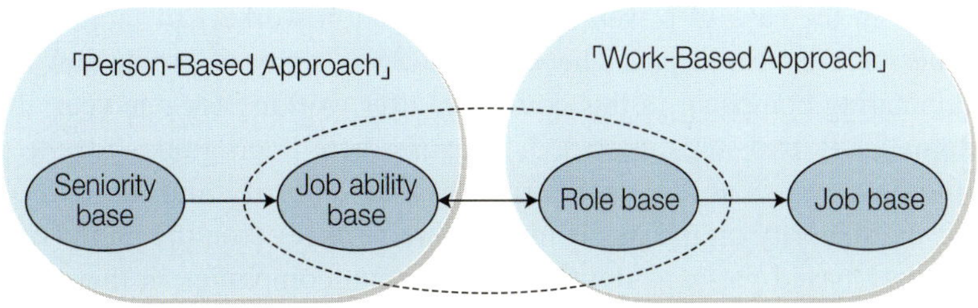

Source: 竹内裕(2013, p. 20).

boards such as staff(Sawon), section deputy(Daeri), section chief(Gwajang), department deputy(Chajang), department head(Bujang). These grade names were formed in the era when the grades corresponded one-to-one with the posts. In that period, grades represented the organizational rank and title of the post at the same time. This grade system was similar to the ranks of the military or of the civil servants in that employees of the same grades got the same pay despite of the jobs they were doing. And employees were called department head even though they did not actually take the post of the department head. These grades represent firstly the relative rank of employees, but it comprehensively reflected each employee's competency, the value of work in position, and the expected role in the organization. However, due to the discrepancy between the increase of the number of employees and limited number of the posts, this match was broken. For that reason, the grades are simply expressed by numbers such as 1st and 2nd level, or a mixture of English and numbers such as J1 and M2 is used these days. The grade levels may vary depending on the needs of the company, but it is a general trend that the number of levels is shortened for the purpose of making quick decisions.[7)]

4.1 Seniority-Based Pay

The seniority-based pay is a representative example of the pay based on the person. It refers to a pay system in which the base salary increases as the number of years of service increases over the years. In some cases, level of education or age are included in the seniority-based pay. Both of them are also an attribute that belongs to person but year of service take more importance in the seniority-based pay. This is because, for example, a new employee who is old but with no experience does not get high pay. However, the number of years of service increases with age after he has joined the company. As a result, there is a high correlation between the number of years of service and age.

Seniority-based pay has been used as the traditional pay system in Korea, but it is gradually decreasing due to the introduction of an annual salary system and the spread of incentive pay. A typical case where seniority-based pay is still used systematically is the pay of public officials and production workers in large corporations. The <Table 8-1> is the pay table for general public officials. The pay of public officials is determined by their grades and seniority step. The grade reflects an individual's experience and competence, and the content or role of the job. The seniority step is the number of years of service. In the case of the public officials, it is promoted to the one step upper after 1 year of service.

Meanwhile, in the case of private sector, production workers of large companies are subject to the seniority-based pay. The <Table 8-2> is a pay of production workers in a large manufacturing company. In this company, after working for one year, the seniority step is automatically two steps upgraded. Because there is no grades for the production workers, the base pay is solely determined by the seniority and the entry level. The influence of the seniority on the pay is much more stronger than the public officials.

The seniority-based pay was dominant in Korean companies in the past because it was beneficial to employees and management in that employees could earn a stable livelihood and management could make them work for a long time without losing

Table 8-1 Pay Table for Public Officials of General Service

(Monthly base pay, Won)

Grades / Seniority step	Grade1	Grade2	Grade3	Grade4	Grade5	Grade6	Grade7	Grade8	Grade9
1	4,122,900	3,711,600	3,348,600	2,870,000	2,564,700	2,115,800	1,898,700	1,692,800	1,659,500
2	4,267,400	3,849,300	3,472,500	2,987,200	2,668,400	2,214,200	1,985,300	1,775,100	1,682,300
3	4,415,600	3,988,800	3,600,100	3,106,300	2,776,000	2,315,800	2,077,000	1,861,800	1,720,400
4	4,567,100	4,129,700	3,728,600	3,228,200	2,887,800	2,419,500	2,173,400	1,950,300	1,773,600
5	4,722,300	4,272,500	3,859,200	3,351,800	3,002,500	2,526,400	2,273,200	2,042,300	1,842,100
6	4,879,400	4,415,500	3,991,100	3,476,500	3,119,600	2,636,200	2,375,400	2,136,600	1,928,200
7	5,038,800	4,560,400	4,124,500	3,602,400	3,238,500	2,746,300	2,478,300	2,231,200	2,013,800
8	5,199,600	4,705,100	4,258,300	3,728,900	3,358,900	2,856,700	2,581,900	2,322,100	2,096,400
9	5,362,600	4,850,800	4,393,300	3,855,900	3,479,600	2,967,500	2,680,400	2,408,800	2,175,400
10	5,526,500	4,996,400	4,528,100	3,982,600	3,601,200	3,071,400	2,774,400	2,490,800	2,251,400
11	5,690,200	5,142,700	4,663,100	4,110,500	3,714,800	3,170,000	2,863,100	2,570,300	2,324,000
12	5,859,300	5,293,900	4,803,100	4,230,900	3.824.400	3,267,100	2,950,300	2,647,900	2,396,100
13	6,029,400	5,446,200	4,933,200	4,343,500	3,928,400	3,358,400	3,033,000	2,722,500	2,465,200
14	6,200,000	5,583,900	5,054,000	4,448,500	4,025,400	3,444,600	3,112,100	2,793,700	2,532,400
15	6,349,000	5,711,000	5,165,300	4,547,400	4,117,000	3,527,500	3,187,600	2,862,200	2,596,400
16	6,481,300	5,827,400	5,269,100	4,640,700	4,203,200	3,605,100	3,259,100	2,928,300	2,658,500
17	6,598,700	5,934,600	5,365,600	4,727,400	4,284,300	3,679,100	3,327,700	2,990,000	2,719,100
18	6,703,200	6,032,500	5,455,200	4,808,300	4,360,900	3,749,100	3,393,300	3,049,900	2,775,500
19	6,796,800	6,123,100	5,538,100	4,883,900	4,433,000	3,815,600	3,455,100	3,107,300	2,831,100
20	6,880,700	6,205,600	5,615,800	4,954,500	4,500,600	3,878,100	3,513,900	3,162,100	2,884,100
21	6,958,000	6,281,100	5,687,600	5,020,600	4,564,200	3,938,200	3,570,100	3,214,400	2,934,100
22	7,026,800	6,350,400	5,754,300	5,082,500	4,623,900	3,994,800	3,623,100	3,264,600	2,982,000
23	7,085,000	6,413,700	5,815,700	5,140,600	4,680,400	4,047,900	3,674,400	3,312,400	3,027,700
24		6,465,500	5,873,100	5,195,400	4,733,000	4,098,400	3,723,000	3,358,600	3,071,500
25		6,515,000	5,920,200	5,245,500	4,782,900	4,146,600	3,769,100	3,402,300	3,113,400
26			5,965,200	5,287,900	4,829,900	4,192,000	3,813,400	3,444,800	3,151,300
27			6,006,900	5,327,100	4,868,800	4,235,100	3,850,700	3,480,200	3,183,800
28				5,364,500	4,906,100	4,271,300	3,885,500	3,514,200	3,215,200
29					4,940,500	4,305,200	3,919,200	3,546,500	3,245,400
30					4,973,900	4,338,600	3,951,300	3,577,700	3,274,800
31						4,369,600	3,981,500	3,608,000	3,303,700
32						4,398,900			

Source: Pay table of 2021, Ministry of Personnel Management(www.mpm.go.kr)

Table 8-2 Seniority-Based Pay for Production Workers

SENIORITY STEP	BASE PAY	HOURLY RATE	DIFFERENTIAL BETWEEN STEPS	NOTES
1	1,335,840	5,566		military service not completed
2	1,349,040	5,621	55	
3	1,362,240	5,676	55	military service completed
4	1,375,440	5,731	55	
5	1,388,640	5,786	55	
6	1,401,840	5,841	55	
7	1,415,040	5,896	55	
8	1,428,240	5,951	55	
9	1,441,440	6,006	55	
10	1,454,640	6,061	55	
11	1,467,840	6,116	55	
12	1,481,040	6,171	55	
13	1,494,240	6,226	55	
14	1,507,440	6,281	55	
15	1,520,640	6,336	55	maintenance worker' starting salary
.				
.				
.				

skilled manpower. In fact, this pay practice has an important advantage in stabilizing the lives of employees as pay rises in time with the increase in costs such as marriage, childcare, and education. These advantages was particularly important during the period of economic development, when companies were growing rapidly. In that period, it was important also for management to lower the turnover rate of skilled workers. In addition, the proportion of young manpower within the companies was so high that they were able to fully utilize these merits of seniority-based pay without bearing large labor costs.

However, due to the low economic growth, low birth rate and aging of the society, employees began to be aging rapidly. This change has braught into relief the latent disadvantages of the seniority-based pay. Above all, the burden of labor costs has increased significantly under this practice. In the seniority-based pay, the base pay increases proportionally depending on the number of years of service, and labor costs is inevitably increased as employees are aging. If the skill or productivity of employees increases in proportion to the tenure, the cost burden may be less, which is not the case in the majority of the cases. In some cases, rather, due to the introduction of new production technology, the skill of the elderly manpower becomes obsolete. The harsh global competition drives all Korean companies to secure cost competitiveness, while it

Table 8-3 Wage Gap of Manufacturing Workers by Years of Service (2010) (unit: %)

	KOREA	GERMANY	SPAIN	FRANCE	ITALY	SWEDEN	UK	JAPAN
Less than 1 year	100.0	100.0	100.0	100.0	100.0	100.0	100.0	100.0
Less than 1~6 year	134.9	128.4	114.6	113.2	126.6	110.9	116.1	129.8
Less than 6~10 years	188.0	157.6	125.0	124.5	129.2	115.7	125.0	148.5
Less than 10~15 year	211.1	166.2	133.5	132.6	136.9	116.1	134.3	168.7
Less than 15~20 year	261.9	170.6	149.8	143.3	140.6	114.6	139.2	202.5
Less than 20~30 years	313.0	191.2	168.2	146.3	152.7	110.8	156.7	241.6

Source: Jinho Jeong, 2013. "International Comparison of Wage Gap by Years of Service in 2010," Unpublished Paper by Korea Labor Institute.

is very difficult to control labor costs under the seniority-based pay.

This can explain why the seniority in the wage system of Korean companies is so high compared to other countries. As can be seen from <Table 8-3>, the seniority of Korean manufacturing workers is higher than that of Japan, which is known as the origin of the seniority-based pay. Due to various difficulties in comparing international statistics, we cannot fully trust the figures, but it is clear that wage increase related to the service year is very strong in Korea compared to other countries.

With the passage of the law requiring the mandatory retirement age to be 60 years or older, the aged employees will increase in number, and the burden of labor costs too will inevitably increase. It is for that reason that the law required labor and management to make efforts to reorganize the wage system. The eventual new extension of retirement age or employment protection for the elderly cannot be effectively achieved without mitigating the strong seniority of the pay system. And the best solution is to change traditional seniority-based pay to a work-oriented one.[8)]

4.2 Ability-Based Pay

Ability-based pay is a pay system that determines the difference in base pay among employees based on the ability for doing jobs. After classifying the ability level of the employees based on the ability level required to perform the jobs, the base pay is paid differently on the each level. There are a wide variety of specific practices, such as how many levels will be designed, whether the ability pay will be set as a single rate or a range, whether the base pay will be composed of only ability pay, or will be composed of other components such as service year and age. In this pay system, what is important is that the base pay is determined by the ability to perform the job possessed by a particular individual. And employees must go through an evaluation in order to climb up the grade. The job ability is an attribute residing in the person like the age or educational level, but it has an important advantage in that the ability has a more clear impact on performance. In addition, this pay can stimulate the ability development of the employees.

The ability-based pay was invented by Japanese companies to attempt to find a way to attenuate too strong seniority in the pay system and to stimulate ability for doing jobs. Various initiatives for changing pay system had been conducted since the 1960s, and this pay system were settled as the dominant pay system representing Japan. According to Isida,[9] the ability-based pay was an alternative solution found after the failure of the transition to job-based pay during 50s and 60s. In this system, the pay raise through ability evaluation was emphasized while influence of seniority and the educational level are weakened. In order to solve the problems of seniority pay system, Japanese companies separated promotion on the ability and promotion on the post, and introduced an ability rating to promote employees having job ability even though they are doing the same job. The main purpose of the management was to improve performance by stimulating employees competency development.

Although there are cases where the base pay consists of only ability pay, but, in general, Japanese companies operate the base pay with multiple components which include seniority or age in addition to the ability pay. This multiple base pay system aims to consider increasing living costs with age, and to promote the development of ability at the same time. It was for reducing unions' resistance to changes in this ability-based pay system. It is because unions often take a negative stance on determining pay through evaluation. The <Table 8-4> is a pay table for a Japanese company implementing the ability-based pay. As can be seen from the table, the employees' ability levels are composed of a total of 9 grades, including 3 junior grades, 3 senior grades, and 3 manager grades. The basic salary consists of age pay, years of service allowance, and skill level.

It was only in the 1990s that the ability-based pay was introduced in Korea. As the era of high growth ended entering the era of low growth, there was a shortage of posts for the employees to be promoted and this absence of the opportunity for promotion became a very serious problem. In particular, it was difficult to ignore the demands of the strong unions which gained power after the galvanizing union movement after 1987. On the other hand, management was worried that seniority-based pay was losing its motivational effect with the course of time. It was, therefore, an important task for management to make the pay system to have a positive impact on motivation and productivity.

Under this situation, in 1990, POSCO firstly introduced the ability-based pay, which are followed by Korea Electronics in 1991, and LG Electronics in 1992.[10] The introduction of the ability-based pay was carried out at the same time as the separation of the rank and position, the establishment of ability grades for career development, and the integration of the rank system between blue and white collar workers. As Korean companies' interest in the ability-based pay has increased, its introduction has progressed since then. A survey in 1998 estimates that about 5% of Korean companies

Table 8-4 **Pay Table of a Japanese Company Based on Ability Grades**

Ability pay

	J-1	J-2	J-3	S-4		M-9
Normal number of years necessary for promotion	2	2	3	3		
Normal age for each ability grade	18	20	22	25		48
Pay raise for the job promotion		1,500	2,000	2,000		6,800
Pay raise for the ability promotion	1,800	2,300	2,800	3,600		11,000
1 step	24,800	27,900	32,500	39,700		179,200
2	25,160	28,360	33,060	40,420	…	181,400
3	25,520	28,820	33,620	41,140		183,400
4	25,880	29,280	34,180	41,860		185,800
5	26,240	29,740	34,740	42,580		188,000
6	26,600	30,200	35,300	43,30		190,200
7	29,960	30,660	35,860	44,020		192,400
8	27,320	31,120	36,420	44,740		194,600
9	27,680	31,580	36,980	45,460		196,800
10	28,040	32,040	97,540	46,180		199,000
11	28,400	32,500	38,100	46,900		201,200
12	28,760	32,960	38,660	47,620		203,400
⋮	⋮	⋮	⋮	⋮		⋮
23	32,720	38,820	44,820	55,540		227,600
24	33,080	38,480	45,380	56,260		229,800

Pay based on age

Age	Age pay
18	93,000
19	94,800
20	96,600
21	98,400
22	100,200
23	102,900
24	105,300
25	108,300
26	111,000
27	113,700
28	117,000
29	120,300
⋮	⋮
40	152,600
41	154,200

Pay based on service year

Service year	Service year pay
0	0
1	400
2	800
3	1,200
4	1,600
5	2,000
6	2,400
7	2,800
8	3,200
9	3,600
10	4,000
11	4,400
⋮	⋮
22	8,800
23	9,200

Source: Yang, B. and H. Ahn, 1993, Theory and practice for the ability-based pay, Labor Economy Institute of the Korea Employers' Federation.

introduced it.[11)] <Table 8-5> shows POSCO's ability qualification system at the time.

There is no change in the rank itself from the past 10 grades to the 10 ability grades, but the types and levels of the ability corresponding to each grade are systematically organized and presented unlike to the past. The decision of promotion depends on the evaluation of the ability skill level and the basic salary is determined accordingly. For reference, the definition and levels of ability for each grade are shown in <Table 8-6>.

However, after the Asian economic crisis of 1997, the need to control labor costs increased, and a majority of companies were busy in introducing various performance pays. As a result, interest in the ability-based pay greatly decreased. Another important reason for the waning of interest was the difficulties of the evaluation arising in the operation of the ability-based pay, especially the evaluation of the ability level. This is because it was not easy to clearly define the difference in ability among different grades or levels. Often, the definitions and explanations for the ability expected are abstract

Table 8-5 Case of the Transition to the Ability-Based Pay (POSCO)

OLD SYSTEM		ABILITY BASED NEW SYSTEM			
GRADES	EXPECTED POSTS	ABILITY GRADE	COMPENSATION LEVEL	ABILITY LEVEL	
		M - 10	Manager-Director	Management and specialization function	Policy decision General management Advanced specialization
1甲	Department Head	M - 9	Department Head		
1乙	Deputy Department Head	M - 8(3)	Deputy Department Head		High level management Advanced specialization
2甲	Section Chief	M - 7(3)	Section Chief		Middle level management
2乙	Deputy Section Chief	S - 6(3)	Deputy Section Chief	Direction and supervision function	Low level management Middle specialization
3甲	Manager	S - 5(3)	Manager		Direction and supervision Low specialization
3乙		S - 4(3)	Employee4		Judgement skill Supervision of subordinates
4甲	Group Leader	J - 3(2)	Employee3	Performing function	Complex routine work
5甲		J - 2(2)	Employee2		Skilled routine work
5乙	Supervisor				
5丙		J - 1(3)	Employee1		Simple routine work
5丁	Supervisor				

and ambiguous. In this situation, in the face of the pressure from the labor unions that constantly demanded an automatic promotion according to the number of years of service, the ability-based pay practically became an seniority-based one.[12)] In Japan, negative views on the ability-based pay have begun to be highlighted recently because of this senioritization of the ability pay. This is one of the reasons why Japanese companies have changed the ability-based pay to the role-based pay since the 1990s. In Korea too, main interest of the companies was to strengthen the line of sight between effort and the performance, and many incentives are introduced to clarify this relationship. As a result, the ability-based pay did not succeed in taking an important place in the Korean pay system.

4.3 Job-Based Pay

Job-based pay is an practice that has historically developed in Europe and the United States. Among Korean companies, it is mainly introduced and used by foreign companies, and not many domestic companies have introduced it. This is because job-

Table 8-6 **Ability Definition and Level (examples)**

GRADE	DEFINITION
M- 8	The ability to independently plan and operate small divisions or similar organizational tasks in accordance with the policies of the entire company and the relevant departments, take practical responsibility for the promotion of the business, manage subordinates, and assist the supervisor at the same time. - Required ability • Organization and cost management capability of the relevant sector • Ability to coordinate interests among members of the relevant department, and the ability to reach out to relevant departments within and outside the company • Command and leadership ability of own department, and development ability to train and guide subordinates • Ability to improve work process within the department in charge • Practical ability of two or more sections within the department
…	…
S- 5	The ability to cultivate and direct subordinates, performing work using judgment and creativity based on one's own professional knowledge and experience - Required ability • Guidance, development, and leadership ability of subordinates • Practical work ability in the relevant sub-sector • Ability to improve work process within the relevant sub-sector

oriented personnel management has been difficult to take root in Korean companies that have traditionally used people-centered personnel management. However, with regard to the issue of discrimination against non-regular workers, the same wage for equal work has emerged as an important policy agenda, and naturally job based pay is gaining a lot of attention. In particular, as the government is promoting a policy to introduce it to public enterprises and institutions, there is a possibility that job pay will spread in the future.

In the job-based pay, the base pay is determined according to the value of the job each individual is in charge of. It can be said that it is a different approach from Japan and Korea in that the value of work is first determined and then the right person is assigned. In order to utilize job-based pay, we have to know the value of the job and job evaluation is used for this. It is common to conduct job evaluation together with job analysis. Job analysis is a process of systematically grasping the content or characteristics of a job, and through this, the main tasks, expected performance and responsibilities, and knowledge, skills, and competencies necessary to effectively perform the job are derived.[13] Job evaluation is conducted based on certain criteria so that job values can be compared using job information secured in the job analysis process. As shown in <Table 8-7>, all jobs are scored for each criterion, and the total score obtained as a result is the value of the job.

It is rare that the job evaluation score itself directly corresponds to the base pay on a one-to-one basis. This is because it is difficult to individually manage pay for each

Table 8-7 **Scoring in the Job Evaluation (example)**

	Factor	Level 1	Level 2	Level 3	Level 4	Level 5
Skill	• Knowledge	14	28	42	56	70
	• Experience	22	44	66	88	110
	• Initiative and ingenuity	14	28	42	56	70
Effort	• Physical demand	10	20	30	40	50
	• Mental demand	5	10	15	20	25
Responsibility	• Equipment or process	5	10	15	20	25
	• Material or product	5	10	15	20	25
	• Safety of others	5	10	15	20	25
	• Work of others	5	10	15	20	25
Job conditions	• Working conditions	10	20	30	40	50
	• Hazards	5	10	15	20	25

job. Therefore, jobs with a certain range of scores are bound together and managed as a group. These are job grades or pay grades. Pay grades are sometimes called pay bands because each pay grade is represented by a bar-shaped band with upper and lower limits. Traditionally, large companies in the United States have operated more than 20 job grades, but they are shifting toward significantly reduced grades to increase flexibility in manpower movement. This is called broadbanding. The most well-known is the IBM case, which has been broadbanding as the past 27 pay grades have been reduced to 10 grades. The [Figure 8-6] shows such a change well.

When the grade according to the job evaluation is determined, competitive pay levels are set for each pay grade through a pay survey in the market. While job evaluation is a tool to ensure internal fairness of pay, pay survey is a means to ensure external fairness of wages. In some cases, pay surveys are conducted directly by companies, but in most cases, it is common to use pay information from government agencies or from a consulting company. Since multiple jobs are included in one pay grade, a pay survey is not conducted for all jobs, but conducted focusing on the most representative job(key job). After that, a specific pay is determined according to the pay policy of the company. The [Figure 8-7] shows the flow in which job pay for an individual is determined in the job-based pay.

Let's look at this process through an example of a company that introduced job-based pay recently.[14)] This company had a pay system based on the seniority, and the content and the value of the job was not reflected in compensation, which made the internal fairness perceived by employees very weak. To solve these problems, job-based pay was introduced. Job analysis was first conducted, and job evaluation was done on the information collected by job analysis. The evaluation factors were determined in consultation with the consulting team and management, which was skill, effort and responsibility. They were set as simple as possible in consideration of the fact that this

Figure 8-6 **IBM's Broadbanding**

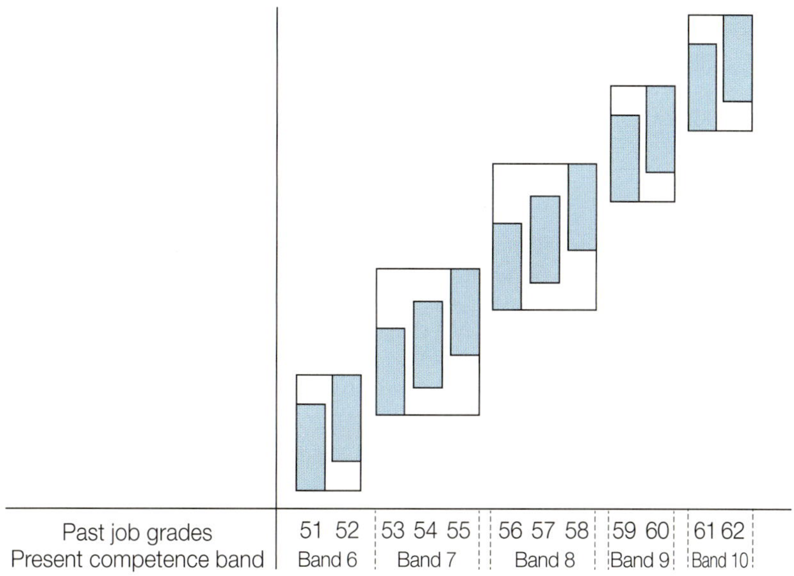

Figure 8-7 **Design Process of Job-Based Pay**

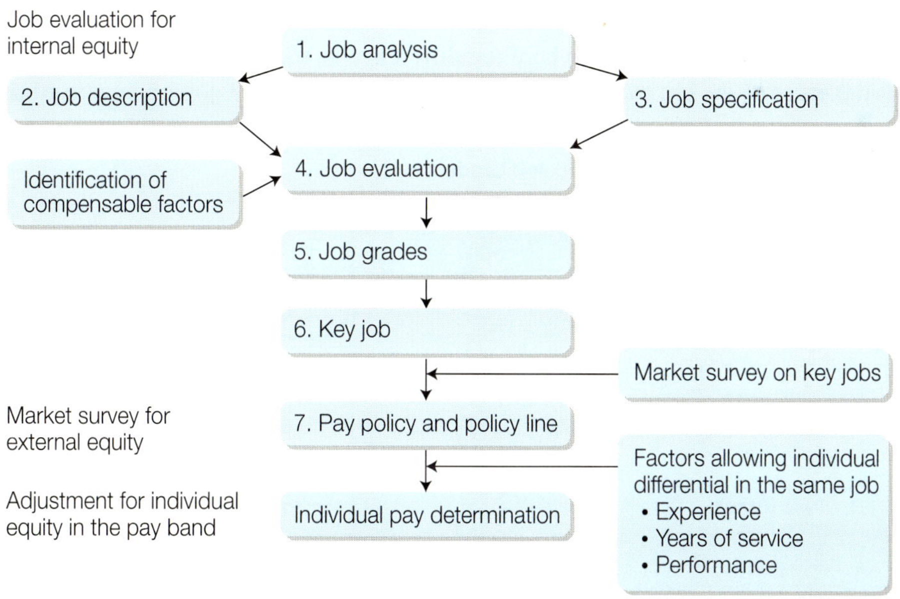

Table 8-8 **Factors of the Job Evaluation**

	FACTOR FOR EVALUATION	DEFINITION FOR EVALUATION FACTORS
Skill	Job expertise	The minimum level of knowledge and skills required to perform the job
	Practical experience	The level of experience required to achieve the overall purpose of the job
Effort	Problem solving ability	The level of ability to accurately identify and solve problems occurring in work processing
	Level of innovation	Effort level to handle work differently than before
Responsibility	Organizational contribution	The degree to which the job contributes to the creation of organizational value
	Performance responsibility	The level of negative impact arising from failing to achieve goals or performance

company was a medium-size with not many employees.

As a result of the job evaluation, a score reflecting the job value was calculated, and based on this, four job grades were determined. The number of job grades to be used was decided by the management in consideration of the characteristics of the job evaluation score distribution and the need for personnel management. In general, job grades are classified at the point where the difference in scores widens. The [figure 8-8] shows the score of the job evaluation and the classification of the job grade accordingly.

Figure 8-8 **Job Evaluation Score and Job Grade**

RAN-KING	TEAM NAME	SCORE (AVG)	JOB GROUP
1	Sales Division	113	
2	Strategic Planning Office	111	G1
3	Institute of Technology	105	
4	Edutech Business Division	89	
5	Production Technology/ Operation Team	76	G2
6	Mass Production Quality/ Development Quality Assurance Team	75	
7	Finance Team	73	
8	Purchase Team	73	
9	HR Team	72	G3
10	PR/IR Team	70	
11	Accounting Team	68	
12	CR Team	61	G4

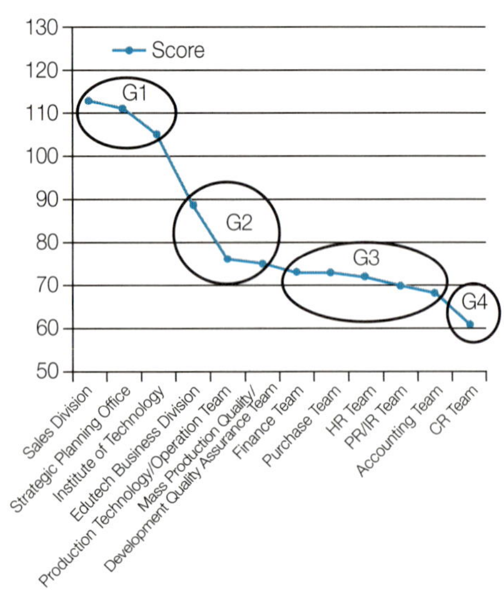

Figure 8-9 Pay Bands by Job Grades

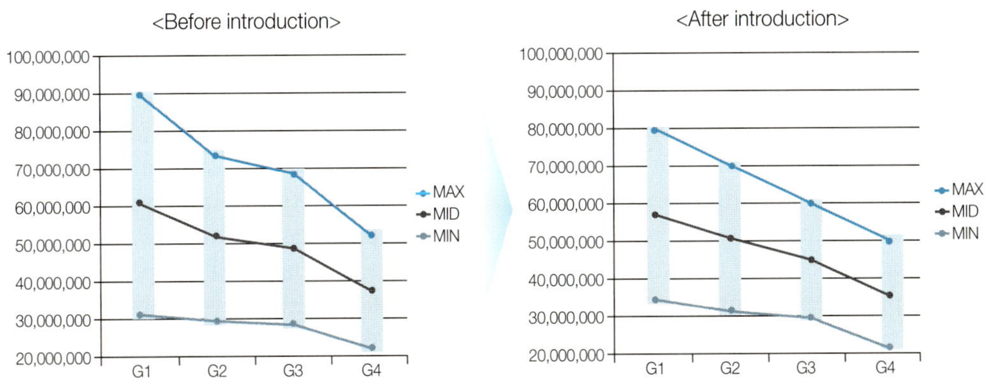

The four job grades set in this way are managed as pay bands, each with an upper and a lower limit. Before the introduction of the job-based pay, individual pays are heavily overlapped by job grades, and the difference in pay reflecting the job value was not properly reflected. Through the job-based pay, the company succeed in aligning the individual pay to the job value while considering market pay level. The [Figure 8-9] shows the process.

In recent years, in line with environmental changes such as low economic growth, aging, and retirement extension, discussions on transformation of the pay system are becoming more active, and job-based pay is being suggested as a promising alternative. That's because job-based pay has the following advantages.

First, it has the easing effect of seniority in pay. In the job-based pay, compensation is determined by job value, so pay raise only occur in principle when there is a change in job duties. Therefore, it is easy to control the seniority effect in pay, which automatically increases pay every year even though there is no change in work. In the job-based pay, a consideration for inflation into compensation is not entirely absent, but it can significantly reduce the effect of seniority compared to the traditional seniority pay. In particular, job-based pay is necessary to relieve the burden of labor costs that will increase due to the eventual extension of the retirement age.

Second, it has the effect of enhancing fairness and preventing discrimination. The competencies and knowledge required, the intensity of work, and the degree of responsibility are all different according to the job the employees have. The job-based pay is fair in that it compensate employees in consideration of the characteristics of the job. In particular, with regard to the non-regular workers, job-based pay guarantees important social fairness. Under the job-based pay, it is difficult to pay them differently just because they are non-regular workers.

Third, it has the effect of reinforcing professionalism. As competition between companies intensifies, specialized knowledge and skills are becoming more important. It is difficult to secure competitiveness in global competition with generalists alone. It is a time when one genius feeds ten thousand people. A company having employees with professional perspectives and capabilities has a competitive edge. The job-based pay reinforces professionalism in the work. This is because it recruits people with the right requirements for work and develops and grows them through a professional career path.

Fourth, it has the support effect of global business development. Korean companies often experience difficulties due to differences in the HR system used by the domestic headquarters and the HR system of the local country where local standard is job-based pay. In this situation, it is difficult to implant the Korean pay system to the local subsidiary. In the reality that mergers and acquisitions with foreign companies are becoming an important strategic means of global business, the fact that the pay system of headquarters can be used in local countries constitutes an important competitiveness.

Despite these advantages, few Korean companies have introduced job-based pay. This is because there are many obstacles to its introduction. The lack of market pay information required to set job pay is an important reason often mentioned by the pay experts. The fact that job analysis and evaluation takes a lot of time and money is another reason that makes it difficult to introduce it. The biggest obstacle, however, is the resistance of labor unions and employees having to give up the yearly pay raise guaranteed on the seniority. In addition, the job-based pay conflicts with the Korean traditional manpower management fostering human resources by taking on various tasks and roles. And the creation and destruction of jobs is accelerated and flexible response is required in a situation where technological and environmental changes are intensifying. It can be said that these are reasons for Korean companies to be cautious about the introduction of the job-based pay.

4.4 Role-Based Pay

Role-based pay is a system that determines the base pay according to the size of an individual's role within an organization. It was invented by Japanese companies in the 1990s to solve the problem of the seniority-based pay or senioritized ability-based pay, and to change their pay system from person-based to work-based one. It was considered as an alternative to Japanese companies that want to introduce job-based pay in the face of the obstacles to the job-based pay. It began to be introduced from the 1990s in Japanese companies, and it is more widely used for the manager-level. In recent years, in the process of pursuing the transformation of the wage system, interest in role pay is increasing significantly in Korea, and it is known that some companies have already started introducing the role-based pay system.

A role includes not only the roles required by the job itself, but also the roles the organization or superior expects. Like job-based pay, role-based pay is a work-oriented pay system, but there are some differences from job-based pay. For our understanding, let's take an example of the HR team leader's job. The value and its grade do not change by who is in charge of the job in the job-based pay. However, in the role-based pay, if he takes an important organizational innovation project this year, his role level can be raised. Although the job remains the same, the role grade can change from the point of view of the role. In this respect, the role-based pay is more flexible than the job-based pay. However, this is not so much different in nature. If the HR team leader continues to take important tasks, then it will be reflected in the job analysis and job grade will be raised accordingly.

The difference between job-based and role-based pay can be explained in terms of the meaning of the grades. The grades in the job-based pay is a group of jobs with similar job values, designed for convenience in pay management. Therefore, job grades reflects the size of job value accordingly. Meanwhile, the role grades in the role-based pay reflects the expected size of the role in the job. However, unlike job grades, it is possible to clarify the expectations that the company has for each role grade, such as the role of learner, role of performer, and role of developer etc. In addition, job grades are always created in a bottom-up method based on job analysis and evaluation, while role grades takes often a top-down method in which the company sets the frame of roles that the company expects from employees and then aligns jobs to them. Therefore, for Korean companies that have traditionally operated manpower by assigning various tasks regardless of individual job duties, role-based pay can be more easily understood and accepted.

The process of setting the role level at the role-based pay is basically very similar to the process of job evaluation at the job-based pay.[15)] This is because the starting point of the role-based pay is the expected role from the assigned job. However, there is a difference that not only the content specified in the job description, but also the size of the mission or role expected from the organization and the boss at that time can be reflected in the grade. Because role-based pay is a wage system based on what one does, like job-based pay, it often leads to confusion about the difference between job-based pay and role-based pay.

Gusuda, an authority on the Japanese wage system, explains the difference as follows.[16)] "If the base salary is determined according to the hierarchies or positions within the organization, it is the position-based pay. Among the various contents related to the job, if a base salary is given based on job responsibilities, it can be said to be a post-based pay. However, in reality, this post-based pay is usually paid in the form of allowances rather than base pay to managers in charge of management. Role-based pay is the case in which a base pay is provided based on the role that includes the job title and expected goals in addition to the job description."

Canon Korea is the first company that introduces and operates role-based pay in Korea. Canon Korea is a joint venture established by investing 50-50 between Canon and Lotte Group. Canon Korea's role-based pay is basically designed and operated in a form similar to that of Japanese Canon's.[17)] The most important motive for introducing it in Canon Korea was to secure competitiveness in labor costs. In the case of production workers, the work done is relatively simple, reaching the peak of productivity after a certain period of time, while wages increase in seniority pay, thus widening the gap between productivity and wages. The role-based pay was sought as an alternative in a situation where this seriously threatened manufacturing competitiveness of the company. This was the same in white collar workers and managers. It was necessary to resolve the phenomenon of receiving high wages compared to roles, and therefore Canon Korea tried to find a solution in the role-based pay where pay increases would not occur unless the expected role changes in each employee's job.

Figure 8-10 Different Pay Systems Based on Work

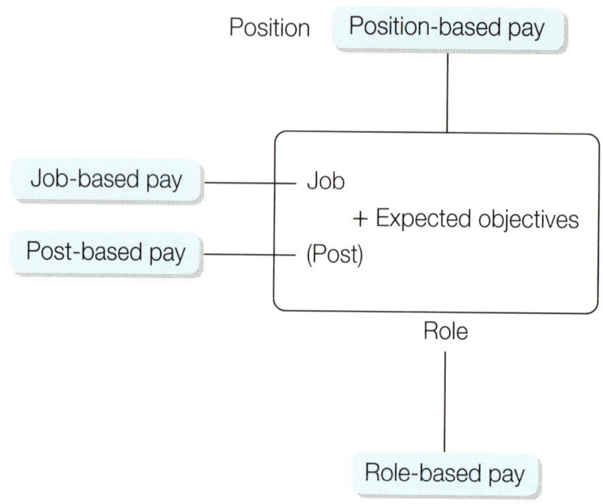

Source: 楠田丘(1998), 役割給と職責給の違いは何か, 労政時報, 第3379号 p. 80.

In order to introduce the role-based salary, the HR team led the job analysis and evaluation. It was an important part to have each employee write all the job descriptions, and then check the contents by the supervisor to determine what role each individual is actually playing and whether they are playing a role appropriate to the position. The job evaluation was conducted by reflecting four evaluation factors, such as job responsibility, difficulty, knowledge requirements for performing the task, and experience. After job analysis and evaluation, the role grade was set as 4 grades from ME to M3 for managers and 4 grades from G1 to G4 for non-managers.

Canon Korea has a position structure for production workers that leads to simple worker → cell leader → group supervisor → model manager. In the case of managerial positions, ME is the role level for the manager who do not have a manager position or have just been promoted by passing the managerial qualification exam. In the process of setting the role level for the introduction of the role-based pay, reorganization of work was carried out so that the roles of the team or headquarters became similar. For example, when the work of a specific team was very important, then the role of that team changed to the level of department. Therefore, all the team or department managers could have the same role grade.

After the introduction of role-based pay, Lotte Canon's wage system has changed as follows. The most important change is that the base salary is determined by the role grades set through job evaluation. Wages are divided into base pay and bonuses, and bonuses consists of minimum bonus, personal achievement bonuses, and company achievement bonuses. Meanwhile, various allowances were integrated into the base pay for the introduction of role pay. Specifically, position allowance, management allowance, and adjustment allowance were all integrated into the base pay, and subsidies for birthday vacation, lunch expenses, transportation expenses, gift expenses, and vacation

Figure 8-11 Setting the Role Grades

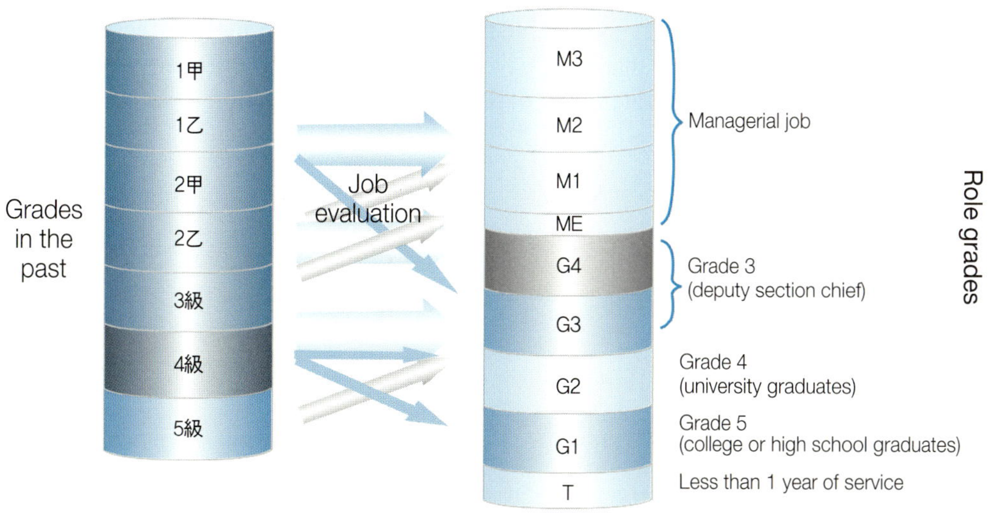

Figure 8-12 Role-Based Pay Structure of Lotte Cannon

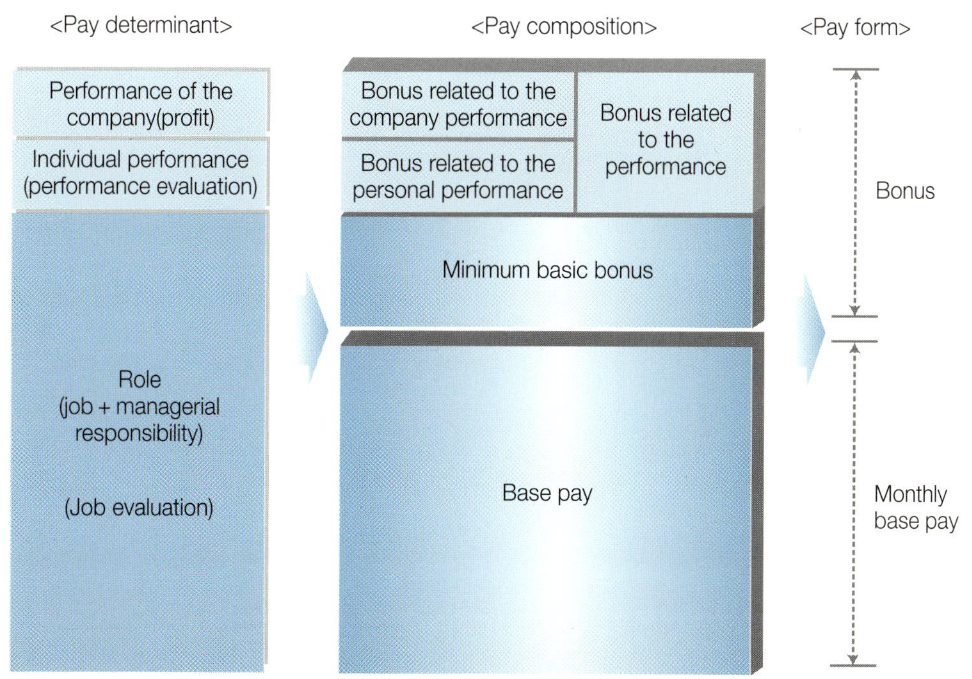

expenses were also integrated into the base pay.

The <Table 8-9> explains the characteristics of the seniority-based, job-based, ability-based and role-based pay system, and compares strengths and weaknesses of the each pay system. Considering that each pay system is suitable in different situations, it is important to select and operate a pay system that fits the situation or strategy of the company.

Table 8-9 **Comparison of Different Pay Systems**

TYPE	CHARACTERISTICS	STRENGTH	WEAKNESS	FAVORABLE SITUATION
Seniority-based pay	• Entrance pay set by education level • Pay raise on the seniority after entrance	• Support living cost • Loyalty for the company • Organizational hierarchy • Easy to understand and administer • Easy for internal transfer • Fewer evaluation problems	• Difficulty in reflecting work value • Difficulty securing professional manpower • Low morale among talented young people • Increased labor cost burden • Labor cost increase not related to productivity • Fail to stimulate ability improvement	• When the job classification is not • When labor shortage is severe • Small and medium size company • Family-oriented organizational culture
Job-based pay	• Pay based on evaluation of job value • High pay for high value job • Consideration for market pay	• Same pay for same value job • Strong internal equity • Objective base of market pay • Efficient cost management	• Difficulty for job evaluation • Rigid internal transfer • Difficult to adapt to rapid environmental change	• When job identification and classification is clear • Sufficient labor supply • Large company under low growth • Individualistic organizational culture
Ability-based pay	• Pay determined by employees' ability (competence) • Classification and evaluation of the ability	• Stimulus for ability development • Retain for competent talent • Opportunity for promotion • Flexible design for pay scheme	• Difficulty for defining ability • Difficulty for evaluating ability • Tendency to senioritization and increased labor costs • Weak tie between ability and performance	• Job requiring high skill • Small and medium size company growing fast • Flexible work flow in which role and duty are overlapping • Team-based organizational culture
Role-based pay	• Pay determined by the role size of the employees • Possibility for different role for the same job or person	• Same role same pay • Flexible transfer and compensation by broadbanding • Easy transition for the job-based pay • Easy to adapt to Korean grade system	• Influence of supervisor on role size • Ambiguous definition of role or meaning • Too much different practices under the role-based pay	• Company under low growth and high labor cost • Too strong resistance to job-based pay • Company who needs flexible utilization of manpower

Source: Adapted by authors from Yoo, G. C. 2014, Wage system of Korean companies: Is job-based pay an alternative, *Labor Review*, February, pp. 37-54.

Ending Case

Samyang Group's Job-Based Pay[18)]

Samyang Group, a representative long-lived company in Korea, has been taking the lead in all personnel systems introduced in Korea as long as it has a long history. In the early years of modern industry after liberation in 1945 from Japanese occupation, due to the shortage of labor and rapid growth, the so-called lifelong employment type of personnel system was predominant practice of the times. It was considered natural that a company takes responsibility for the person's life once he or she enters the company. During this period, Samyang's HR system, like other companies, was a seniority-based HR system. There was a strong belief that after joining a company, various experiences would lead to improved performance. This seniority-based personnel system was applied until the end of the 1980s.

However, in the late 1980s, many employees couldn't go up to the higher positions because there were not enough positions. As a result, the morale of employees declined, and to compensate for this, Samyang introduced an ability-based personnel system and job-ability qualification practice. This system can be said to be a system that makes use of the merits of the seniority-based personnel system of Eastern thinking and the merit-based personnel system of Western thinking. Through this system, if a person after a certain number of years of service is recognized as having the ability to perform a job, he will be promoted with increased pay even if there is no upper-level position.

Meanwhile, in the course of the 1998 Asian financial crisis, many companies having realized the importance of the competitiveness and performance for survival, were introducing various pay-for-performance. Samyang Group was no exception. In the past, Samyang's seniority-based personnel system or ability-based qualification system were both not related to the actual contribution to the company. And high performers were particularly dissatisfied in these systems. Some initiatives were examined to cope with this problems while maintaining the precedent systems but it was difficult to sufficiently recognize high performers.

Accordingly, Samyang needed to change the minds of employees by attempting a drastic change to job-based personnel system. However, there was a serious obstacle to this transition. In the existing person-based personnel system, tasks with different values were mixed in one job, and there were many cases where the workload was assigned differently according to individual abilities. For example, planning or strategy tasks and simple routine tasks are often set as a single person's job, and too many tasks are concentrated on the person who gives performance. In this situation, it was difficult to make fair evaluation and compensation according to job value. Therefore, it was necessary to rearrange the necessary duties from upper to lower work units and all individuals working in them, and to clearly assigning role and duties for each job.

In order to construct job-based personnel system, the company identified and standardized all the tasks that must be done to achieve the business vision and the relative value of the job is evaluated. The job grade was divided into four grades according to the relative value. In the case of research and development jobs, it was difficult to draw job value because their tasks were conducted on the projects lasting as little as 3 months to as long as 2 years. Accordingly, job grades were classified into four stages in consideration of individual competency levels. In the case of on-site production workers, the contribution to productivity is different according to the individual's skill proficiency, so the grades were assigned to four levels according to the individual skill level.

For compensation of employees, the basic annual pay, the qualification pay, the position pay, and the performance pay were all integrated into one base pay. And a target incentive was introduced to set the company-wide financial performance goal and provide incentives according to the achievement level. Under the job-based pay, the employee's annual compensation is determined by the position within the pay band and his performance. The pay band is adjusted annually by comprehensively considering many factors, such as the economic growth rate and inflation rate, job value in the market, the trend of competitors, and the company's ability to pay. The job grade can be changed according to changes in strategy or work contents. If there is a change in job value due to changes in company strategy, in work processes, the job evaluation committee evaluates them and reflects the results into the job grades.

The company's job-based personnel system, emphasizing employee's own job instead of the vertical position system, has created an opportunity to transform into a horizontal organizational culture. However, due to the introduction of the job-based pay, which was not implemented by most domestic companies, the company had to face many problems. The company did not have enough experience in the recruitment how to reflect the characteristics of the job and how to judge the suitability for the job. There were also many difficulties in the early stage because applicants did not know exactly what kind of personnel system the job-based system was.

Despite the fact that a long time has passed since the introduction, there are still some problems to be solved. Samyang's compensation system was far from being implemented by other domestic companies, so it often took some time for new employees to understand and accept the system. Moreover, if the growth of the organization is not supported, it is impossible to move to a higher-level job, and the promotion stagnation cannot be resolved. Also, the principle of equal compensation for equal-value work is good by itself, but it is also somewhat difficult to accommodate in the egalitarian Korean culture. Because of these problems, Samyang's job-based personnel system was not welcomed by employees at the beginning of its introduction even it was implemented after a long preparation period. In particular, when relocating the job after the job analysis and redesign, a consideration for seniority was done and a refusal to move from a higher value job to a lower one happened. Some employees requested for job reevaluation even though there was no change in the job. In response, the company tried to faithfully apply the principle of the job-based personnel system.

Just as all systems cannot be perfect, the job-based personnel system can have various problems and limitations. In particular, it is very difficult to accurately grasp the market value of a job in a situation where there are not many domestic companies that implement job-based pay and there is no accurate wage information for the job. However, as a result of the experience of operating a job-based personnel system, the company think that if more detailed and standardized wage information is provided at the government level in the future, it will not only help to extend the retirement age, but also allow companies to respond effectively to challenges the aging society pose in the future.

Discussion Questions

1. Since the late 1980s, Samyang introduced an ability-based pay with ability qualification system to solve the problem of lowering morale caused by promotion stagnation. This system was also the dominant pay system in Japan at that time. What are the problems with this system?
2. Why is job-based pay a work-oriented pay, not people-oriented one?
3. In the case of Samyang, job-based pay is applied to white collar employees, but compensation grades are determined based on competency level or skill proficiency level for production and research jobs. What is the reason?
4. Although the necessity of job-based pay has been emphasized for a long time, there are not many cases of introducing it among domestic indigenous company. What are the factors that make it difficult for Korean companies to introduce job-based pay?

CHAPTER

9

Pay for Performance

1. Environmental Change and Pay for Performance
2. Pay for Performance and Motivation
3. Types and Characteristics of Pay for Performance
4. Strategic Use of Pay for Performance

Learning Objectives

1. Understand environmental changes requiring pay for performance.
2. Understand the various theoretical foundations of pay for performance.
3. Understand the side effects of pay for performance and the ways to avoid them.
4. Understand the conditions supporting the motivating effect of pay for performance.

Introductory Case

In January 2021, when SK Hynix decided to pay an amount equivalent of 400% of the base salary as performance incentive, it was engulfed in an unexpected ripple. This is because employees' dissatisfaction has been pouring out like an explosion. Employees expressed dissatisfaction with the fact that the amount did not properly reflect their contribution to the company's profit. In fact, while operating profit in 2020 exceeded 5 trillion won, an increase of 84% compared to the previous year, the level of incentives remained at the same as the previous year. In addition, employees were also dissatisfied with the fact that the incentive was significantly lower than that of Samsung Electronics. The lack of transparency in the process for determining incentive was also an important factor in amplifying dissatisfaction. It was known only that the size of the incentive is measured in terms of economic value added (EVA), and the exact number of each element that actually constitutes it or how the final incentive is determined from the EVA was not known to the employees at all.

As the situation worsened, Chairman Choi announced that he would return his annual salary of 3 billion won, while President Lee Seok-Hee tried to explain directly to the employees, but the situation did not calm down. Employees expressed their distrust of the management in a strong tone through internal and external social media, and even criticized the management for their performance being exploited. The labor-management conflict over the incentive has spread beyond Hynix to SK Telecom. It was a very difficult situation for the SK Group and Hynix, which valued the happiness of its members and tried to create a happy success story. The conflict related to the incentive has also spread to Samsung Electronics and LG Chem, and behind the scenes there are young generations who can't stand the unfair situation. They were at the center of raising the issue of unfairness through public mail to the management and showing strong cohesion while communicating through SNS.

SK Hynix held a labor-management council meeting and decided to change the formular from EVA to operating profit to increase its predictability, and to provide additional welfare benefits to the employees. However, not all problems have been solved. This is because it has not yet been clearly determined what percentage of operating profit will be paid as an incentive, and the trust of the employees in the management has not been fully restored. This case suggests that the transparent criteria and process for determining pay for performance are as important as the amount of the incentive itself.

Discussion Questions

1. Why did SK Hynix employees become dissatisfied with the incentive despite the fact that they were paid a considerable amount of money?
2. What factors determine economic value added(EVA)? Why are employees dissatisfied with that formular?
3. Is it appropriate for the company to change the formular of pay for performance to operating profit and provide some benefits?
4. If you are the HR manager of SK Hynix, how would you like to improve incentive system? What are the necessary conditions for the incentive to work as expected?

The era has come when everyone talks about performance. It is natural from a management point of view to emphasize performance because it is impossible for a company to survive without performance. In Korea, traditionally firms have preferred long-term growth to short-term performance. However, this approach lost its influence after Asian financial crisis in 1997, and short-term performance and shareholders' interest began to be seriously considered and actively pursued. These changes gained great momentum under the name of global standards. Pay for performance is one of the remarkable change representing this new tendency. If the base pay is a reward that is determined according to the value, role of the job or ability of each individual, pay for performance is a reward based on performance in addition to the basic reward. Performance-based compensation includes a variety of methods and systems. The incentives based on company performance are the most common, but sales allowances and productivity incentives can all be included in the pay for performance. In a broader sense, an increase in the base pay according to performance can also be considered as a form of pay for performance.

The reason why companies actively use pay for performance is the belief that performance-based rewards can promote motivation of the employees. If there is no difference in rewards according to performance, the will to work hard and achieve good results will be weakened. Therefore, most companies have implemented and operated a reward system based on performance. However, performance pay is a double-edged sword. If it is well managed, it can contribute to performance improvement through motivation, but if it is not, conflict and dissatisfaction may arise and fail to improve performance. In particular, if the criteria for determining performance pay are not established clearly and fairly, the side effects may be great. It is not rare to find the firms experiencing the unexpected negative effects of the performance pay. For example, in a car repair company, the shorter the maintenance time, the more incentives were paid. As a result, the maintenance was rushed, resulting in increased customer dissatisfaction.

Performance cannot be rewarded only in cash. Let's recall the total rewards perspective discussed in the previous chapter. It is possible to give praise and recognition for outstanding performance, and it is also possible to provide educational opportunities in lieu of cash or to reflect on promotions. Emphasizing only cash rewards for hard work may actually weaken intrinsic motivation. This is because the intrinsic motivation feeling that work itself is interesting can be turned into working for money. This does not mean, however, that cash compensation is unnecessary. Therefore, it is more effective to properly combine various reward methods rather than stick to rewarding performance only in cash.

1. Environmental Change and Pay for Performance

Pay for performance, which determine the size of rewards based on performance, are rapidly spreading. Profit sharing(PS), introduced by Samsung Electronics in 2000 after the Asian financial crisis, has attracted a lot of attention from the media in that up to 50% of annual salary is paid according to the amount of profit generated in the business. It ushered in an era of full-fledged pay for performance. Samsung Electronics' PS was introduced with the purpose of reinforcing business unit-oriented management strategies after the economic crisis, and is a system that embodies performance-based compensation in an uncertain environment.[1)] Under different names, various types of pay for performance have been introduced and operated in many firms. In the past, the portion of performance-related pay was small. However, in recent years, the proportion of performance-related pay has increased. Such changes are being facilitated by the following environmental changes.

1.1 Increased Market Pressure for the Performance

Performance pressure from the market felt by companies is increasing significantly. In particular, in the stock market, the amount of profit a company has shown or expected in a given period plays a very important role in determining the stock price. The top management, who is obliged to keep the stock price at an appropriate level, cannot but pay attention to the company's performance. A decline in corporate performance and a drop in stock prices endanger the position of the CEO. The size of the dividend also affects the share price and a company's performance need to be sufficient in order to provide appropriate dividends to shareholders.

In the past, Korean companies were not very sensitive to pressure from the stock market. Until just before the Asian economic crisis, the management of Korean companies was characterized by growth expansionism. By giving priority to growth and utilizing external funds as much as possible with a small amount of equity capital, they have pursued actively expansion in non-related businesses. The economic crisis inevitably destroyed the unrelated diversification strategy represented by the high debt ratio and circular shareholding, and since then, business management that places importance on shareholder interests has taken root.[2)]

1.2 Rapid Change and Uncertainty of the Environment

The reason companies reinforce performance-based rewards stems from the fact that the environment is changing rapidly and uncertainty is growing. As the environment changes and it is difficult to predict the company's performance according to it, paying wages on a fixed basis is burdensome for companies. Therefore, a portion of the compensation is provided as a performance pay with a variable nature is preferred. If the company's performance is bad, no incentives are paid, so the labor cost burden is reduced. It can be said that uncertainty is shared by the company and its members. However, it should be noted that this type of pay for performance may impair employee wage stability making his livelihood difficult.

1.3 The Decline of Long-Term Employment

Changes in which long-term employment gradually disappears and turnover between companies increases significantly are also factors that promote pay for performance. In the long-term employment with the company, compensation is possible through promotion, even if it is not cash compensation. In fact, in the past, the most important compensation in Korean companies was promotion rather than wages. While giving wages similar to those who joined the company at the same time for the harmony between them, the companies have offered a fast promotion to the high potential. However, if the long-term relationship between the employee and the company disappears, the employee prefers to be compensated in cash for the current performance. If company fails to provide such immediate compensation, it risks losing the necessary manpower, so it tries to compensate promptly for performance.

1.4 Securing Key Talents

Pay for performance are also being actively used for the purpose of securing key talent. When hiring external talent, providing a large fixed wage is the surest method as an inducement, but in this case, pay equity with internal workers become often an issue. Performance pay can solve this problem because newly hired can justify the large amount of pay they receive by showing the high performance. The company can pay a signing bonus at the time of the contract, but in this case it is difficult to stimulate sustained performance after hire. Performance pay can be helpful in that situation also because it gives continuously a stimulus to the talents to work hard to get the compensation he expects. Therefore, introducing and operating a performance-based pay system can promote the recruitment of external talents by enabling bold compensation for them according to their performance.

2. Pay for Performance and Motivation

Previously, we looked at the changes in the environment that led to the active use of performance pay. In order to respond to such changes in the environment, a company must promote the motivation of its employees to work hard. An important reason performance-based pay is emphasized and spread is that it can increase motivation. The basic principle of the motivating effect of performance pay is as follows. If a company decides individual or group rewards according to performance, employees will increase their motivation to work, and when the motivation to work increases, they work harder, resulting in higher organizational performance. As organizational performance increases,

Figure 9-1 Relationship between Performance and Compensation

rewards increase accordingly, which in turn creates a virtuous cycle between rewards, motivation, and performance improvement.

2.1 Theoretical Basis of Pay for Performance

The theoretical claim that performance pay can contribute to improving the performance of individuals, groups or organizations is mainly based on the diverse motivation theories of psychology, and agency theory in economics. These theories are useful not only in predicting motivational effect of the pay for performance, but also in drawing important implications for how firms should design performance pay to increase its motivational effect. The outline of each theory and its implications are summarized in <Table 9-1>.

Table 9-1 Theories on the Motivational Effect of Performance Pay

	CONTENT OF THE THEORY	IMPLICATIONS OF THE THEORY
Expectancy theory	• Expectation of performance realization • Linkage between performance and rewards • Expected compensation different among employees	• Education and capacity for realizing performance • Consistent and visible rewards based on performance • Offering of compensation desired by employees
Equity theory	• Compensation compared to one's own effort and outcome • Compensation level compared to other people's efforts and outcome • Satisfied if the ratio is fair, dissatisfied if it is not	• Fairness based on the comparison with others • Procedural fairness • Distributive fairness
Goal setting theory	• Influences of goal setting on motivation • Importance of characteristics of planned goal • Importance of process of goal setting	• Importance of clear, achievable and challenging goals • Communication and endorsement on the goal • Linking performance and rewards
Reinforcement Theory	• Power of rewards in reinforcing desired behavior • Unexpected rewards have a strong effect • Immediate compensation is effective	• Reinforcement must be well planned • The importance of timely compensation • Stimulus intensity that exceeds the threshold
Agency theory	• Compensation strategy when it is difficult to directly observe the work performance • Control the process by rewards for results	• Different compensation system according to the characteristics of jobs • Alignment of personal and organizational goals through compensation

1) Expectancy Theory

Although it is possible for several theories to explain the motivating effect of performance pay on individual employees,[3] this can be explained most easily through expectancy theory. According to expectancy theory,[4] motivation level is determined by the expectation that an individual can achieve a specific performance if he or she works hard (expectancy), the belief that he will be rewarded for the performance (instrumentality), and the importance of such a reward (valence) to the individual. Therefore, when performance pays are introduced and operated, compensation should be offered whenever a performance occurs, thereby increasing the instrumentality of compensation and motivating employees to work hard. If the individual is a person who has a strong sense of value for money, the motivating effect will be stronger.

Expectancy theory asserts that when employees are well aware of the performance goals they need to achieve, and if a company conduct performance-based rewards, the expectation of high rewards strengthens the motivation to improve individual or group performance. At this point, what is important is that the employees have the ability to produce results. Otherwise, the motivating effect is lost because there is no expectation that the goal will be achieved. Therefore, as much emphasis is placed on performance rewards, investment in education and training is essential. In addition, when performance is achieved, compensation must be provided. If rewards are not provided despite achievements, it is difficult to expect the same motivation next time. Finally, the motivating effect increases only when the reward should fit to what the employees are looking forward to. For example, for employees who want to be promoted, giving a promotion rather than a monetary reward has a stronger motivating effect.

2) Equity Theory

According to the equity theory, it is claimed that people feel satisfied when the results of their efforts are fair to those of other people, but when not, they become dissatisfied and lose their motivation to work.[5] In other words, if the reward is appropriate for one's own efforts and outcome compared to others, the motivation to work hard will last, but if not, the motivation does not occur. An implication of the equity theory with respect to performance pay is that employees always compare the efforts and outcome of his own with those of others. Therefore, it is important to make employees feel fairly compensated among themselve, and the incentive must commensurate with the effort and outcome of each employee. This is called distributive fairness. Compensation should be distributed fairly in proportion to effort and performance. It is to note that distributive fairness has a highly correlated with procedural fairness. In order for such a distribution to be felt fairly, the efforts and results must be evaluated according to predetermined standards or procedures. This is procedural fairness. In the end, the equity theory tells us that in order for the performance pay to have a motivating effect, the company's evaluation system should be fair, while the size of compensation should also be determined in proportion to effort and performance.

3) Goal-Setting Theory

Goal setting theory asserts that if the goal set by the employee and his superior is objective, clearly defined, achievable, and challenging, the motivating effect will be high.[6)] In addition, the goals should not be excessive, and it is effective to focus on a major area or task, and a measurable goal that can be achieved within a set time is desirable. Goal setting theory provides the theoretical basis for the management by objective(MBO) used in most companies today. This theory provides important implications related to the operation of performance pay. First of all, the performance goal, which is the base for evaluating the performance, must be clear, objective, challenging, and achievable at the same time. In addition, continuous communication and feedback between superior and subordinates are very important. The effect of performance pay can be maximized through continuous communication such as checking the degree of goal achievement and providing feedback on improvement measures from the goal setting stage to the implementation process.

4) Reinforcement Theory

Reinforcement theory claims that if positive or negative rewards for a specific behavior are provided, that behavior can be further reinforced or reduced.[7)] For example, if an employee who shows good results through hard work is rewarded with a sufficient bonus, he will continue to work hard after that. Reinforcement theory does not focus on what motivates people, but on how to reinforce positive behavior while to eliminate negative behavior. For reinforcement to occur effectively, a reward must be paid only when the expected behavior or outcome is observed, and must be given immediately. From this point of view, a bonus that is customarily received by anyone or a bonus that one has to wait for one year has a low reinforcing effect. Incentives that are paid monthly according to accurate performance evaluation are more effective in motivating employees. Also, the larger the reward, the more likely reinforcement will occur. When the size of the incentive is small, the motivation to try to do the expected behavior is less and reinforcement is not achieved.

5) Agency Theory

The agency theory starts from the relationship between the owner of the organization and the agent who has the delegation from the owner to manage it. Typical examples are shareholders and professional managers such as CEO. Shareholders entrust the management of the company to the professional manager and reward them in return. The problem is that it is impossible for the shareholders to directly observe and control whether his management decision is right because the manager's work is highly sophisticated and the execution process is complex. Even if the agent is lazy or neglected, the owner has no way of knowing it. In such a situation, find a kind of compensation system preventing the agent's negligence and making the interests of the owner and the agents coincide is the core of the theory. The implication of the agency theory in relation to the design and operation of performance pay is that performance-oriented compensation is appropriate for a complex job which is difficult to understand and control. This is because, if sufficient compensation is given for the result instead of giving up control of the process, the owner's interest will be enhanced as a result in the process of the agent pursuing his own interest. The agency theory strongly suggests that the effect can be maximized only when the individual goal, which is the basis for compensation, is consistent with the organizational goal.

3. Types and Characteristics of Pay for Performance

The pay for performance is a pay determined by performance, and various types of performance pay exist. The method in which pay are determined can be divided into two types according to whether it is related to the base pay or only related to the incentives. The former determines the raise of the base pay, in which the increased amount becomes new base pay. Therefore, the effect of pay increase is cumulative. In the case of incentives, cumulative effects do not occur because they are paid only during the fixed period according to performance.

On the other hand, performance standards can be classified according to whether they are based on individual performance or group performance. The individual performance pay may increase acceptability and motivational effects because only performance that an individual makes is considered. However, there is a risk that the performance of the group may be sacrificed for individual performance. The performance pay based on group performance has the advantage of facilitating cooperation between individuals or teams. This again includes base-up, which determines the rate of base pay increase according to the company's performance, and various types of group incentives. [Figure 9-2] shows how performance pays can be classified according to the two criteria described above.

3.1 Pay Raise Based on Individual Performance

3.1.1 Yeonbongje

The Yeonbongje is a system that determines the base pay increase in consideration of individual performance, and this is a kind of Korean adaptation of merit pay which is commonly used in American and European companies. Let's explain how this works

Figure 9-2 Types of Pay for Performance

	Individual performance	Group performance
Raise of base pay	Merit pay Yeonbongje (Korean merit pay)	Across-the-board increase
Incentives	Piece-rate pay Commission Allowances and award	Team incentives Gain sharing Profit sharing

Figure 9-3 Trend of Introduction of Yeonbongje

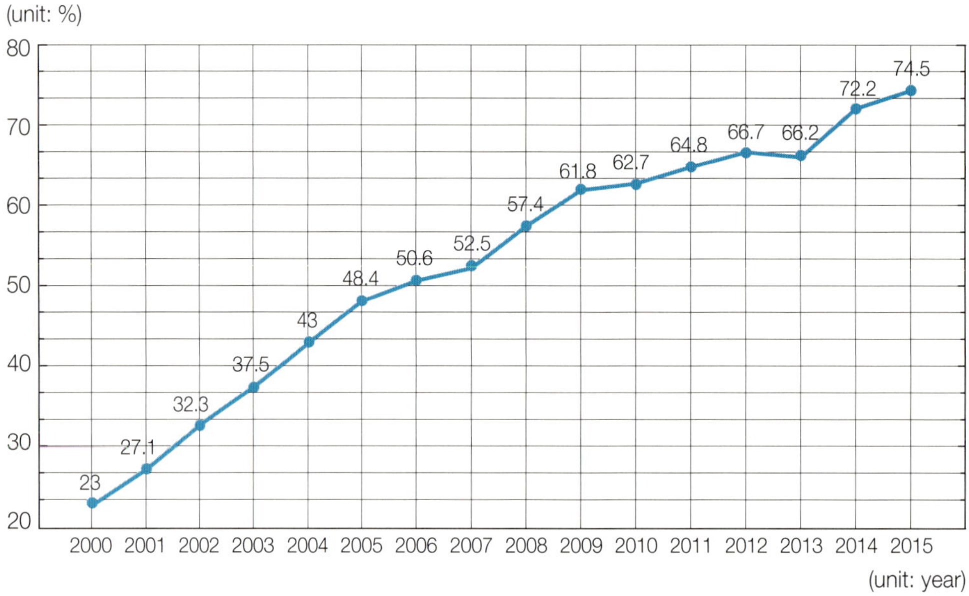

Note: establishment with 100 or more regular workers
Source: wage and working hour information system(www.wage.go.kr)

with a simple example. If the financial budget for a pay has increased 5% this year, a 9% raise is applied to high-performing individuals while 3% to low-performing individuals. The system can be designed in various ways, but the most important thing is that the increase of the base pay is different according to the individual evaluation result.[8)] The Yeonbongje was introduced by some companies just before the economic crisis that occurred at the end of 1997, but it spread rapidly after the economic crisis, and in 2006, more than 50% of companies with 100 or more employees introduced it. This is because Korean companies reorganized their compensation system to emphasize performance while witnessing serious crisis in which even large corporations went bankrupt due to sluggish performance. The Yeonbongje served as a representative example of such a new trend towards performance based pay.

The most important feature of the Yeonbongje is that the pay raise of base pay is different for each individual according to the evaluation result, and the determined pay increase has a cumulative effect. For example, as shown in [Table 9-2], a pay raise of 9% for those who received an S grade, 7% for an employee with an A grade, 5% for a B grade, and 3% for a C grade is applied. The high-performing employees receive more pay increases than low-performing employees, and the effect of such wage increases will be cumulative. Under the Yeonbongje, the pay raise is affected not only by the performance evaluation, but also by the level at which the employee's pay is located in the pay band to which his or her pay belongs. The higher the position of the pay in the pay band, the smaller the applied pay increase rate. This is because, in the case of

Table 9-2 **Pay Raise According to the Performance (example)**

		EVALUATION GRADE AND PAY RAISE				
Evaluation grade		S	A	B	C	D
Average pay increase		9%	7%	5%	3%	0%
Position in the pay band	Upper 1/3	7%	5%	3%	1%	0%
	Middle 1/3	9%	7%	5%	3%	0%
	Lower 1/3	11%	9%	7%	5%	0%

the same performance, it means that a person with less experience and years of service in the relevant position made more effort and contribution than a person with high experience and years of service. Also, this is to provide a message that employees who are already in a high position in the pay band should develop their competencies and be promoted to a higher job grade and pay band in order to receive a higher pay increase.

From the current point of view, the Yeonbongje seems like a pay system with nothing special about it. However, the differential increase in the base pay according to individual evaluation was very new in the late 1990s, when most of the employees received the same wage increase rate across-the-board. Employees often felt insecure about the Yeonbongje at that time. Such anxiety was mainly caused by distrust in the fairness of evaluation. For this reason, unions strongly opposed its introduction, and as a result, it was introduced mainly for white collar employees except production workers. Of course, this is also a result of considering the fact that the Yeonbongje can have a meaningful effect only when there is a certain degree of autonomy in job. Because it is difficult to differentiate pay according to individual performance in the case of production workers whose work speed or procedure was collectively determined by technical necessity.

Is the Yeonbongje achieving the expected motivational or performance improvement effect in Korean companies? Although there are not many empirical studies related to this, in the case of Jang (2003), the empirical results show that a reward system centered on individuality has a positive effect on employees' job performance efforts. It appears that it increases even more when it is combined with a bundle of commitment-based human resources practices.[9)] On the other hand, a study by Yu and Park (2007) found that although the Yeonbongje did not have a meaningful effect on the effectiveness of human resource management evaluated by strategic planning officers of the company, it had a positive effect on the financial performance of companies measured by per capita added value. It shows also that the positive effect is further increased when implemented together with MBO.[10)]

3.1.2 Base-Up Increase

In Korean companies, if there is a union, the wage increase is determined and applied through wage negotiations between management and union, and if there is no union, the wage increase rate is determined and applied by the company. For example, if a 3%

Pay for Performance: Confidence in evaluation is important

Does history repeat itself? Like the opposition to the Yeonbongje in the past, in 2015, it was a strong opposition to the reform of public institutions under the Park Geun-Hye administration. One of the pillar of the reform was the introduction of performance-based pay consisting of differentiate base pay according to the performance. It is very similar to the Yeonbongje implemented in private companies. At the end of 2015, the Ministry of Human Resources and Innovation decided to expand the performance-based salary system to civil servants with a rank of 5 or lower. And in early 2016, the Ministry of Economy and Finance presented the 「Recommendation for the Performance Salary System of Public Institutions」 and has exerted strong pressure to introduce it to the public sector. However, this provoked strong protests and strikes of the majority of unions such as railways and finance unions. And even after almost all public institutions completed the introduction, the conflict has been intensified. The reason labor unions oppose the performance-based salary system is that the difference between individuals causes competition, is not suitable for the public sector, where the public interest must be emphasized. But the biggest reason of the opposition was distrust in evaluation. In the end, the performance-based salary system was abolished with the arrival of the Moon Jae-In administration, but it was an opportunity to make realize once again that the evaluation system is more important than the pay system itself.

wage increase was decided, the base pay of all employees would increase by 3%, and so on. In Korea, it is called "base-up" meaning the raise of the base pay itself, while in USA, this is called across-the-board increase in the sense of a wage increase applied to all employees. This kind of pay increase has been used as a general rule in Korea very long time.

Base-up is generally not considered as a performance pay because of the fact that the increase rate is determined by labor-management negotiations. One of the reasons requiring a base-up is to compensate for inflation. This is because real wages decrease if wages do not rise to reflect this. However, the most important consideration in base-up is the company's performance. This is because the demands of the union are determined in consideration of the company's performance.

The base-up does not differentiate the wage increase according to individual or group performance, but distributes the company-wide performance equally to the employees ex post. Even if individual and group wage increases are not differentiated, the base-up can be applied flexibly and rationally in consideration of economic conditions and corporate performance. For example, Japanese companies have controlled labor costs while freezing or minimizing base-up during the recession called the lost 20 years.

However, it should be noted that if the wage increase is mainly based on the base-up method, it may negatively affect the motivation of high performers and may cause difficulties in retaining key talents. According to one study, a flat wage increase according to the base-up method makes competent employees feel that they are not being compensated enough, and as a result, they reduce the effort or try to change jobs.[11)]

3.2 Individual Incentive

3.2.1 Individual Special Reward

Most companies operate a system in which special one-time bonuses are paid to people who have made special achievements or contributions. The difference between this practice and other incentives to be discussed below is that the performance goals or indicators to be achieved are not systematically set in advance in the special reward. It is operated in such a way that rewards are given to the small number of people who have made outstanding contributions over the course of a year. For example, the Samsung Group awards the Samsung Award each year in four categories: Achievement Award, Technology Award, Design Award, and Special Award to executives and employees who showed outstanding achievements. The winner receives a special promotion to the first rank and a cash prize of 100 million won. SK Group is also implementing a reward system for individuals or teams who pursue Supex[12)] with the belief that excellent performance is rewarded with certainty in order to inspire the spirit of challenge among employees and energize the organization. The reward for the pursuit of Supex is 200 million won per case, and an unprecedented 1 billion won is given to the grand prize.

The reward prize is a temporary cash reward of variable nature whose payment cannot be determined in advance, and the purpose of the reward is to promote morale and motivation of employees by providing exceptional rewards for outstanding performance. The amount of compensation is large, but more importantly, the recognition for individual efforts and achievements through rewards is also very important. Although the data is a bit outdated, in 2004, job portal site Job Korea (www.jobkorea.co.kr) conducted a survey on the reward system of 633 companies based in Korea. According to it, 480 companies (75.8%) had employee reward systems. As a form of reward, incentives (bounties) accounted for the most at 39.3%, followed by reflection in personnel evaluation 14.6%, award of prizes (gold or gift certificate, etc.) 13.1%, additional points of promotion at 12.2%, awards certificates and plaques at 9.5%. Overseas travel or training opportunities were given in the order of 8.9%.

On the other hand, there is a job invention reward. A job invention refers to a technology invented by an employee in the course of his job and it falls within the business scope of the company (Article 10 of the Invention Promotion Act). As the importance of technology as a source of competitiveness becomes more prominent, the need to systematically recognize compensation for job inventions is increasing. Korean companies, like Japanese companies, have a strong tendency to regard job inventions as company property because they were developed by the company's facilities and working time, and thus tend not to compensate for them sufficiently. However, in this case, the risk of excellent technical manpower leaving the company may increase. Therefore, it is necessary to introduce and operate the job invention system in order to create an atmosphere that is devoted to technology development. The fact that the job invention

Litigation over Job Invention

A very famous example related to job invention is a Japanese American who won the 2014 Nobel Prize in Physics. The lawsuit was filed by scholar Shuji Nakamura against the company. The story begins with the blue light emitting diode (LED) he invented when he was a young researcher. It had worth trillions of dollars and the invention became a stepping stone for a chemical industry company in which he was working for to take off as a global company. However, the only compensation he received in exchange was a special promotion for the manager and 20,000 yen. He eventually resigned from the company. Then, after going to the United States as a professor, the company sued him for divulging business secrets, which was dismissed by the court. After that, Nakamura files a lawsuit against the company at the Tokyo Court. In the first trial, the court ordered the company to pay 20 billion yen in compensation, but the court of appeals decided it to 840 million yen through a reconciliation. During this process, he said as follows: "Japan is not a place that spurs researchers' motivation and creativity. When I brought huge profits for the company, nothing came back to me. Japanese egalitarianism culture and system can't revive the motivation of researchers. I love Japan, but I am disappointed with the Japanese system."

system has recently been systematically introduced and operated by IT companies and large corporations reflects this reality.

3.2.2 Individual Performance Pay

Unlike the previous special reward, individual performance pay is a pay in which a clear performance standard is set in advance and incentives are paid according to it. A typical example is piece-rate, in which a unit wage is set for one product and wages are paid according to the output. Individual performance pay has historically been used in various forms. It can be divided into the following four types depending on whether the pay rate is the output or the time required, and whether a single rate or multiple rates are applied.

1) Piece-Rate Pay

Piece-rate is a method of paying wages by applying a fixed wage rate to a single product. Its advantage is that it is easy to understand and simple to calculate. People are rewarded according to the achievements represented by the number of produced items and the wage increases in proportion to the amount of production. It is very effective in stimulating people to improve performance. Because of these advantages, piece-rate was widely used in the early days of capitalism.

There is also a kind of piece-rate in which multiple rates are created in order to make the stimulus effect on the performance of remuneration even stronger. In this pay, a target level which can be achieved only when people work hard is set-up. Then, a higher wage rate is applied when you achieve more than the target, whereas a normal rate is

Figure 9-4 **Types of Individual Performance Pay**

	Number of product per unit time	Required time per unit product
Single rate	Piece-rate	Standard time-rate
Multiple rates	Multiple-rate piece-rate (Taylor, Merrick)	Multiple-rate time rate (Halsey, Rowan, Gantt)

Source: Milkovich and Newman, 2002, p. 313.

applied when the target is not reached. A representative example of this is the multiple rates suggested by Taylor, who is called the father of scientific management. In the case of the Merrick method, it is basically similar to the Taylor method, but there is a difference in that the wage rate is divided into three and applied different rates according to three cases such as exceeding the target level, in the case of 83% to 100%, and in less than 83%.

Piece-rate was the dominant wage of production workers before job-based pay was established in the United States. In the United States, according to a 1920 survey by the National Industrial Conference Board, it was reported that 60% of responding manufacturers were using piece-rate pay, and it was reported that 80% of workers worked with piece-rate pay.[13)] In the case of Korea also, the proportion of individual performance pay was not small in the 1960s. According to a 1962 survey by the Korea Productivity Center, 39% of businesses used piece-rate pay.

However, piece-rate can be a very harsh wage system for low-performing people for diverse reasons. In particular, it can seriously threaten the stability of wages for those who lack the necessary physical strength or skills to achieve performance. There is also a risk of neglecting quality by over-focusing on quantity. On the other hand, modern production technology and work organization have made it difficult to apply piece-rate in the work place. This is because it has become difficult to measure individual output as the work organization changed into the Ford-style production in which individual worker has no control over the speed and quantity of products. For this reason, piece-rate tends to disappear in modern large-scale work organizations. However, it can still be found in the secondary labor market.

2) Time-Based Performance Pay

Whereas in the piece-rate the amount of wages is determined according to how much production is done in a fixed time, in the case of time-based performance pay, the size of wages is determined by how much time is taken to complete the job. For example, let's say that the standard working time is 6 hours for a mechanic in an auto repair shop to change an engine. In this case, the standard working time is the time it takes for a mechanic with normal abilities to work at a standard speed. The standard time rate is to pay the hourly rate of 6 hours even if you completed the work in 5 hours, which

Double-Edged Sword: incentives

Brennan, who became CEO of Sears Roebuck in 1990, pursues powerful reforms to increase profits while cutting costs drastically by $600 million. The pressure on performance has affected a very wide range, from top management to the lowest level. The auto repair division also began to strongly apply incentives to achieve individual repair sales targets to increase profits. Sales increased as a result, but Sears was accused of making unnecessary repairs to customers by the California Consumer Protection Agency. That's because, according to the results of a survey through disguised customers, in 34 out of 38 cases, Sears increased sales by making unnecessary repairs, costing an average of $235 to the customers. In the end, strong incentives to increase sales lowered customer trust, and Sears was faced with a serious crisis. Sears is no exception. These problems occur very often. There is also a case where a hygiene-conscious food company paid incentives for bugs found in the process, and employees caught bugs from their homes and claimed that they were found in the process. Performance pay is a double-edged sword that must be used with caution.[14)]

is shorter than the standard 6 hours. Although you worked for only 5 hours, you will receive a wage equivalent to 6 hours. Therefore, in this time-based performance pay, all employees make an active effort to complete the task as fast as possible than the standard work time.

Unlike single rate pay, where the hourly wage is fixed at one, compensation for time reduction can be implemented more aggressively using multiple rates. The representative examples are Halsey, Rowan, and Gantt premiums, which are named after the designers of the plan. Halsey method is to make employees work earlier than standard working hours, and the company and employees share 50% of the direct labor cost saved due to the shortened time. Therefore, the faster the work is performed, the more the hourly wage rate increases. Rowan premium is same with Halsey in that the company and individual employees share the labor costs saved due to the shortened working hours, but the difference is that the wage rates are systematically designed and applied according to the working speed. For example, if the standard working time is 10 hours, the incentive rate will vary depending on the amount of time savings, such as 30% of the savings if the job is done in 9 hours, 50% if completed in 8 hours, and 70% if finished in 7 hours. In Gantt plan, if the work is completed earlier than the standard work time, the wages for the standard work time and 20% of the amount are paid. Therefore, lesser the time taken to accomplish the job, higher the wage rate because employees receive the pay for the standard working time and 20% premium.

The objective of strongly stimulating an individual's efforts to realize performance is the same for both piece-rate pay and time-based pay. However, time performance pay is more effective than piece-rate when a task takes a long time to complete, the task is not repetitive, and requires many different skills. It should be noted that using time-based performance pay runs a risk of quality problems such as defects due to focus on time

Table 9-3 **Advantages and Disadvantages of Individual Performance Pay**

Advantages	• Provides strong motivation for performance • High wages and low labor costs can be realized • Reduces the need for observation and supervision of the workers
Disadvantages	• Concentration on immediate performance may hamper other important performance, such as quality or safety. • Competitive atmosphere can be created with no consideration for newcomers or OJT. • Disagreement between the company and employees over the setting of standard production volume or standard working hours may occur

reduction. Therefore, it is important to operate this pay while simultaneously considering other important evaluation indicators such as defects and safety. As the modern work organization changes to a collective process, time-based incentive is also being used significantly less, except for some workplaces where individuals can directly control the production process.

As can be seen in <Table 9-3>, individual incentives have advantages and disadvantages. In order to reduce side effects and increase motivation, the process of setting performance indicators such as standard workload and standard working hours should be reasonable and fair. This is the reason why scientific analysis such as motion studies and time studies were historically used in the introduction of individual incentives. In addition, it should not be forgotten that individual incentives can be easily accepted and effective when there is trust between the company and its employees.

3.3 Group Incentive

The difference between group incentives and individual incentives is that incentives are paid based on group performance rather than individual performance. In group incentives, performance indicators are set and operated to reflect group performance. Group can be a team, a division, a business unit, or the entire company. In the case of group incentives, like individual incentives, incentives are paid according to the degree to which goals are achieved based on a predetermined group performance standard. Which of the two is more effective, individual incentives or group incentives, depends on the content of the work and the characteristics of the work organization. Individual incentives are appropriate when the job can be performed independently, such as a salesperson, and the individual can control his performance. Group incentives are appropriate in situations where work speed or performance is collectively determined, or where it is difficult to clearly measure individual performance, such as a production job in a continuous work process. Individual incentives have a strong motivating effect that promotes performance improvement, but may hinder collective cooperation. Therefore, the best way is to use an appropriate combination of individual incentives and group incentives. In fact, most companies have introduced and operated both types of incentives at the same time.

Group incentives can take various forms, but they can be classified based on the target to which the incentive is applied and the type of performance indicator that determines the incentive. The target is at which level the incentive system will be applied among teams, divisions, business units, and the entire company. The smaller the scale of the target, the greater the motivating effect and the less free-riding problem occurs, but there is a risk that the scope of cooperation and the perspective on performance are limited. For example, if a team incentive is implemented, cooperation within the team will be strong, but competition with other teams may intensify. On the other hand, the types of performance indicators can be broadly divided into profit and productivity. Profit is easy to understand as the final financial performance, and from the company's point of view, it has the advantage that it is not financially burdensome because it is to pay the earned money. However, the profit has the disadvantage that the market environment or special circumstances unrelated to the efforts of the employees can have a great influence. Since productivity indicators are mainly affected by the degree of effort of employees, they can have a stronger effect on motivation than profit indicators. However, it can put a strain on the company's ability to pay in the case when productivity has improved but sales are not good.

3.3.1 Team Incentive

Team incentives are a form of cash pay that sets performance goals for each team and pays a corresponding amount when they achieve them. In Korea, the introduction rate of team incentives is not high compared to group incentives for the entire company. According to a 2008 survey by the Labor Institute, as shown in <Table 9-3>, 80.8% of the incentive system applied company-wide while only 10.3% is targeting to departments. There may be several reasons for this, such as that it is difficult to calculate performance goals for each team, or that the purpose of the group incentives is often to promote cooperation at the company level rather than competition between teams.

However, there are some companies that use team incentives very effectively. Nuri Media, a small and medium-sized Korean business operating in the academic research database field, is actively operating various types of performance compensation systems.[15] Among them, team performance pay is the most important, especially in terms of the size of the bounty and the impact on employees. A total of 13 teams decide performance goals and incentive levels in consultation with management at the beginning of the year. As a result, team performance pay is paid at the end of the year.

Table 9-4 **Introduction Level of the Group Incentives**

TARGET LEVEL	FREQUENCY	INTRODUCTION RATE
Company	1,988	80.8%
Business unit	221	9%
Department	253	10.3%

Source: Korea Labor Institute, 2008, A survey on the wage system.

Team Incentive at Nucor

Nucor is the world's number one producer of steel beams and decks, and the number one steel producer in the United States. Nucor implements four incentive systems and operate a strong team incentive system targeting production workers. Generally, a teams consist of 12 to 20 people. There is no upper limit on the team bonus, but it is usually set between 100% and 220% of the base salary. On average, it is determined between 170% and 180%. Team bonuses are based on the production of each team, specifically by the ton of product. Defects are deducted from the production volume in order for employees not to lose interest in quality. All employees at Nucor, even if they are not production workers, are receiving various types of performance bonus systems. And bonuses based on profits are provided to all employees. Through this performance-oriented culture and system, Nucor have never recorded a deficit and conducted a layoff.

Source: HRMagazine, 2007 Feb 1.

In the case of 2015, one team received a performance bonus of 100 million won, and 50% of the 13 teams received a performance bonus of tens of millions of won. Through various types of performance reward and welfare systems, including team incentives, the company has been able to be successful in business since its establishment.

3.3.2 Gain Sharing

Gain sharing is a group incentive in which productivity goal is set in advance and bonus is distributed to employees when the productivity goal is achieved. In simple terms, productivity is the ratio of output to input, and it has the advantage that it can include a wide variety of fromular as productivity indicator. Except for profit-based incentives, all other incentive programs can be considered as productivity incentives. In general, quantity, sales, and cost reduction are often used as productivity indicator, but it is also possible to use indicators such as quality or customer satisfaction.

The advantage of gain sharing is that various performance indicators are possible, but consultation with employees or unions is very important in selecting indicators. This is because there may be serious conflicts over the validity of the performance indicators. In order to reduce such conflicts, it is good to set and operate productivity indicators that can have an clear motivational effect while reducing ambiguity or uncertainty to interpret.

Factors affecting productivity are very diverse, and various performance indicators can be introduced in consideration of company characteristics and circumstances. By far the most popular productivity incentive schemes are the Scanlon plan, the Rucker plan, and the Improshare plan. All three plans are common in that they aim to improve productivity and use a predetermined ratio that represents productivity. The input indicator is labor-related cost or working hours, and the output indicator is sales or added value. The specific performance indicators used for inputs and outputs in these schemes are as follows.

Table 9-5 Productivity Indicator of Scanlon, Rucker and Improshare

	Scanlon Plan	Rucker Plan	Improshare
Input indicator	Labor cost	Labor cost	Used working hours
Output indicator	Sales value	Added value	Standard working hours

1) Scanlon Plan

The scheme was devised by Scanlon, who worked as a field worker and union steward at a steel company. After calculating the ratio of the sales value of products sold or in stock to the labor cost, if the labor cost paid in a specific month is less than the ratio, the saved labor cost is shared between the company and its employees. In fact, overtime work is a very common phenomenon in the production field, and premium wages are paid to it. So if employees work hard to increase production, overtime and related labor cost will be reduced. The Scanlon plan is an attempt to increase work efficiency by distributing a portion of the reduced labor cost to employees.

<Table 9-6> briefly explains the process for calculating bonuses in the Scanlon plan. The calculated cost savings is 50 million won, of which 75% is distributed to employees. In addition, not all of them are paid out, but about 25% of it is generally saved in case when there is no productivity improvement.

2) Rucker Plan

Rucker plan is the same as the Scanlon plan in that it uses labor costs as an input index, but it is different from the Scanlon plan in that it uses added value rather than sales value as an output index. According to Rucker, who devised it, increasing more added value with a given labor cost or realizing the same added value with less labor cost means improved productivity. In Rucker plan, the standard ratio of labor costs in the added value of a company is set, and incentives are paid based on the difference between the labor costs according to the standard ratio and that of actual labor costs. The <Table 9-7> shows the procedure for calculating incentives in the Rucker Plan. The ratio

Table 9-6 Example of Incentive Calculation (Scanlon Plan)

Calculation of standard ratio based on historical data		
① Product sales value	=	KRW 10,000,000,000
② Labor cost	=	KRW 4,000,000,000
Standard ratio(②÷①)	=	0.4
January 2022 bonus calculation		
① Product sales value	=	KRW 1,000,000,000
② Labor cost (①×0.4)	=	KRW 400,000,000
③ Actual labor cost	=	KRW 350,000,000
④ Savings (incentive pool)	=	KRW 50,000,000

Table 9-7 **Example of Incentive Calculation (Rucker Plan)**

Calculation of standard ratio based on historical data		
① Value of output	=	KRW 10,000,000,000
② Raw material purchase cost	=	KRW 6,000,000,000
③ Value added (①−②)	=	KRW 4,000,000,000
④ Standard labor cost (③×0.3)	=	KRW 1,200,000,000
⑤ Actual labor cost	=	KRW 1,000,000,000
⑥ Incentive pool (④−⑤)	=	KRW 200,000,000
⑦ Employee group incentives (⑥×0.5)	=	KRW 100,000,000

0.3 used to calculate the standard labor cost is a number resulting from the value added divided by the labor cost using historical data at the company.

3) Improshare

Improshare is an abbreviation for improved productivity through sharing and was created by Mitchell Fein, an engineer. In this system, after setting the standard time required to produce one product, if the product is completed sooner than this time, the saved time is converted into money and shared between labor and management in half. When employees work hard and efficiently and shorten the required time, the productivity increases, so the fruits are distributed. It is effective to introduce and operate Improshare in industries where the product itself is large and complex and time is a more understandable indicator than production, for example, turbine or aircraft manufacturing.

3.3.3 Profit Sharing

Profit-sharing distributes a portion of a company's profits to its employees according to a pre-determined distribution formula. The profit-sharing has the advantage that it is easy to obtain calculation indicators and simple to calculate the bonus. However, it carries the risk that corporate profits will be affected not only by the efforts of the employees but also by the external environment over which the employees or the company cannot control. Nevertheless, the profit-sharing system is being introduced and used by many companies due to the objectivity of the indicator and convenience of application.[16)]

In the United States, according to the results of a study by the American Chamber of Commerce, it appears that the profit-sharing system has been introduced in about 20% of American companies since the 1960s, and there is no significant change in the penetration rate.[17)] In Japan, among the performance-sharing systems introduced, bonus based on corporate profits account for the highest proportion.[18)] In Korea, it is known that the profit-based formular occupies the highest proportion among companies that are introducing the group incentive system.[19)]

The most well-known example of a profit-sharing system in Korea is Samsung Electronics' PS. Samsung Electronics introduced the profit-sharing in 2000, and it received a lot of attention from the media because of the fact that total 400 billion won in cash was paid to its members as profit-sharing bonuses. It is not that Korean companies do not have a practice for distributing a portion of corporate profits to employees, but in the case of Samsung Electronics, depending on the size of the profits, up to 50% of the individual's annual salary can be paid, which is very unconventional. Samsung Electronics' PS system uses 20% of the economic value added (EVA) realized by each business unit as a financial source.[20)]

3.3.4 Stock Option

A stock option is the right to purchase stocks at a predetermined price within a certain period of time, and it is provided by a company to its executives and employees. Employees who received stock options may or may not exercise their rights when the time has come to exercise their rights. A stock option is an option and not a stock grant. An individual who owns a stock option will exercise his right and make a profit only when the stock price is higher than the exercise price, and will not exercise the right if the stock price is lower than or equal to the exercise price. Therefore, in the case of stock option, unlike employee stock grant, there is no financial loss due to a fall in the stock price.

The [Figure 9-5] shows how stock options work.[21)] At the time the stock option is granted (grant time), the stock option contract stipulates how many stocks can be purchased at certain price during determined period. For example, the right to purchase 1,000 shares at the time of exercise is granted to executive A at an exercise price of 20,000 won. The exercise time is the time at which the stock option can be exercised,

Figure 9-5 Working Mechanism of Stock Option

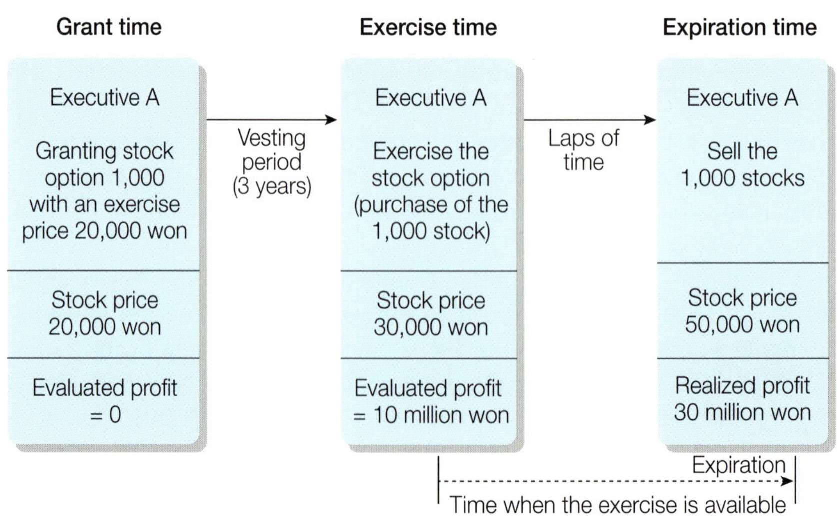

which usually begins 3 years after the grant. When executive A exercises his stock option, the company provides 1,000 shares of the stock to executive A at the previously agreed exercise price of 20,000 won, and executive A pay the corresponding amount of 20 million won to the company. As a result, executive A gets an estimated profit of 10 million won by subtracting the 20 million won he spent to purchase his own stock from the 30 million won value of the stock evaluated at the current market price. He can realize a profit by selling it on the stock market. Rather than an individual carrying out such a cumbersome process by himself, it is more often for the company to take care of the operation and pays the cash profit to him. Stock options have an expiration date when the right expires. After this period, the right to exercise the stock option is lost, so the individual who has been granted the stock option must exercise the right before it.

Although a stock option is a type of performance pay, it is characterized as a long-term incentive unlike other performance pay. This is because once the stock option is granted, the exercise of the option is prohibited during the vesting period, so the individual who is granted the stock option strives to improve the company's performance during this long period. This feature has a great effect in promoting motivation and preventing turnover for a long period of time for people who are doing long-term projects such as new drug development. When stock options are used as a reward for past performance, the period for exercising it can be shortened. In that case, however, there is no difference from the traditional incentive system, and the long-term effect of stock options can be halved.

4. Strategic Use of Pay for Performance

There is no doubt that the performance pay is an important practice that greatly contributes to increase employee motivation. However, as discussed earlier, performance pay is not a panacea. And if it is operated inappropriately, there are many side effects. In order to achieve the expected effect of performance pay, it is necessary to pay attention to the following points.

4.1 Pay for Performance and Education

As seen in the expectancy theory, for performance pay to have a motivating effect, there must be an expectation that performance can be achieved through effort. At this time, it is the competence of the employees that has an important influence on such expectations. If employees lack the capacity, no matter how hard they try, they will not be able to produce results. In this regard, a company that introduces performance pay should make sufficient investments and efforts to develop the competency of its employees. If performance pay is introduced in a state where the employees' competence is insufficient, the employees will show frustration or give up rather than work hard.

4.2 Pay for Performance and Pay Stability

It has to be cleary understood that performance pay is a variable pay. Variable pay tends to increase income instability because the size of the reward is not fixed. In particular, performance pay can increase anxiety in situations where the level of base pay is insufficient to guarantee a livelihood. It should not be forgotten that such insecurities may make employees desperate and do their best, but conversely, these may lead to expedient behavior or turnover. Therefore, it is necessary to find an appropriate ratio of fixed and variable pay, and it is desirable to design performance pay so that the size of variable pay according to performance does not become excessive in the case of low-ranking employees.

4.3 Pay for Performance and Performance Indicator

In order for performance pay to have a motivating effect, employees must clearly understand performance indicators and accept them. If employees don't understand very well or distrust performance indicators, the motivating effect disappears. All performance indicators have their pros and cons. Therefore, the important thing is to make the employees accept them while helping them to understand the characteristics of the performance indicators. To this end, it is more desirable for the company to actively develop suitable performance indicators together with the employees from the start rather than designing and applying them unilaterally.

4.4 Pay for Performance and Evaluation

Performance pay is determined by performance in principle, but it is often evaluation that determines actually the degree of performance achievement. In the case of the merit pay, for example, the evaluation result determines the pay raise in base pay. In the case of group incentives, the incentive pool is determined according to the group performance, but there are some cases in which differential distribution is made according to evaluation result of the employees. Therefore, it is important to create reasonable performance indicators, but it is also important to evaluate employees fairly. It is necessary to remember that the motivating effect of performance pay disappears when there is a great deal of distrust in evaluation system.

Ending Case

The Shadow of Pay for Performance: Fujitsu case[22)]

Fujitsu was the first among Japanese conglomerates to introduce performance-based management. Fujitsu's bold introduction of performance-based management, rejecting the traditional life-time employment and seniority-based system, was a major event that shook the foundation of Japanese society. However, contrary to high expectations, Fujitsu's performance-based management ended in disastrous failure. In 1993, when Fujitsu first introduced this system, after the effects of the collapse of the bubble economy did not go away, and the negative aspects of Japanese-style management were further emphasized. Fujitsu recorded its first operating loss in 1992. Concerned about this, executives dispatched people to Silicon Valley to study the computer business. They saw American engineers there who worked harder than Japanese homologues, and a system of performance pay that supported their high motivation to work. Fujitsu's management anguished by performance deterioration, strongly believed that everything would be fine if they switched from a Japanese system to an American one. Fujitsu's reform for the performance-based management started with the introduction of merit pay for managers in 1993 and expanded it to middle-level employees and above from 1997. The key point was the evaluation based on objective indicators of performance management, which is different from the existing employee evaluation system based on the seniority or skill.

The company promoted the virtue of performance-based management extensively in order to secure excellent manpower. At company briefing to recruit newly graduated people, this phrase is emphasized without exception: "At Fujitsu, you are rewarded for your performance. Fujitsu is a company where you can fully realize your abilities." At that time, Fujitsu's performance-based management was regarded as an exemplar case of new personnel system in Japan. The objective performance evaluation system consists of the following three. The first is a objective management system in which goals are established for each department and individual. It is to set goals for each semi-annual period and evaluate them at the end of the term. Naturally, the goal should be set at the same height to ensure fairness between each employees, and an interview should be conducted with one's own supervisor. In addition, the goal must match the work of the department and must have a certain level of difficulty.

Second, the evaluation grade is reflected in the bonus and promotion. After the introduction of a new system, there was a difference of up to ten times in the performance pay between employees at Fujitsu except the base pay. If you get the best annual rating, your annual income almost doubles. This can inflame the competitive spirit of employees who are accustomed to a stable life and stimulate their greed for performance. This will naturally increase the company's performance. This difference of performance pay between employees starts to widen from the third year of joining the company, so the competitive system is set up early enough. Third, the discretionary labor system was introduced. It is a new system that was born from the idea that wages are not in return for working hours, but for performance. There is no room for overtime in the discretionary work system. There is no fixed commuting time, and there is no minimum working hours required in the flexible working system. In this system, all that was required of the employees was to achieve the goal.

As Fujitsu's performance-based management became widely known, it began to spread quite a bit of repercussions throughout Japanese companies. There was no one among personnel managers of large corporations who did not mention Fujitsu, because such reforms were not yet tried or achieved in the typical large corporations. Under these circumstances, Fujitsu's bold introduction of performance system was a significant event that symbolized the change of Japanese society.

However, in the 2000s, Fujitsu's growth rate began to drop sharply. It was as if a car running at 150km/h had hit the brakes abruptly. The employees, who were expected to be full of high motivation and had to constantly run towards their goals, ended up getting worse results than before. Many employees who were loyal to the company until a few years ago, savagely criticized the company in various magazines and the Internet. What was most unexpected was the rapid increase in employee turnover. The more talented, they are the more often they leave the company. While Fujitsu hires talents from other companies in units of 100 people every year, more Fujitsu natives have changed jobs. Why did this happen? There may be numerous reasons, but the boldly introduced performance system was at the center of the problem. It cannot be said that performance-based management itself is bad. However, Fujitsu's performanceism did not work at all.

Fujitsu's performance-based management already began to show some flaws in 1998. Every half year, employees are evaluated on their goal achievement through a meeting with their direct supervisor. Of course, if the goal is achieved, they get an A, and if it exceeds the goal, an SA. After that, a meeting called the Evaluation Committee is held. However, each evaluation from SA to E was allocated according to the distribution ratio determined in advance by the Human Resources Department. Even if all the employees achieved their respective goals, in the end, the rankings were based on relative evaluation with other employees. Naturally, the downgraded employees were not convinced at all by this result.

Goal setting itself was also a problem. In the rapidly changing IT industry, it is almost impossible to make and maintain a plan during six months. Even if you set a perfect goal in the beginning, it is difficult to guarantee that it will be effective even after six months. Goals have to be changed according to new trends, rival companies' movements, and market conditions. If employees stick to the goal that was fixed at the beginning, they cannot respond to this fast move. Also, one of the things that had a bad reputation for Fujitsu employees was the discretionary labor system. Originally, this system allows free working hours, but there is no overtime pay because it is not based on hourly wages. During a recession, Fujitsu try to cut labor costs at maximum, but the method of operating the system was not fair to the eyes of the employees. According to Fujitsu's Human Resources Department, employees should arrive on time, leave on time, and the company prohibited their overtime. This was completely different from the free use of working time which is the purpose of the discretionary labor system. The introduction of performance-based management in a state where the traditional organizational culture was not changed was also a big problem. Although the company emphasized performance, superiors still regarded subordinates who worked late and took fewer annual leave as motivated employees. This is because people who were promoted in the past occupied most of the managerial positions. In addition, managers who were promoted smoothly from the seniority system often made the employees feel disconnected from the performance-centered rhetoric.

Discussion Questions

1. What motivated Fujitsu to introduce performance-based management? Was it a wrong decision by the management at the time to introduce a performance-based compensation system?
2. What are the problems or side effects of performance-based pay that can be seen through the case of Fujitsu?
3. One of the reasons why performance-based compensation has not been effectively established at Fujitsu was related to the evaluation system. What do you think was the problem? Could the problem be solved by using absolute evaluation instead of relative one?
4. What are some examples of Korean companies that did not achieve the expected effect or failed after introducing the performance-based pay? What lessons can we learn from this?

CHAPTER

10

Designing and Administering Benefits

1. Role of Employee Benefits
2. Change of Environment and Employee Benefits
3. Types of Employee Benefits
4. Flexible Employee Benefits
5. Strategic Management of Employee Benefits

Learning Objectives

1. Understand the purpose and role of employee benefits.
2. Understand environmental changes that affect benefits.
3. Understand diverse types of employee benefits.
4. Understand characteristics of flexible benefits.
5. Establish efficient and effective benefits strategy.

Introductory Case

Mr. Han, a manager of the marketing team of a Korean chemical company used pensions and rental cars this summer vacation with 'welfare points' offered by the company. By using them, he was able to significantly reduce vacation expenses. It was also very convenient because he could easily search and make reservations for hotels, condos, and pensions across the country just by accessing the in-house welfare system. The company offers more than 20 programs to choose from in four categories: health promotion, self-development, leisure and welfare stores.

The employee benefits operated in this way is called the cafeteria benefits or flexible benefits plan. Employees can select benefits according to their own needs or preferences within the limits of preassigned points. That plan was well received by the employees. According to the HR department, satisfaction with benefits program increased significantly after its introduction. In the past, the benefits were mainly monopolized by senior and old workers. But now, anyone can choose the benefits they need, so it is natural to see the satisfaction of the employees for benefits to rise. It is also good for the company to be able to stably control the benefits every year through welfare points.

Mr. Han thinks that the system is a good thing for him too. However, he feels not quite satisfied still. Above all, there are only a few welfare points that can be used for one year. Of course, it's better than nothing, but the points are equivalent for only a few hundred thousand won. So, there are cases the stress increases after entering the welfare system when he realize there are not much things he can choose with his points. And there are still too many considerations for employee grades when allocating points. If an employee belongs to a high grade, he gets a lot of wages. Why the company need to give him extra consideration in welfare points on top of that? Mr. Han thinks also that it would be better to gives exceptional points to a family with many children like his.

Discussion Questions

1. What is the purpose of the companies to introduce the flexible benefits plan?
2. How can financial resources be prepared for the introduction of the flexible benefits plan?
3. What do you think can be a reasonable standard for allocating welfare points in this company?
4. What are the side effects of the flexible benefits plan, if any?

As explained through the concept of total compensation in chapter 8, benefits are one of the various rewards that companies provide to their employees. Benefits includes all forms of services or benefits provided on the status of a membership of the company, in addition to wages paid directly in cash in return for labor. Broadly, it includes both legal statutory welfare benefits such as employment insurance or medical insurance, and non-statutory benefits voluntarily provided by companies. In the statutory benefits, there is no room for companies to design the contents.

In general, it is true that companies and employees are less interested in benefits compared to wages paid directly to employees in the form of cash. Companies often do not show special interest to the benefits plan while just maintaining existing benefits that have been introduced before. In addition, when an employee changes his job or a newly graduated searches a job, the level of benefits of the company is not the most considered in their decision. Moreover, with the recent establishment of the Yeonbongje as the dominant wage system, the trend of greater interest in annual salary is also making the interest in benefits decrease.

If so, wouldn't it be the most effective alternative to pay all the compensation as wages while abolishing the benefits plan? By doing so, the company can reduce the burden of putting in manpower and spending money to operate it. In other words, is the benefits still necessary for the company in the rapidly changing environment? Or, if benefits plan is necessary, how can it be designed and operated in a way that can satisfy both the company and its employees? And it is common that employee benefits are mainly operated for regular employees, but is it unnecessary to provide them to non-regular employees?

This chapter is intended to examine these questions and to help design and operate an effective benefits plan. First, the purpose and role of benefits will be reviewed, and then environmental changes making companies to pay attention to them will be discussed. Based on this basic understanding, various benefits plan currently introduced and operated by Korean companies will be examined. The flexible benefits system, which has recently been attracting attention as an important innovative practice will also be examined. Finally, we will discuss how to strategically manage benefits plan in consideration of its purpose, and environmental changes.

1. Role of Employee Benefits

1.1 The Concept and Characteristics of Employee Benefits

Specific form of employee benefits vary widely, from dormitories and sports facilities to health insurance and resorts. Paying a certain amount of money for marriage and funeral is a unique employee benefit for Korean companies that are different from those in Europe and America. It is not easy to theoretically define what employee benefits is. Diverse scholars have different definitions on the employee benefits. For example, Ivancevich defined employee benefits as "any benefit or service that is an indirect compensation other than wages related to direct reward for labor offered."[1] Meanwhile, Gomez-Mejia et al. explain employee benefits as "collective rewards based on the organizational membership that provide safety for members and their families."[2] In this book, we define employee benefits as "any kind of monetary or non-monetary benefits and services that are paid based on the membership of the company, other than wages paid directly in cash in return for labor offered."

Employee benefits have various characteristics different from wages. First, employee benefits are provided in principle because of their membership to the company rather than individual or job characteristics. For example, in the case of the student financial aid, which is considered a very important benefit for Korean employees, any employee can receive it as long as he has children enrolled in college. No other conditions than being member of the company are required to obtain this benefit. In case of family allowance also, employees don't need any other condition but have family members.

Second, employee benefits are indirect compensation. If wages are paid directly to employees in the form of cash in return for their labor, employee benefits are generally provided in the form of benefits or services rather than cash. For example, providing a company house does not directly provide money, but offer benefits of living in the safe and comfortable space. In some cases, certain money is paid for congratulating for marriage or mourning death but it is not rewards for the work done but a consideration of the company for their members.

Third, unlike wages which are generally paid on a monthly basis, employee benefits are paid only when circumstances requiring them arise. For example, in the case of student financial aid, benefit is provided only to the employees having college students children. Likewise, congratulatory money or condoling money are offered only when such events like marriage or funeral happen. Therefore, some employees receive benefits and others do not in a fixed period of time, but it is important to note that employees have the same opportunity to get the benefit if that event happens.

Fourth, unlike wages, employee benefits are very diverse in terms of benefits that companies can provide. The number and types of benefits can be increased as long as employees need them and the company is willing to invest expenses. In fact, some Korean companies offer several dozens of employee benefits to their employees.

1.2 Necessity and Role of Employee Benefits

1.2.1 Necessity of Employee Benefits

Why should a company work on employee benefits? If sufficient wages are paid to the employees, shouldn't they directly purchase the benefits they need? What is the need for a company to run employee benefit programs at a cost and effort? These questions are very important for an accurate understanding of the employee benefits, and through these questions, the role of employee benefits can be understood more clearly. The reasons why a company should operate employee benefits apart from wages are as follows.

First, there are cases where it is impossible for an individual to purchase benefits in the market. For example, resort condos are now common and anyone can make a reservation online, but in the past, there was a time when they were not widely developed in Korea. Therefore, companies have constructed and operated their own resort facility. Commuter buses in the era when private cars were not widely used are also a representative example of this. In addition, employee benefit can be offered at an affordable price by using discounted price based on group purchase power.

Second, when employee benefits are not offered and if this budget is distributed as wages, there are cases in which employees do not purchase benefits that are very important from the point of management of the company. For example, even though the management believes that the health and safety of its employees matters a lot and a health check-up is essential, the employees may not want to spend money to receive the check-up. In this case, the need arises for the company to provide comprehensive medical examinations to its employees through a benefit system.

Third, employee benefits are necessary for a differentiated compensation strategy. In the case of a company that cannot pay sufficient wages due to financial constraints, it can be very helpful in securing or maintaining manpower to identify employees' needs for benefits and supporting them. For example, companies that operate day-care centers to ensure work-family balance in order to secure and maintain female professional manpower fall under this category. If it is limited to wages, it is impossible for a company to make strategic choices, but if employee benefits are included, various strategic choices can be possible.

Lastly, regardless of whether a company wants it or not, in the case of statutory benefits stipulated by law, its enforcement is mandatory. Therefore, even if a company wants to pay all compensation with wages without employee benefits, there is no choice but to operate statutory benefits at all times. As time goes by, statutory benefits are becoming more and more important.

1.2.2 Role of Employee Benefits

Employee benefits focused on the livelihood support, which played an important role in the era when income levels were low, have lost their meaning and role at present. It might be better to make this kind of benefits included into wages. However, as we saw earlier, the employee benefits can play an important role now and in the future. If so, what role does the employee benefits play in the management of human resources? Considering that employee benefits are one of the important rewards provided to employees and an important subsystem of human resource management, the role of employee benefits can be summarized as securing and maintaining human resources, and improving their motivation and productivity. Let's take a look at each in detail.

First, the benefits system is used as an effective means to secure excellent manpower. This is because, if the wages are at the same level, companies with well-prepared employee benefits are more likely to secure excellent manpower than those without them. For example, the most important reason of Korean companies running dormitories and schools in the economic development era was to secure diligent female production workers. Now that the times have changed, employee benefits that facilitate work-family balance are being used as a means of securing competent female workers.

Second, the employee benefits makes an non-negligible contribution to preventing the turnover of excellent manpower. In particular, benefits that is well-suited to the needs of individual employees are not easy to replace. In addition, employee benefits, which is operated based on the membership to the company performs the function of making the workplace atmosphere and human relationships friendly and cooperative. As a result, the opportunity cost that must be given up in case of a job change increases, which can contribute to preventing turnover and maintaining excellent manpower.

Third, a well-designed and well-operated employee benefits have the effect of increasing employee motivation and enhancing productivity. Traditionally, benefits have focused on enhancing the stability of life and organizational commitment of employees. It is difficult to say that employees who are satisfied with the company will necessarily achieve high performance, but it is also difficult to expect high performance from employees who lack stability and commitment. In particular, if employee benefits are well tailored to the needs of employees, they can contribute to the productivity by increasing satisfaction and commitment of employees.

2. Change of Environment and Employee Benefits

In relation to employee benefits, the environment surrounding Korean companies has changed significantly in recent years. These changes are not limited to Korean companies, but are common to all developed countries including the United States and Japan. Such changes in the environment pose new challenges related to management of employee benefits.

2.1 Increase of Benefits Costs

One of the most direct reasons that management should pay attention to employee benefits is that their costs are increasing significantly. For example, in the case of U.S. companies, the share of employee benefits in the total compensation cost has expanded from 3% in 1929 to 29.4% in 2021 for private companies, and 38.3% for government. The expenses of the employee benefits directly compared with the salaries paid to employees in 2021 are 41.6% for private companies and 62.1% for government employees respectively.[3)] In Korea, the proportion of the employee benefits is not as high as in the United States, but the proportion of benefits expenses compared to salary has risen from 9.8% in 1985 to 14.7% in 2019. In particular, the proportion of statutory welfare expenses compared to salary increased significantly from 2.2% in 1982 to 9.0% in 2019.[4)]

The cost of employee benefits continues to increase because the companies have expanded various benefits to secure competent manpower.[5)] And various benefits plans have been devised and introduced to increase the motivation and morale of the secured employees. Another important factor is the influence of labour unions. In order to improve the working conditions of union members, the union has demanded that various benefits plans be included. As a result, the employee benefits and their costs have increased significantly. In addition, the tax law can be said to be one of the causes of augmenting the scale and cost of employee benefits. The employee benefits are generally regarded as expenses and subject to tax deductions, thus reducing taxes to pay. Lastly, the expansion of statutory benefits also contributed to the increase in benefit expenses. Especially in Korea, four statutory insurances consisting of employment, health, pension and occupational safety have been expanded. Therefore, how to effectively design and manage the costly employee benefits has become a very important task for the human resource department. In particular, there is an increasing need to find ways to effectively control costs while increasing the benefit satisfaction of the employees. The flexible benefits, which will be described later, can be said to be an attempt to take on this challenge.

2.2 Changes in Benefits Needs

Another important environmental change surrounding employee benefits is that employees' needs for benefits are changing in various ways. These changes in needs are due to the increase in income level, the proliferation of leisure culture, the spread of the Internet, and the diversification of the workforce. As their needs change more and more, it becomes an important and difficult task to quickly and flexibly introduce and operate various benefits plans that satisfy them efficiently.

2.2.1 Improvement of Income Level

As the income level increased, the role and importance of many employee benefits operated by the company was greatly reduced. For example, as incomes of the employees increase and privately-owned cars become commonplace, the role of commuter buses has been reduced to an auxiliary means. The situation is the same for the condominiums and resorts in that the company owned facility lost its role because they can be easily used anywhere in the country through the Internet. Therefore, the utilization rate of benefits related to leisure facilities of the company, has sharply lowered while incurring unnecessary cost to maintain them.

2.2.2 Diversification of Benefits Need

Along with the increase of income level, the benefits need of employees are also diversifying significantly. For example, in the past, the hobbies of the Korean employees were mainly hiking or fishing, but now they are showing a lot of variety such as skin scuba, restaurant trips, music clubs, and dancing. Also, with regard to health, the desire for precise diagnosis beyond simple health examinations is increasing mainly among the middle-aged and elderly, and the preference for meditation, fitness and pilates is also continuously increasing.

2.2.3 Diversification of Types of Employment

The workforce composition of Korean companies is diversifying and the proportion of female workers is increasing. In particular, as employment flexibility is emphasized recently, the number of people in the middle of career externally hired is rapidly increasing, and the number of non-regular workers is also expanding significantly. Divers workforce show meaningful differences in their preferences for benefits. For example, female workers have a strong need for work-family balance, and young people tend to prefer benefits that can be enjoyed each year rather than a benefit that require a long wait such as student tuition aid for children. The diversification of the workforce means diversification of their benefit needs, which poses a difficult task to the company on how to satisfy them flexibly.

2.3 Changes in the Benefits-Related Laws

Significant changes are also taking place in the benefits-related laws. As society develops, the legal system to protect workers is being strengthened, and the mandatory implementation of basic benefits tend to expand. As a result, statutory benefits costs are increasing. This is because the insurance premiums has increased as the target of insurance has expanded and insurance services have enriched. The exemplar cases are the four major social insurances that are health insurance, employment insurance, industrial accident insurance, and national pension.

An important law related to employee benefits is the Labor Welfare Framework Act. In 2009, the Basic Workers Welfare Act and Employee Welfare Fund Act were combined into Basic Workers Welfare Act, and provisions on advanced benefits practices such as flexible benefit plan and employee assistance program were added. The flexible benefit plan is a practice in which workers can select from among various benefit items according to their preferences and needs. The employee assistance program protects workers by supporting and helping them to resolve stress and personal grievances and provides a series of services such as counseling.

3. Types of Employee Benefits

As described above, unlike wages, which are uniformly paid in cash, employee benefits are characterized by being provided in a variety of forms. If so, what kind of employee benefits does the companies actually provide to their employees? Let's take a look at benefit practices in detail.

In a broad sense, corporate welfare which is another name of employee benefits is a part of the overall welfare of society. Scholars who study welfare at the societal level define social welfare as "a state in which people can enjoy happiness through good health, a prosperous life, and a comfortable environment."[6)] Social welfare is divided into public and private welfare according to the entity that provides welfare benefits. Private welfare is further divided into company welfare provided by a corporation,

Figure 10-1 **Types of Welfare Benefits**

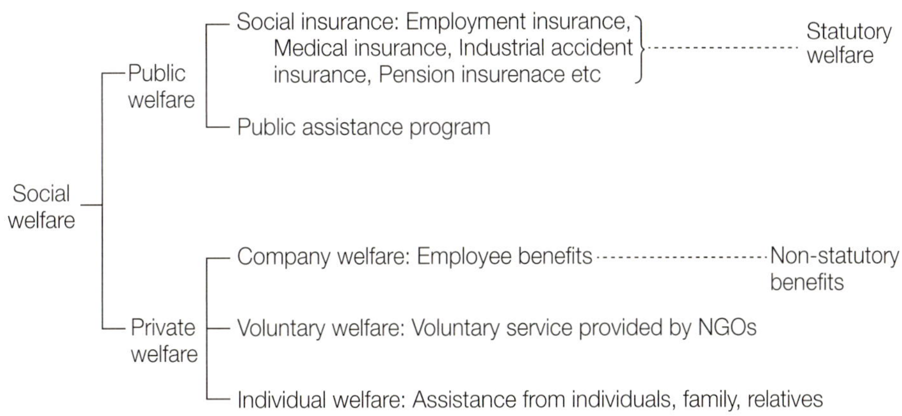

Source: Song 1995, Korean Corporate Welfare Study, Korea Labor Institute.

voluntary welfare provided by non-profit private organizations, and individual welfare provided by individuals, families, and relatives. The following [Figure 10-1] shows the types of social welfare.

From a human resource management point of view, employee benefits include social insurance within public welfare and corporate welfare among private welfare. The former is called statutory welfare in the sense of welfare stipulated by law, and the latter is called non-statutory welfare because its design and operation is free without regulation. In a strict sense, only non-statutory welfare benefits should be included in the employee benefits. In many cases, however, statutory and non-statutory benefits are covered under title of employee benefits. In addition, since companies are obliged to collect and pay social insurance premiums on behalf of the state, it is necessary to understand such contents.

3.1 Statutory Employee Benefits

The central part of statutory benefits is national employment, health, industrial accident, and pension insurance. In Korea, wage workers are obliged to take these insurances through the company. The contents of the benefits are stipulated by law, and the operation is carried out by each public institution specialized on the function. The companies play a role of informing and collecting the insurance premium according to the legislation. In the case of severance pay, it can be regarded as statutory benefits in that it contributes to the stability of life after retirement, although there is argument that it must be regarded as deferred wages. Since the minimum standard for paid leave is also provided by the Labor Standards Act, the company is obliged to provide these benefits to its employees in accordance with such standards. In particular, in the case of severance pay and paid leave, providing additional benefits beyond the legal minimum stipulated by the law falls under the voluntary authority of the company, so it can be regarded as employee benefits outside the statutory provisions. Although statutory benefits are very important to employees, companies cannot design and operate the programs proactively.

1) National Health Insurance

The health of employees affects their work motivation and productivity, and also affects workplace atmosphere and morale. The national health insurance plays a very important role in preventing and detecting diseases of workers so that they can maintain their health, and in the event of an outbreak, it utilizes the insurance function to provide treatment at an affordable price. In Korea, the national health insurance was first implemented in establishments with 500 or more workers in 1977, and since then, expanded to the establishments with 300 or more workers in 1979. Now, every Korean is insured either workers in the company or self-employed and the insurance is managed by the National Health Insurance Service.[7)]

The insurance premiums for employees are levied on the basis of remuneration and a 6.99% premium must be paid for the monthly remuneration. Half of the insurance premium is to be borne by the employer and the other half by the employee. Insurance rates are determined annually by the Health Insurance Policy Review Committee of the Ministry of Health and Welfare. Meanwhile, since 2008, the long-term care insurance system for the elderly has been introduced and is being implemented. It provides long-term care benefits such as physical activity or housework support to the elderly who have difficulty in performing daily life alone due to old age or geriatric diseases. The insurance premium rate is 12.27% of the previously calculated health insurance premium, and the employer and employees must each bear it. Since January 2011, the National Health Insurance Service has implemented a system in which the notification, receipt, and arrears of the four major insurance premiums are collectively managed.

2) National Pension

The national pension is a type of social insurance that aims to promote the stability of people's livelihood by compensating for the income loss due to the retirement, the death and the illness or accident. In Korea, the pension system was implemented for establishments with 10 or more employees from 1988, and the application was expanded to establishments with 5 or more employees in 1992. In 2006, it became compulsory to all Korean employers employing more than one worker.

Employees' pension insurance premiums are 4.5% of the monthly remuneration and to be paid by employee and employer respectively. Overall, it is equivalent to 9% of monthly remuneration, which is the highest level compared to other insurance premiums. As with health insurance, the employer pays half of the premium. With the aging population, it is certain that the number of pension recipients that the current working workforce must support will increase. Therefore, pension reform in the direction of paying more than now and receiving less after retirement is inevitable. The reforms of civil servants' pensions and private teachers' pensions have already been implemented in this direction. Therefore, it is highly likely that the pension premium will continue to increase in the future, which is expected to be more burdensome to the employees and the company.

3) Industrial Accident Insurance

It was introduced in 1964 to protect workers from industrial accidents, which had been rapidly increasing with the progress of industrialization. Industrial accident insurance is a compulsory insurance that the state is responsible for ensuring the livelihood of industrial accident workers and their families. The state collects a certain amount of insurance premiums from employers and uses the funds to compensate industrial accident workers on behalf of employers. Korea's industrial accident insurance started in 1964 as only applicable to mining and manufacturing industries with more than 500 employees, and has been expanded to all workplaces with one or more employees on July 1st 2000 through. Unlike other social insurances, it requires

Table 10-1 Insurance Premium Rate by Industry in 2021 (Unit: per thousand)

Industry type	Premium	Industry type	Premium
1. Mining		**4. Construction business**	36
Coal Mining and Quarrying	185	**5. Transportation, warehousing, and telecommunications**	
Limestone, metals, non-metals, and other mining	57	Railway/air/warehousing/ transport related service	8
2. Manufacturing		Land and water transport	18
Food manufacturing	16	Telecommunications	9
Textiles and textile products manufacturing	11	**6. Forestry**	58
Wood and paper products manufacturing	20	**7. Fishing**	28
Publishing, printing, and bookbinding	10	**8. Agriculture**	20
Chemical and rubber product manufacturing	13	**9. Other business**	
Pharmaceuticals, cosmetics, briquettes, and petroleum products	7	Facility management and business support service	8
Machinery, metal and non-metallic mineral products	13	Miscellaneous business	9
Metal smelting	10	Professional/health/education/ leisure-related services	6
Electrical machine tools, precision tools, and electronic products	6	Wholesale and retail, food and lodging	8
Shipbuilding and repair business	24	Real estate and leasing	7
Handmade and other products	12	Business of the state and local governments	9
3. Electricity, gas, steam, and water services	8	**10. Finance and insurance**	6

* Overseas dispatchers: 14/1,000

the company to pay the entire premium. The employer must pay the premium based on the monthly remuneration of the employees, applying the insurance premium rate for each industry determined through the notification of the Ministry of Employment and Labor every year. The insurance premium rates by industry in 2021 are as shown in <Table 10-1>.

In relation to industrial accident insurance, one of the most frequent complaints from insured workers is that it is not easy to be recognized as an industrial accident even if it results from the work activity. As industrial accident insurance is, in principle, insurance against occupational accidents, in order to be covered by insurance, therefore, proof that an injury, disease, disability, or death occurred due to the person's work-related reasons is required. From the perspective of workers, it is difficult to prove such a cause, so lawsuits surrounding it are increasing. A representative example is musculoskeletal disorder. Many lawsuits have been filed against the Korea Workers' Compensation and Welfare Service, which decides whether or not to recognize it as a industrial accident. In addition, disasters when commuting to work by private car or depression also become frequent conflicts over the recognition of industrial accidents.

4) Employment Insurance

Employment insurance is one of the four major social insurances, which is particularly closely related to both personnel managers and employees. Therefore, it is very important to understand and utilize the contents and benefits of the insurance well. Historically, employment insurance started from unemployment insurance in most countries. This is because the payment of unemployment allowances for the livelihood of workers who have lost their jobs for involuntary reasons was a very urgent task not only for individual workers but also for society. However, there is growing social awareness that not only paying unemployment allowance, but developing vocational competency to facilitate job change is very important. Based on this point of view. social insurance called employment insurance was introduced in Korea in 1995, and in 1998, three years later, employment insurance was expanded and applied to all workplaces with one or more employees.

The activities of employment insurance is largely divided into four categories: employment stabilization, vocational competency development, unemployment benefit, and maternity protection. First, the employment stabilization aid allows employers to maintain employment without firing workers or to increase employment making hire the unemployed by subsidizing a portion of the labor cost. Second, in the vocational competency development, when an employer provides vocational training to workers or when workers receive training for self-development, expenses are covered by the insurance. Third, the unemployment benefit program pays unemployment allowance to the unemployed and their families for a certain period of time when they lose their jobs. Specifically, if a worker works at a workplace for more than 180 days out of the 18 months before he loses his job against his will, such as the company's closure, bankruptcy, or reduction in staff, he can receive job search allowance. However, if he resigns voluntarily to change jobs, he cannot receive it. According to the age at the time of laid-off and the insurance period, 50% of the average wage before unemployment is paid for 90 to 240 days.

Lastly, the maternity protection program includes parental and maternity leave benefits. In the case of parental leave, workers with infants under the age of one can take childcare leave for at least 30 days in accordance with article 19 of the Equal Employment Opportunity Act, and receive 400,000 won each month if certain conditions are met. In the case of maternity leave before and after the childbirth, an amount equivalent to the ordinary wage under the Labor Standards Act is paid for a total of 90 days of leave. The first 60 days are covered by the employer and the remaining 30 days are covered by the employment insurance.

Insurance premiums are calculated based on monthly remuneration, and in the case of unemployment benefits, workers and employers must each bear 0.8%. However, in the case of employment stabilization and vocational competency development, workers do not pay insurance premiums and insurance is operated entirely at the employer's expense. Premium rates are applied differently depending on the size of the business, so large companies are expected to pay higher premiums. For details, refer to <Table 10-2>.

5) Severance Pay

Korea is probably the only country that makes severance pay a mandatory provision by law. In Japan, which introduced and operated the statutory severance pay before Korea, it was changed to a voluntary severance pay in 1944. However, Korea still operates it as a statutory pay. The demand to convert the statutory severance pay into a voluntary one like in Japan has been raised from the business since long time, but it has not been realized. Severance pay plays a very important role in securing the livelihood of workers who leave the company, whether voluntarily or involuntarily. In particular, for workers who are about to retire, the existence of severance pay has a more important role than anything else.

In Korea's severance pay system, 30 days of average wages are accumulated as severance pay when one year of service is completed, and severance pay is calculated and paid according to the period of service at the time of retirement. For example, when a worker who has worked for 25 years retires, the average wage is calculated at the time of retirement, and the monthly average wage multiplied by 25 is the severance pay

Table 10-2 Premiums of Employment Insurance

CATEGORY		WORKER	EMPLOYER
Unemployment allowance		0.8%	0.8%
Stabilization of employment and vocational ability development	Companies with less than 150 employees	-	0.25%
	Companies with 150 or more employees (including priority support target companies)	-	0.45%
	Companies with 150 or more and less than 1,000 employees (excluding priority support target companies)	-	0.65%
	Companies with 1,000 or more employees and businesses directly operated by the state and local governments	-	0.85%

to be paid. In this case, the average wage is the amount obtained by dividing the total amount of wages paid to the worker in the preceding three months from the time when the cause for calculating the average wage occurred, divided by the total number of days during the period (Labor Standards Act Article 2). In the past, there were a number of companies that operated a progressive system that multiplies a certain premium as the number of years of service increases. Currently, with the exception of some companies, such system is not being operated.

After 2005 when the Act on the Guarantee of Workers' Retirement Benefits was established, it has been possible to introduce and operate a retirement pension in place of the traditional severance pay. The main reason for its introduction is that, although severance pay is required to be deposited within the company, there were not many companies that actually comply with it, and retirees often do not receive severance pay. To solve this problem, the Wage Bond Guarantee Act was enacted, guaranteeing severance pay equivalent to the final three years. However, it cannot be a fundamental solution. In the case of retirement pensions, it eliminates the insolvency risk by allowing the severance pay to be deposited and managed by external specialized financial institutions. In addition, unlike severance pay, which is paid in lump sum upon retirement, retirement pension is paid in the form of an annuity or lump sum, so workers can choose according to their needs or preferences.

Retirement pensions are divided into two types: defined benefits (DB) and defined contribution (DC). In the case of the defined benefit, as is the existing severance pay system, the severance pay to be paid to workers is fixed, and the employer bears the profits or losses resulting from the financial results of the operation. The company manages the funds by entrusting workers' severance pay to a financial institution, and depending on the results of managing funds, the contribution that the company has to pay may increase or decrease. For workers, there is no difference from the past as they will receive the same severance pay, but the advantage is that the risk of not receiving severance pay is greatly reduced because the severance pay is not deposited within the company but at a specialized financial institution. It can be said that this type is suitable for companies with high business stability and high employment security.

On the other hand, in the case of defined contribution, the company deposits an amount equivalent to the employee's severance pay in a financial institution, and the employee manages the funds to receive the accumulated amount as an annuity or lump sum upon retirement. The amount of severance pay an employee will receive depends on the performance of the fund. If the fund is well managed, the employee can earn more profit than the defined benefit plan, but if it is poorly managed, the amount of severance pay can be lower than that of the defined benefit plan. Therefore, it is an important difference from the defined benefit plan that the amount of severance pay received varies depending on the financial knowledge of the worker or the expertise of the financial institution. Unlike defined benefit plans, defined contribution plans have the advantage of being able to withdraw early if certain conditions are met. It is suitable for cases where there is a risk of arrears due to insufficient stability of the company, or when the amount calculated as severance pay changes every year due to the variable wage, or for workers who change jobs frequently.

Table 10-3 **Comparison between Defined Benefits and Defined Contribution Pension**

	DEFINED BENEFITS(DB)	DEFINED CONTRIBUTION(DC)
Concept	The level of severance pay to be paid upon retirement is determined in advance. When a worker retires, the employer pays the severance pay agreed.	The level of contribution to be born by the company has been determined in advance. When a worker retires, he receives severance pay according to the performance of the fund.
Responsible for managing fund	Employer	Worker
Corporate burden	Depending on the results of the fund performance, the company's contribution may change.	Each year, the company's contribution is fixed at an amount equal to or more than 1/12 of the total wages of workers.
Retirement benefits	Fixed	Variable
Early withdrawal	Impossible	Available under certain conditions
Suitable companies and workers	Company with no bankruptcy risk and stable employment	Companies that introduced the Yeonbongje(merit pay) Companies at risk of default Workers who move frequently

Neither the defined benefit plan nor the defined contribution plan is unilaterally advantageous, and pros or cons may differ depending on the expertise of the investment manager or long-term stock market conditions. In addition, the investment propensity of individual workers also plays an important role. However, in general, workers prefer the defined benefit plan, while employers tend to prefer the defined contribution plan. Retirement pensions have spread rapidly since the introduction of the system, and as of the end of 2020, the accumulated amount exceeded 252.3 trillion won, and among them, defined benefit pensions occupy a dominant position at 61%.[8] However, compared to 67.8% in 2016, the proportion of defined benefit plans has decreased and that of defined contribution plans has increased.

6) Paid Leave

Minimum standards for paid leave are also stipulated by the Labor Standards Act (Article 60). According to this, the employer should grant one day of paid leave to workers who have worked continuously for less than one year for each month of work, and 15 days of paid leave to workers who have worked for 80% or more in one year. In addition, a worker who has worked continuously for three years or more should be given one day of paid leave for every two years of continuous service exceeding the first one year. According to the law, workers with more than one year of service are entitled to at least 15 days and maximum of 25 days of paid leave from the company. Article 61 of the same Act provides for an obligatory provision for employers to facilitate paid leave for workers.

Before the law was amended, the employer was supposed to settle the unused paid vacation days in January every year and pay them in money. As a result, contrary to the purpose of the paid leave system, which is the reproduction and self-development of the labor force through sufficient rest, a side effect of hindering its use and increasing the labor cost has occurred. To solve this, compensation for unused paid leave was prohibited. Instead, it become mandatory for employers to make efforts to promote paid leave for workers.

The Labor Standards Act sets minimum standards, and it is possible to offer to the employees more than the minimum to improve their morale and motivation. For example, in addition to basic paid leave, more paid leave can be given as a means of rewarding employees with excellent work and performance. A representative example of this is reward vacations that provide travel packages with paid leave.

3.2 Non-Statutory Employee Benefits

Non-statutory employee benefits refer to various benefits that are not compulsory by law, but that companies voluntarily provide for their employees. Therefore, they have different forms depending on the industry to which the company belongs or the characteristics of the workforce composition. For example, in the case of KEPCO(Korea Electric Power Corporation) and KT(Korea Telecom), which have business sites across the country and have many internal transfers, corporate housing has been used as an important benefit. Also, in the case of factories where single workers are numerous, the dormitory constitutes an important benefit. Non-statutory benefits of voluntary nature require additional costs, but have the advantage of designing flexible plans in consideration of the characteristics and circumstances of the company.

Non-statutory benefits can be divided into those that provide additional benefits in addition to the legal minimum, and those that provide benefits that are not legally required at all.[9] In the former case, for example, the provision of additional insurance coverage to compulsory health insurance, the progressive severance pay system, and paid leave as rewards fall into this category. In the latter case, a separate benefits plan is designed and operated reflecting the characteristics of the company and the needs of workers. Although it costs money and effort, it is necessary for the companies that want to motivate their employees.

1) Residence-Related Benefits

There are cases where facilities such as company houses and dormitories are built for free or low-price use, or loans are provided to the employees for house purchase or rent. In Korea, where it is very difficult to buy a house because of the exorbitant price, support for housing stability has played a very important role in securing and retaining employees and enhancing their motivation. However, this plan requires a lot of money which explains that only large private and public companies could offer it. And with the development of diverse loan products in the financial market, such benefits are gradually disappearing.

2) Health and Safety Related Benefits

This includes life insurance provided for the health and safety of employees or additional health checkups that are provided in addition to legal medical insurance. In some cases, a health center is installed within the company to provide support for simple diagnosis and treatment at work. Large companies often operate sports facilities, fitness centers, playgrounds, and recreation rooms to maintain the employees' health. And more and more companies are introducing an employee assistance program (EAP) to more actively check and maintain the mental health of employees.

3) Living Support

This includes paying congratulatory or condoling money to the employees having marriage or funeral in the family requiring a lot of money for that event. In some cases, meals are provided at low prices by operating a company restaurant, or the cost of meals is paid when the company do not run restaurants. The case of a company offering its own products at a discount price to the employees falls into this category. Operating a commuter bus is an important living support that helps employees commute to work. The most costly for living support is student financial support. Full support was generally provided to prevent difficulties in living due to the burden of tuition fees for college students in the family. Living support played a very important role in times when wages were low and livelihoods were difficult, but recently their importance has been decreasing.

4) Entertainment and Leisure

While the importance of living support is relatively decreasing, that of the entertainment and the leisure is increasing. By supporting various in-house club activities or operating libraries, and recreation facilities, companies are helping their employees to get away from work and enjoy various cultural experiences and rest. Some companies are trying to hold concerts or run liberal arts lectures in company spaces. In recent years, the number of cases in which the design or operation of the cultural and leisure system is entrusted to an external professional firms is increasing significantly.

5) Work-Family Balance

Recently, the employee benefits related to work-family balance is receiving the most attention from companies and employees. It is not that there were no such plans in the past. The operation of childcare facilities is a typical example. However, in recent years, work-family balance is regarded as a very important social agenda due to the low fertility and aging population in Korea. Accordingly, efforts to support work-family balance are increasing more than ever. For reference, even in the United States and other developed countries, work-family balance accounts for a very large proportion of the employee benefits provided voluntarily by companies.

6) Flexible Working System

The flexible working system, which allows employees to flexibly select work hours and locations, is also receiving a lot of attention recently. The flexible working system breaks away from the standardized work practice of having to work at a fixed time and a fixed place. Flexible work allows employees to adjust their commuting time according to their circumstances without having to commute at a fixed time, so they can adjust their work hours in consideration of their personal or family-related needs. It is possible to set only the total amount of working hours and give all the discretion to the employees. However, because of the need for face-to-face contact such as meetings and information sharing, it is more often that the company set a core time for all employees to be in the company and gives discretion for the rest time.

4. Flexible Employee Benefits

4.1 Appearance Background

The flexible benefits plan has attracted a lot of attention of domestic and foreign companies because it has the potential to solve the problems that many companies are facing with regard to manage benefits program today. As we have already seen, many companies are under strong pressure from the cost burden due to the steep rise in benefits costs. They are also not so sure that the extant benefits plans are effective in motivating employees. In fact, there is often a discrepancy between the existing benefits and the changing needs of employees.

It is difficult to meet various benefits needs with the traditional plan that presupposes a standard workforce centered on married men and operates a uniform service for all of them. In this situation, wouldn't it be better to pay cash in the form of wages rather than a benefit and let employees choose their benefits needs on their own? The flexible benefits plan takes this kind of approach to satisfy the diverse benefits needs of employees in that it provides credits to them as if paying cash and then allows them to solve their own benefits needs within that limits.

In Korea, the flexible benefits plan was first introduced in 1997 by IBM Korea, followed by LG Distribution and CJ in 1998, and has continued to spread among private companies in the 2000s. In particular, in 2003, some government agencies introduced it as a pilot, and since then, it has been applied to all civil servants. As of 2009, it is estimated that there are about 500 companies that independently operate a flexible benefits plan, and about 1,000 companies use outsourcing operated by specialized companies.[10)] The market size of the flexible benefits plan has continued to increase since then. Although there is no survey data indicating the exact size of the market, according to Easywell, which is the No.1 operator having about 50% of market share, its entrusted benefits budget is 1.4 trillion won and the number of customers is 1,700.[11)]

The spread of the flexible benefits plan is not only a phenomenon in Korea. It has been used in developed countries earlier than in Korea. For example, in the case of the United States, tax benefits for the flexible benefits plan began to be provided through the 1978 tax law revision, and since then it has begun to spread rapidly.[12)] Meanwhile, in German companies, 64.5% of managers and 22.5% of employees were already receiving the flexible benefits plan in the 1990s.[13)] Even in Japan, where the introduction of the flexible benefits plan was relatively late, 104 companies, or 17.1% of the companies were implementing it in 2019.[14)]

4.2 Effect of the Flexible Benefits Plan

This popularity of the flexible benefits plan can be explained by the fact that it allows employees to choose the benefits they want on their own. Various advantages that can be obtained from this feature are as follows.[15)]

① As employees can choose the benefits that best suits their needs and preferences, satisfaction with welfare benefits can be increased.
② The changing needs for benefits can be reflected in a timely manner.
③ By having employees and their families participate in their benefits design, it is possible to enhance their understanding of benefits.
④ By easily introducing a new benefit without additional cost, it is possible to broaden the range of choices for employees.
⑤ By limiting the level of total benefits cost while satisfying the needs of employees, the increase in labor cost can be controlled stably.
⑥ Labor-management cooperation can be enhanced by having the labor union or worker representatives participate in the process of planning the flexible benefits plan.

In sum, the flexible benefits plan can increase the benefits satisfaction of employees while stably controlling the benefits cost. This means that it can offer a good solution to the problems that the traditional benefits plan had. According to an empirical study in the United States, after the introduction of the flexible benefits plan in a financial company, overall job satisfaction has increased, and in particular, the satisfaction related to benefits has risen significantly.[16)]

4.3 Types and Characteristics of the Flexible Benefits Plan

4.3.1 Core Plus Option

The core plus option makes essential benefits (core items) compulsory to all employees and then employees can increases the coverage of core items or freely select other benefits than the core items within a credit limit. Core items are benefits that the company consider essential for all employees. This is the most common type of the flexible benefit plan. The core plus option type has the advantage of satisfying the different benefits needs of employees by ensuring freedom of choice while maintaining a basic benefits plan for all employees. In this type, however, there is a possibility that employees' choice is biased on a specific item, and the burden of managing the plan may increase when the choice is much diverse.

Core plus option

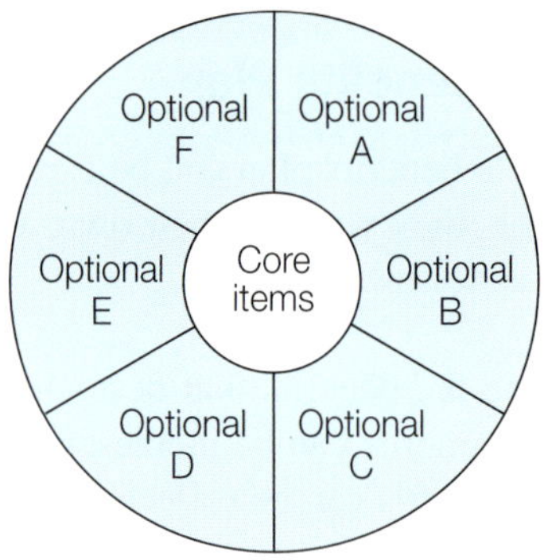

4.3.2 Modular Plan

The modular plan is a system in which employees select one of several modules composed of a combination of various benefits. In general, there is not much difference in the contents of benefits themselves between modules, and only the level of each benefit is different. The sum of the total cost of benefits does not also differ between modules.

The modular plan has the advantage that employees can easily choose one module that suits them because the company classify the benefits needs of employees in advance through modular design. In addition, while a lot of time being invested in design, it is easy to manage and operating costs are low once design is established. However, since everything is set in advance, it is rigid in nature and has the disadvantages of limiting employees' choice to limited number of modules. It is desirable to introduce the modular plan type when employees have a low understanding of the flexible benefits plan and lack the ability to design benefits plan that suits them. Also, it is desirable to use it when employees are clearly divided into several groups with similar benefits needs.

Modular plan

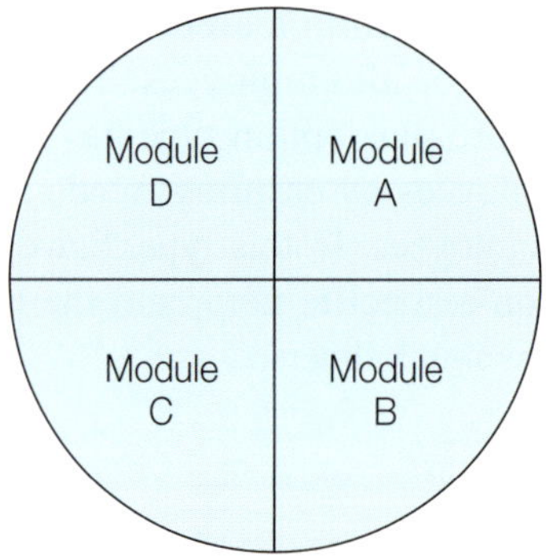

4.3.3 Mixed and Match

Mixed and match is a method in which individual employee can choose not only benefit items but also benefit levels according to his own needs. Among the types of the flexible benefits plan, it is the type in which individual choice is guaranteed the most. In addition, since a benefit account is set for each individual and the total budget for all benefit services is set and operated, stable control of the budget can be achieved. However, if employees focus their choices on specific items, it may become difficult to offer a balanced and comprehensive benefit service. For example, if an employee does not choose the health-related benefit service that the company expect them to select, it may go against the company's policy to protect the health and safety of its employees. Since it is difficult to predict the choice of members in advance, this kind of situation may increase the difficulty in managing the system.

4.3.4 Flexible Spending Account

In the flexible spending account, the amount of benefit credit provided by the company to its employees and the amount drawn out by each employee are deposited in the employee's individual benefit account. And then, employees can freely choose and purchase various benefit services suggested by the company within the amount of this account. Under this system, if employees claim the cost after purchasing the benefit item or service, the cost will be covered within the amount of each employee's spending account.

4.4 Precautions for the Introduction and Operation

The flexible benefits plan can have adverse effects if mismanaged. Its potential disadvantages are as follows. First, the employees may not choose the benefits they really need or the company want them to choose. Second, the design of the flexible benefits plan is very costly and time consuming, and the cost of management and the workload of the HR department may be important. The introduction of the flexible benefits plan necessarily requires the help of a computerized system, so the introduction of the human resource information system is a prerequisite. Third, since employees choose the benefits that they actually use, the utilization rate increase compared to the traditional benefits plan, which make the actual cost grow than expected at the design stage. Fourth, in order to provide the flexible benefits plan, it is necessary to secure a certain amount of credit that can be used by each individual. However, after excluding statutory welfare benefits, which account for a significant portion of welfare budget, there may be few discretionary credits that can actually be distributed to employees, which make it impossible to provide meaningful benefits.

As a way to solve these problems, a professional service company that operates the flexible benefits plan has emerged. Various specialized companies such as Benepia, led by Easywell which holds a dominant market share, are operating the flexible benefits plan on consignment. A company that wants to introduce a flexible benefits plan can design the most suitable contents with the help of a service provider, and then pays the necessary expenses to the service company. When the flexible benefits plan is entrusted to an external service company, it has the advantage of solving various problems encountered in designing and operating the plan directly. Service companies that have multiple companies as customers supply a variety of products and services to employees of various customers. Commissions for welfare services and profits from sales of products and services are important sources of income for these service providers.

5. Strategic Management of Employee Benefits

5.1 The Need for Strategic Management

Employee benefits, which cost a lot of money, must be managed effectively. When the benefits are not based on the needs of the employees, only money are spent without any meaningful effect. Strategic management of benefits is to increase employee benefits satisfaction and organizational productivity by designing benefits systems in response to environmental changes while considering corporate management philosophy or policies. In order to implement and strategically manage benefits, it is necessary to clearly set the goals that the benefits aims to achieve. Most of the problems that many companies are currently facing with benefits arise from the fact that the purpose or goal of the benefits has not been set and the benefits programs has been created and operated ad hoc according to the circumstances. Of course, such goals are bound to vary from company to company, but at least external competitiveness, satisfaction of employees and cost effectiveness must be included in common.

5.1.1 External Competitiveness of Employee Benefits

As we have already seen through the previous two chapters related to compensation management, external fairness or external competitiveness is very important in compensation. In terms of employee benefits, the level of benefits provided by the company must be competitive compared to the level of benefits of other companies. Weak competitiveness make it difficult to secure, retain, and motivate competent human resources.

In order to review the external competitiveness of employee benefits, a benefit survey is necessary. A company need to research benefits programs of direct competitors. For that purpose, human resource managers may share information on benefits with those of other companies. Or, there may be cases where more specialized and detailed materials are provided through professional consulting companies. With the survey, it is possible to know in detail the types and contents of the employee benefits provided by competitors and to understand the relative level of benefits provided by the company.

In relation to the external competitiveness of benefits, the choices that a company takes can be broadly divided into four categories just like wage: a lead strategy, a match strategy, a lag strategy, and a focus strategy. First, the lead strategy is a strategy that provides various types of benefits to employees by applying a very high benefit coverage. It is a strategy to secure and retain excellent manpower. The match strategy refers to a strategy in which the company offers a similar benefits compared to other companies in the labor market. Therefore, this does not give to the company a special advantage over other companies but does not put the company at a disadvantage.

On the other hand, the lag strategy provides employee benefits that are lower than the average benefits offered by other companies, and it is difficult to see it as an intentional strategy in a strict sense. This is because the company is forced to adopt such a strategy due to the difficult financial situation. Small and medium-sized enterprises (SMEs) and venture companies are typical examples. Therefore, a focus strategy is appropriate as a strategic choice for these companies. Focus strategy refers to a strategy to get the maximum effect with limited resources by concentrating on specific employee benefits needed by the company rather than matching all benefits provided by competitors. In the case of venture companies, focusing on self-development and travel, which young employees prefer, can be a good example of this strategy.

5.1.2 Satisfaction of Employee Benefits

Satisfaction with employee benefits is determined not only by the overall level of benefits, but also by how well the benefits match the needs of employees. If the external competitiveness of welfare benefits mainly affects the securing of excellent manpower, whether the needs of employees related to the benefits are actually being met has a great influence on the retention and motivation of the employees. What is important here is that the benefits needs of employees can vary greatly from individual to individual.

In the case of wages, the overall level of wages is important, and these do not vary greatly depending on the characteristics of individual employees. In the case of benefits, however, the contents of the benefits should be different depending on the needs of the individuals. For example, for employees who are still raising young children, benefits related to childcare are important, but for employees who are old, benefits related to health and pension are more important. Therefore, the company needs to pay attention to the match between individual needs and benefits plan.

In order to increase employees' satisfaction with benefits, it is necessary to accurately understand their benefit needs. Individual and focus group interview, questionnaires can be used to understand what benefits employees want to receive from the company. It is also important to analyze and figure out the patterns of the individual needs according to demographic characteristics. This is because, based on this information, it is possible to accurately design and provide the main contents of the benefits that the company must provide.

5.1.3 Cost Effectiveness

It is a very important task to efficiently manage costs in the design and operation of the benefit system. While the need to effectively control the cost of benefits is increasing, it is not easy to do it. As mentioned above, benefit costs are increasing rapidly in almost every country, but the satisfaction or productivity does not justify the cost. Therefore, the human resource management department must effectively control the cost while enhancing the external competitiveness of benefits and increasing benefit satisfaction. In practice, the HR department must solve the difficult task of securing external competitiveness and internal satisfaction with a given budget.

In order to effectively control costs, continuous review is necessary to find the benefit programs that are expensive but not satisfactory, and that are desired by employees even though they cost not much. This must be based on the results of the benefit needs and satisfaction identified in advance by the survey. In addition, it is necessary to actively seek ways to reduce existing benefits costs. For example, some American companies that need to cut excessively expensive medical costs provide a service that sends employees to countries with low medical costs, such as India.[17)]

5.2 Efficient Operation of Employee Benefits

After a specific benefit plan is designed and introduced according to the benefit strategy and goals, it is very important to operate it efficiently. It is true that design is important, but operational aspects should not be overlooked. In relation to operation, what is essential is communication with employees and continuous revision and improvement of the plan.

5.2.1 Communication

One of the reasons why the company does not get the expected effect despite investing a lot of financial resources for employee benefits is that employees don't have a good understanding of existing benefit plans in the company and the costs they incur to the company. According to some researches, it is reported that employees underestimate the cost that the company has to bear for the benefits provided to them. In this situation, it would be much more effective for the company to pay individuals in the form of wages rather than to inject more benefit resources. As we have already seen, since wages and benefits have different expected goals and characteristics, it is of importance to make an accurate understanding of benefits through communication.

It is common for most Korean companies to simply explain benefits plan as part of the orientation process after hiring new employees. After that, employees are often unable to properly utilize the existing benefits plans because they rarely receive accurate information about them. To prevent this, one alternative is to create and provide material in the form of a one-page brochure or a desktop calendar that can be placed on a desk. The key is to make it readily available for immediate reference whenever employees need it. It is also necessary to introduce the contents once a week or every month using e-mail or web. Basic contents are introduced through brochures or e-mails, and then the employees can promote their understanding and utilization of benefits by referencing to the web.

5.2.2 Update of the Benefits Plan

As we have already discussed, the benefit needs of employees change as the environment changes, or as an individual's career or age changes. Accordingly, the company's benefit system must be continuously updated in accordance with it. To this end, it does matter to investigate the importance and satisfaction of each benefit plan through regular surveys, and to create and provide plans that can satisfy new benefit needs while abolishing plans with low satisfaction. New benefit needs are also caused by the emergence of professional service providers who offer new benefit services that did not exist in the past. Therefore, the person in charge of benefits in the HR department must also pay attention to the supply status of various benefit services in the market.

Ending Case

LG Chem's Flexible Benefit Plan[18)]

LG Chem prepared to introduce the flexible benefit plan in 2005 and implemented it in 2006. The main reason for introducing it was that the existing benefit programs did not adequately meet the changing workforce structure and the needs of its employees. In particular, the company paid attention to the newly joined employees who was rapidly increasing and will become the core workforce of the company in the future. The HR department, realizing that the most dissatisfied issue for them is benefits, felt the need to reorganize the benefit plan. In fact, the extant benefit programs did not sufficiently satisfy the benefit needs of young workers, and that the benefit choices were very limited. Therefore, it became urgent to satisfy the various needs of young employees. The flexible benefit plan was regarded as an important alternative and its introduction was promoted.

The HR department examined the existing benefit programs, and it turned out that the overall benefit level was higher than that of other companies, but the need for improvement in cost effectiveness and employee satisfaction was clear. Despite the fact that benefit expenses were quite high, employees perceived the company's benefit investment very low, and satisfaction with the benefits was also lower than that of other comparable companies. This results from the fact that most benefits were concentrated on employees with long service year, usually married and having children, and the needs of young employees were not sufficiently met. Also, in some cases, benefits were recognized as vested interests, so new programs were continuously added regardless of cost effectiveness, while satisfaction or effectiveness analysis was not secured properly.

Starting from the analysis of the current situation and problems, LG Chem set the goals of the benefit reform as improvement of benefit equality and cost efficiency, and active reflection of individual preferences, and decided to introduce the flexible benefit plan for that purpose. The first decision to make was whether to put all benefits in the framework of the flexible benefit plan or whether to maintain essential benefit items as before while combining the rest benefits into the flexible benefit system. If all benefit items are integrated as the flexible benefit plan, it has the advantage of broadening the range of employee choices, thus increasing employee satisfaction with benefits. However, there may be confusion due to sudden changes or resistance due to the abolition of the previous programs. Also, there is a concern that, if everything is left to the employees' choice, employee benefits for life stability, health, and self-development may not be sufficiently chosen. After taking these issues into serious consideration, LG Chem decided to keep the benefits related to a stable and healthy life as common items and make rest benefits related to different individual needs and life style as flexible choice items.

Common items include housing and living stability support (housing funds, congratulatory and condoling money, student financial aid), and medical and health support (medical expenses, comprehensive health checkups, regular health checkups). On the other hand, the flexible benefits are designed to reflect the choices according to an individual's lifestyle as much as possible. The flexible benefits were composed of four categories: health, self-development, leisure, and e-shop.

In order to increase the equality of benefits, it is designed to distribute the same benefit budget to all employees, and the number of points is quantified so that the individual can recognize the benefits he or she receives. All incumbents are eligible to receive points. At the beginning, the period of use of points was set to one year, but at the request of employees, unspent points could be carried over to the next year. However, the company is encouraging the regular use of points so as not to miss the period of using points. The operation of the system was entrusted to an external specialized company for the purpose of efficiency. The company provides points to its employees, and they can use the benefit card to choose benefits provided by consigned companies online and off-line. The used point information goes to the consigned company, the usage details are delivered to the employee again.

LG Chem conducted continuous communication with employees in the process of designing and introducing the flexible benefits plan. In order to share the basic concept and purpose of the plan with employees, a preliminary survey and interview were conducted, and a labor-management joint task force was formed and operated. During the design phase, a briefing session was held about the characteristics of the plan, selectable items, and use method, and the HR had time to fully explain to the representative of the employee council. After the plan is confirmed, manuals are distributed to employees and briefing sessions are held again, while detailed information is intro-

	Category	Contents
Flexible Benefits	Health Care	additional health checkups, additional medical expenses, and purchase of glasses
	Self Development	education expenses, book and record purchase expenses physical fitness expenses (sports club, golf class)
	Leisure & Life	resort, leisure, domestic and foreign travel, cultural life (theater, performance, movie), theme park, gifts (flowers, cakes, rice cake delivery, etc.), family dining out programs
	e-Shop	LG Mall (LG Electronics, LG Household & Health Care, etc.) Household goods, health/beauty, etc.

duced through the internal bulletin board. And system improvement is continuously carried out by receiving feedback from employees.

Through the introduction and operation of the new system, employee satisfaction with benefits has greatly improved. In addition, significant improvements also have been made in terms of efficiency. The fact that employees can choose what they want contributed to the increase in satisfaction. The HR department will not be satisfied with the current performance and will continue to exert efforts to operate an efficient benefit system.

Discussion Questions

1. If all existing benefit programs are integrated into an flexible choice plan, employees have the advantage of greatly expanded benefit options they can choose. Nevertheless, why did LG Chem choose to operate its new benefit plan as a core plus option type?
2. In the process of reforming the benefit system, why did LG Chem consider continuous and systematic communication so important and thoroughly implement it?
3. The benefit needs of employees change according to the times, and the level of careers and age. What kind of efforts should the HR department make in order for the flexible benefit plan to effectively satisfy these changing needs?
4. The flexible benefit plan is being introduced and spread mainly by large corporations that have already operated a high-level benefit programs. Is it possible to introduce this system even for SMEs with little financial capacity?

CHAPTER
11

Turnover

Learning Objectives

1. Can understand and explain types of turnover.
2. Can explain what is the optimal turnover rate in a company.
3. Can explain the efforts that managers can make to prevent the brain drain.
4. Can explain the background of downsizing actively in companies.
5. Can suggest alternatives to avoid layoff for managerial reasons.
6. Can explain the basic principles of discipline that managers must follow.
7. Understand the attitudes and roles leaders should assume in the process of discipline.

Introductory Case

ABC's CEO Soobin Lee and executives have been contemplating the final decision for several days. ABC Distribution has grown rapidly over the past 5 years as a result of innovatively improving online and offline services and distribution stages to provide high-quality products at low prices. In 1999, when CEO Soobin Lee and some early founding members came up with ideas and started a business, they experienced a very difficult time for a while. In the 10 years from 1999 to 2009, when it was founded, the number of stores increased by only 10, and the sales also took a turbulent pace. However, through new services and distribution innovation, sales increased more than tenfold from 2010 to 2015, and the number of stores reached more than 100 across the country. The total number of employees of ABC Distribution, including the head office, was only about 50, but it increased rapidly as the company grew. Currently, there are about 500 employees nationwide, with 30 employees at the head office and 5 employees per store. Based on the CEO's management philosophy, the company maintains a HR policy of hiring full-time employees whenever possible. However, depending on the store, part-time employees required during busy hours were hired by the store manager after autonomous judgment. About 10% of the store's 500 employees are non-regular employees.

However, in 2016, the decrease in Chinese tourists due to the deployment of THAAD, the appearance of similar competitors, and the economic downturn, the sales began to drop sharply. Until the beginning of the year, they managed to survive by cutting costs by tightening the belt. However, as the summer came and the economy became more difficult, the deficit accumulated and it became impossible to maintain 100 stores any more. Accordingly, CEO Soobin Lee and the management fell into trouble. Without downsizing, the company itself was at risk. First of all, it was decided to close the store, where it became meaningless to run the store any longer due to a sharp drop in customers. The number of such stores was about 30% of the total nationwide. However, the reason why the CEO and the management were not able to make decisions easily was about what to do with the employees who worked hard together and contributed to the growth of the company. Once the number of stores is reduced, the HR team has been instructed to figure out how many employees will need to be laid off.

Discussion Questions

1. What alternatives can the company choose in this situation?
2. In case of layoff, what kind of procedure should the company go through?
3. What HR strategy should the company choose to grow again?
4. What would you do if you were the CEO of this company?
5. What would you do if you were the store manager?

Hiring deals with the meeting between individuals and organizations, while turnover deals with the separation between individuals and organizations. Many companies spend a lot of money trying to recruit good talent, but they are often insensitive to the phenomenon of top talent leaving the organization. One of the most common reasons why mergers and acquisitions (M&A) of companies fail is that excellent talents of the acquired company leave. Acquisition of a company is often due to the unique capabilities and technology of the company, but most of the capabilities and skills are inherent in people rather than machines. However, if talented people leave after the takeover, it will end up buying a company that is only a shell, paying a high price.

In the case of Korean companies, the turnover rate of new employees is serious. Although the youth unemployment rate is very high, according to statistics, the turnover rate of new college graduates within one year of joining the company reached 27.0% as of 2016.[1)] On the other hand, despite low competency or performance, it is impossible to send out low performers due to rigid labor laws. Also, there are difficulties in organizational management due to employees who do not perform their roles properly. This chapter deals with the turnover management issues that companies and managers face in human resource management.

1. Types of Turnover

There are voluntary turnover and involuntary turnover, depending on who makes the decision about turnover. Voluntary turnover occurs when individual members make the decision to leave. It is the decision to leave the company on their own if they are dissatisfied with the organization or seek other personal opportunities outside the organization. On the other hand, involuntary turnover refers to a case in which the decision to leave is made by an organization, not an individual. Various management problems arise because in involuntary turnover, employees leave the company due to the company's decision even though they have no intention of leaving the company. Involuntary turnover is further classified according to who provides the cause of turnover. When an individual member provides the cause of turnover, it is called dismissal. Another is the case where layoffs are made for business reasons of the company even though there is no cause attributable to individual members, which is often referred to as downsizing.

2. Voluntary Turnover

Voluntary turnover is when employees leave the company on their own. There are two main reasons for leaving the company. The first occurs because organizations and individuals misfit. Individuals who enter through the hiring process go to work for the first time with various expectations about the company. When you write an application for a job and go to an interview, you think that your various expectations will be suitable for this company, so you enter the company with inflated dreams. However, the reality does not necessarily live up to expectations. You will encounter an environment that is quite different from what you originally expected, such as the work environment, wages or benefits, working conditions, the company's unique organizational culture that you did not know from outside, your relationship with your boss, and the time and distance it takes to commute.

The second reason for voluntary turnover is external opportunities. The greater the number of external opportunities, the higher the voluntary turnover rate. For example, if the unemployment rate in the labor market is low and the talent shortage is severe, it is easy to find another job. On the other hand, if the youth unemployment rate is high and it is very difficult to enter a good company, as in recent years, it is difficult to make a decision to change jobs. In addition to these labor market conditions, external opportunities are also personal. There are various reasons, such as entering graduate school to continue studying, working in a field of interest as a freelancer, or taking charge of a family-run company and transforming into CEO or an executive. In addition, although it cannot be seen as an opportunity, some leave the company for various reasons, such as health or psychological problems.

2.1 Optimal Turnover Rate[2)]

The turnover of top talent is sometimes fatal to the organization. However, voluntary turnover is not necessarily a bad thing. Proper turnover also helps to keep the organization healthy. The turnover rate is used as an indicator to determine whether an organization is properly managing turnover. The turnover rate is usually calculated on a yearly basis. It is calculated by taking into account the number of turnover in one year among all employees. If the total number of employees was 1,000, and 100 of them had changed jobs, the turnover rate was 10%. If the employee moves frequently, add the total number of employees who joined the company for one year to the number of employees at the beginning of the year, and then calculate it by taking into account the total number of employees who changed jobs during the year. For example, if there were 1,000 people as of January 1, 2017, and 100 people newly joined in 2017, the total number of employees for one year would be 1,100. And if 100 people resigned voluntarily during 2017, the total number of employees at the end of December 31, 2017 is the same as that of January 1, but the turnover rate is 9.1% (100/1,100×100).

There is no consensus on what level of turnover is appropriate. Most companies judge whether the company's average turnover rate is high or low compared to the average turnover rate in its industry or compared to that of its competitors. In addition, the turnover rate of specific member groups such as new employees, female talents, leader-level talents, and R&D core talents is calculated separately and compared with the overall average turnover rate. A concept that contrasts with the turnover rate is the retention rate. As shown in [Figure 11-1], the theoretically optimal turnover rate is when the company's total cost can be kept at the lowest level. The higher the turnover rate, the higher the turnover cost. Conversely, when the turnover rate decreases, the retention rate increases and the maintenance cost increases. The theoretical appropriate turnover rate

Figure 11-1 **Optimal Turnover Rate**

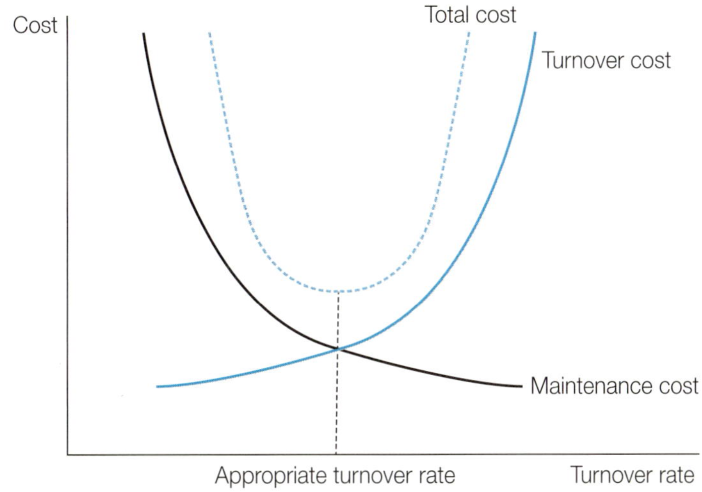

is the point of contact that minimizes the total cost by properly harmonizing the two in consideration of the turnover cost and the maintenance cost.

2.2 The Function of Voluntary Turnover

Voluntary turnover has both positive and negative functions. As mentioned, voluntary turnover is not always bad for the organization. A certain degree of turnover is also necessary for proper manpower circulation. On the other hand, there are costs associated with voluntary turnover. As seen in the previous section, an organization needs detailed human resource management to achieve an appropriate turnover rate while minimizing the adverse effects of voluntary turnover.

2.2.1 The Positive Function of Voluntary Turnover[3)]

1) Reduction of Labor Cost

The share of labor costs in the total cost of an organization varies from industry to industry, but is never insignificant. Labor cost is proportional to the number of employees in the organization. In order to reduce costs when management becomes difficult, labor costs should be considered. As will be discussed later, one of the various alternatives to reducing labor costs is the reduction of manpower. However, voluntary reduction of manpower through voluntary turnover is helpful because forced manpower reduction can have side effects.

2) Replacement of Low Performers

Voluntary turnover does not only happen to talented people with excellent performance. Low performers who fail to adapt to the organization for various reasons will also consider changing jobs. From an organization's point of view, the company wants to retain talented people. At this time, if the low performer voluntarily leaves the organization, the burden of forcibly leaving the organization is reduced.

3) Opportunities for New Change

Proper turnover brings vitality to the organization. Organizations must always have new blood transfusions to keep them active. If new talent fills in the void caused by the turnover of existing workers, the organization can try new changes. In particular, the turnover of members in leadership positions, including executives, leads to a change of leadership and becomes an opportunity for organizational change.

2.2.2 Dysfunction of Voluntary Turnover[4)]

1) Occurrence of Turnover Cost

It is not easy to accurately and financially calculate the cost of turnover. However, the fact that the calculation is not accurate does not mean that it does not incur costs. In terms of human resource management, it is necessary to know exactly what the cost of turnover is, and to be able to infer how much it is. The cost of turnover can be divided into direct cost and indirect cost.

Direct costs are costs that arise from the inability to properly perform the job that the person was performing when the person left the job. When turnover occurs unexpectedly in an organization, it is not easy to find replacement workers immediately. Then, the job performed by the new employee is left vacant, or urgent work is shared with other colleagues in the vicinity. As a result, it is more likely that the productivity or quality of the job will not be maintained at the previous level. Also, there is a risk that the customer will move to another company if there is a strong network with the customer. Also, even after hiring a replacement worker, it will take a certain period of time to reach the level of job performance performed by the previous person in charge. Problems with productivity or quality or with customers may still arise until the replacement worker performs the job smoothly. Another direct cost is the time and administrative costs of HR managers from exit interviews. Many companies conduct exit interviews as a way to prevent the outflow of excellent talent. This isn't free either.

On the other hand, the indirect cost is the recruitment cost that an organization must pay to select talent and the training cost to improve competency after selection. In order to hire a talented person, it is necessary to go through several stages of selection process, including recruitment advertisements, document screening, tests, and interviews. This process can sometimes take several months. Recruitment through a headhunter costs more. In addition, when new employees are hired from outside, whether they are new or experienced employees, the company puts a lot of effort into adapting to the organization and improving their competencies, including orientation. It is a huge loss for a company to lose the talents it has hired and nurtured in this way. In order to fill vacancies caused by turnover, a similar process must be repeated.

2) Deterioration of Organizational Climate

The side effects of turnover are not limited to those who change jobs. It can also negatively affect other colleagues who remain in the organization. In particular, if the person is recognized as excellent within the organization and the relationship with colleagues is strong, the negative impact will be greater. If the cause of turnover is caused by the organization rather than the individual, this negative effect is amplified and the atmosphere of the organization deteriorates. In addition, if a person who can replace the job is not hired as soon as possible, the burden of sharing work among the remaining colleagues increases, and problems with productivity, quality, and customers may arise, leading to a risky atmosphere throughout the organization. Additional turnover among remaining workers may occur in this case.

2.3 Activities to Prevent Voluntary Turnover

Failure to retain top talent can be catastrophic for an organization. Companies are making various efforts to prevent the turnover of talented people. Evaluation, training, and compensation covered in this textbook also directly or indirectly contribute to retaining excellent talent. Here, we will look more directly at how organizations can retain excellent talent.

1) Mentoring

Mentoring is a process in which senior employees (mentors) demonstrate their experiences and capabilities to help junior employees (mentees) overcome various difficulties in the organization and develop their potential competencies to the maximum. As discussed in Chapter 7, although mentoring may take place at an informal level, many companies are introducing it as a formal system. Mentoring plays a positive role, especially in helping new hires adjust to a new environment. For example, as shown in <Table 11-1>, Company C, a large Korean conglomerate, supports various activities through mentoring for new employees: sharing group values, department orientation, work guidance, and individual counseling and support for personal anniversary events, etc.

Table 11-1 Examples of Mentoring Activities for Large Korean Company C

Sharing Corporate values	Activities to help the members properly acquire and practice the culture of values pursued
Department orientation	Orientation so that the members can understand and adapt early to the department in which they are placed
Work guidance	Activities that guide the members to understand their future tasks and acquire relevant competencies
Personal consultation	Activities to support the overcoming of troubles and difficulties in organizational life
Anniversary event	Activities to encourage and care for activities experienced for the first time in organizational life

2) Exit Interview

An exit interview refers to an interview with an employee who has already decided to leave in order to identify the cause of the turnover.[5)] The reason for conducting an exit interview is to find out the internal cause of the turnover and prevent the turnover of excellent talent in the future rather than to change the mind of an employee who has decided to leave. As employees who have decided to leave the organization, they want to give their final advice to the organization for the sake of their attachment to the organization they worked for and for the rest of their colleagues. For this reason, in order for an exit interview to be successful, it is necessary to thoroughly analyze the causes within the organization pointed out by them and make visible improvement efforts. Otherwise, there will still be employees leaving the organization for similar reasons. And when they leave, they no longer frankly advise the company.

3) Orientation

Orientation for new employees or newly recruited experienced employees is also useful in preventing early turnover. Orientation is a socialization process that helps new employees become familiar with and provide information about the company's policies and practices. As a member of a new organization, you must be able to understand and match the expectations of the company. Orientation is important because each organization has different internal norms and disciplines that cannot be known from outside the organization. New employees who join the team without knowing this may make mistakes and may be reprimanded by internal members for this. A poorly entered first impression can persist during organizational life and can even lead to organizational maladjustment.

4) Realistic Job Preview

A realistic job preview is to provide practical information including negative information about the organization or job to applicants during the hiring process. It is an activity to match the expectations of the applicant and the company by providing accurate information on what the organization expects, the work environment, and what kind of job is actually performed in advance. In this way, it is possible to provide criteria for applicants to select a company on their own, and to prevent unexpected situations in advance due to different expectations even after joining the organization. In particular, by providing even negative information, it is possible to prevent employees who have already joined the company from leaving because of this. <Table 11-2> is an example of a realistic job preview used by Company C, a large Korean company.

3. Involuntary Turnover

Involuntary turnover, unlike voluntary turnover, is when the company decides who leave the company. This is called dismissal. It refers to the dismissal of a member at the discretion of the company despite the intention to continue the employment relationship with the company. Depending on who gave the cause, dismissal is divided into ordinary

Table 11-2 **Example of Realistic Job Preview of Company C (Sales Support Analyst Job of Food Sales Division)**

▶ Job contents

I am in charge of directly supporting the sales activities of the Sales Division. My work can be divided into three main categories. First, it is the task of supporting the strategy establishment of the sales division. We analyze and plan data so that we can establish a one-year management plan for the sales division and establish an effective sales strategy to achieve it. For example, after analyzing performance on a monthly, weekly, and daily basis, we provide feedback to the field and suggest countermeasures, and we manage the contribution margin by analyzing the organization's profit and loss on a monthly and quarterly basis. Second, we support salespeople to conduct sales activities smoothly. Specifically, it is in charge of event planning and management, promotional material management, customer credit/collateral confirmation, and deposit management, and supports on-site sales activities by establishing sales strategies that meet the unmet needs of consumers according to regional characteristics. Third, there are one-time tasks: e.g., participation in a TF promoted by the company in the mid to long term or support for the operation of a team meeting.

▶ Daily routine

I go to work at 8:30 am, establish a work plan for the day, and start my day by checking the progress of sales (by department and product) up to the previous day. In the morning, we check the progress of the sales indicators to check the areas where the sales performance is poor, identify the cause and give feedback, or establish a new strategy. In addition, business cooperation with related departments is checked through e-mail or phone calls, and sales support such as product supply and demand changes, event changes, and credit adjustment are carried out. In the afternoon, tasks ordered by the boss are mainly performed. Mid- to long-term promotion tasks such as meetings with related departments and sales organization structure improvement are performed, and data collection, processing, and analysis for the operation of the meeting body are performed.

▶ How to do work

When a new strategy is established and supported by discovering a weak point in sales performance, it is often discussed with department members or related departments, and mid- to long-term projects are carried out in cooperation with department members. Most of the other support work and tasks ordered by the boss are handled by myself. I make my own decisions on most matters if it do not materially affect sales strategy. On the other hand, due to the nature of the sales support business, there is little contact with external customers as all tasks are performed within the office. However, I communicate with in-house customers such as salespeople/executives, marketing-related departments, screening teams, and general affairs teams that are directly related to sales activities. On the other hand, due to the nature of the sales support business, all tasks are performed within the office, so there is little contact with external customers. The main things I communicate with are: from time to time with salespeople and executives; at least twice a day, with marketing-related departments, discussing related product strategies and new product information, market trends, and product supply and demand; 3 times a day or more with the event staff management department for event planning and execution and staff management.

▶ Qualifications and skills required for work

Analytical decision-making ability and planning ability to establish a strategy by integrating economic trends, market conditions, and competitor trends are required. In addition, enterprise-wide resource management system (ERP) operation ability and computational utilization ability are required to process and analyze data. Above all, speedy and accurate data provision is vital, so accuracy and timing are important. And since it deals with the sales and expenses of the sales organization as a whole, financial accounting knowledge to read profit and loss statements is required, and negotiation skills to persuade the other party in the communication process with other departments for sales support work are required.

▶ Job characteristics and opportunities and vision for self-development
Sales support work usually involves multiple tasks and tends to lack professionalism. Also, as a coordinator of sales and marketing, it is often difficult to reconcile the opinions of both sides, and there is a disadvantage in that the sense of the field is lowered because the sales are not conducted directly in the field. However, it has the advantage of being able to form a wide range of interpersonal relationships and experience various business areas, and learn the flow of sales as a whole. In addition, you can perform your duties as the subject of various pending issues, and you can utilize various factors for business management in the field. While performing various tasks, you can find a job that suits your aptitude, or you can acquire specialized knowledge through internal and external educational opportunities such as marketing-related fields or financial accounting.

dismissal, disciplinary dismissal,[6)] and managerial layoff.

Prior to the 1997 Asian financial crisis, Korean companies had a strong concept of a lifelong workplace in that if an employee joined the company as a new employee, he or she could stay at the same company until full retirement unless there was an accident or crime. Of course, they did not draw up an official contract, but they had a psychological contract that both the organization and the members tacitly agreed to. However, after the financial crisis, this psychological contract was broken, and neither the organization nor its members had a lifelong job in mind.

This does not mean that dismissal or layoffs are free. Involuntary turnover is painful for both the organization and its members, and it can be the most difficult experience of their lives, especially for employees. Labor market flexibility refers to the time it takes to find another job after leaving one company. In countries with high flexibility (mainly British and American countries), dismissal is relatively free. On the other hand, in Korea and Japan, the labor market is not very flexible and dismissal is not free. In Korea, the Labor Standards Act strictly restricts dismissal to protect workers.

3.1 Ordinary Dismissal and Disciplinary Dismissal

3.1.1 Definition

Disciplinary dismissal is when a cause attributable to the employee occurs to such an extent that the employment relationship cannot be continued. On the other hand, ordinary dismissal usually refers to cases where unavoidable reasons such as illness or injury occur. In both cases, the employment relationship is terminated by the employer's decision. Ordinary dismissal and disciplinary dismissal have in common in that they depend on the cause attributable to the employee, so there is no significant difference in legal effect. However, it has a different meaning in cases where the nature of the reasons for dismissal is different and the retirement compensation is paid differently in a collective agreement.[7)]

Article 23 [Restrictions on dismissal, etc.] Paragraph 1 of the Labor Standards Act stipulates that "an employer shall not dismiss, suspend, change jobs, reduce wages, or punish employees without justifiable reasons." The interpretation of this provision and the court's decision are controversial. On the one hand, there is an argument that it should be interpreted more strictly by emphasizing "cannot". On the other hand, there is an argument that the scope of "just cause" should be broadened to broadly admit cases where ability is lowered or performance does not meet expectations. An employee may apply for relief to the Labor Relations Commission if it is judged that disciplinary action such as dismissal is not justifiable (Labor Standards Act, Article 28). Requests for relief through the Labor Relations Commission for unfair dismissal are on the rise. The number of dismissals in Korea is increasing, and it is also proof that it is becoming an important issue in Korean society.

As explained in Chapter 2 previously, it is unclear in the current legal system whether dismissal for low performers is a disciplinary dismissal or an ordinary dismissal. In relation to the dismissal of low performers, performance management through GE's vitality curve has been benchmarked by Korean companies a lot. GE, where Jack Welch served as chairman, divided its employees into three groups, A, B, and C, through relative evaluation, and provided support to those who fell into grade A to maximize their potential to grow as core talents and managers. The employees in the B grade were motivated to move up to the A grade and continuously provided with a training program. Lastly, the bottom 10% of the C grade members are given the opportunity to perform other jobs, and if they still remain in the low grade despite providing several opportunities, they are subject to dismissal. However, as the CEO changed, GE's policies were relaxed, and recently, it is undergoing a change to abolish relative evaluation.

Figure 11-2 GE's Vitality Curve

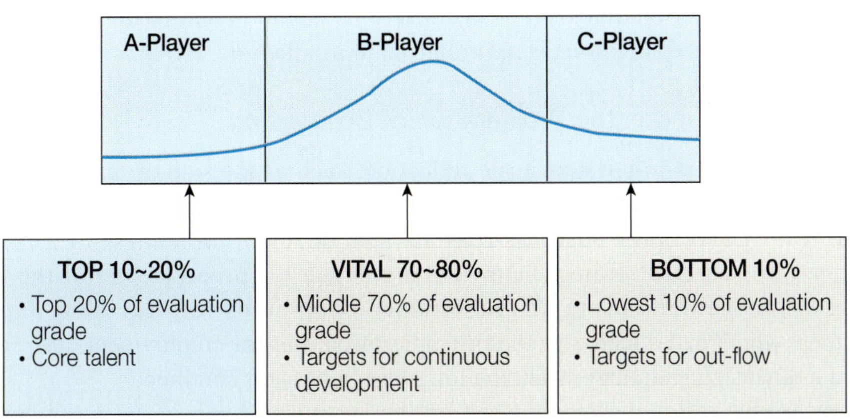

3.1.2 Fair Disciplinary Dismissal

Dismissal is the heaviest form of discipline. The law also sets strict requirements for the justification of dismissal. Administrative procedures for dismissal are generally stipulated in the company's employment rules, and the disciplinary process is supervised by the HR department. However, since it is the workplace where disciplinary action, including dismissal, actually occurs, managers must deal with it carefully at the forefront. The principles of guidance and discipline that managers should pay attention to will be discussed later.

Fairness is important in the process of disciplinary dismissal. Fairness must first be fair as a result. The party to the disciplinary dismissal must acknowledge that the cause of the disciplinary dismissal is serious enough to cause the dismissal. It should also be fair in comparison with other cases and people. When a similar situation arises, the company must make the same personnel decision no matter who it is. Second, it must be procedurally fair. The decision of dismissal must be made according to an objective procedure, and if the parties object to it, it must be accepted so that the decision can be made again with caution. The Labor Relations Commission and the courts value procedural fairness as much as consequential fairness, and many cases are dismissed due to procedural problems. According to the Labor Standards Act, an employer must give at least 30 days' notice to dismiss a worker (Article 26), and must notify the reason and time of dismissal in writing (Article 27).

3.2 Dismissal for Managerial Reasons

3.2.1 Definition

Dismissal for managerial reasons can be defined as "the layoff of some of the employees of the company under certain conditions based on business necessity and on the premise of maintaining and surviving the company."[8)] Article 24 [Restriction on Dismissal for managerial reasons] Paragraph 1 of the Labor Standards Act states, "In order for an employer to dismiss a worker for managerial reasons, there must be an urgent business need. In this case, the transfer, acquisition, or merger of business to prevent business deterioration shall be deemed to be due to urgent business necessity." A dismissal for managerial reasons is also referred to as a layoff.

3.2.2 Background of the Proliferation of Downsizing

Downsizing refers to physical scale reduction, such as the sale of buildings or land, reduction of business units, or closure of factories when a company is in business difficulties.[9)] Layoffs for business reasons also occur in the course of a company pursuing a downsizing strategy. Downsizing began to spread as one of the human resource management strategies in Western companies in the 1980s. Japanese companies, which had adhered to the principle of permanent employment, also recently adopted a downsizing strategy when the long-term recession continued.

There are the following reasons behind the spread of downsizing in the corporate field, and the business environment is not expected to change significantly in the future.

1) Securing Competitiveness by Reducing Labor Costs

When the supply of manpower exceeds the demand, the firm becomes burdened with costs. As labor costs account for a higher proportion of total costs, it is necessary to reduce labor costs in order to reduce costs. Since labor cost is proportional to the number of workers, the method of reducing the number of workers is considered in order to reduce the labor cost.

2) Introduction of New Technologies

When factories become automated by introducing artificial intelligence or robots to work previously done by humans, the demand for manpower decreases. The demand for manpower is expected to decrease due to the 4th industrial revolution, which is being discussed recently. The advent of new technologies, such as the 4th industrial revolution, creates new jobs, but also increases the number of jobs replaced by machines.

3) Corporate M&A

As uncertainty in the business environment increases and the speed of technological change accelerates, companies want to respond quickly to new demands. One of these strategies is to acquire companies that possess technology, design, or capabilities that it does not have, or merge between companies that can create synergy with each other. In case of mergers and acquisitions (M&A) of companies, duplication occurs as the job fields that were required for each company. A typical example is the staff department.

4) Relocation of the Factory

This also has to do with labor costs. If possible, companies will look for places where labor costs are low. Korea is no longer a country with low labor costs. Many companies have moved their factories to China or Southeast Asia, where labor costs are low. When a factory is relocated, the existing factory is closed or the operation is reduced, thus reducing the demand for manpower.

3.2.3 Why Downsizing Fails

The goal that companies want to achieve through downsizing is to overcome temporary crises and create new opportunities by changing the atmosphere. In practice, however, many studies have been published that downsizing is not as successful as expected.[10)] In particular, in the short term, when costs are reduced by downsizing, profitability seems to improve, but this is a temporary optical illusion, and in the long run, productivity is lowered and competitiveness deteriorates. There are several reasons why downsizing fails.

1) Loss of Required Manpower

Unlike disciplinary dismissals, layoffs for downsizing occur in large numbers. As a result, there are cases in which the necessary personnel for the company are also laid off. These people are often in charge of important tasks behind the scenes, so it is judged that they are not needed right now. And after they disappeared, the company realizes how much they needed them. This leads to re-employment, sometimes with higher compensation.

2) Loss of Organizational Network

The task of an organization is to achieve results through an invisible collaboration system while each person performs their assigned task. This invisible force that moves the organization is called social capital. The release of people through downsizing sometimes has the unexpected result of not only releasing the workforce, but disrupting the invisible organizational network with which they were associated.

3) Decreased Morale of Survivors

After downsizing, in order for the organization to exert new power again, the remaining members must be motivated to carry out their work. On the contrary, the remaining workers may experience serious psychological difficulties. The psychological pain suffered by the remaining workers may be compared with the pain experienced by those who survived major accidents such as building collapses or subway disasters. The psychological phenomenon they feel is called survivor's syndrome. Survivor's syndrome is a psychological phenomenon in three stages. First, it is a feeling of guilt, and co-workers feel sorry that only they survived after being fired. Second is an anger. Dismissal for managerial reasons is different from disciplinary dismissal, in which the company suffers from hardship despite the fact that there is no fault of the employee. This causes the remaining workers to feel resentful towards the management over the dismissal of their co-workers. Third is anxiety. It is said that people who survive a major accident even go out wrong because they fear not knowing when and how they will get in an accident. Likewise, the remaining workers suffer from the anxiety of not knowing when they, like their colleagues, will be fired. If the remaining members are experiencing this psychological state, it becomes very difficult to revitalize the company after downsizing. Therefore, in order for a company to overcome difficulties through downsizing and normalize again, a cautious approach to layoff is required.

3.2.4 Management of Dismissal for Managerial Reasons

Any dismissal is painful for both the organization and its members. However, in particular, layoff is dismissal for business reasons even though there is no fault on the part of the employee. In addition, while disciplinary dismissals apply only to one person or a small number of people, dismissals for managerial reasons are made in large numbers, so it is a problem not only for the person concerned but also for society.

For example, the issue of Ssangyong Motor's layoff in 2009 was partially resolved 10 years later. Ssangyong Motors announced a restructuring plan in 2009 due to a business loss, and the number of personnel reduction plans amounted to 2,700. Severe labor-management conflict was expressed, and many union members were arrested, leading to physical clashes. In the end, nearly 1,000 workers were subject to dismissal for managerial reasons. After that, efforts to avoid dismissal continued through labor-management agreement, but a significant number of workers were forcibly dismissed. Since then, several laid-off workers have committed suicide, and the aftermath is still a social issue.[11)]

Although dismissal for managerial reasons is a human resource management strategy that companies can choose, careful management is required in the implementation process. Even in the case of downsizing due to changes in the business environments discussed above, various other possible alternatives should be considered, and dismissal should be selected as the last resort. In addition, even if dismissal is chosen, fair procedures must be followed. [Figure 11-3] presents various alternatives that organizations can take when the need to reduce staff to reduce labor costs arises.[12)]

1) Alternatives to Dismissal

If the ultimate goal of dismissal for managerial reasons is to secure new business opportunities through cost reduction, there are various alternatives besides dismissal. Organizations are advised to consider these various alternatives first before making a dismissal decision.

① Employment Policy

An alternative to dismissal through employment policy is to allow attrition to occur without filling any more vacancies when retirement or turnover occurs. Also, in the case of a company that has increased its staff every year, a plan to freeze hiring may be considered to prevent further increase in staff. In addition, there is a plan to reduce employment by not extending the employment of non-regular workers such as dispatched workers, contract workers, or part-time workers, which companies often use as a way to cut costs through employment policies. In addition, there is a plan to carry out the work within the company without outsourcing any more work that has been

Figure 11-3 Alternatives to Dismissal for Managerial Reasons

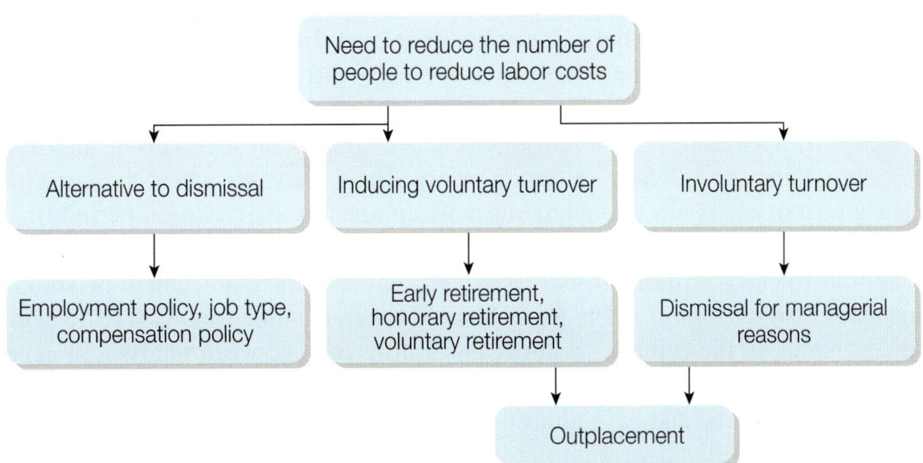

outsourced. Reducing overtime or weekend work, or even shortening working hours altogether, can be an alternative. In addition, temporary expansion of unpaid leave also helps to cut costs.

② Job Management

If a general job management type is for one person to perform one job, an alternative to dismissal through a change in job type is to use various job management. For example, when there is no work to the extent that all employees cannot work full-time due to a temporary shortage of demand, a job sharing system in which two people share the same job is also possible. This is a method frequently used by airlines. Rather than firing a crew member when the number of flights is reduced, two crew members perform a single task, so that compensation is reduced but employment is maintained. In addition, a method of shifting from a high-paying job to a low-paying job (job transfer) or a job relocation method of relocating from a factory or region with reduced demand to a factory or region with high demand is also possible.

③ Compensation Policy

If the alternatives through changes in employment policy and job management were to reduce costs indirectly, a method to directly reduce labor costs as an alternative to dismissal can also be considered. For example, it is possible to freeze the wage increase. When wages are frozen, nominal wages remain the same, but real wages, adjusted for inflation, decrease. Another option is to go one step further and cut wages altogether. There are cases in which many companies cut wages from executives during the Asian financial crisis. In addition to this, measures to reduce overtime pay or reduce welfare benefits are also used by suppressing overtime work, weekends and holidays in connection with employment policy. More fundamentally, a compensation strategy to prepare for uncertainty in the business environment by reducing the proportion of fixed pay and expanding variable pay can also be an alternative to dismissal.

2) Inducing Voluntary Turnover

Inducing voluntary turnover is a method to find applicants to change jobs in advance by using certain incentives before forcible dismissal. In countries where there is no mandatory retirement system, companies use early retirement. The early retirement system refers to a case in which workers are encouraged to retire earlier than their intended retirement date. Early retirement is encouraged through certain incentives, such as providing several years' worth of salary. There are cases where the opportunity for early retirement is always open, but most companies set a certain period of time and notify them. In the case of Korean companies with a mandatory retirement system, it is similar to early retirement, but uses the terms honorary retirement or voluntary retirement to induce turnover. The terms honorary retirement or voluntary retirement are used depending on the company without much difference between the two. In general, honorary retirement provides an opportunity to retire with honor to members who have worked for a long time and have almost reached the retirement age, as seen in the term. On the other hand, voluntary retirement is a measure to induce turnover of all employees regardless of age.

3) Fair Dismissal Management

Although the importance of fairness was emphasized in disciplinary dismissal, the same is true in dismissal for managerial reasons. Rather, fairness may be more important because it was caused by the management crisis without the fault of the workers.[13)]

① Notice of Dismissal

As in the case of disciplinary dismissal, when dismissing for managerial reasons, as stipulated in Article 26 [Notice of Dismissal] of the Labor Standards Act, notice of dismissal must be given 30 days in advance.

The United States and other countries with more freedom from dismissal than Korea also strictly restrict the notice of dismissal. For example, in the United States, 60 days notice is required. The reason for regulating the notice of dismissal in this way is to provide workers with minimum stability in life and a period to find another job, even if dismissal for managerial reasons is unavoidable.

② Criteria for Selection of Persons Subject to Dismissal

Unlike disciplinary dismissals, dismissals for managerial reasons occur in large numbers. For example, if you close a factory, you can fire all workers in that factory. However, in most cases, it is necessary to overcome the crisis and normalize management after downsizing, so the necessary manpower remains. Because of this, some workers are subject to dismissal and others are left behind. Therefore, in the process of dismissal for managerial reasons, it is very important how to set the standards for dismissal and retention. When Korean companies, which had little experience in the past, faced the economic crisis in 1997 and dismissed them for business reasons, they used unreasonable standards such as priority for workers with low economic difficulties and priority for female employees when a married couple works together.

The criteria for dismissal can be divided into seniority, individual performance, or individual competency. In the case of the year of employment as the basis, there is little room for controversy because the standards are clear. However, in Korea, which has developed a seniority-based wage system, unlike countries that send out employees with less experience first, it is necessary to send out workers with high seniority in order to reduce costs. In this case, the backlash from workers increases, and there is a side effect that excellent and experienced workers are included. On the other hand, in the case of individual performance or competency, it is possible to select workers who are expected to remain in the company, but there is a possibility that the judgment of who has high performance and who has high competency may not be objective. Which criteria to use should be carefully selected by managers, taking into account the effects and side effects.

③ Notification of Dismissal

Informing the person who is being dismissed that he or she has become a victim must be prompt and formal. In the process of dismissal for managerial reasons, many controversies and rumors arise. In-house rumors can not only harm the organizational atmosphere, but also hurt both those who are being fired and those who remain. All decisions on dismissal and selection of candidates must be strictly kept confidential, but once a decision has been made, it must be executed promptly. For those subject to dismissal, it is desirable to receive the details of decision-making directly from the HR manager or, if possible, from the immediate supervisor, rather than through informal channels such as 'they said that they have become a target' to fellow workers.

4) Outplacement

As downsizing became common, outplacement emerged as a way to minimize the side effects. Outplacement was first devised in 1969 by Exxon (then Standard Oil) in the United States to support older workers who were laid off due to downsizing. Since then, it has been adopted by most global companies to the extent that 75% of Fortune 500 companies regularly provide outplacement services. Outplacement is a worker support program to minimize employment problems caused by dismissal for managerial reasons and to quickly normalize the organization after downsizing. Although it is called a job search assistance service in Korea, outplacement includes various programs in addition to job change support. [Figure 11-4] shows an example of a program of a multinational consulting company that provides outplacement services. As shown in the figure, outplacement shows the characteristics of a comprehensive career management service. Assisting laid-off or prospective workers to look back on their careers and find new ones. Entrepreneurship is one of the important options in this process.

Outplacement may be performed internally within the company, or it may be entrusted to a consulting company that provides outplacement service as shown in [Figure 11-4]. In the case of Samsung Electronics, a career consulting center has been established within the company since 2001, providing a variety of outplacement services at all times. It has provided services to about 6,400 people so far, and it is reported that about 5,500 of them have succeeded in re-employment.[14] In addition, the Government Employees Pension Service (GEPS) provides services to public officials scheduled to retire, and the Ministry of Employment and Labor has established specialized agencies in each region to support re-employment of middle-aged and older adults.

Outplacement services can be divided into two support programs, such as psychological support and job search assistance.

① Psychological Support

Laid-off employees suffer from various psychological anxiety because the person suffers the pain of being dismissed despite no fault of his own. Professional psychological counselors provide support for psychological problems such as hostility, anger, or loss of self-confidence through counseling. Its main purpose is to help restore self-confidence and return to society. In this process, if it is deemed necessary, the family will receive psychological support together. Many studies say that the first pain experienced by laid-off workers is not the economic issue, but the feelings of regret for the family or the family's reaction.[15]

Figure 11-4 Example of Outplacement Service from a Multinational Consulting Company

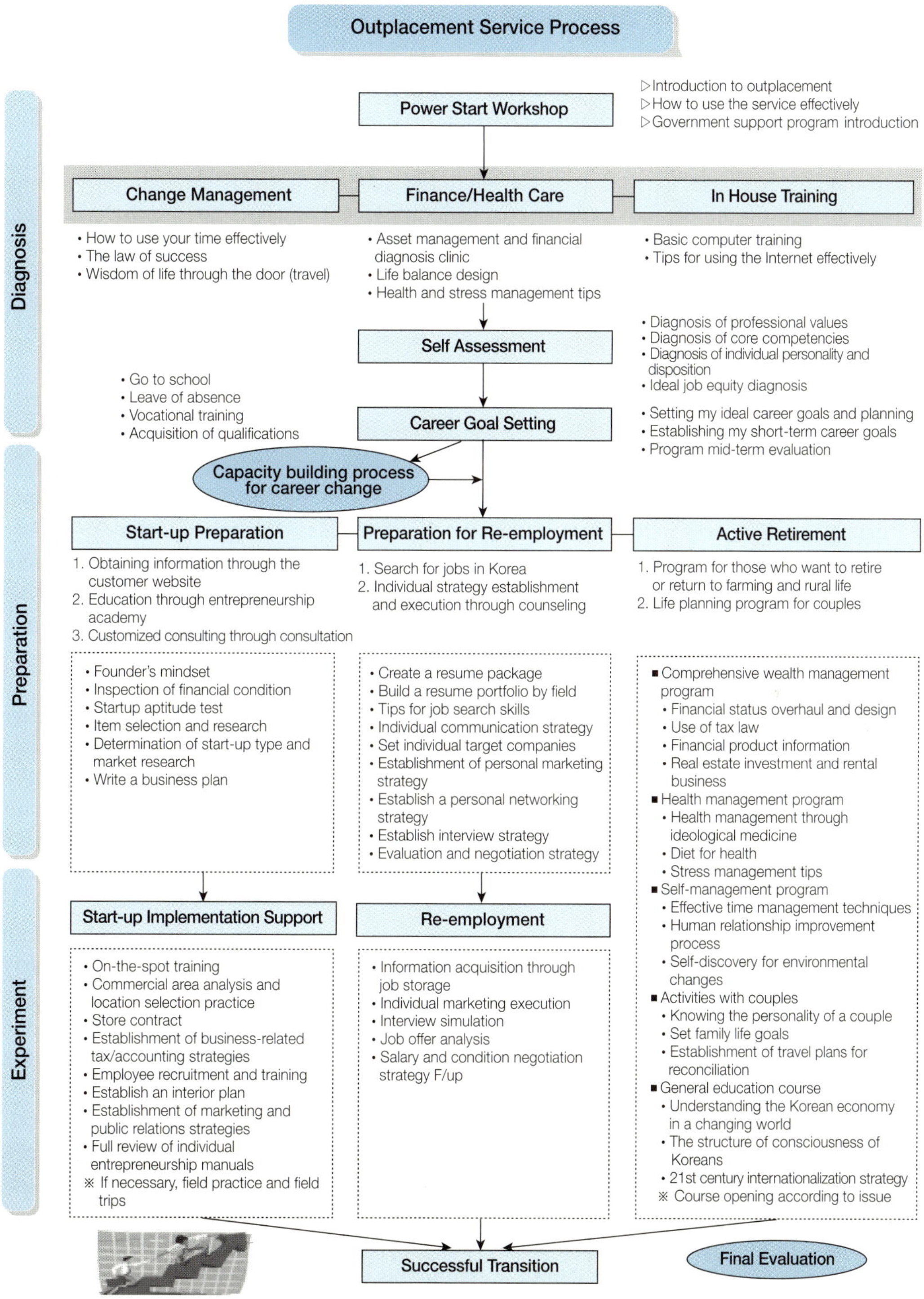

② Job Search Assistance

Outplacement service provides a variety of support needed for job change. First of all, it is common to provide an office space where laid-off workers can go to work. It supports work in the office, such as phone, computer, fax, and office supplies. Having a place to go to work provides great psychological comfort to laid-off workers. In addition, with the support of a professional consultant, they re-examine their aptitude, personality, and competency from the perspective of starting anew from the beginning. Rewrite their resume by emphasizing what they can highlight as their strengths. In addition, training is provided on the details necessary for re-employment, such as how to interview and negotiate salary. In some cases, companies directly support re-employment. For example, companies such as GE and GM hold job fairs and advertise them through the media or provide services that connect laid-off workers with companies in the same industry or subcontractors.

4. Discipline

Discipline is a tool for leaders to communicate with members in the organizational management process to reinforce company policies or rules. Discipline includes not only the negative meaning of punishment for wrongdoing of members, but also the meaning of edification for improvement of behavior.

4.1 Management Rights

As workers have labor rights, managers have management rights. Labor rights refer to rights that are not infringed upon by others, including managers, in labor relations.

Labor rights include the basic rights guaranteed in the Constitution and the three labor rights, as well as rights protected by private contracts such as employment contracts, collective agreements, and rules of employment. For example, Article 33 of the Constitution stipulates that "workers have the right to autonomously organize, bargain collectively, and act collectively in order to improve working conditions."

On the other hand, the right to management is a right widely recognized in western countries, corresponding to the right to work[16)], but in Korea, it has not been clearly defined.[17)]

In the case of the United States, through precedents, etc., management rights related to employment are referred to as the "employment at will", and just as workers have the right to freely choose a company, managers also have the right to freely choose workers. Each country has different regulations and permissible scopes for management rights. However, in most countries, management right is generally recognized as a manager's right that can be exercised within the scope stipulated by law in order to conduct business and acquire profits from it. This includes human resource management to recruit, promote, place, evaluate, and reward employees. It can be said that the right to discipline employees with problems covered in this chapter is also included.

4.2 Problematic Employees

It can be said that managers have a right and a duty to manage problematic employees in an organization. Of course, which cases should be considered as problematic employees or which processes and procedures to be managed must be dealt with in detail from the viewpoint of fairness and legality. In most enterprises, if there is a labor union, it is stipulated in the collective agreement, and if not, it is stipulated in the employment rules. <Table 11-3> is an excerpt of some cases listed as grounds for disciplinary action in the employment rules of a large Korean company.

As the table shows, there are members within an organization who have problematic behaviors for a wide variety of reasons. The content of the disciplinary action may vary depending on the severity, but if such problems occur frequently, they may negatively affect not only the worker himself or herself but also those around him or her. If problematic members are left without discipline, the following bigger problems arise.

① It negatively affects the entire organization.

Problematic employees make the atmosphere of the whole organization bad. This negatively affects not only one's own performance but also the performance of other members, thereby lowering the overall performance of the organization.

② It causes a huge loss to the company.

If small problems are left unattended, these problems can accumulate and turn into bigger problems. This, in the end, can inflict significant losses directly on the organization beyond the negative impact of reduced performance.

③ The individual problematic employee is also unhappy.

It is rare for an employee who causes a problem to be a problematic employee in the first place. Active guidance from organization and managers from the beginning of a problem can prevent it from getting worse. Otherwise, if left unattended, it will eventually reach a state where it cannot be improved any more, which is unfortunate not only for the organization but also for the individual.

4.3 Purpose and Effect of Discipline

The purpose of disciplinary action is to improve the behavior of members. Organizations spend a lot of time and effort to find the best talent. Sometimes, they enter the company through competition of hundreds of jobs. However, not all members match the expectations of the organization. As time passes, some members lose their original motivation when joining the company, fail to achieve the expected results of the company, or do things they should not do. In this case, it is not desirable to simply fire them, and also it is not easy to fire them under Korea's labor law. If the company fires them, as we saw earlier, a lot of money is wasted for hiring, educating, and training them, and the productivity problem during the absence period and the cost of hiring replacement workers must also be added. Therefore, what is most desirable for the organization and for the members is to convert their behavior into the behavior expected by the company, and discipline is a tool for that purpose.

Table 11-3 **Some of the Reasons for Disciplinary Action Presented in the Employment Rules of a Large Korean Company**

- If you accept the employment of another company without the company's permission
- If the reason for disqualification is discovered after joining the company
- If it is found that the employment has been made by cheating on career or other important matters or using sorcery
- A person who has been sentenced to prison by criminal prosecution
- A person who has caused customer dissatisfaction or damaged the company's reputation by violating work attire due to unkind or inappropriate customer service
- A person who intentionally divulges or tries to divulge the secrets of the company and business partners
- A person who engages in other business that is contrary to the interests of the company
- A person who disobeys or delays implementation of the company's personnel order
- A person who does not comply with the instructions and orders of the company and superiors in the course of business, or who unreasonably refuses or rebels
- A person who behaves in a way that interferes with or interferes with the operation of the company
- A person who intentionally damages or destroys the notices posted by the company, or affixes handouts without permission
- A person who uses the company's facilities other than its intended purpose, such as graffiti on the company's walls or walls
- A person who defrauded or misappropriated the company's money or other similar acts
- A person who manufactures or repairs personal items in-house or has others do it
- A person who intentionally or negligently commits a serious business mistake
- A person who intentionally attempts to lower work efficiency or interfere with work
- Persons who are recognized as having remarkably poor performance or performance and no prospect of improvement or improvement
- A person who manipulates sales performance, such as transferring or taking over sales performance
- A person who gambles inside the company or disturbs public morals by other acts
- Those who are recognized as lacking enthusiasm for work due to frequent tardy, early leave, and absenteeism
- Those who have been absent from work for more than 5 days per month and 15 days per year without justifiable reasons
- A person who eats or prepares food during working hours or prepares for closing before closing time
- A person who neglects to work while sleeping or lying down during working hours
- A person who works while under the influence of alcohol or who encourages or abetted drinking or drinking during working hours
- A person who reports false or delayed work hours
- Persons with markedly poor conduct on a daily basis

The effects of discipline are as follows.[18]

① It has a preventive effect.

By clarifying the principles of discipline in the organization and sharing them with members, members recognize which behaviors are desirable and which behaviors are not. In addition, the effect of self-regulation arises by observing surrounding colleagues being punished through discipline.

② There is an effect of improving behavior.

Leaders can improve the behavior of members by using discipline as tools of appropriate organizational management. When a leader observes that members engage in undesirable behavior, he or she can utilize human resource management such as performance management and competency development in parallel with disciplinary action, as we saw earlier.

③ There is an effect of deterring behavior through punishment.

If the leader does not improve the member's behavior despite making various efforts, the behavior can be suppressed through punishment.

4.4 Basic Principles of Discipline

There are basic principles that an organizational leader must follow with discipline. This is called the red hot stove rule, and it comes from the meaning that the disciplinary principle that a leader must follow is just like informing young children that a hot stove is dangerous.[19)] The principles of discipline based on the hot stove rule are as follows.

① (Immediate) It must be done immediately when a problem occurs.

Just as touching a hot stove immediately burns you, if you break the rules, you should be disciplined immediately. Otherwise, as time passes, they either don't know what wrong they have done or try to rationalize their own mistakes.

② (With warning) If the problem is repeated, it should be done with a warning as to what consequences will follow.

Just like telling a child that touching a hot stove will cause burns, you need to warn them in advance. When a rule is violated, it must be clearly notified in advance of what punishment will follow. Otherwise, employees will be dissatisfied with the company's rules, like a child trying to blame the stove rather than his or her own fault.

③ (Consistent) When a similar problem occurs, it should always be done consistently.

Just as touching a hot stove always causes burns, violating pre-established rules always requires discipline. When applying rules, if sometimes nothing happens and sometimes severe punishment follows, the leader loses the trust of his members.

④ (Impersonal) Anyone who causes problems will be guided without exception.

Just as anyone who touches a hot stove will get burns without exception, anyone who violates the rules must be disciplined without exception. If the application of the rule differs from person to person, the rule cannot be a hot stove. Regardless of the relationship with the leader or the position or rank within the organization, anyone who violates the established rules should be fairly and appropriately disciplined without exception.

4.5 Disciplinary Procedure

There are two approaches to the disciplinary process.[20] There is a progressive discipline which is a traditional approach, and a positive discipline, which emphasizes the improvement of members' behavior rather than punishment. As shown in <Table 11-4>, there is no difference in going through the 4 steps, but the message to be delivered to the employee is different at each step.

In the progressive approach, it proceeds as a process in which the manager handles the necessary matters at each step with discipline in mind. In the first verbal warning stage, the manager verbally warns the relevant member what the consequences will be if the problem persists. In the second document warning stage, if the problem is not improved despite verbal warning, a warning is given through official documents. In the 3rd waiting order step, to provide the problem employee with a last chance within the organization, he/she has to withdraw from his/her current job and the company issues a stand-by order. From this point on, measures shall be taken so that the relevant member does not affect the company's confidentiality or important assets. In the fourth stage of disciplinary dismissal, if it is determined that improvement is no longer possible at the company despite providing the last opportunity, the final notice of dismissal is given.

The difference between the positive approach and the progressive approach is that in the first verbal warning and the second written warning stage, rather than emphasizing discipline, the employee clearly recognizes which behavior is the problem so that he or she can awaken himself or herself. The employee is informed of the company's policy in detail and identified which actions are in violation of the company's policy. In the third stage, in a progressive approach, the company unilaterally issues a standby order, but in a positive approach, it supports workers to make their own decisions. For example, the company can give him or her a few days of free time, and in the meantime, suggest things he or she can do to improve behavior, or a request he or she would like the company to support. He/she can write a new employment contract or switch to a part-time job. In the end, if a change in behavior does not follow in spite of providing such an opportunity, it will ultimately go through the process of dismissal.

The final decision of dismissal must follow the procedures described in the employment rules or collective agreement. Most companies hold HR committees and provide opportunities to those involved. If the dismissal decision is made without these procedures, the dismissal may be invalidated due to the problem of procedural fairness, regardless of the seriousness of the problem.

Table 11-4 Approaches to Discipline

	PROGRESSIVE APPROACH	POSITIVE APPROACH
Step 1	1st verbal warning	1st oral confirmation
Step 2	2nd document warning	Secondary document confirmation
Step 3	3rd standby order	Provision of third-order decision-making opportunities
Final step	4th disciplinary dismissal	4th disciplinary dismissal

4.6 The Role of the Manager

Unit managers who are responsible for organizational management play an important role in the discipline process. The final dismissal decision is made at the company level, but the role of the manager is very important in terms of reasons for dismissal and procedural fairness. Managers should pay attention to and carefully observe the work performance of members on a regular basis. Since the most desirable thing is to prevent the occurrence of problematic employees, in order to prevent small problems from becoming bigger, active intervention in even the smallest problems is required from the beginning. In addition, managers should always keep in mind that there may be problematic employees in any organization, even to varying degrees. In addition, as mentioned in Chapter 6, performance management, it is necessary to examine the circumstances in which such a problem occurred before the individual problem. It should be recognized that managing problematic employees is both the responsibility and the right of the leader, who is the manager.

Ending Case

LG CNS Management of Low Performers[21)]

In all organizations, there are high performers who create and lead performance, while there are also low performers who do not meet expectations. In order to improve organizational performance, securing and nurturing key talent is important, but the competencies of all members, including low performers, must be increased together. The lack of competencies of low performers does not end in itself and negatively affects the work of other members. There are internal costs such as demoralization of the organization, reduced productivity, and impaired teamwork. Moreover, if these low performers are managers of the organization, the harm becomes more serious. There is a risk of coaching team members in the wrong direction, and the department continues to underperform, eventually degrading all members of the team to low performers.

In general, low performers are 'members whose personal achievements are lower than the required level and also have insufficient potential for future growth', which usually means those who belong to the bottom 10% of the organization. In the case of LG CNS, based on the three-year evaluation results, those whose performance and competency results are in the bottom 1% are classified as low performers. After going through several stages of verification process, they are finally reclassified into the number of expelled personnel and the number of fostering personnel for management.

There are two approaches to managing lowperformers: an exit approach and a competency development approach. The exit is to dismiss a certain percentage of low performers (for example, the bottom 10%) every year. One example is GE's vitality curve to regularly fire 10% of its workforce every year. On the other hand, the competency development approach provides various opportunities for possible members to develop their potential and supports them to overcome the sluggish performance caused by low performers or job suitability due to environmental influences. As shown in <Table 1>, the exit approach includes dismissal and job change support, and the competency development approach includes career improvement and changes in employment conditions. Among them, LG CNS is using the job search support as the exit approach and career improvement method as the competency development approach for a management for low performers.

At LG CNS, most of the low performers do not achieve proper results due to the different visions of individuals and organizations, but consider them to be human resources that are never inferior to their competitiveness in the labor market. Although their performance at LG CNS is low, there is sufficient potential to create new performances if the conditions and opportunities that are suitable for the individual are giv-

<Table 1> How LG CNS Manages Underperformers

DIVISION		PURPOSE	METHOD	CHARACTERISTIC
Exit approach	Fire	Eliminate inefficiencies immediately	Layoffs Recommended resignation	• Effective in situations where urgency is needed • Decreased sense of belonging to remaining members
	Job change support	Eliminate inefficiencies in the long run	Outplacement	• Linkage with policy support from the Ministry of Employment and Labor • Minimize the impact of survivors and retirees
Competency development approach	Career improvement	Providing opportunities for underperforming competency development	Career improvement program	• Long-term development plan required • Costs due to the introduction of the development program
	Changes in employment conditions	Motivation or voluntary retirement	Change of identity (contract worker)	• Giving new positions to underperformers • Voluntary development effort required

en appropriately. Under this philosophy, the company provides job change support to low performers or the outplacement service necessary for starting a business. Through a specialized outplacement company, the job change support service provides various job search assistance activities such as management of change to a new job, emotional treatment, and career goal setting, as well as various services such as start-up, financial technology, and liberal arts lectures. And for mid-level professionals (manpower at the manager level or higher) who change to subcontractors, LG CNS supports part of the labor cost to subcontractors to manage ex-employees and enhance the competencies of subcontractors.

The competency development approach begins by declaring that the entire organization will make an effort to nurture the relevant members for one year by having all line managers, from the field department heads, business department heads, and business division heads, prepare, review, and approve the development plan together. Thereafter, the department head shall record the evaluation results semiannually to see if the relevant member is diligently devoted to nurturing activities such as job development, so that the person concerned is not re-selected as a low performer in the future. In addition, the head of the department determines whether the member is suitable for the current job, and if not, he or she may change the job or request a transfer assignment. In this case, if necessary, the HR department provides consulting or inter-organizational mediation.

LG CNS is implementing the following five core principles for effective lowperformer management. First, it is the clarity of the reasons for the management of the low performers. It is to make the field clearly aware of the reasons for managing low performers. Explain that the management of lowperformers is not aimed at expulsion, but is ultimately a way to build a performance-oriented culture. Its main purpose is to provide an opportunity for members who cannot fully demonstrate their abilities to take a leap forward by giving them another chance.

Second, it is the continuity of management practices of low performers. In order for low performer management to succeed systematically, continuous execution is the key. If an organization implements the system inconsistently, it will cause distrust among its members. LG CNS continuously and consistently induces the expulsion of low performers to create a virtuous cycle of manpower and healthy tension within the organization, and to establish a performance-oriented corporate culture.

Third, it is the establishment of an objective and fair evaluation system and culture. The biggest characteristic of a company that does not properly manage low performers is that members have low trust in the fairness of evaluation. The reasons for this include the unclear evaluation criteria and the sharing-type evaluation operation. To solve this problem, LG CNS is working hard to prepare an objective evaluation system, provide appropriate feedback, enhance the evaluation capacity of the evaluator, and build trust between the evaluator and the member. On the other hand, lowperformer management measures can help establish a fair evaluation system. The head of the field department should not give an unfair evaluation to a specific employee even if he is afraid of lowperformer management. An objective and fair evaluation system and a management plan for low performers are necessary and sufficient conditions for each other.

Fourth, it is a field-oriented, lowperformer management principle. Performance management, including low performers, does not focus on distinguishing between good and bad employees, but rather aims to help all members improve their performance. To this end, LG CNS is wary of rigid evaluation and provides an opportunity to select a job that suits aptitude and competency evaluation for performance improvement. The role of the department head in the field is important in this process. All authority from the confirmation of low performers to change management and expulsion of the subject is delegated to the field department head. The HR department guides and coaches the field department head to perform his or her role, and plays a mediating role in communication with other departments that the field department head may find difficult.

Fifth, it is the principle of appropriate support and consideration. LG CNS has prepared a 'job change support program' that includes support for re-employment and stress management for the entire process of low performers until they find another job that suits their abilities and aptitudes. The company is doing its best to provide support and human consideration.

Discussion Question

1. What are the characteristics of LG CNS's management plan of low performers?
2. Does the objectivity and fairness of evaluation arise when selecting low performers like LG CNS?
3. Why do Korean companies need to manage low performers, and what are the necessary conditions for successful implementation of this HR strategy?

CHAPTER
12

Globalization and Human Resource Management

1. Stages of Globalization and Management
2. Characteristics of International Human Resources Management
3. Types of International Human Resource Management
4. Culture and International Human Resources Management
5. Management of Expatriates
6. Challenges for Korean Companies

Learning Objectives

1. Understand the characteristics of international human resource management compared to domestic human resource management.
2. Understand the types of four strategies for international human resource management.
3. Understand the impact of culture on international human resource management.
4. Can understand and utilize management of expatriates in selection and compensation.
5. Figure out the challenges Korean companies are facing and find a way to coping with.

Introductory Case

Company A is a representative electronics company in Korea. The company actively promoted local advancement in Eastern Europe by establishing a production factory to secure market opportunities after the communist system collapsed and Eastern Europe countries were incorporated into the EU. In the early days, the headquarters operated the local factory by sending expatriates to most major positions, including the head of the factory. However, as it became difficult for local workers to find a career vision, problems began to arise, such as lowering morale and increasing turnover of middle-managers.

As this problem also occurred in local subsidiaries in other countries, the company's management began to recognize the need for a localization. And various personnel policies for localization were implemented. As a result, the morale of the locals increased, but this time, a new problem emerged like a lack of prompt communication with the head office and the inability to properly implement the strategy in connection with the head office. This is because, in the case of local workers, it is common to build their own careers while moving companies, so personal career goals are prioritized rather than headquarters strategies, and they prefer short-term performance to the long-term one. Moreover, as the personal corruption of the head of a local operation has recently surfaced, the localization strategy is about to be abandoned. But it is also clear that going back to the old way is not the solution to the problem. What is the best alternative in this situation?

Discussion Questions

1. What can be the problems that arise when managing a local corporation under the strong direction of the head office?
2. What are the eventual problems with operating a local corporation according to the localization strategy?
3. What could be the ways to reconcile global integration with autonomous local management?

Globalization has already become a reality and a daily routine for us. This is because the products and services of foreign multinational companies such as McDonald's, iPhone, and Instagram are a part of our lives. In addition, although they still use Korean names, such as Renault Samsung and SC First Bank, there are a number of companies whose management is in the hands of foreign capital. In particular, during the economic crisis in 1998, management of many Korean companies were transferred to multinational corporations. Even if we do not go out into the world, the world has already entered us deeply. As a result, the number of people employed by multinational companies has increased significantly compared to the past, and their management systems and human resources management methods are no longer unfamiliar. In particular, in relation to the wage system, job-based pay is being actively used mainly by foreign companies.

It is, however, the companies that directly establish and operate corporations abroad that are acutely feeling the problem of human resource management due to globalization. It is difficult to apply the human resource management system they have in the home country to the local corporations, and it is not easy to secure and utilize human resources in the situation where the culture, legal system, labor market are significantly different as well as the geographical distance. It is a widely known that Lincoln Electric of the United States, which was very proud of its piece-rate and incentive system, expected them to work abroad as well as in USA, but it turned out to be a major failure in the end.[1)] Meanwhile, it is not always a good idea to follow the local HR management practices, because multinational companies may lose their differentiated strengths in people management.

In this chapter, we look at alternatives to the human resource-related issues that Korean companies face as they enter overseas markets. To this end, we will first explain the stages of globalization that companies go through as they grow, then examine the differences between domestic and international human resource management. We will also examine generic types of international human resource management. Next, we will cover the culture, which has an important influence on the organization and management of people abroad. In addition, various issues about the management of expatriates who play a key role in the operation and management of overseas subsidiaries will be reviewed. Lastly, the tasks that Korean companies must solve for successful globalization will be presented.

1. Stages of Globalization and Management

Samsung, Hyundai, LG, and SK Group, the four largest corporate groups in Korea, are now very active in global markets and have grown into global companies that satisfy customers all around the world. Less well-known Korean companies such as CJ, POSCO, Naver, Kakao, Lotte, Hanwha, Doosan, and Daelim are also doing a brisk global business. After having established a firm position in the domestic market, they gradually expanded their scope of activities abroad and become a global company. Recently, there are cases where, like game companies and bio ventures, some companies

Figure 12-1 **Five Stages of Globalization**

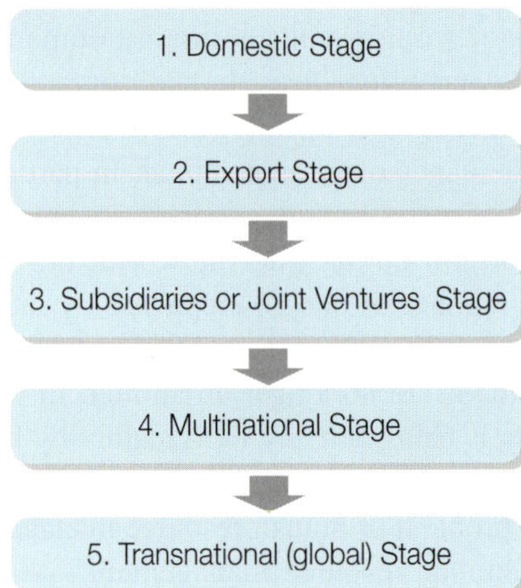

start their business targeting the global market from the beginning. But most companies start with a domestic business at first and go through the following five steps to develop into a truly global company.[2)] And as management expands beyond the domestic market to global business, the roles and activities of human resource management to support this also evolve and change according to each stage.[3)]

1.1 Domestic Stage

In the domestic business stage, all business is carried out in one country. The types of products are also simple in most cases. For example, when Hyundai Motor Company (HMC) first started manufacturing automobiles in 1967, products were offered only to customers in Korea. Parts and technology were imported from overseas, and sales of products were limited to Korea. Most global companies are those that started out as domestic businesses and grew up after that. In this stage, human resource management activities such as recruitment, evaluation, compensation, and training are also limited to domestic area. Therefore, international human resource management activities are not required at this stage.

1.2 Export Stage

Companies with stable domestic business try to find more opportunities and explore overseas markets. The first thing they do is to export products or services abroad. Some companies skip the domestic business stage and start offering products and services to the foreign countries fom the beginning. HMC first exported six Ponys to Ecuador in 1976. In 2004, 28 years later, its cumulative exports exceeded 10 million units of cars. An important issue of human resource management in the export business stage is to secure manpower with professional competency to be in charge of overseas export, and for this purpose, a department dedicated to export is often created within the company.

1.3 Subsidiaries or Joint Ventures Stage

If the export business is successfully developed and export volume increases while the needs of overseas customers are diversified, it will be difficult to satisfy the needs of foreign customers just by exporting from Korea. This is because it is difficult to accurately understand the value expected by customers and to respond quickly to them by simply supplying a product with a specification demanded by a buyer. To solve this problem, companies establish overseas branches or make joint ventures with local companies. As automobile exports increased, HMC set up local sales subsidiaries in Canada and USA in the late 1980s, and in the 1990s built automobile manufacturing plants in Turkey and India. In this stage, management of expatriates who lead local branches or joint ventures while carring out the decisions of the head office become of strategic importance, and human resource management activities that can foster, select, and manage them are strongly required. At the same time, it is also an important task for human resource management to effectively manage locals hired in the host country.

1.4 Multinational Stage

Entering the multinational stage, the scope of the company's activities is extended all over the world. As the size of the company grows and the market expands to the global market, the company can not be able to sufficiently meet global demand with a limited number of foreign operations. Therefore, the company creates and operates necessary local organizations for each region or country around the world. Research institutes or design centers may be established in each region, and sales or production corporations can be set up in each country. HMC has 6 technology research centers and design centers in various regions, and operates 20 sales subsidiaries and 7 production plants across various countries. Human resource management becomes more complex at the multinational level. This is because companies have to manage a large number of employees with diverse culture in different locations across the globe. Although the role of expatriates remains important, local manpower management becomes equally important. The trasnfer of people occurs not only between local operations and headquarters, but also among local organizations, making it necessary, for example, for US personnel to work in Europe or for Chinese personnel to work in Australia. In the head office also people with various nationalities work together in the same teams. In order to effectively manage such complexity and diversity, it becomes very important to establish a strategy that can unite organizations around the world and share core values, while utilizing human resources strategy suitable for the local labor market.

1.5 Transnational Stage

The final stage is transnational corporations. At this stage, the nationality of the head office becomes less important, and the identity of the company on the global stage becomes more important. In terms of business, it is the stage where management activities transcends national boundaries. The head office is in charge of making important strategic decisions while maintaining a small size, and the vision or philosophy to maintain the corporate identity is shared by the entire company, but locally appropriate and autonomous decision-making is emphasized for each business unit or regional group. The balance between the global integration strategy and the local response strategy becomes a big strategic issue, and this is well represented by the expression Glocalization. In this stage, talents with diverse nationalities are more actively utilized compared to multinational companies, and the talents who 'think globally and act locally' is emphasized. Most of the global companies such as Netflix, Google, SAP, Nestlé, and IBM are such transnational corporations. Large Korean companies like Samsung Electronics, LG Electronics, and Hyundai Motor Company are currently in the stage of transitioning from multinational companies to transnational companies.

2. Characteristics of International Human Resource Management

Human resource management of international companies is not fundamentally different from human resource management of domestic companies in that it is an activity that enhances competitiveness of companies through efficient selection and development of human resources and compensation. However, the dimension of a nation is added because business activities are carried out across national borders. In other words, the human resource management of an internationalized company must consider the human resource management environment and system specific to the head office and the local country at the same time. Here again, the dimension of diversifying the composition of human resources within an organization is added. For example, in the case of a local subsidiary in Singapore, expatriates dispatched from Korea, local Singaporean and Malaysian or other nationality coexist and work together. In the end, human resource management of international companies consists of three dimensions: the function of human resource management, the country and the composition of employees.[4)] As a result, the following peculiarities of international human resource management are generated, which are different from domestic human resource management.[5)]

First, human resource management of international companies performs much more diverse functions than that of domestic companies. For example, exchange rate fluctuations, tax issues, education and training for overseas expatriation, and relationships with local government agencies are special activities of international human resource management that are not covered by domestic human resource management.

Second, the high risk of decision-making is also an important feature of international human resource management. Ill managed human resource management can cause labor-management conflicts resulting in economic loss as well as fatal damage to the corporate image. In particular, labor-management disputes combined with national emotions tend

Figure 12-2 **Three Dimension Model of International HRM**

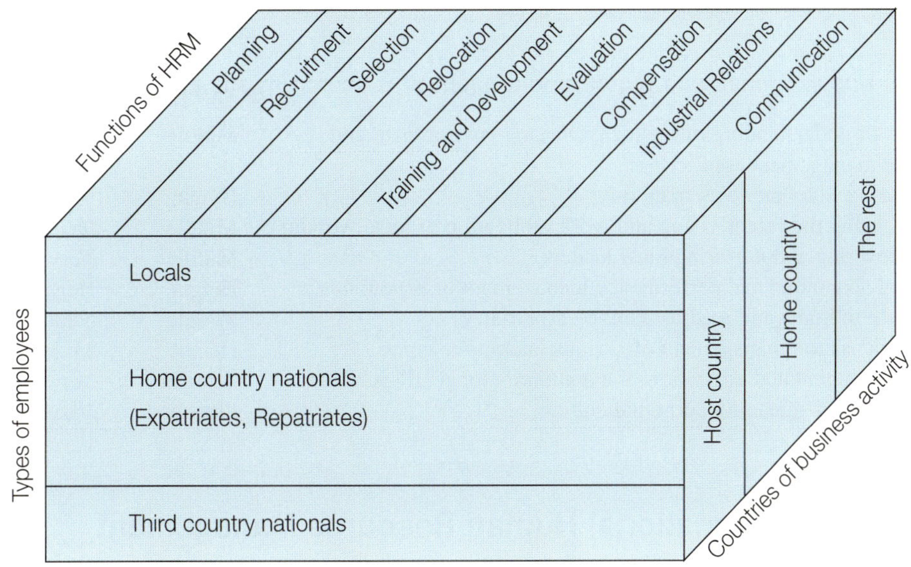

to be very intense and prolonged. If an expatriate manager fails to perform his duties in the host country, it will have a significant adverse effect on the performance of the local organization as well as the individual concerned.

Third, international human resource management is affected by variables that companies cannot control compared to domestic human resource management. Local country's policies, labor-management relations, tax system, safety management regulations, etc. are exogenous variables that originate from the local environment and have a decisive influence on overseas production and business activities. Nevertheless, the influence of companies on them is extremely limited, and difficulties in international human resource management arise from that fact.

Due to these characteristics, international human resource management requires a very broad perspective compared to domestic human resource management. Therefore, the person in charge must not only be fully familiar with the culture, tradition, practices and law of the host country, but also have knowledge of the international environment such as international political situation and trade trends. And he needs to be sensitive to change in the global environment. Otherwise, it will be impossible to design and operate a human resources management system suitable for a complex overseas environment. Specifically, international companies face various human resource management tasks and issues that are not covered by domestic human resource management. The following <Table 12-1> summarizes the major issues of human resource management that occur in international companies, unlike domestic companies.

Table 12-1 Major Issues in International Human Resource Management

ISSUES IN INTERNATIONAL HUMAN RESOURCE MANAGEMENT	FREQUENCY OF OCCURRENCE	IMPOR-TANCE
• Lack of understanding of the local working environment and labor-management conflict	Middle	Height
• Securing excellent local manpower	Height	Middle
• Enhancing the career vision and work motivation of local workers	Middle	Height
• Discovering and nurturing local leaders	Middle	Very high
• Local adaptation and performance management of expatriates	Height	Height
• Return to home and readjustment of expatriates	Middle	Middle
• Compensation management of various manpower types	Height	Middle
• Establishment and utilization of a common global HR platform	Lowness	Very high
• Sharing and spreading corporate culture	Lowness	Very high

3. Types of International Human Resource Management

International companies are adopting various international HR management strategies according to their internationalization experience, business goals and competitive strategies. Human resource management that an internationalized company pursues can be largely divided into home country centered, host country centered, region centered, and global centered, and its characteristics are as following <Table 12-2>.[6)]

• Ethnocentric Approach

The ethnocentric approach prefers home country nationals over locals, dispatches expatriates to run overseas branches, and gives them preferential treatment over locals in role, responsibility and compensation. International companies that have adopted the ethnocentric strategy usually apply the personnel management practices and strategies developed in their home countries to overseas branches as well, and the head office tends to have strong control over the overseas branches. If the country where the headquarters is located is a developed country and the local country is an underdeveloped country, it is likely to take this approach. And companies lacking experience in international business also tend to adopt it.

• Polycentric Approach

The polycentric approach is basically a strategy based on the assumption that each country has its own culture and customs, and it is difficult for foreigners to understand them. Therefore, international companies that have adopted a polycentric strategy entrust the operation of foreign subsidiaries to locals and try to minimize the intervention of the headquarters unless there is a major problem in its operation. In this approach subsidiaries basically maintain relatively an independent relationship with the head office. And in terms of personnel management, rather than imitating or transplanting the

Table 12-2 **Types of International Human Resource Management**

	ETHNOCENTRIC	POLYCENTRIC	REGIOCENTRIC	GEOCENTRIC
Organizational Structure	Complex organizational structure of the headquarters and simple one in local operation	Independent and different structure from country to country	Highly correlated among operations in the same region	High complexity and correlation on the global basis
Authority of Decision	Concentrated on home headquarters	Relatively low authority and intervention from headquarters	A lot of authority to regional headquarters	Worldwide cooperation between headquarters and foreign operations
Evaluation and Control	Apply criteria and method of headquarters to local operations	Depends on the specific situations of the local country	Appropriate criteria and method according to the regions	Criteria and method reflecting global needs and local situations
Compen-sation	Favorable treatment for the home country nationals	Highly diverse according to the local countries	Compensation based on the contribution to the regional objectives	Compensation based on the performance of local operation and its contribution to the global objective
Communi-cation	Many direction and advice from the headquarters to local operations	Low degree of information sharing between headquarters and local operations	Close communication among local operations within the region	Interactive and close communication on the global basis
Sense of Belonging	Location country of headquarters	Local country	Corresponding regions	The true global company
Staffing	Expatriates manage the local operations	Local managers lead the local operations	Develop human resources need in each region	Development of human resource at the global level

system of the home country as it is, the companies tend to accept the prevailing system or practices in the local country and try to adapt to the local situation.

• Regiocentric Approach

The regiocentric approach is a strategy that divides the world into several geographic regions and selects, educates and trains, deploys, and evaluates manpower to manage according to the specific regions. In addition, human resources management policies and systems are developed and utilized within the region to maintain the integrity inside the region as much as possible. This strategy focuses on rationalizing personnel management activities within one region beyond the borders of one country, unlike the local one.

Therefore, although communication and coordination within each region are active whereas communication and coordination between regions and the head office tend to be relatively insufficient.

- Geocentric Approach

The geocentric approach is a strategy to optimize the use of resources at the global level, and to integrate human resource management activities into one system targeting the world. In this strategy, a lot of effort is put into making the headquarters and overseas subsidiaries form a single organism. Therefore, the nationality of the executives becomes meaningless, and ideas and human resources move freely across borders and regions. Under this strategy, personnel management policies and practices are also developed to achieve these goals. And although the culture and management principles are common throughout the all organizations scattered around the world, specific systems are developed and operated flexibly according to the local situations and needs. This strategy can be used by international companies whose business is spread all over the world and has a lot of experience in managing overseas organizations and personnel.

In general, as internationalization progresses, the human resource management of international companies tends to change from a ethnocentric towards a geocentric strategy. However, such changes do not occur in all companies, and the human resource management strategy of a specific company should be determined after considering the company's internationalization stage, its unique culture, the company's global manpower level, and the company's globalization strategy. The home country-oriented ethnocentric strategy currently adopted by most Korean companies should be changed in the long run. However, it is necessary to understand that there is no single choice in choosing an appropriate international human resource management strategy. A geocentric strategy cannot be an unconditional goal, and it is more important to choose a strategy taking into account the specific circumstances of each company.

4. Culture and International Human Resources Management

One of the biggest difference between international and domestic HR management is that people and organizations have to be managed in a country with a different culture from their home country. No one does not recognize the importance of culture, but it is very difficult to properly define and understand what culture is. The most widely known definition of culture is that of Kluckhohn and Kroeber, where culture is 'a patterned way of thinking, feeling, and reacting, acquired and transmitted through symbols'.[7] On the other hand, according to Schein, organizational culture consists of three layers: basic assumptions that everyone in that culture takes for granted, principles and values advocated by members, and observable artefacts or symbols.[8]

If international companies do not properly grasp the values of local people, which are not observed easily to the outsiders' eyes, they are most likely to make a serious management mistake. In fact, there are many cases of international companies that

Figure 12-3 **Three Layers of Organizational Culture**

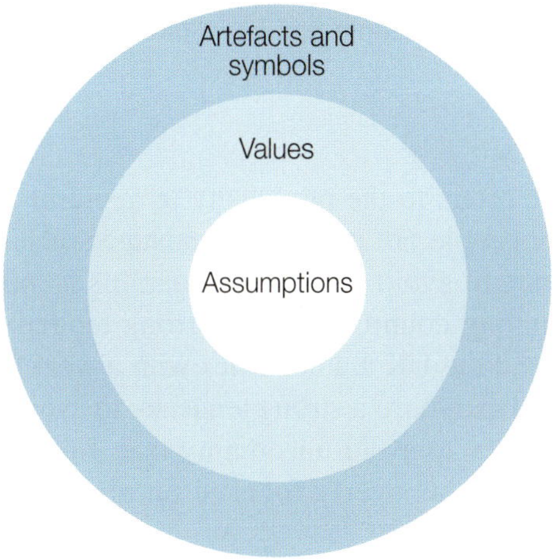

have suffered a great failure because they do not understand the local cultural code well. Understanding the local culture is essential not only to avoid mistakes, but also to actively seek and exploit market opportunities. It is also very helpful in managing local people and organizations. If a system introduced is contrary to the local assumptions or values, there must be a great resistance to it and it will be difficult to achieve the expected effect even after the introduction. In this sense, understanding and effective management of culture cannot be overemphasized.

4.1 Cultural Dimensions of Hofstede

The difficulty in understanding and utilizing culture mainly comes from the fact that although we know the importance of culture, it is difficult to accurately grasp it concretely. For example, it is clear that cultural differences have an great impact on market entry and manpower management, but it is not easy to figure out clearly how values affect them. Hofstede's work is of great value in this respect.[9)] His research is based on a large-scale survey of IBM employees around the world and presents four dimensions for comparing cultures across countries. The four dimensions are power distance, uncertainty avoidance, masculinity and femininity, and individualism and collectivism, respectively.

- Power Distance

Power distance is the extent to which people accept the existence of inequalities of power among people, which may vary from country to country. When the power distance is high, the hierarchical organizational structure is easily accepted and authority and responsibility are concentrated in the superior. A country with a very strong power distance is Malaysia, and the Nordic countries including Netherlands have a low power distance. Neither Korea nor Japan have a very high or low power distance compared to the average, but since Japan has a stronger power distance than Korea, from the perspective of Koreans, Japanese people can be regarded as conforming to the hierarchy more easily.

- Uncertainty Avoidance

Uncertainty avoidance refers to the propensity to avoid uncertain situations, and in cultures where it is high, people are planning in advance or clearly defining roles and responsibilities in advance to avoid uncertain situations as much as possible. Korea, Japan, and France are among countries with a strong tendency to avoid uncertainty, while Singapore, China, and the UK are countries with a weak tendency to avoid such a tendency. Both Korea and Japan have a strong tendency to avoid uncertainty, but because Japan has a stronger tendency to avoid uncertainty than Korea, in the eyes of Koreans, Japanese people may be seen as overly focused on planning and unable to respond flexibly to uncertain situations.

- Masculinity vs. Femininity

Masculinity is a culture that emphasizes goals and achievements, and femininity is a culture that emphasizes quality of life and relationships. Japan, Mexico, and Austria have strong masculine cultures, whereas the Netherlands and Norway have strong feminine cultures. Korea is a country where masculinity is not high. In countries with strong masculinity, women's social advancement is limited, and in cultures with strong femininity, gender discrimination is low and women's social influence is strong. In a culture with strong masculinity, applying strong financial incentives to achieve goals may be effective, whereas in a culture with strong femininity, a work-family balance policy may be more effective than monetary compensation.

- Individualism vs. Collectivism

In the individualistic culture, the individual is recognized as the most important basic unit of society, whereas in the collectivist culture, the individual has a primary meaning as a member of the group. Countries with strong individualism are Anglo-Saxon countries such as the United States, United Kingdom, and Australia, and the tendency of individualism in Latin and Asian countries is low. Among European countries, the Netherlands, Germany, and France show strong individualism, while Portugal and Greece show a strong collectivism tendency. In an individualistic culture, rewards based on individual abilities and performance are easily accepted, whereas in a collectivist culture, incentives based on collective performance may be more effective.

Hofstead presents the relative strength of the four value dimensions by making it possible to compare them through an index for each country. The following <Table 12-3> shows the results.[10] Many studies examining the influence of culture make use of this index. For example, the cultural distance between Korea and the United States is the sum of the absolute values of the differences in the four value dimensions. Although there are a lot of critics about whether measuring cultural distance in this way is correct,

Table 12-3 **National Index of Four Cultural Dimensions**

COUNTRY	POWER DISTANCE		INDIVIDUALISM VS. COLLECTIVISM		MASCULINITY VS. FEMININITY		UNCERTAINTY AVOIDANCE	
	INDEX	RANKING	INDEX	RANKING	INDEX	RANKING	INDEX	RANKING
Guatemala	95	2-3	6	53	37	43	101	3
Greece	60	27-8	35	30	57	18-19	112	1
South Africa	49	36-7	65	16	63	13-14	49	39-40
Netherlands	38	40	80	4-5	14	51	53	35
Norway	31	47-8	69	13	8	52	50	38
New Zealand	22	50	79	6	58	17	49	39-40
Denmark	18	51	74	9	16	50	23	51
Germany	35	42-4	67	15	66	9-10	65	29
Malaysia	104	1	26	36	50	25-6	36	46
Mexico	81	5-6	30	32	69	6	82	18
Belgium	65	20	75	8	54	22	94	5-6
Brazil	69	14	38	26-7	49	27	76	21-2
Salvador	66	18-19	19	42	40	40	94	5-6
Sweden	31	47-8	71	10-11	5	52	29	49-50
Spain	57	31	51	20	42	37-8	86	10-15
Singapore	74	13	20	39-41	48	28	8	53
Argentina	49	35-6	46	22-3	56	20-1	86	10-15
Ireland	28	49	70	12	68	7-8	35	47-8
Ecuador	78	8-9	8	52	63	13-14	67	28
UK	35	42-4	89	3	66	9-10	35	47-8
Austria	11	53	55	18	79	2	70	24-5
Iran	58	19-20	41	24	43	35-6	59	31-2
Israel	13	52	54	19	47	29	81	19
Italy	50	34	76	7	70	4-5	75	23
India	77	10-11	48	21	56	20-1	40	45
Indonesia	78	8-9	14	47-8	46	30-1	48	41-2
Japan	54	33	46	22-3	95	1	92	7
Jamaica	45	37	39	25	68	7-8	13	52
Chile	63	24-5	23	38	28	46	86	10-15
Canada	39	39	80	4-5	52	24	48	41-2
Costa Rica	35	42-4	15	46	21	48-9	86	10-15
Columbia	67	17	13	49	64	11-12	80	20
Panama	95	2-3	11	51	44	34	86	10-15
Pakistan	55	32	14	47-8	50	25-6	70	24-5
Peru	64	21-3	16	45	42	37-8	87	9
Portugal	63	24-5	27	33-5	31	45	104	2
France	68	15-16	71	10-11	43	35-6	86	10-15
Finland	33	46	63	17	26	47	59	31-2
Philippine	94	4	32	31	64	11-12	44	44
Korea	60	27-8	18	43	39	41	85	16-17
Australia	36	41	90	2	61	16	51	37
Hong Kong	68	15-16	25	37	57	18-19	29	49-50

Hofstead's research is being used extensively because it provides a ground to explain in what dimension and how much differ cultures between countries.

4.2 Cultural Dimension of Trompenaars and Turner

Trompenaars and Turner are also well-known researchers in the discussion of cultural differences between countries.[11)] Their research relatively lacks some theoretical framework and methodological rigor compared to Hofstead's research, but has the advantage of being preferred by practitioners in that it is easy to understand by experience and intuition. They divide culture into seven dimensions: universalism versus particularism, individualism versus communitarianism, neutral versus emotional, specific versus diffusionism, achievement versus ascription, sequential versus synchronic view of time, and internal versus outer orientation. Of these, the first five dimensions relate to the relationship between people, and the latter two dimensions are perspectives on time and nature, respectively.

- Universalism vs. Particularism

Universalism is the belief that what is right and good should always be the case under any circumstance, while particularism is the view that such judgments can vary according to social or interpersonal contexts. In a universalistic culture, there is only one reality, and formal rules are emphasized. In particularitic cultures, reality is understood as subjective, and the importance of relationships rather than rules is emphasized.

- Individualism vs. Communitarianism

Whether people view themselves as individuals or as members of a group by default varies from culture to culture. While individualism is a society centered on individuals, communitarianism is a culture that prioritizes groups. In an individualistic culture, individual freedom or achievement is considered important, and recognition and reward for this is effective. In a communitarian culture, collective consultation is more important than the individual, and rewards for collective performance may be more effective.

- Neutral vs. Emotional

In a neutral culture, people try to suppress emotions in daily life or work, and reason and objective logic is emphasized. In contrast, in emotional cultures, expressing emotions is considered natural and actively encouraged. In the eyes of the people in a neutral culture a person from an emotional culture may appear to be distracted and unprofessional, whereas a person in an emotional culture may feel a person from a neutral culture as uninterested in their peers or lacks humanity.

- Specific vs. Diffuse

Specific centered culture strictly separates the realms of work and personal life, and believes that people can work together even if their relationships are not good. However, in diffuse based culture, work and personal life are overlapping, and good relationships are essential to work well together. In the specific oriented culture, clear instructions

Figure 12-4 **Seven Dimensions of Culture**

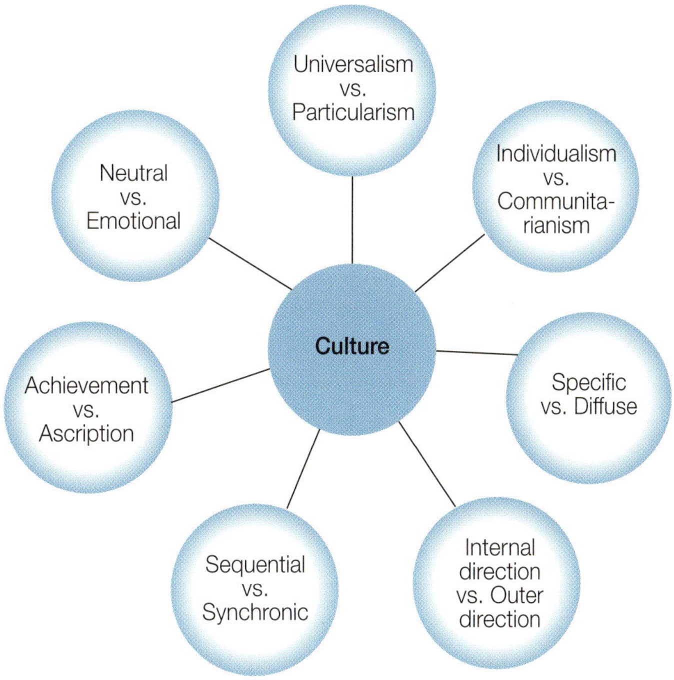

and feedback are emphasized for work, whereas in the diffuse oriented culture, out-of-work dinners and gatherings have an important meaning.

Achievement vs. Ascription

In an achievement culture, individuals are judged by the achievements, and social status is determined by that. However, in an ascription culture, social status is determined by things that are given by birth status, age, and gender. In an achievement culture, the individual's ability and achievement are appreciated and emphasized, not the position or power that he or she has. In an attribution culture, a position or authority determines the importance of an individual, and corresponding courtesy is naturally expected.

Sequential Time vs. Synchronic Time

In a sequential time view, one activity or action is expected to happen at one point in time, and more than two events are not natural and should not happen at the same time. In a synchronic time view, it is natural and desirable that several activities are unfolding simultaneously. In a culture with a sequential time line, it is important to be on time, and adherence to schedules according to plan is strongly emphasized. Wasting time in this culture is something to be avoided at all costs. In a culture with a simultaneous time perspective, plans and schedules can be adjusted according to circumstances, and

Measuring Adaptability to the Local Culture

Samsung Electronics has been using the Samsung Cultural Adaptation Index since 2013. SCAI examines whether expatriate candidates who will be dispatched overseas have the cultural capacity to adapt to local countries, and provides feedback to those who are likely to have difficulty adapting abroad in advance, so that they can prepare more thoroughly in advance. Expatriation may be reconsidered if cultural adaptation competence is remarkably low. SCAI also includes the fit test between local culture and individual cultural values using Hofstede's cultural dimension. If the gap between the characteristics of the local culture and the characteristics of an individual is very large, there is a high possibility that an adaptation problem will occur. Such efforts like Samsung Electronics did are rare not only in domestic companies but also in overseas companies, and it is an important example of considering and utilizing culture in the human resource management.

flexible time allocation is accepted as natural.

- Internal vs. Outer Direction

Internal direction refers to the belief that nature or environment can be changed or overcome through individual or organizational efforts, and outer orientation stands for the tendency or behavior to see such external influences as something to conform in acknowledging and accepting them. In an internal oriented culture, it is natural to attribute success and failure to the individual or the organization rather than to the environment, and aggressive behavior to succeed is well accepted. In an outward-oriented culture, short-term failure or loss is relatively easily accepted, and a greater meaning is placed on harmony with the environment or relationship-building for long-term success.

5. Management of Expatriates

The manpower subject to the international human resource management is divided into three groups: workforce from the country where the local operation is located (host country nationals), expatriate employees dispatched from the head office to host country, and people sent from local operations to other local countries to work (third country nationals). In reality, local workforce recruited on the spot accounts for the largest number, but their management method is not much different from managing workforce at home country except for variables such as the local working environment or culture. On the other hand, the number of third country nationals is very small and the strategic importance is not so great. Therefore, an important group in international human resource management is expatriates who are dispatched from the headquarters and work in local operations. Although the absolute number is not large, most of them play central roles as managers or key persons in local operations, and they are key links of communication channel between the headquarters and local operations. With that in mind, the following will focus on the management of expatriates.

5.1 Advantages and Disadvantages of Using Expatriates

In order to secure the necessary human resources for overseas subsidiaries, it is necessary to decide from which group to fill the managerial positions in local operations. Recruitable workforce includes home country nationals (expatriates), local and third-country employees, but the key decision-making is primarily about the choice between expatriates and host country employees. The following <Table 12-4> shows the advantages and disadvantages of using expatriates.

Utilizing expatriates has the advantage of making communication with the head office smooth and operating a local corporation in line with the head office's strategy. In addition, it is possible to reduce management errors and failures by allowing competent personnel with proven experience and ability at the headquarters to take over the management. Utilization of expatriates is not only related to the smooth operation of local corporations. Expatriate experience can also contribute to developing the global perspective and competency of the head office workforce. The use of expatriates can sometimes become an unavoidable choice when the company is not well known in the local country or the labor market is not well developed.

On the other hand, making use of local nationals has the opposite advantages and disadvantages to the method of using expatriates. Use of local manpower has advantages in terms of localization, but disadvantages in terms of control and coordination from the headquarters. Specifically, the utilization of local manpower can avoid language and cultural barriers, and can expect them to work for a longer period than expatriates. In addition, as the opportunities for promotion and career management of locals increase, the morale of the locals mounts up accordingly. However, there are a number of disadvantages to this as well. For example it becomes difficult for the headquarters to control and coordinate local operations, and by using local employees, the opportunities for the headquarters managers to get a overseas experience may be lost.

Table 12-4 Advantages and Disadvantages of Using Expatriates

ADVANTAGES	DISADVANTAGES
Control and coordination of the entire international enterprise can be promoted.	Local national employees are less likely to be promoted.
The head office staff can acquire international sensibilities and experiences.	It can be obstacles to localization.
The experience and abilities necessary for the job have already been verified.	The management style of the headquarters is pursued unnecessarily.
The management goals and policies of the headquarters can be pursued quickly.	There can be conflicts due to the difference in compensation between expatriates and local workers.

Whether or not to utilize expatriates is a matter that should be decided by the strategy and situations of the company. For example, it is desirable for a company that adopts a strategy emphasizing the control of overseas subsidiaries to actively utilize expatriate personnel. And it is desirable for a company that pursues localization strategy to make use of local personnel. Of course, in this process, the local market and legal environment must be carefully considered. In addition, companies that are not well known abroad and are in the initial stage of overseas expansion have no choice but to actively utilize expatriates, because it is difficult to secure competent manpower when the company is not well known locally. And it is more effective to use expatriates when the local labor market is in short supply of competent manpower.

5.2 Selection of Expatriates

The selection of employees to go abroad and work as expatriates is an important factor in determining the success or failure of overseas operation. An expatriate failure often refers to a case in which a person returns home midway without accomplishing a scheduled overseas work assignment. The premature return is mainly explained by the failure of the expatriate or his family to adapt to the local work and life environment. In the case of failure, not only the cost of finding a new expatriate candidate and training and relocate him will occur, but there may be problems with the relationship with the local government or customers, which will have a major impact on local operation.

In order to prevent the failure of expatriation and to lead overseas business successfully, it is necessary to put a lot of effort into the selection of expatriates. The job competency is a basic criteria that the candidates should have, but it is not enough. <Table 12-5> below shows the factors that affect the effective adaptation to the local environment and job performance. These factors need to be considered in a balanced way through the selection decision.[12)]

Meanwhile, an additional consideration in the selection of expatriates is the issue of the expatriate's family, especially the spouse. Family maladjustment is an serious factor that makes it difficult for expatriates to adapt to overseas, but at the same time, active support and cooperation from the families is essential for successful overseas work. In some cases, the family serves as an important window for understanding the local

Table 12-5 Core Competencies for Expatriates

CORE QUALIFICATION FOR EXPATRIATES
• Strategic mindset • Ability to adapt to new environment • Sensitivity to other cultures • Ability to work on an international team • Language proficiency • Understanding of international marketing • Human relationship skills • International negotiation skills

culture. For example, networking with the parents of their children's friends or attending school events provide expatriates with a very precious opportunity to get out of their working relationship and get to know the local people and their culture. Nevertheless, compared to international companies in other countries, Korean companies still lack support for family adaptation.

5.3 Training and Development of Expatriates

Cross-cultural training is of importance in training and development of expatriates. Expatriates working abroad should be aware of not only the language of the country but also cultural traditions and customs in preparation for a successful adaptation. The following <Table 12-6> shows the main contents of education and training that international managers think they hope to receive to prepare for overseas dispatch.[13)]

However, the local environment of the host country differs from country to country, and even in the same country, the economic and business situation may be different depending on the time of dispatch. In other words, it is desirable to adjust the content and intensity of the training according to the local situation every time the expatriate is trained. For example, if there is a large cultural difference between the home and the host country, active education is required proportionally. However, if the cultural differences are not large and the expatriates have overseas work experience, the intensity or duration of education does not need to be too high.

Meanwhile, training and development of host and third country nationals are also important for the success of the overseas operations. They generally lack understanding of the management techniques of the headquarters and the culture of the home country, so education and training should focus on that matters. For this purpose, it can be helpful to send local employees to the headquarters to receive that kind of training. It is known that the education for locals held at the headquarters is very effective for forming a sense of unity and sharing management perspective and culture. Focusing of these education on committed and competent local workers can increase the motivation of local workers while providing them with an opportunity to network at headquarters.

Table 12-6 **Training Need for Expatriate Preparation**

PREPARATION CONTENTS	RESPONSE FREQUENCY (%)
• Opportunity to visit the country to be dispatched in advance	79
• Language training	73
• Prior briefing by the repatriate worked in the host country	67
• Overall management training of the company	44
• Cross-cultural education for expatriates	42
• Cross-cultural education for the families	38
• General management education at the Business School	29
• Language training for families	23
• Training on negotiation skills in the host country	17

5.4 Compensation of Expatriates

Compensation management of expatriates belongs to a very technical and professional field. This is because it is necessary to calculate the difference in purchasing power between the home and the local country, and design the compensation level and compensation formular in consideration of the double taxation prevention agreement or tax system between countries. However, in the broad framework of the principle of compensation, the compensation method is divided into the method based on purchasing power at the home country and the method based on the wage level of the host country.

5.4.1 Home Based Approach

The home-based approach stands on the basis of the level of purchasing power in the home country. It is designed to maintain the standard of living that the expatriates and their families enjoy in their home country to the local country. It draws up the compensation of expatriates starting from the wage received by expatriates in their home country, and pays additional expenses in the form of allowances. In this way, this method trys to respect the principle that there should be no decrease in real purchasing power just because they are dispatched abroad. This is the most widely used method by multinational corporations because it has the advantage of facilitating the transfer of manpower abroad by ensuring that expatriates can maintain the standard of living in their home country elsewhere.

However, this method has several disadvantages. First, it may lead to an unfair wage gap between expatriates and local workforce. Also, it is more expensive compared to other methods. In this method, various allowances for overseas dispatch tend to be set excessively high to compensate for the relocation abroad. For example, maintaining a living standard similar to that in the United States in areas such as Japan and Hong Kong could be very expensive. In addition, it is complicated and difficult to compare the price level of various countries and calculate the appropriate pay level for expatriates in consideration of exchange rates.

5.4.2 Host Country Based Approach

Another way to determine the compensation of expatriates is based on the wage level of the host country. In this method, the pay of expatriate employees is determined to be the same as the wage level of local workers performing similar jobs. And various allowances related to overseas dispatch are added here, and the total amount is paid in the local currency. While this method has the advantage of reducing the unfairness in wages between expatriates and local workers and reducing the cost of compensation management, it is necessary to negotiate wages with individual expatriates when expatriating abroad, and is sensitive to changes in exchange rates.

On the other hand, a special feature in compensation management for expatriates is the variety of employee benefits. Since living conditions in the host country are very different from those in the home country, it is common to provide various benefits for expatriates and their families. For example, subsidies for the rental of a local residence, support for air trip to the home country, allowances for children's education abroad, and aid for moving expenses are considered basic benefits for expatriates and their families.

5.5 Exile Syndrome and the Problem of Repatriation

Exile syndrome refers to the feeling that expatriates feel alienated from the head office. As expatriates are dispatched overseas to work in a geographically distant location, communication with the head office becomes difficult. As a result, it is easy to be anxious about being disadvantaged in promotion and to feel "exiled." This phenomenon is called exile syndrome. To solve this problem, it is effective to give an opportunity to maintain a connection point or network with the head office through regular meetings or business trips at the head office, and let the superior, who has important roles and responsibilities at the head office, act as a mentor for their career.

On the other hand, the repatriation of expatriates to the headquarters in their home country after completing their work overseas is a very important process. Just as the problem of adaptation occurs when going abroad, there may also be a problem of adaptation in the case of returning home. For example, the expatriates have to adapt to a changed headquarters organization or atmosphere and build new networks again. In addition, it is necessary to adapt to the situation in which the authority and autonomy enjoyed in the local corporation can be suddenly diminished in the head office. However, most companies put a lot of effort into sending expatriates abroad, whereas they do not take any measures for their return. As a result, the repatriates coming to the headquarters can have difficulties in re-adaptation. It could be a great loss not to able to actively utilize the valuable experiences and knowledge gained by expatriates from overseas experience.

Therefore, companies have a lot to gain by recognizing the importance of adaptation of the repatriates. In order to help their readjustment, an orientation for adaptation to the home country should be conducted to make them familiar with the changes in the organization and management of the head office. Companies may allow them to submit reports or briefing materials so that the head office can utilize the valuable experience and knowledge gained through overseas work, and help their adaptation and increase their self-esteem. And it is effective to start preparing for a successful return to home while working abroad. To this end, it is desirable to appoint mentor who will advise on their careers even while working abroad to provide counseling on career management after returning to work.

6. Challenges for Korean Companies

Although the history of internationalization of Korean companies is short, it is difficult to say that large Korean companies have a lower degree of internationalization compared to other foreign advanced companies. Korean groups, mainly centering on the electronics industry, have established and are operating production and sales corporations in several dozens of countries, and the proportion of overseas sales in total sales is increasing significantly. Also, recently, small and medium-sized enterprises (SMEs) are also active in overseas expansion, so there are many cases of establishing a local production facilities together with large corporations or independently. However, with the progress of globalization, there are many challenges to be solved in human resource management. In the following, we will look at the tasks necessary for the globalization of Korean companies.

6.1 Headquarters Centered Strategy of Korean Companies

In the case of Korean companies, there are many cases where a clear strategic direction has not yet been established on the issue of how to manage local organizations and human resources abroad. And many problems are exposed in the actual management process. The type of international human resource management of Korean companies that are currently pursuing can be generally characterized as home country oriented. In the home country-oriented type, the head office constitutes the central point of decision-making and has strong control over local organizations. In addition, expatriates dispatched are mainly used to manage overseas organizations. This type of human resource management is a strategic choice for many Korean firms to take advantage of the strength of quick and consistent execution on the global dimension. And in some case, they had not much room but to choose it because there was a lack of integrated management mechanism to support localized management by delegating authority to local people.

The problem is that there are non-negligible side effects of home-based human resource management. In this type of management, quick and flexible responses to the local circumstances often become difficult. In addition, the opportunities for career development of local employees are inevitably limited, making it difficult to foster and secure competent local manpower. The high probability of misunderstanding with local laws or labor-management conflicts with local employees is another problem for the headquarters-oriented strategy.

6.2 Harmony of Global Integration and Localization

The most important task that Korean companies pursuing internationalization must solve in the long term is how to harmonize global integration and localization. In order to strengthen the competitiveness expected through internationalization, localization of the organization and management is desperately needed. At the same time, organizations and people across the globe must be effectively integrated to enable rapid decision-making on the global dimension. Business performance and competitiveness can be secured through internationalization only when locally responsive decision-making is made in accordance with an integrated globalization strategy. It is for this reason that advanced multinational corporations emphasize 'think globally, and 'act locally'.

In order for global integration and localization to be well balanced, an integration mechanism that can support and consolidate decentralized organizations and human resources must be implemented. This is because the degree of localization tends to be determined by the degree of these integration means. Localization should be consistent with the strategic objectives of the entire enterprise. Advanced international companies basically localize business operations and delegate their authority to a large extent, but they are developing and using various integration methods to integrate them. In terms of organizational structure, regional organizations that can perform integration and coordination functions are required. In terms of management process, a unified performance evaluation system, global manager, and corporate culture are the main means that Koreans companies have to make use of.

- Regional Organization Structure

Most advanced international companies are using regional organizations to coordinate several local organization with same geographical area. While the basic decision-making authority is held by each business unit, regional organizations focus on the coordination and human resource development needed between different business units in the same region. In addition, regional organizations play a role in discovering and promoting agendas that require a joint response in relation to the government, customers, labor market, and suppliers, which are important for each region.

- Performance Management System

Each local operation should be evaluated based on the strategic goals of the business unit to which it belongs, and the competence and performance of local managers have to be determined according to the global evaluation format and evaluation procedure. In particular, a common evaluation system for leadership competency is essential for leadership level manpower who must work on the global arena. Only with such a performance evaluation system, consistent global business promotion is possible while extensive localization is being pursued.

- Development of Global Leaders

A leader who understands the culture and strategy of the headquarters and can lead change in overseas organizations is an essential condition for localization. Many advanced companies point to the lack of global leaders as the biggest obstacle in the process of globalization. It is for this reason that advanced companies are strategically interested in nurturing global leaders. Localization is possible only if the company can nurture leaders who can think globally and act locally.

- Organizational Culture

When there are shared values, decentralization and rapid decision-making are possible, and operations around the world can be united towards a single vision and goal. Therefore, international companies are putting a lot of effort into spreading corporate culture in the operations and units located all over the world. From this point of view, one of the most important roles of the CEO should share the corporate culture with them. Overseas work is also being used as a means to share and spread corporate culture in the all organizations.

Samsung's Regional Expert Development

Samsung's regional expert program, which started in 1990 with the goal of nurturing leaders in globalization, has been continuously promoted despite various difficulties for the next 23 years, and has developed about 5,000 regional experts so far. Candidates for regional experts are usually selected from young people at the level of assistant managers or managers, and when selected, they are dispatched to the chosen local country after 12 weeks of intensive language training. During the first six months, the main mission is to intensively learn the language, history, and culture of the local country, and to actively create a network with the locals. For the remaining 6 months, they plan and execute the project they had prepared before the departure. The company invests a year of time and money for each of the candidate for their learning and growth.

The effect of the regional expert system has already begun to show from the beginning of its introduction. Regional experts dispatched to Thailand and Indonesia have made significant contributions to Samsung's rapid growth in the country based on their understanding and network of the local market. Regional experts have played an essential role in Samsung's globalization, enhancing the understanding of the local area within the headquarters after returning to Korea, and then returning to the local area to serve as organization heads. Such a program is a rare case that is difficult to find even in advanced global companies.[14)]

6.3 Globalization of Headquarters

For successful globalization, the head office workforce must be globalized. The problem that Korean companies with little experience in globalization are facing is the lack of globalization in the headquarters. One of the reasons why Korean companies choose the home country oriented human resource management strategy is that the head office workforce itself is not globalized due to lack of international working experience. Just as local leaders working at local subsidiaries need to understand the strategy and culture of the head office, managers working at the head office must also have an understanding and sensitivity to the local market. Here are some ways to globalize the head office workforce.

- English as Corporate Language

In order for the head office personnel to communicate with local personnel smoothly and efficiently, the language as a means of communication must be unified. However, in reality, it is difficult to make Korean the official language of the company. In such a situation, the method of specifying the official language of the enterprise as English can be helpful. In fact, some non-English speaking multinational companies have officially designated English as their company language. Although no Korean companies have adopted such a policy yet, there are cases where the headquarters had implemented a policy to hold meetings in English at headquarters. But unfortunately most of them have failed. This is partly because the English meeting was requested not only for departments that needed English communication with local personnel, but also for all employees, and partly because the English level of the staff at the headquarters was not yet at the level for the smooth meeting. Because of these problems, a weird incident of having a brief meeting in English and then meeting again in Korean often occurred at the companies implementing the meeting in English. Taking the lessons from the past failures, it is necessary to consider designating English as the official language within the headquarters in the long term, but it must be first applied to the departments and personnel who absolutely need communication with overseas organizations.

Development of the Local Talent

Another effective way to globalize headquarters is to actively recruit and utilize overseas talent at headquarters. By allowing foreign talents of different languages, cultures, and values to work together with domestic people at headquarters, the company can enhance the openness and diversity of domestic people and provide opportunities to understand local perspectives even if they do not work abroad. In this area, too, many Korean companies have made their own efforts. They create and operate a specialized organization that discovers and recruits overseas human resources, recruits senior executives for the vice president level as foreigners, and recruits young talents from overseas. However, there are still few cases in which these efforts have yielded expected results. This is because, in many cases, recruited overseas personnel did not adapt well to Korean culture and organization and left the company without making the anticipated contribution. The problem of homogeneous and collective culture and communication difficulty due to language in Korea is an important cause. As much effort is put into recruiting, it is necessary to support their adaptation while making necessary information

Bitter Experiment of Recruiting Foreign Talents

Vice Chairman Nam Yong, who took office as CEO of LG Electronics in early 2007, set a vision to make it into a true global company, and radically transformed the organization. And for this purpose, C-level foreign managers were suddenly appointed in key areas such as strategy, marketing, human resources, purchasing, and supply chain. However, after three years, they all left LG Electronics as their contracts were terminated. The main reason for their leaving was the sluggish performance of not keeping up with the market change to smartphones. However, communication problems were also an important cause. Korean workers criticized them that they only emphasize the basic approach and solutions without understanding the accurate situations while they are complaining that Korean employees do not understand and respect the basic principles and systems. The reason for this wide difference in perspective was that language communication was difficult and that the appointment of foreign executives was perceived as an obstacle to the promotion of domestic personnel. It can be useful to recruit foreign executives, but before that, the company should prepare a culture and system where both groups can work effectively. This is an important lesson that LG electronics got from failure.

be documented and communicated in English.

Utilization of the Repatriates

Expatriates get a very practical and intense cross-cultural experience in the local country. Leveraging their experiences, they can play a vital role in the globalization of the headquarters. However, it is more common for these valuable experiences to be lost after returning to the head office. Therefore, it is necessary to make an active effort so that the experience and knowledge of those who have worked abroad can be utilized in the head office. For this purpose, it will be helpful to support effective communication and coordination by sharing the experiences of repatriates, and allowing them to take on jobs related to overseas organizations.

Promotion Qualifications and Overseas Work

A time-taking, but highly effective way to globalize headquarters is to make international work experience a prerequisite for executive promotion. This method can help to understand the local perspective and issues by linking overseas work with career management so that personnel with local experience can rise to important positions at the head office. In addition, it can expand the pool of expatriates by enabling talented people to apply for overseas work for their career development. With this in mind, there are many companies that systematically specify overseas work experience as an important condition for executive promotion among advanced foreign companies. However, it seems that Korean companies are not making active efforts in this field yet.

Cross-Cultural Training for Head Office Personnel

The progress of globalization is making frequent contact and communication with organizations and people from other cultures, even for those working at the headquarters. Therefore, it is necessary for them to understand the culture of the other countries for effective work performance. Considering this, it is desirable to increase the understanding of different cultures and viewpoints through cross-cultural education and training for head office personnel. In particular, cross-cultural education is important

Intel's Cross-Cultural Education

Intel, which produces and sells main computing devices and memory chips for personal computers in various regions of the world, has a very diverse culture within its headquarters in the United States as well as its overseas subsidiaries around the world. This is because the company selects the manpower it needs from various regions and countries. The diverse cultures within the company and the cooperative relationships it has with other companies around the world served as a momentum to develop a systematic cross-cultural education program. Intel's intercultural education, which started as a cultural adaptation education for foreign-born members in 1983, is an intercultural awareness program that systematically implements contents to raise awareness of cultural diversity in the curriculum for all employees of the headquarters.

for companies that are actively trying to recruit foreign manpower. In the case of Intel, where people from various countries are working together, it is known that it has been conducting cross-cultural education for a long time.

Ending Case

CGV's Entry into Vietnam through International M&A[15)]

As of 2015, out of a total of 377 movie theaters in Vietnam, CJ CGV (hereinafter CGV) had 196 and Lotte Cinema had 86, and the proportion of Korean operators was close to 75%. In particular, CGV first entered the Vietnamese market by acquiring Megastar, a local theater operator, in 2011, three years later than its competitor, Lotte Cinema. However, CGV's overseas business did not go smoothly from the beginning. The first overseas market entry was made in the form of a joint venture in China in 2006, but due to the Chinese government's discrimination and regulation against foreign companies and strong competition with local companies, only 10 theaters were released during 5 years after entering the market.

In order to make up for the sluggishness in the Chinese market, CGV entered Vietnam, a new emerging market, by acquiring local operators. In the early stage of the entrance, it faced many difficulties, such as the immaturity of movie viewing culture due to low national income, government regulations on politically sensitive movie screenings, a non-systematic movie rating system, and illegal downloading and distribution of movie files. Nevertheless, CGV established its position as the No. 1 theater operator in Vietnam in a relatively short period of time through the head office's active commitment and localization policy.

CGV, Korea's No. 1 theater operator, recognized early on that it was difficult for film companies to have explosive growth opportunities in the mature Korean theater industry. CGV entered the Vietnamese market in 2011 following China and the United States. Unlike the previous preference for joint ventures or direct investment, CGV chose to acquire a local theater business in Vietnam. At that time, none of the Korean entertainment companies succeeded in international acquisitions, and despite the fact that it was the first international acquisition in the history of CGV, the Vietnamese business achieved remarkable results with increasing sales and recording net profit within 8 months of the acquisition. M&A for local companies had the great advantage of eliminating strong potential rivals and acquiring advantageous theaters pre-occupied by incumbents. In addition, it helped CGV to enter the local market relatively quickly compared to other entry methods such as new establishment or joint venture.

At the time CGV entered the market, three companies, Megastar, Galaxy, and Platinum, were considered for acquisition among Vietnamese theater companies that were on sale for M&A. Among them, CGV judged that Megastar was the most suitable for the company's entry goals and business characteristics. Unlike Galaxy and Platinum, which operated a small number of theaters in Hanoi and Ho Chi Minh at the time,

Megastar was a large-scale operator with 7 theaters nationwide. In addition, most of its theaters are located in shopping malls, so compared to other local companies, it is closer to the multiplex operator that CGV is pursuing. Therefore, it was expected that the acquisition of Megastar would make it easier for CGV to realize the strategic goal of preoccupying the local theater market through rapid business expansion. Megastar was already the largest operator in Vietnam with 7 theaters, occupying 60% of the market share, and two of them were enjoying great success with 1 million audiences visiting each year. CGV selected Megastar as a target for acquisition through a prompt decision-making process, started the M&A process in earnest, and made a large-scale investment of about $74 million to acquire Megastar in July 2011. Through this, CGV gained more than half of the market share as soon as it started business in Vietnam.

After the acquisition, CGV carefully promoted organizational integration so that the newly acquired organization could be efficiently controlled without compromising its excellent local manpower and business base. It is well known that no matter how good company is acquired, it is difficult to create the expected synergy if proper organizational integration is not achieved. CGV made a lot of effort in implementing deverse actions. First, CGV reorganized the existing structure by dividing it into program management which decides and adjusts films to be screened, and media sales which is in charge of theater, video, DVD, and broadcast distribution, etc. And a regional store manager position was created so that rational and prompt decisions could be made. In HR management, a system was established to clarify performance evaluation criteria and differentiate incentives accordingly. In financial management, the headquarters system emphasizing accuracy and transparency was introduced in Vietnam.

In addition, since it is difficult to secure local manpower who can speak English and have experience in the film industry in Vietnam, most of Megastar's existing manpower was inherited as it was, and the actual decision authority selecting films to be screened was given to Vietnamese managers. This was to increase their loyalty to the company and strengthen work motivation by giving them decision-making power while taking advantage of the fact that they can understand the tastes of Vietnamese audiences and government regulations better than expatriates from Korea. By introducing a weekly meeting system, which was not implemented in the headquarters, all employees, regardless of their positions, such as store managers, headquarters employees, and theater managers, had time to gather and understand the company's status and major issues. Through this meeting, managers of lower ranks also actively participated in communication, and their fresh ideas and field knowledge were reflected in major decision making, and their sense of ownership and satisfaction improved.

CGV also recognized the cultural differences between the headquarters and the Vietnamese subsidiary even after the acquisition, and respected Megastar's unique corporate culture maintaining events such as "End of Party" and "Company Trip" held at Megastar. Lastly, the theater industry requires a lot of initial capital investment, so if location selection is wrong once, huge losses is inevitable. In order to reduce such risk, the theater positioning process and manual created through the experience of the Korean headquarters were introduced in Vietnam. After acquiring Megastar, the brand name was not changed immediately and the existing brand was maintained for 2 years and 6 months. It was also time for CGV to learn the culture, and the competitive advantage of Megastar while minimizing the confusion that existing employees may feel. During that time, CGV prepared enough to differentiate the brand image of CGV, which it want consumers to recognize in the future, not that of the existing Megastar.

After the acquisition of Megastar, CGV effectively applied its knowledge and know-how of the theater business it had built in Korea to its Vietnamese business, while pursuing the localization of movie content in order to respond to the tastes of Vietnamese audiences. In addition, while effectively responding to the strong regulations of the Vietnamese government on the film industry, many social contribution activities were carried out to overcome the disadvantages as a foreign film business operator. Through this series of strategic efforts, CGV was able to achieve remarkable business expansion and excellent business performance in Vietnam in a short period of time.

Discussion Questions

1. As CGV entered Vietnam, why did it choose to acquire a local company instead of a green site or joint venture?
2. What is post-merger integration (PMI) in international M&A and why is it so important?
3. What specific actions did CGV carry out for organizational integration?
4. As explained in this chapter, in order for Korean companies to achieve successful globalization, global integration and localization must be integrated in good balance. How did CGV solve these difficult challenges?

References and Sources

CHAPTER 1

1) Dessler, G. 2011. *Human Resource Management.* Boston: Pearson.
2) Drucker, P. F. 1973. *Management: Tasks, Responsibilities, Practices.* New York: Harper.
3) *Ibid.*
4) Seok-cheol Yoon. 2006. *Princepia Menezimenta.* Gyeongmunsa.
5) Kaufman, B. E. 2007. The development of HRM in historical and international perspective. In P. Boxtall, J. Purcell, & P. Wright (Eds.). The Oxford Handbook of Human Resource Management: 19-47. Oxford: Oxford University Press.
6) Kaufman, B. E. 2007. University of Wisconsin-Madison, University of California-Berkeley, etc. were the first universities in the U.S. for which majors related to personnel management or industrial relations were created.
7) Taylor, F. (translated by Young-Ho Bang). 2010. *The Principles of Scientific Management.* 21st Century Books.
8) Korea Labor Institute. 1999. *21st Century Human Resource Management: New Paradigm and Action Task.* Myeonggyeongsa.
9) Wright, P. M. & McMahan, G. C. 1992. Theoretical perspectives for strategic human resource management. *Journal of Management* 18(2): 295-320.
10) In the early stages of his presentation of the resource-based theory, Professor Jay B. Barney selected non-substitutable as the fourth element, but later, in the process of elaborating the theory, the fourth element was changed to organizational ability to complete the VRIO model.
11) Jeon Sang-gil. 2016. *Human resource management for creative management, asking the way.* Changmyeong.

CHAPTER 2

1) Lim, J. Y. 2014. *Labor Law*, Parkyoungsa, p. 3.
2) *Ibid.*, p. 17.
3) Article 93 of the Labor Standards Act (Preparation and Report of Employment Rules).
4) The contents of the Labor Standards Act, which apply even when the number of regular workers is 4 or less, includes preparation and issuance of labor contracts, weekly holidays, payment of severance pay, and compliance with the minimum wage. For more information on this, refer to the following. Ministry of Employment and Labor (2019), Essential Labor Law for workplaces with 4 or fewer employees.
5) For more information on the employment insurance system, refer to the Employment Insurance website (/www.ei.go.kr).
6) For major activities of the Labor Relations Commission and recent important decisions, refer to the Central Labor Commission's website (www.nlrc.go.kr).
7) Ahn J. Y. 2005. "Labor Market Discrimination Practices: Focusing on Hiring Discrimination,"

Labor Review 1(4): 3-18.
8) Women's Labor Law Support Center, 2011, A survey on discriminatory practices in the process of hiring companies, National Human Rights Commission's Research Report.
9) Seoul newspaper, 2015.5.16. "The height limit for female flight attendants was officially abolished but... airline not hiring persons whose hight is under 162cm."
10) Newsis, 2011.10.23. "Long way to go for a fair society: not easily broken discrimination against region, education and age."
11) News Mission, 2015.3.10. "Job season, faith is also a spec?... Side effects of preferential employment for Christians."
12) Herald Economy, 2015.8.5. "The Glass Ceiling Still High."
13) Kyunghyang Shinmun, 2013.10.10. "Restriction on recruitment of women in recruiting candidates for police officers is a discrimination."
14) A person who violates Article 26 of the Act shall be punished by imprisonment for up to two years or a fine of up to 10 million won.
15) Gender Equality Employment and Work-Family Balance Support Act, Articles 12 and 13.
16) JoongAng Economy Co. 2014, Practical Labor Glossary.
17) Ministry of Gender Equality and Family, 2019. 2018 Sexual Harassment Survey Results.
18) Refer to the following for the purpose and content of the revision of the Labor Standards Act on workplace harassment. Kim G. J. 2019. "Current Status and Tasks of the Workplace Bullying Prevention Act," *Labor Review* 47-52.
19) Ministry of Employment and Labor, 2019. Manual for judgment, prevention and response to harassment in the workplace.
20) Hankyoreh, 2020.6.28. "Is it the "Law of Neglect of Harassment at Work?"
21) The standard employment rate is set differently by industry. Manufacturing is 2%, transportation, real estate and leasing is 6%, and other industries are 3%.
22) Regarding Japan's mandatory continuing employment system, note Park W. S. 2016. "Human Resource Management Response to Changes in Labor Market Environment: Japanese Cases," in Human Resource Management Measures to Respond to Changes in the Labor Market Environment such as Extension of Retirement Age, Korea Labor Institute.
23) Kim K. S. 2016. "Legal Problems of Smart Device on the Labor," in Workers who are scared of Kakao Talk: Working hours without boundaries of workers, 127th Labor Forum of the Korea Labor and Social Research Institute.

CHAPTER 3

1) Hakjong Lee and Hyukseung Yang. 2012. *Strategic Human Resource Management*. Orae.
2) www.merck.com, www.merck.co.kr
3) Internal information of an anonymous company in the Korean IT industry.
4) Coca-Cola has also changed recently. Current CEO, James Quincey, was hired from a consulting firm, unlike previous CEOs.
5) www.cocacola.com, www.cocacolar.co.kr, www.pepsicola.com,www.pepsicola.co.kr
6) Gomez-Mejia, L. R., Balkin, D. B., & Cardy, R. L. 2012. *Managing Human Resources* (7th edition). Boston: Pearson.
7) Wright, P. M. & McMahan, G. C. 1992. Theoretical perspectives for strategic human resource management. *Journal of Management*, 18(2): 295-320.
8) Gomez-Mejia, L. R. et al. 2012. *op. cit.*
9) Gomez-Mejia, L. R. et al. 2012. *op. cit.* pp. 56-58.
10) Sejin Jang. 2002. *Management strategy*. Pakyoungsa.
11) Porter, M. E. 1980. *Competitive Advantage*. New York: Free Press.
12) Miles, R. E. & Snow, C. C. 1984. Designing strategic human resource systems. *Organizational*

Dynamics 13(1): 36-52.
13) Gomez-Mejia, L. R. et al. 2012. *op. cit.,* pp. 59-60.
14) Gomez-Mejia, L. R. et al. 2012. *op. cit.,* pp. 61.
15) Bechet, T. P. 2002. *Strategic Staffing: A Practical Toolkit for Worforce Planning*. (Translated by Jeongsik Yoo). Geoleun. pp. 110.
16) Wikipedia. https://en.wikipedia.org/wiki/%ED%8F%AC%EC%8A%A4%EC%BD%94.
17) POSCO internal data revision.
18) POSCO. *HR Insight*. 2019. August. pp. 41-45.

CHAPTER 4

1) Im Chang-hee. 2013. *Organizational Behavior* 5th Edition. B&M Books.
2) For more detailed competency modeling, see 「Development and use of core competency model」 (Spencer & Spencer (by Min Byeong-mo, Dong-gun Park, Jong-goo Park, Jae-chang Jeong). 1998. PSI Consulting) and 「The secret to improving work performance: competency」 (Duois (as Lee Dong-bae and Lee Chang-soo), 1993. See EDS Consulting).
3) Heneman, H. G., Judge, T. A., & Heneman, R. L. 2000. *Staffing Organizations*. Boston: Irwin McGraw-Hill.
4) As a recruitment test conducted by Samsung Group, the name was changed from SSAT to GSAT in May 2015. (See NAVER Knowledge Encyclopedia).
5) https://sempio.recruiter.co.kr. In Sampyo Foods,
6) Chosun Ilbo. March 1, 2017. "Every year in the second half of the year, new employees are recruited.. Like a food company, from a cooking interview to a chopstick interview."
7) Electronic company's internal information.
8) Son Tae-won. 2012. *Introduction to Organizational Behavior*. B&M Books. p. 75.
9) Aldag, J. R. & Kuzuhar, L. W. 2002. *Organizational Behavior & Management*. South-Western. p. 234.
10) *Ibid*. p. 277.
11) Im Chang-hee. 2013. *op. cit*., pp. 238-239.
12) Baek Ki-bok. 2014. *op. cit*., p. 125.
13) Baek Ki-bok. 2014. *op. cit.,* pp. 134-139.
14) Park Kyung-gyu. 2016. *Rookie management*. Hong Moon-sa.
15) Dessler, G. 2011. *Human Resource Management*. Boston: Pearson.
16) Dessler, G. 2011. The content has been slightly revised.
17) Jeong Yeon-Ang. 1996. Job analysis and job evaluation. Korea Labor Institute.
Gomez-Mejia, L. R., et al. 2012. *op. cit.*
Brannick, M. T., Levine, E. L., & Morgeson, F. P. 2007. *Job and Work Analysis: Methods, Reserach, and Applications for Human Resource Management*. Los Angeles: SAGE.
18) Brannick, T. M. et al. 2007. *op. cit.*
19) Gyu-chang Yu, Sang-min Lee, Hye-jeong Lee, and Se-ri Noh. 2014. A study on the development of job evaluation model for Korean-style small and medium-sized enterprises. Labor-Management Development Foundation.
20) Woo-Seok Seo. 2017. "Example of improved work productivity and employee satisfaction through the introduction of flexible working system: Hana Tour" *Wage Study* 25(2): 102-107.

CHAPTER 5

1) Jobvite, 2010, 2011, 2012, 2013, Social Recruiting Survey.
2) Agencycentral, 2020.5.24. Social Recruiting: Survey, Statistics and Infographics, www.agencycentral.uk.com.

3) Korean Chamber of Commerce, 2018. The top 100 companies' talent image.

4) For details on the development history of the personality test and the structure of the personality factors of the five-factor theory, see Dae-Hyun Ha, Hae-ik Hwang, and Sang-in Nam, 2008. "The development of the five-factor personality test and its relationship to academic, adaptation, and career-related criteria," *Educational Psychology Research* 22(3): 609-929.

5) Korean Educational Evaluation Society, 2004. Educational Evaluation Glossary, Hakjisa.

6) Kim, S. M. 2019. The reality of fair hiring and improvement measures, Korea Labor Institute.

7) For more information on the assessment center, see Han Tae-Young, 2013. *Personnel Evaluation and Performance Management*, Sigma Press, Chapter 11.

8) Korea Economic Research Institute, September 6, 2019. Plans of major Korean companies to recruit new university graduates.

9) Yang, J., Im, M., Choi, S., Kim, J., & Ko, D. (forthcoming). Artificial Intelligence-Based Hiring: An Exploratory Study of Hiring Market Reactions, Japan Labor Issues.

10) Kyunghyang Shinmun, September 7, 2018, "AI recruitment, personnel in charge of 70% oppose."

11) For detailed theoretical information on organizational socialization, refer to the following. Chao, G. T., O'leary-Kelly, A. M., Wolf, A., Klein, H. J. & Gardner, P. D. 1994. "Organizational Socialization: Its content and Consequences," *Journal of Applied Psychology* 79(5), 730-743.

12) Magazine Hankyung, August 2020, "Annual salary doesn't matter,": HR manager knows applicants lie.

13) Son B. W. and J. H. Choi, 2015, "A Study on the Improvement Plan for Human Resource Management Using NCS-based Recruitment System of Human Resources Development Service of Korea" Proceedings of the Korean Society for Human Resource Management Spring Conference.

CHAPTER 6

1) Hankyoreh. July 7, 2017. 7 out of 10 office workers "Do not trust personnel evaluation."

2) Gomez-Mejia, L. R. et al. 2012. *op. cit.*

3) Kevin R. Murphy & Jeanette N. Cleveland. 1995. *Understanding Performance Appraisal: Social, Organizational, and Goal-based Perspectives*. Sage Publications.

4) IBM Korea internal performance management explanatory material.

5) Gubman, E. 1998. *The Talent Solution: Aligning Strategy and People to Achieve Extraordinary Results*. McGraw-Hill. pp. See also 306-308.

6) Milkovich, G. T., & Widgor, A. K. 1991. *Pay for Performance: Evaluating Performance Appraisal and Merit Pay*. National Academy Press: Washington, D. C.; Landy, R. & Farr, J. Performance rating. *Psychological Bulletin* 87(1): pp. 72-107.

7) Schuler R. S. & Huber, V. L., 1993. *Personnel and Human Resource Management*. West.

8) John Door. 2019. *OKR*. (Translated by Park Se-yeon). Sejong.

9) Locke, E. A. & Latham, G. P. 1990. *A Theory of Goal Setting and Task Performance*. Englewood Cliffs: Prentice Hall.

10) Bacal, R. 2001. *Performance Management* (*The skill of performance management that makes an ordinary team leader achieve extraordinary performance*. Translated by Gyu-Chang Yu). Communication Books.

11) Rockart, J. F. 1979. Chief executives define their own data needs. *Harvard Business Review*, March-April: 81-93.

12) Moon Kwon-mo. 2008. Child molestation incidents and KPIs (key performance indicators). *Dong-A Business Review*.

13) Gomez-Mejia, L. R., Balkin, D. B., & Cardy, R. L. 2010. *Managing Human Resources* (6th edition). Boston: Pearson.

14) Kulik, C. T. *Human Resources for the Non-HR Manager*. Mahwah, New Jersey: Lawrence Erlbaum Associates.

15) Hyuk Kim, 2015. "LG Display's Human Resource Evaluation System Operation Case," *Wage Study* 23(4): 84-90.

CHAPTER 7

1) Generation M is a collective term for millenniums born in the early 1980s to early 2000s and Generation Z born in the mid-1990s to early 2000s.
2) Werner, J. M. & DeSimone, R. L. 2006. *Human Resource Development* (4th edition). Thomson Southwestern. pp. 11-12.
3) Kulik, C. T. *op. cit.*, pp. 137-141.
4) Hall, D. T. 1996. Protean careers of the 21st century. *The Academy of Management Executive* 10(4): pp. 8-15,
5) Newsis. June 25, 2017. Large corporations removed their ranks and destroyed their titles.... Samsung followed by LG.
6) Bartlett, C. A. & McLean, A. N. 2006. GE's talent machine: the making of a CEO. Harvard Business School Case.
7) Charan, R., Drotter, S., & Noel, J. 2001. *The Leadership Pipeline: How to Build the Leadership Powered Company*. window of the future.
8) Dubios, D. D. 1998. The Competency Casebook. HRD Press & International Society for Performance Management.
9) Naver Knowledge Encyclopedia. Psychological Glossary.
10) Reference was made to the internal manual for developing leaders of Philips.
11) Rothwell, W. J. 2001. *Effective Succession Planning*. New York: AMACOM. pp. 1-9.
12) Thornton, G. G. & Rupp, D. E. 2006. *Assessment Centers in Human Resource Management*. Mahwah, NJ: Lawrence Erlbaum.
13) Moravec, M. 1993. How BPX implemented dual career ladders. *Research Technology Management*, 36(1): pp. 39-44.
14) Dong-A Ilbo. June 29, 2016. Hanwha "Study for an hour every day after work."
15) Jeong Seung-guk. 2009. Workplace Innovation and Learning: A Yuhan-Kimberly Case Study. *Industrial Labor Research*. 15(2): pp. 385-418.
16) Greenhaus, J. H., Callanan, G. A., & Godshalk, V. M. 2010. *Career Management*. LA: Sage. p. 394.
17) Whitmore, J. 2007. *Coaching for Performance* (*Coaching Leadership for Performance Improvement*, translated by Youngsoon Kim). Kimyoungsa.
18) Kram, K. E. 1983. Phases of mentor relationship. *Academy of Management Journal* 26: pp. 608-626.
19) Ortega, J. 2001. Job rotation as a learning mechanism. *Management Science* 47(10): pp. 1361-1370.
20) Reference was made to the internal manual for developing leaders of Philips.
21) Bong Hyeon-cheol. 2011. *Action learning to be successful*. planetary ratio. p. 57.
22) Jaehee Lee. 2021. *A2M Human Resource Development for Education Professionals*. Yang Sung Won. pp. 17-18.
23) *Ibid.*
24) Wood, D. F. 2003. ABC of learning and teaching in Medicine. Problem based learning. Clinical Review. Vo. 326. 328-330.
25) Gomez-Mejia, L. R., et al. 2012. *op. cit.*
26) Yunhap news. "Amazon staff retraining 800 billion won....100,000 retraining within 6 years" July 12, 2019.
27) Kirkpatrick, D. L. 1996. Great ideas revisited: revisiting Kirkpatrick's four-level model. Training & Development. pp. 54-57.

28) Park Ji-young, 2016. “Renault Samsung Motors’ Talent Development Strategy and Performance Management Plan,” *Wage Study* 24(2): 100-109.

CHAPTER 8

1) “Total compensation are all forms of financial returns and tangible services and benefits employees receive as part of an employment relationship,” Newman, Gerhart and Milkovich(Compensation, 12th Ed. 2017).
2) Chosun Biz, 2020. 6. 8. “Kakao, the No. 1 company that college students want to work for... beat Samsung Electronics.”
3) Goler, L., J. Gale, B. Harrington, G. Adam, 2018. “The Real Reason People Quit Their Jobs,” HR News Jan 23, Society for Human Resource Management.
4) Kim, J. 2011. War for talent between Google and Facebook, SERI Management Notes, Samsung Economic Research Institute.
5) Korea Labor Institute, 2019. ‘The difference in working conditions according to the rate below the minimum wage,’ Monthly Labor Review, April, Statistics Prism.
6) Economic, Social and Labor Council, 2015. Wage Report: Understanding the Wage System, p. 14.
7) For the historical background and status of Korean companies’ grade system and recent changes, refer to Yoo Gyu-Chang(2014), Grade and promotion system in a retirement age of 60, in Ahn Eds. Human Reosurce Management in a Retirement Age of 60, Hodunamu, 2014.
8) Economic, Social and Labor Council(2017), 2016 Wage Report: Searching for alternatives to reform of the wage system.
9) 石田光男(2003), 仕事の社会科学: 労動研究のフロンティア, ミネルヴァ書房.
10) Refer to the following for an example of a company that introduced the ability-based pay at this time. Park, J. 1992. A Case Study of Improving the Wage System of Korean Companies, Korea Productivity Center. Yang, B. and H. Ahn. 1993, Theory and practice for the ability-based pay, Labor Economy Institute of the Korea Employers’ Federation.
11) Yoo, G. 1998. Measures for Improving the Evaluation System for Introduction of the Ability-based pay, Korea Labor Institute.
12) Kim, D. B. 2015. Changes and Prospects of the Wage System in Korea, Wage Conference: The Wage System in Korea, Korea Labor Institute.
13) There are many different ways to do job analysis. For more information on job analysis, refer to Newman, Gerhart and Milkovich (Compensation, 12th Ed. 2017), Chapter 4 Job Analysis.
14) For more information on this case, refer to the following. Choi, Y. J. 2020, Cases of Wage System Reorganization, Wage Information Brief No. 7 pp. 6-11, Korea Labor Institute.
15) Refer to the following for how to set the role class and design the role-based pay in practice. Jaewook Shin and Kwangwoo Kim, 2016. Role-level design methods and examples, PNC Media.
16) 楠田丘, 1998. 役割給と職責給の違いは何か, 労政時報, 第3379号 pp. 80-81.
17) For details on Canon and Korea’s role-based pay, refer to the following. Park, W. and D. B., Kim (2016), Role-based pay in Japanese companies: examples and implications, Korea Employers Federation.
18) Kwon, Y. S. 2013. “Samyang Group’s Job-based Personnel and Wage System and Organizational Culture Innovation,” Wage Research, Labor Economic Research Institute, Korean Employers’ Federation, Vol. 21, No. 2, 76-82.

CHAPTER 9

1) For more information on this, refer to Woo-Sung Park and Byung-Ha Lee, 2003. Changes and Implications of Samsung Electronics’ Compensation System, *Korea Business Review* 6(2): 148-166.

2) For the change in the corporate management paradigm after the economic crisis, refer to Young-Ho Cho, 2000. "Environmental Change and the Great Transformation of Corporate Management," in 「Human Resource Management for the 21st Century」, Korea Labor Institute (ed.).
3) Theoretical discussions on the motivating effect of performance pay are available in Milkovich and Newman, 2002. *Compensation*, 7th edition, Chicago: Irwin., pp. 283-287.
4) Vroom, V. H. 1964. *Work and Motivation*, New York: John Wiley & Sons.
5) Adams, J. S. 1963. Toward an understanding of inequity. *Journal of Abnormal and Social Psychology*, 67, pp. 422-436.
6) Locke, E. A. 1968. "Toward a theory of task motivation and incentives," *Organizational Behavior and Human Performance* 7: pp. 157-189.
7) B. F. Skinner, 1938. The Behavior of Organisms. Skinner, B. F. 1972. *Beyond freedom and dignity*. New York: Vintage Books.
8) For the definition and theoretical basis of the Yeonbongje, Gyu-chang Yoo and Woo-seong Park, 1999. "A theoretical review on the introduction and effect of the Yeonbongje", *Korean Journal of Management*, Vol. 7, No. 2.
9) Eun-mi Jang, 2003. "A Study on the Effect of Individual Performance-Based Compensation System on Job Performance Effort: Focusing on the Moderating Effect of the HR Bundle," *Korean Journal of Management* 11(1), pp. 133-158.
10) Gyu-Chang Yu and Woo-Sung Park, 2007. "Factors Influencing the Introduction of Performance-Based HR System and Organizational Performance", *Korean Journal of Management* 15(3).
11) Keaveny, T. J. and R. E. Allen, 1983. "The Implications of an Across-the-Board Salary Increase," *Research in Higher Education* 19(1): pp. 11-24.
12) According to SK, Supex means super excellent representing the highest level achievable by human abilities.
13) Economic, Social and Labor Council, 2016, 2015 Wage Report: p. 73.
14) Kelly, K. and E. Schine, 1992. "How Did Sears Blow This Gasket," June 29. p. 38.
15) The Chosun Ilbo, 2016.5.3., "A 3-person team year-end bonus of 100 million? Unconventional welfare of a company of 80 employees."
16) Woo-Sung Park and Kwang-Dong Lim, 1999, Profit Sharing, Korea Labor Institute.
17) Kruse, D. L. 1992. "Profit Sharing and Productivity: Microeconomic Evidence from the U.S.," *The Economic Journal*, Vol. 102.
18) Hak-Soo Oh, 「The Japanese performance-sharing system」, Park Young-Beom (ed.), 「The performance-sharing system of major advanced countries」, Korea Labor Institute, 1994.
19) Korea Labor Institute, 2008. A survey on the wage system.
20) For Samsung Electronics' PS system, refer to the following. Woo-Sung Park and Byung-Ha Lee, 2003, Changes and Implications of Samsung Electronics' Compensation System, *Korea Business Review* 6(2): 148-166.
21) Park Woo-Sung, 2000. Stock Option System, Korea Labor Institute.
22) Shigeyuki Joe, 2005. Fujitsu Performance-based management Report, Deulnyuk.

CHAPTER 10

1) Ivancevich, M. 1998. *Human Resource Management*, 7th ed., New York: MiGraw-Hill. p. 376.
2) Gomez-Mejia, L. R., Balkin, D. B. and Cardy, R. L. 2009. *Managing Human Resources,* 5th ed., Pearson.
3) The compensation cost consists of salaries and employee benefits, and is surveyed and announced annually. For the detailed information, refer to the followings. Bureau of Labor Statistics, 2021 June, Employer cost for compensation cost, www.bls.gov.
4) KLI Labor Statistics, 2021. Labor cost per worker, Korea Labor Institute.
5) Rosenbloom Eds., 2001. *The Handbook of Employee Benefits* 5th Edition, Ohio, U.S.A.: McGraw-

Hill.
6) Ho-Geun Song, 1995. Korean Corporate Welfare Study, Korea Labor Institute.
7) For detailed information about the national health insurance and services that National Health Insurance Service offers, consult the home page of NHIS. (https://www.nhis.or.kr/english/index.do).
8) Shim Soo-yeon, 2021. Recent domestic retirement pension market trends, Capital Market Focus, Korea Capital Market Research Institute.
9) Youngjae Kim, Seongguk Kim, and Kangsik Kim, 2005. *Human Resource Management*, Samyeongsa.
10) Choi Soo-chan, 2009. A study on the rational introduction and operation model of flexible benefits system, Korea Workers' Compensation and Welfare Service.
11) New Daily Economics, 2020. Hyundai Department Store Group's acquisition of Easywell Why?.
12) Gye-Jeon Song and Gwi-Hyeon Park, 1997. A study on the introduction of cafeteria-style welfare system, LG Economic Research Institute.
13) Park Kyung-gyu and Ahn Hee-tak, 1998. Comparison of Human Resources Management in Korean and German Companies, Korea Employers Federation.
14) 日本経済団体連合会, 2020. 第64回 福利厚生費調査結果報告.
15) Milkovich & Newman, 1996. Compensation, 5th edition, McCaffery, R. M. 1992. Employee Bebefit Programs: A Total Compensation Perspective, PWS-Kent.
16) Barber, A. E., Dunham, R. B., & R. A. Formisano, 1992. The Impact of Flexible Benefits on Employee Satisfaction: A Field Study, *Personnel Psychology*, Vol. 45.
17) Shelly, J. 2008. "Transformation Vacation," *Human Resource Executives*, Nov 1.
18) Korea Employers' Federation, 2013, Cases collected of Personnel Wages.

CHAPTER 11

1) Korea Employers' Federation (KEMCO) '2016 New Employee Recruitment Survey'. Re-quoted from Edaily May 1, 2017 article (http://www.edaily.co.kr/).
2) Alelsen, M. A. & Baysinger, B. D. 1984. Optimal and dysfunctional turnover: toward an organizational level models. *Academy of Management Review* 9: pp. 331-341.
3) Gomez-Mejia, L. R. et al. 2012. *op. cit.*, pp. 228-232.
4) Park, Gyeong-gyu. 2016. *New Human Resource Management*. See pp. 553-556.
5) Ahr, P. R. & Ahr, T. B. 2000. *Overturn Turnover*. St. Louis, Missouri: Cause Publishing Company.
6) According to the Labor Law (Labor Standards Act) in Korea, involuntary turnover is divided into dismissal and layoff for managerial reasons.
7) Ha, G. R. 2021. *Labor Standards Act*. JoongAng Economic Co., Ltd.
8) Ha, G. R. 2012. *Labor Standards Act*. Central Economics. p. 656.
9) Datta, D. K. Guthrie, J. P., Basuil, D., & Pandey, A. 2010. Causes and effects of employee downsizing: a review and synthesis. *Journal of Management* 36(1): pp. 281-348.
10) Datta, D. K. Guthrie, J. P., Basuil, D., & Pandey, A. 2010. Causes and effects of employee downsizing: a review and synthesis. *Journal of Management* 36(1): pp. 281-348.
11) Seungyoon Lee and Seungseop Kim. 2015. Ssangyong Motors layoffs and slides in Korean society. *Korean Social Policy* 22(4): pp. 73-96.
12) Gomez-Mejia, L. R. et al. 2012. *op. cit.*, See pp. 236-242.
13) Kulik, C. T. 2004. *Human Resources for the Non-HR Manager*. London: Lawrence Erlbaum Associates, Publishers. See pp. 188-191.
14) JoongAng Ilbo. July 5, 2017. [More, longer] Pricking into a lecture on "How to be treated by your wife after retirement."
15) Cascio, W. F. Human Resource Planning Employment & Placement. Washington D.C.: The Bureaue of National Affairs, Inc.

16) Gomez-Mejia, L. R. et al. 2012. *op. cit.*, pp. 499-500.
17) Sungjin Kim. 2013. Whether management rights are subject to collective bargaining. *Labor Law* 45(3): pp. 191-231.
18) Hak-Jong Lee and Hyuk-Sung Yang. *op. cit.*, p. 392.
19) Kulik. C. T. *op. cit.*, pp. 161-162.
20) Kulik. C. T. *op. cit.*, pp. 162-166.
21) Park Kyung-gon, 2012. "LG CNS Management of Underperformers," *Wage Study* 20(1): 90-95.

CHAPTER 12

1) Hastings, D. F. 1999. "Loncoln Electric's Harsh Lessons from International Expansion," *Harvard Business Review* 79(8): 1-11.
2) Hill, C. W. 2012. *International Business*, New York: McGraw-Hill.
3) Gomez-Mejia, L. R., et al. 2012. *op. cit.*
4) Morgan, P. V. 1986. International Human Resource Management—Fact or Fiction, *Personnel Administrator*, Vol. 31, No. 9, pp. 43-47.
5) Briscoe, D. R. 1995. *International Human Resource Management*, Englewood Cliffs: Prentice-Hall.
6) Heenan, D. A. & Perlmutter, H. V. 1979. *Multinational Organization Development*, Addison-Wesley, Massachusetts.
7) A. L. Kroeber and C. Kluckhohn, 1952. *Culture, A Critical Review of Concepts and Definitions*, New York, NY, Random House, p. 181.
8) E. H. Schein, *Organizational Culture and Leadership*, Sanfrancisco Jossey-Bass, 2004.
9) G. Hofstede, 1980. *Culture's Consequences: International Differences in Work Related Values*, Sage.
10) G. Hofstede, 1991. *Culture and Organizations: Software of the Mind*, McGraw-Hill.
11) F. Trompenaars and C. Hampden-Turner, 2002. *Riding the Waves of Culture*, London Nicholas Brealey.
12) Barham, K. & Devine, M. 1990. The Quest for the International Manager: A Survey of Global Human Resource Strategies, Ashridge Management Resource Group/The Economist Intelligence Unit, Special Report No. 2098.
13) Barham, K. & Devine, M. 1990. *op. cit.*
14) Khanna, T., J. Song and K. Lee, 2001. The Paradox of Samsung's Rise, *Harvard Business Review*. July-August pp. 142-147.
15) Choi Soon-gyu and Kang Ji-hoon, 2017. CJ CGV's strategy to dominate the Vietnamese theater market through mergers and acquisitions, *Korea Business Review* 21(3): 115-146.

Index

E

F

G

H

I

J

K

L

M

N

O

T

U

V

W

Y